FOOD SERVICE
IN INDUSTRY and INSTITUTIONS

FOOD SERVICE
IN INDUSTRY and INSTITUTIONS

Second Edition

JOHN W. STOKES, 1897–

John W. Stokes and Company
Food Service Management Consultants
Newtonville, Massachusetts 02160

WM. C. BROWN COMPANY PUBLISHERS

44.330

Contents

Foreword

By Donald E. Lundberg, Ph.D., Head,
Department of Hotel, Restaurant and Travel Administration,
University of Massachusetts, Amherst, Massachusetts

"Here is a first"—the first book to be published which is entirely devoted to a detailed explanation of food service as it should be conducted in hospitals, schools, colleges, and industrial plants. It is also a first in another regard. Collected here are dozens of photographs of equipment, kitchens, and food-service areas which in themselves are a remarkable contribution to the literature. For those interested in origins and antecedents, Chapter I offers a well-documented account of the beginnings of food service in institutions and industry.

The author, John Stokes, is uniquely qualified to write this book. He is a teacher, a food-service consultant, and was for many years president of a large food-service enterprise. His comprehension of the subject is equaled by few other people, and he is one of the few who has the perseverance to painstakingly set down the details necessary to cover this broad and complex subject.

This book will be a valuable contribution to the library of anyone interested in food service. It is so organized and written as to be an excellent textbook for classes in institution management, hospital management, and classes in hotel and restaurant management.

I personally am grateful to Mr. Stokes for writing this book, grateful for the several years of effort that went into its writing, and for a work which can save so many mistakes and hours of work on the part of teachers and food-service managers.

Acknowledgments

To establish sound management principles and practical operating procedures for the far-flung and growing industrial and institutional food-service field poses a task far beyond the capacity of any single individual. Although I have relied in part upon my own experience as a food-service operator and as a consultant, and have visited many food services in the United States, Canada, Latin America, and Europe during the past thirty years, this book would not have been written without the assistance of others. To all who have contributed to its usefulness, I wish to extend my sincere appreciation.

Following are those who specifically assisted with the first edition: Frances Buzzell, First National Bank of Boston; Marie Casteen, former Chief Dietitian, Newton-Wellesley Hospital; Elizabeth Cornwall, Dietitian, Wellesley College; Blanche Fickle, Librarian, Cornell School of Hotel Administration; Louise Hatch, Chief Dietitian, Massachusetts General Hospital; Gertrude Loud, Personnel Director, Newton-Wellesley Hospital; Anne M. Tracy, Director, Residence Halls, Columbia University; Ruth Yakel, Executive Director, American Dietetic Association; Sister Mary Perpetua, Chief Dietitian, St. Peter's Hospital, Albany, New York; Mrs. Lois Gilson, Chief Dietitian, Worcester City Hospital, Worcester, Massachusetts; Mrs. Hattie Smith, former Assistant Commissioner of Labor and Industry, Boston, Massachusetts; Charles Banino of the Ritz-Carleton Hotel, Boston; Alexander Armour, Steward, McLean Hospital, Waverly, Massachusetts; J. P. Craig, Sonesta Hotels, Boston; Robert M. Cunningham, Jr., Editor, *Modern Hospital*; Thomas M. Day, Restaurant Manager, Bell Telephone Laboratories, Whippany, New Jersey; Professor Peter Dukas, Department of Hotel and Restaurant Management, Florida State University. Also assisting with the revised edition have been Dr. Arthur C. Avery, Purdue University; Gertrude Bernard-Fraser, Bernard & Associates, Montreal; Joseph T. Greco, Assistant Administrator, Barnes Hospital, St. Louis; C. Graham Hurlburt, Director, Harvard University Food Services; Wm. R. Mumma, Assistant Vice-President, Chicago Wesley Memorial Hospital; John C. Stalker, Director, Bureau of Nutrition, Education and Food Services, Massachusetts Department of Education; Helen J. Recknagal, Ph.D., Managing Editor, Cornell Hotel and Restaurant Administration Quarterly; Jane Young Wallace, Editor, *Institutions Volume Feeding;* Henry Ehle, Editor, *Restaurant World;*

Gilbert Van Houten Jr., Director, Undergraduate Dining Halls, Princeton University; and Theodore W. Minah, Director, Dining Halls Operations, Duke University. Credits to those parties furnishing illustrative material for this book accompany the illustrations.

Last but not least, tribute should be paid to the following of my associates for the cooperation and assistance rendered by them: the late Howard Tochterman and the late W.J.L. Roop, and to C. Dixon Matthews, C.P.A. and member of the Massachusetts Bar, and Richard P. Troyer. To Dr. Donald E. Lundberg, who edited the first edition and wrote the Foreword, my gratitude for his wise counsel and guidance.

John W. Stokes

CHAPTER 1

How Industrial and Institutional Feeding Developed

It well has been said that "We learn from history that we do not learn from history." As applied to man's progress in learning to live in peace with his neighbors, this is undoubtedly true. Yet, a knowledge of how the present widespread industrial and institutional food services have evolved from early and often primitive beginnings is basic to an understanding of the larger problems.

To detail the progress in this great field over the centuries would require many pages, far beyond the purview of this book. We do well, at least, to consider in brief the main facts, and to note some of the outstanding pioneers whose achievements blazed the way. We can only view their accomplishments with pride, and seek to emulate their vision and leadership.

EMPLOYEE FEEDING

The feeding of employees is an important part of all institutional food services. Industrial food services are concerned almost wholly with this problem.

Employee feeding is not new. It dates back to that first day in the dim and distant past when an outside worker joined some prehistoric family group. This prototype of the American farmer's "hired girl" or "hired man," like all workers since, had to be fed.

Undoubtedly the hordes of workers whose toil brought forth the pyramids on the Nile, or who constructed other fabulous monuments of antiquity, required food-service facilities commensurate with the tremendous scope of these projects.

From the time the first primitive tribe hit the war path and the first ship set sail on a voyage, provision has had to be made for food. Ever since, armies have "traveled on their stomachs," and the ship's galley has been an essential piece of nautical equipment. In many respects the soldier's rations and the sailor's mess are analogous to the meal provided for the worker in the shop or office.

Even before the Industrial Revolution brought about the transfer of industry from the household to the factory, it was customary in many trades for the employer to provide board and lodging for apprentices and other workers. A similar practice was followed over the centuries in the mercantile establishments of the great cities of England and continental Europe.

Robert Owen, Father of Industrial Catering

Beginning in 1800, Robert Owen, an astute young mill operator in Scotland, appalled by the exploitation of children in the British textile industry, created an extensive welfare system in his mill at New Lanark. About 1815 he established a large "eating room" for his employees and their families. Owen's methods were so successful that they spread over the civilized world and gave impetus to the welfare movement that culminated about the turn of the present century. Robert Owen has well been called "the father of modern industrial catering." He and others were responsible for the first "Factory Acts" in Great Britain, the forerunners of later child labor legislation.

In the United States

In this country, when the first cotton mills were established in the 1820s along the Merrimack River in Massachusetts, boarding houses were erected to house and feed the women employees who were recruited from nearby and distant communities.

Subsidization

Nicholas P. Gilman, an American student of industrial welfare, in a survey made in 1899, pointed out that on the Continent, food services were operated under more paternalistic policies than in England. In Europe, he stated, many employers provided places where food brought from home might be prepared or reheated, and supplemented by beverages or other items sold at cost.

American employers, on the other hand, provided meals *below cost*, or in some cases *free*. This, he emphasized, represented an important addition to real wages. Thus, the policy of subsidization has been characteristic of employee feeding in the United States from early times.

Lumber Camps

Lumbering is one of the oldest industries in America, going back to the 1600s in Virginia and Maine. In the early days, the cooking and eating were done around the open fireplace in the bunkhouse of what was known as the "State Of Maine" type of camp.

As the forests of the East became depleted, the logging operators moved to Michigan, Wisconsin, Minnesota, and later to the Northwest and the South. During all of these migrations, the feeding of the "lumber jacks" has always been an integral part of the logging operation. A combination cook-shanty and dining room was usually erected by the logging operator, who hired the cook and provided the food.

The author visited lumber camps in Idaho in 1925, and can testify to the substantial quantity and good quality of the meals served at that time. From all accounts, this emphasis on quantity and quality still persists.

In the old time lumber camp, the cook's call to breakfast started the day, as witness this North Wood's doggerel:

"Wake up," yelled Cookie.
"It ban mornin," say he.
"It ban daylight in swamp all youse guys." "So outa
   warm bunk, we skall fallin kerplunk, and rubbin'
   like blazes our eyes."

EARLY INDUSTRIAL FOOD SERVICES

By the 1890s many factories, department stores and telephone exchanges in the United States were providing food services for their employees. The Seaside Institute, an employees' clubhouse established in 1887 by Warner Brothers, corset manufacturers of Bridgeport, Connecticut, contained a lunchroom where sandwiches, desserts, and beverages were supplied at cost.

The National Cash Register Company opened a dining room for department heads at Dayton, Ohio, in 1891. In 1895 service of hot soup and coffee for women employees began. A year later this service was extended, and by 1905 an employees' dining hall seating 1800, reportedly the largest in the world at that time, was opened. Speaking of the first lunchroom for women workers, John H. Patterson, the company's founder, said at the time: "Of course we lose money on this, but we get the loss back in better work done."

Construction of Canals and Railroads

Construction of canals, which began in 1792 in this country and reached its zenith about 1837, necessitated food service for workers. The building of railroads began in 1829 and continued during the remainder of the 19th century. On the first transcontinental line, completed in 1869, and on other Western lines, the feeding of construction workers was accomplished in camps and from rolling kitchens. On many occasions, the caterers, engaged by the railroad contractors, had to abandon their pots and pans for rifles when Indian war parties attacked. At present there are several catering companies which specialize in feeding and lodging railroad maintenance-of-way workers.

Railroad Y.M.C.A.'s

The Railroad Department of the Young Men's Christian Association established "Y" buildings at terminals where railroad workers could be housed and fed. In 1889 there were 136 of these Railroad "Y's." Their number has been greatly reduced in recent years as junction points have disappeared with the advent of diesel engines and longer runs and the decline in railroad passenger traffic. Of the 1815 American Y.M.C.A.'s today, 519 operate food services with total annual sales volume of $14,575,000, not including income from vending machines.

Maritime Workers

Diets on early sailing vessels were notoriously poor. The absence of fresh fruits and vegetables, containing what we now know as Vitamin "C," caused scurvy to be a common disease at sea. From 1795 lime and lemon juices were issued by the British Navy as anti-scorbutics; hence, the term "limey" applied to British sailors.

Modern refrigeration and galley equipment make the food of the present day sailor a far cry from that of the past. Demands of seamen's unions and the desire on the part of shipowners to attract and hold desirable workers have given to sailors on American flag ships meals equal to those served to the passengers. To maintain our merchant marine, the U.S. Government subsidizes ships of U.S. registry. This subsidy is based upon the higher wages and better food provided our seamen as compared with those of other nations. For example, on a large passenger liner the cost of subsistence, for the crew alone, will amount to $1,000,000 or more annually.

Hotels and Restaurants

Inns and hostelries also date back to the dim and distant past. Their advent came when trade and commerce made overnight travel necessary. The Biblical account of the birth of Jesus in a manger because there was "no room in the inn" reveals the existence of inns nearly 2000 years ago.

Always there has been the necessity of feeding hotel and restaurant employees, formerly without charge. As food costs increased, and methods of control became necessary, separate dining rooms were set up for employees in larger hotels and restaurants. In smaller places, employees may be served in the public dining room before or after regular meal hours. Frequently employees are limited in their choice of items. The practice of charging employees for their meals is becoming more prevalent, such charges being made at either half price or the actual cost of the food.

U.S. Food Services Overseas

Many American companies conduct food services for their employees engaged in overseas operations. Typical of these is United Fruit Company of Boston. Since the turn of the century this company has operated hotels, restaurants, and hospitals for its employees in Panama, Costa Rica, Honduras, Nicaragua, Guatemala and Jamaica.

United Fruit also founded a unique educational institution, *Escuela Agricola Panamericana* (Pan-American Agricultural School) at Zanmorano, Honduras. Here, young men from twelve Latin American countries are trained in scientific agriculture and modern methods of food handling.

Arabian-American Oil Company in Saudi Arabia and Creole Petroleum Corporation in Venezuela are other examples of the many American companies maintaining food services overseas.

THE CAFETERIA

The cafeteria, the generally accepted type of employee food service today, originated in the Kansas City, Missouri, Young Women's Christian Association in 1891. Seeking to provide working girls with good food at low cost, the Association's managers visited the Ogontz Lunch Club for young women which had been organized in Chicago a year ealier. Combining some of the self-service methods in use there with features of their own devising, they called the new service a "cafeteria," from the Spanish, "a place where coffee is sold at retail."

At first, cafeterias were set up in organizations like the YWCA's and YMCA's. It was not until after the turn of the century that cafeteries became the accepted pattern for employee feeding. In 1902, Edward R. Harris, the largest stockholder of the former Plymouth Cordage Company, Plymouth, Massachusetts, erected at his own expense a building housing a kitchen, two cafeterias, and recreational facilities for the benefit of the Company's employees. Prior to this time, lunchrooms and table service dining rooms had been the accepted types of food service in use in industry.

The Hollow Square, Free Flow, or Shopping Center Cafeteria

The "Hollow Square, "Free Flow," "Shopping Center," or, as it is called in the West, "The Scramble System" type of cafeteria came into vogue in the 1930s

Main Serving Area (Free-flow or scramble). Dining Rooms, University of Alaska, College, Alaska. (Courtesy Flambert & Flambert, Inc., San Francisco, California.)

Cashier's Stand and Beverage Service. Dining Commons, University of Alaska, College, Alaska. (Courtesy Flambert & Flambert, Inc., San Francisco, California.)

in commercial eating places like the Colonnade Cafeterias in Cleveland, Cincinnati, Pittsburgh, Philadelphia, and Newark, and the Grace Smith Restaurants in Toledo. Colonnade cafeterias were located in the basements of office buildings and catered to clerical workers and business people. Some of these patrons wished a complete meal while others desired only a sandwich or beverage. For this reason it proved advantageous to provide a substitute for the single cafeteria line. Customers were free to carry their trays to the various sides of the hollow square and to select whatever they desired.

It is believed the hollow-square principle was first applied in 1951 to an industrial cafeteria in the Western Electric plant at Winston Salem, North Carolina. It was termed a "shopping center" cafeteria because of the similarity in going from counter to counter in a supermarket or shopping center to get the foods one wishes. Since then the idea has increased in popularity and is being widely applied in the construction of new industrial cafeterias, as well as in schools and colleges.

MEAKIN'S SURVEY

In 1905, Budgett Meakin, a British student of industrial conditions, made an extensive survey of employee welfare systems then in effect in various parts of the world. He listed some fifty firms in the United States which were providing food service to employees at that time. The majority were manufacturing plants, although the list included department stores and telephone companies.

The cafeteria principle was used in a few of the above instances. Most of the food services were company-operated, but in a few plants outside caterers were engaged. Some were operated by employee-associations which, Meakin felt, fostered a greater sense of appreciation on the part of the patrons. He agreed with earlier observers who pointed out that a greater degree of subsidization of food services existed in America than abroad. Meakin also stressed that the accommodations for workers should be clean and attractive, and the food as good or better than that obtained at home.

BEFORE WORLD WAR I

In the present century, before World War I, the growth of employee feeding in this country was slow. The Panic of 1907 was undoubtedly a deterrent to economic activity, and it was not until 1914, when the war started in Europe, that American shipyards and munition plants began to hum with activity.

WORLD WAR I (1914-1918)

At the outset of the War, the welfare motive was dominant, and food service had become an accepted part of personnel work in many industries. When the United States entered the war in April 1917, it has been estimated that about one-half of the larger companies maintained some sort of employee feeding facilities. More of these were dining rooms rather than cafeterias. About 85% were company-operated. The remainder was divided between those managed by employee associations and those served by outside contractors. During the war, lunch periods were shortened. As plants expanded and labor became scarce, it was found that food services were a means of attracting and holding desirable workers. As a result, many new food services were instituted during the nineteen months that this country was engaged in the conflict.

BETWEEN THE WARS

The economic growth of the United States following World War I led to the enlargement of old plants and the building of new ones. The advent of good roads which accompanied the development of the automobile, as well as other improved transportation facilities, made it possible for plants to attract workers from a wider radius; hence it became *necessary* to provide food service.

The cafeteria had proven its worth in the war plants. It enabled large numbers of employees to be fed quickly, required fewer workers to operate, and gave satisfaction to patrons because they could select the food they wished at prices they were willing to pay. As a result, cafeterias were set up in many business firms and in institutions as well.

By 1928, a study of 4,075 manufacturing plants showed that of those employing 1,000 or more people, 75 percent maintained food service. Of those employing 50 to 100 workers, less than 5 percent had such facilities. Both in large and small plants, the majority of the food services were company-operated.

WORLD WAR II (1939-1945)

Although there had been a marked increase in industrial activity in this country after the start of the war in Europe in 1939, it was estimated that in early 1941 less than 2,000,000 were employed in plants providing food service.

After Pearl Harbor, in December, 1941, our industrial capacity increased by leaps and bounds. By the end of the European War in 1944, there were approximately 12,500 war plants in the United States employing 12,600,000 workers. In addition, there were an estimated 3,900,000 workers in plants not directly engaged in war work. In all, there were some 16,000,000

people employed in industry. Of these, it is estimated that about one-third, or 5,500,000 workers, were served food on the job in one way or another. At the time, food-service facilities were also being planned for an additional 1,500,000 industrial workers.

FOOD-SERVICE CONTRACTORS

An outstanding phenomenon of World War II was the impetus given to the development of industrial catering. Many plant executives, preoccupied with their own problems, were glad to turn over the operation of their cafeterias to outside caterers. Many restaurant and hotel men became contractors during the war period, and industrial feeding came into its own as an industry.

This was not a new field, for as early as 1897 N. W. Cease gave up his job in a locomotive plant near Richmond, Virginia, to sell lemonade during the warm months at a penny a dipper to his former fellow workers. Noting a reduction in the accident rate, management prevailed upon Mr. Cease to extend his operations. By 1904, with the help of a brother, W. M. Cease, he opened a cafeteria in American Locomotive Works at Dunkirk, N. Y. Figure 1.1 shows the menu in effect at that time. Shortly thereafter, the Cease brothers were operating cafeterias in locomotive plants in Richmond, Schenectady, and Montreal.

During the war years men of diverse backgrounds, including Fred B. Prophet who had been a hotel steward in Elmira, New York; John H. Slater, an English teacher at the University of Pennsylvania; Andrew J. Crotty, Boston, a candy salesman; and John and Martin Harding, sons of a Chicago restaurateur, to name a few, entered the catering field. These men developed large organizations and, in some instances, entered the school and hospital field.

Within the past decade, however, there has been a marked trend toward mergers and amalgamations. Many of the independent catering companies became parts of large food-service corporations or divisions of great conglomerates. Some, however, have retained their original identities and through successful operation have grown to take their places among the leading companies. Figure 1.2 lists ten of the largest catering companies together with their 1970 sales volumes and number of units served as of July, 1971.

Saga Administrative Corporation is an example of the latter type of catering organization. It began in 1948 with three young men: Bill Laughlin, Hank Anderson, and Bill Scandling, who operated the campus cafeteria at Hobart College, Geneva, New York, where they were seniors. Upon graduation they branched

OUR MENU - 70 YEARS AGO

DINNER

Chowders	3c
Vegetable Soup	3c
Vermicelli Soup	3c
Split Pea Soup	3c
Tomato Soup	3c
Queen Olives	3c
Lamb and Beef Stews	3c
Roast Pork and Apple Sauce	3c
Roast Prime Beef, Dish Gravy	3c
Spring Lamb and Mint Sauce	3c
Cold Ham	3c
Pickled Pigs' Feet	3c
Mutton	3c
Mashed Potatoes	3c
Sweet Potatoes	3c
Turnips	3c
Peas	3c
Corn	3c
Salads	3c
Tomatoes	3c
Boiled Onions	3c
Beets	3c
Boiled Cabbage	3c
Pies, (all kinds) per slice	3c
Custards	3c
Plum Pudding with Hard Sauce	3c
Jellies	3c
Cakes	3c
Domestic Cheese	3c
Swiss Cheese	3c
Fruit	1 and 2c
Coffee	3c
Milk	3c
Horseradish	Free
Pepper Sauce	Free
Worcestershire Sauce	Free
Table Sauce	Free
Catsup	Free

BREAKFAST and SUPPER

Fruit in Season	3c
Coffee	3c
Milk	3c
Tea	3c
Chocolate	3c
Oatmeal	3c
Force	3c
Shredded Wheat Biscuit	3c
Cod Fish Balls	3c
Small Steak, Potatoes, Bread Butter	10c
Sugar Cured Ham	3c
Chops	3c
Liver and Onions	3c
Hamburg Steak	3c
Bacon	3c
Fried Oysters, two for	3c
Hot Frankforts, two for	3c
Porterhouse Steak	15c
Sirloin Steak	15c

EGGS (One)

Boiled	3c
Scrambled	3c
Fried 3c, Poached on Toast	3c
Boston Baked Beans	3c
Potato Salad	3c

SANDWICHES

Ham	3c
Chicken	3c
Domestic Cheese	3c
Swiss Cheese	3c
Egg	3c
Oyster Sandwiches	3c

POTATOES

French Fried	3c
Hashed Brown	3c
Baked	3c

BREAD

Pullman Loaf, Boston Brown Rye	—
Corn Cakes	3c
Buckwheat Cakes	3c
Syrup and Butter	3c
Buttered Toast	3c
Waffles	3c
Bread or Rolls with Butter	3c

SOAP, PEPSIN GUM, TOBACCO and CIGARS at Low Prices.

AMERICAN LOCOMOTIVE WORKS

Cease Lunch System

Any inattention or uncivil remarks of Waitresses reported to Manager will be appreciated.

MAY 5th, 1904—

Fig. 1.1. An early industrial menu.

out into the catering business, first in the college field, where they now operate food services for some 270 colleges and universities. Later they entered the hospital area where they now serve some 40 hospitals and health care units. They also manage approximately 140 industrial food services in plants and offices. In all, they operate more than 570 accounts in 43 states, the District of Columbia, Canada, and Puerto Rico.

The College and Hospital Divisions operate largely upon contracts providing revenues based upon a fixed price per day for food service. In business and industrial establishments Saga usually receives a management fee for providing food service and sells food to the employees for cash. Vending machine service is also provided in many of these business food services. In an increasing number of establishments Saga is now operating the facilities at a fixed price per day with a ceiling upon profits. In their various operations, space and equipment facilities are generally supplied by the customer.

Saga is known throughout the industry for the emphasis it places upon the training of its employees. Four "orientation centers" are located in New Jersey, Michigan, Arizona, and California, where newly hired managers spend four weeks learning Saga's operating systems.

	Volume in $ millions 1971	*Food Service Units 1971*
1. Marriott Corporation, Washington, D. C.	$605	1,122
2. A.R.A. Services, Philadelphia, Pa.	496	1,426
3. Canteen Corporation, Chicago, Ill.	340	500
4. Servomation Corporation, New York, N. Y.	293	450*
5. Interstate United Corp., Chicago, Ill.	167	600
6. Saga Administrative Corp., Menlo Park, California	166	555
7. Ogden Corporation, Toledo, Ohio	150*	6,500
8. Greyhound Food Mgmt. Inc., Detroit, Michigan	120	436
9. The Macke Co. Cheverly, Md.	110	2,142
10. Morrison, Inc., Mobile, Alabama	94	262

*Estimated

Fig. 1.2. Ten leading food-service contractors. (Courtesy Institutions/Volume Feeding Magazine, July 15, 1972.)

THE COFFEE BREAK

The development of the "coffee break" in business, industry, and institutions was another wartime phenomenon which by now has become universal. Because of the waste of valuable time involved in going to and from the cafeteria during these coffee breaks, many companies have devised methods of bringing the coffee to the employees by means of baskets, mobile carts, or by the use of vending machines.

VENDING MACHINES

Vending machines have been developed to such an extent that in many small offices and plants they take the place of cafeterias. Each of these machines, costing from $600 to $2,400, serve hot coffee with or with-

"Der Keller" serves German cuisine at University of Guelph. (Courtesy Prof. George D. Bedell, Director, School of Hotel and Food Administration, University of Guelph, Ontario, Canada.)

Standard Oil (Ind.) Research Center, Naperville, Ill., showing "cafeteria on the lake." (Courtesy Harding-Williams Business & Industry Group. Saga Administrative Corp., Menlo Park, Cal.)

The Blue & White Room (Free-Flow Cafeteria), Duke University, Durham, N. C. (Courtesy Theodore W. Minah, Director of Dining Halls Operation.)

Placing Roast in Oven. International Harvester Co. Cafeteria, Melrose Park, Ill. (Courtesy Middleby-Marshall Oven Co., Morton Grove, Ill.)

Student Cafeteria, University of Guelph, Guelph Ontario, Canada. (Courtesy Prof. George D. Bedell.)

Cashier's Station, Blue and White Room (Free-Flow Cafeteria), Duke University, Durham, N. C. (Courtesy Theodore W. Minah, Director Dining Halls Operation.)

out sugar or cream, milk, soft drinks, sandwiches, hot canned soups, ice cream, pastries, etc.

NUTRITION AND INDUSTRIAL FOOD SERVICE

Another wartime contribution was the development and popularization of the science of nutrition. The world has been made food conscious, and words like "vitamins" and "calories" are household terms. Much was done during the war to induce workers to eat balanced diets including fruits and vegetables. Posters issued by the U.S. Department of Agriculture stressing the "Seven Basic Foods" were widely circulated. However, it takes time to change eating habits and individual preferences. Furthermore, as the employee food service usually supplies only one of the worker's three daily meals, it has been difficult to make that one meal the balancing factor.

Nevertheless, the industrial cafeteria has undoubtedly played a vital role in inducing workers to eat foods to which they had not previously been accustomed. The United States is often called "the melting pot," after Zangwill's famous play of the same name, stressing the amalgamation of races and customs in this country. Because of the intermingling of dishes with various racial and regional backgrounds, the author has characterized industrial cafeterias as "epicurean melting-pots."

COMPANY OPERATED FOOD SERVICES

Along with the development of industrial feeding on a wide scale, the manager of the company-operated food service is playing an increasingly important role. He is constantly seeking ways to make the food service meet the needs and desires of the employees it serves. At the same time, in light of constantly increasing costs, he is endeavoring to improve the effectiveness of his operation.

Managers of company-operated food services have their own national organization, to-wit, The Industrial Cafeteria Managers Association. There are also a number of regional associations. Frequent meetings are held at which common problems are discussed. The purpose of these associations is to enhance the professional status of the industrial food-service manager.

POST-WAR TRENDS

Few employee food services were discontinued after World War II and in addition many new ones were introduced as industries migrated to small towns and to the suburban areas of the cities, where other food-service facilities were virtually nonexistent. Vending machines were introduced to serve meals in plants too small to support a cafeteria.

Men and women who had formerly worked in war plants or had served with the Armed Forces had been accustomed to food service and naturally expected it as a condition of employment.

Many small catering companies were set up after the war to serve offices, stores, garages, and small manufacturing plants. Some of these operated mobile canteens—trucks serving coffee, sandwiches, and desserts. Others furnished hot food and beverages in insulated containers from small central kitchens.

Until recently many industrial cafeterias had been highly subsidized by management and in some cases free meals supplied to office workers in banks, insurance companies, and other establishments. However, as wages have increased and fringe benefits extended, the trend has changed to serving employees' meals at cost or at nominal prices.

FOOD SERVICE IN BANKS

What is believed to be the oldest employee food service still in operation is that instituted by the Bowery Savings Bank of New York City in 1834. Meals

Fig. 1.3.   Early building of Bowery Savings Bank.

have been served daily without charge to employees for nearly 140 years. Today as in the beginning, waitress service is provided.

The First National Bank of Boston has maintained its own food service for employees at its head office since 1924. A cafeteria is provided for employees and buffet service for officers and guests. Nominal prices are charged. The restaurant manager is assisted by a staff of 100 in serving about 2,500 meals daily between 10:30 A.M. and 2:30 P.M.

One of the largest food services is that of the Chase-Manhattan Bank in New York City which was instituted in 1915. Approximately 1,500,000 meals are served annually to employees.

The First National Bank of Chicago began serving meals to its employees as early as 1893. Some 2,750 meals are served daily. Another large Chicago financial institution, Continental-Illinois Bank & Trust Company, has served meals to employees since 1929 at nominal charges.

Cafeteria service is provided for 1,100 employees as well as table service for officers and guests at the Philadelphia National Bank. This food service dates back to the late 1890s.

The Bank of America established two cafeterias for its head office employees in San Francisco in the early 1930s. These are operated by a local restaurateur. Nominal prices are charged and price increases are subject to approval by the bank's management committee.

TELEPHONE COMPANIES

In the 1890s the New York and Chicago Telephone Companies began to provide lunchrooms for women operators. Because telephone company operations are literally continuous day and night, food service has become a special consideration. Employees need food or refreshments at hours and on days and in locations where public food accommodations are not readily available.

Consequently, Bell companies in the United States and Canada provide several forms of in-house food service, including more than 450 cafeterias, both company and contractor-operated; over 550 additional food-service centers, primarily banks of vending machines, more than 100 kitchenettes in which employees may prepare snacks, and many other isolated soft drink and/or candy vending machines.

INSURANCE COMPANIES

Metropolitan Life Insurance Company of New York has maintained food services for its head office em-

ployees since 1893, serving approximately 15,000 meals daily. Fifteen straight-line cafeterias are used to feed the majority of employees on weekdays between 11 A.M. and 1:20 P.M. Various other groups are served around the clock seven days a week. Cafeteria menus include choice of one hot or one cold plate along with a wide variety of other foods and beverages. Table service is provided for executives and for special events.

The Prudential Insurance Company of America started its food service in 1923. Currently the Prudential serves approximately 4,100,000 meals annually to its Home Office and Regional Home Office employees.

The cafeteria of the New York Life Insurance Company serves its 4,000 Home Office employees between 11:30 A.M. and 2:30 P.M. on weekdays, using the "shopping center" or "free flow" arrangement. Soiled dishes are self-bused to trayveyors. Nominal prices are charged and the service is operated by a contractor. In addition to the cafeteria, coffee service is provided each morning by means of mobile carts.

The Atlantic Companies in New York supplied free meals to employees until 1960, but now provide low-cost cafeteria service.

The Insurance Company of North America has provided food service for the employees of its head office in Philadelphia for more than 34 years. Cafeteria service is also available to employees of its New York and Los Angeles Service Offices. Nominal prices are charged. Over 475,000 meals are served at the head office annually. For the smaller offices in the United States and Canada, consisting of from 25 to 250 employees, lounges are maintained, containing vending machines, where employees may eat their lunches brought from home.

John Hancock Mutual Life Insurance Company provides some 5,000 luncheons daily in it's cafeterias for the employees of its head office in Boston. Table service is available for officers and guests.

The Kemper Insurance Companies serve some 200 breakfasts and 1,150 luncheons daily for employees at their new quarters at Long Grove, Illinois. Nominal prices are charged.

Connecticut General Life Insurance Company of Hartford feels that because of its location it has the responsibility of providing adequate food service for its employees. Consequently it subsidizes the cafeteria operation. Breakfast and luncheons are served daily and the cafeteria is open from 6:00 A.M. to 6:30 P.M. A waitress serving area is provided which is open to all employees at an extra charge of 50¢; tipping is not permitted. Private dining rooms are also available for various company group meetings. In lieu of daily coffee breaks, beverage wagons bring coffee, tea, milk, hot chocolate, bouillon, and fruit juices to employees shortly after nine each morning.

The Travelers Insurance Company serves more than 1,250,000 meals annually at its Hartford headquarters. Nominal prices are charged. A new employees' restaurant is at present under construction with a "shopping center" or "free flow" cafeteria planned.

AIRLINE CATERING

Meeting the food needs of passengers and crews on airlines has become a big business. Marriott Corporation of Washington, D. C. is the largest airline caterer. Although it operates only 90 industrial and institutional food services, Marriott is a diversified food and lodging company, serving some 1100 units. In 1971 it did a total business of 605 million dollars.

The company had its beginning in 1926 in Washington in the form of an A & W Root Beer stand operated by J. Willard Marriott, a graduate of the University of Utah, his bride of a few months, and a partner whom he later bought out. With the assistance of Mrs. Marriott, he changed the root beer stand into a drive-in restaurant called The Hot Shoppe. By 1930 there were five Hot Shoppes. In 1937, the company became the first airline caterer, putting up meals in cardboard boxes for American and Eastern Airlines passengers out of Washington. In 1971 Marriott served some 50 airlines from 28 domestic flight kitchens and 18 overseas airports.

Marriott is identified for its approach to effective employee training known as the "Audio/Visual" concept. Each unit manager is provided with an audiovisual machine and a library of skill and attitude films pertaining to the operation of his unit. This audiovisual system is not a substitute for personal on-the-job training. It is an *aid* to supervisors in developing well-trained, courteous, and motivated employees. In 1972 Marriott launched a programmed approach to personalized learning and development of management trainees known as "I.D." (individual development).

Another important airline caterer is Sky Chefs, Inc., of New York City, a subsidiary of American Airlines. Sky Chefs serves other airlines as well and operates some 21 catering kitchens on the mainland and in Hawaii. It also operates hotels and food services for the public at various airports.

In these catering kitchens the food may be chilled or frozen after preparation and is reheated on the planes by convection ovens and in some cases by microwave ovens. Figure 1.4 shows a typical airline menu.

Airline caterers seem to have little difficulty in securing and holding employees. This is due to the fact that the caterers' employees have the same flight privileges as the employees of the airlines, traveling at low cost but on a standby basis.

Breakfast Snack
Butter Pecan Coffee Cake
Cinn. Nut Coffee Cake
Strawberry Twist
Crinkle Cup

MS First Class Lunch/Dinner
 1. Shrimp Gruyere
 2. Beef Brochette
 3. Parslied Buttered Rice
 4. Peas W/Pimento
 5. Basic Salad Mix
 6. Garnish #6
    A. Cheddar Cheese
    B. Radish Rose (Medium)
    C. Parsley Sprig
 7. Chef Italian Dressing
 8. German Chocolate Cake
 9. Varietal Roll
10. Butter 72 cut

MSL First Class Dinner
 1. Shrimp Cocktail Supreme
 2. Cocktail Sauce
 3. New York Sirloin
    A. Anna Potatoes
    B. Carrots/Peas
 4. Chicken Kiev
    A. Anna Potatoes
    B. Carrots/Peas
 5. Seafood Au Gratin
    A. Buttered Rice
 6. Basic Salad Mix #2
 7. Salad Dressing Tray
 8. Ice Cream Sundae
 9. Varietal Roll
10. Butter 60 cut

Fig. 1.4. Typical airline menus. (Courtesy Sky Chefs, Inc., New York, N. Y.)

HOSPITAL FOOD SERVICE

In considering the development of hospital food service one does well to remember that the words "hospital," "hostel," and "hotel" are derived from the same Latin word, "hospes," meaning a guest. All three terms suggest a place where guests, whether well or ill, are lodged and fed.

Crude hospitals were known to exist in India and Egypt as early as six centuries before the Christian era. Temples provided refuge for the sick in early Greece and in Rome. As in hospitals today, food was provided for the patients.

Although the first hospital in England was established in 1004 A.D. and the first on the American continent in Mexico in 1524, it was not until the middle of the 19th Century that modern standards of treatment and diets began to take form.

Hospital Diets in 1687

A diet table approved by the governing board of St. Bartholomew's Hospital in London in April, 1687 has been preserved as shown in Figure 1.5.

	Dyett Appointed
Daily	10 oz. of Wheaten Bread and 3 pts. of Shilling Bread.
Sunday	6 oz. of Beefe boiled without bones 1 pt. and a halfe of Beefe Broth 1 pt. of Ale Cawdell
Monday	1 pt. of Milk Pottage 6 oz. of Beefe 1½ pt. of Beefe Broth
Tuesday	Halfe a pint of Boyled Mutton 3 pts. of Mutton Brothe
Wednesday	4 oz. of Cheese 2 oz. of Butter 1 pt. Milk Pottage
Thursday	Same allowance as Sunday (plus) 1 pt. of Rice Milke
Friday	1 pt. of Sugar Soppes 2 oz. of Cheese 1 oz. of Butter 1 pt. of Water Gruell
Saturday	The same allowance as Wednesday

Fig. 1.5. An early diet table.

Although a substantial diet considering prevailing standards, the foregoing illustrates the lack of fruits and vegetables which was characteristic of the meals of the English lower classes of that day.

Florence Nightingale

It was an English nurse, Florence Nightingale, who laid the foundation for modern hospital organization. During the Crimean War, Miss Nightingale was sent to the front by the British War Office to relieve the distress of the wounded. Arriving in the Crimea in 1854, she organized nursing services and reorganized the army hospitals and kitchens so efficiently that the high mortality rate was soon reduced.

After the war, Miss Nightingale devoted her efforts to the improvement of hospital conditions in England, which at the time were said to be little better than those existing in the worst type of prisons. Florence Nightingale can well be called the *first modern hospital administrator* and also the *first hospital dietitian in the modern sense.*

Assisting Miss Nightingale in the Crimea was a little-known hero, Alexis Soyer, a London chef, a native of France, and a flamboyant, many-sided genius. Soyer invented a camp stove, developed recipes, and taught the soldiers how to cook. He can well be termed the *first army dietitian.*

The Dietitian

In the earlier hospitals in the United States, the preparation of the food was in charge of the cook, the housekeeper, or the head nurse. As the importance of food from a *therapeutic* as well as a *nutritional* standpoint became recognized, it was realized that special study must be given in this field. Physicians began to seek among women engaged in food service those who could assist in the diets of patients. At a Home Economics Conference held in 1899 at Lake Placid, New York, the title of "Dietitian" was chosen for those engaged in this new profession. At first the dietitian worked only in the diet kitchen preparing special diets.

Fig. 1.6. Florence Nightingale, the first hospital dietitian. (Courtesy The Modern Hospital, Chicago, Ill.)

Later her services were extended to include the feeding of all patients and staff.

The American Dietetic Association was founded in 1917 and has grown from a membership of 98 in that year to 22,463 as of May 31, 1971. Most of the members are women, but there are a number of male dietitians as well. In 1927 a program of Dietetic Internships was instituted by the Association.

During the two world wars, dietitians distinguished themselves by their ability to provide suitable food for patients in military hospitals. In World War II, 1,998 dietitians were commissioned by the Armed Services of the United States.

Professional dietitians may be distinguished as follows: (1) Administrative Dietitians; (2) Therapeutic Dietitians; (3) Teaching Dietitians; (4) Consulting Dietitians; and (5) Nutritionists. One or more of these roles may be filled by one individual, however. By passing an examination at the completion of internship and meeting continuing educational requirements, a dietitian may become a "Registered Dietitian" with the letters "R.D." following his or her name.

Recent Trends In Hospital Feeding

Many changes have taken place in hospital feeding in the past decade. The wage scale of dietary employees has been increased and recently hospitals have been brought under the provisions of the Federal Employment Security Act. This has made it necessary that kitchens and serving areas be efficiently arranged for effective labor utilization and that other steps be taken to control labor costs. Some hospitals have gone over to the use of convenience foods, for example. Special Diet Kitchens have been eliminated in most hospitals, all food being initially prepared in the Main Kitchen.

Selective menus have been introduced, giving the patient the opportunity to choose between two or more entrees at noon and evening meals. In some hospitals "five meals" are being served to patients, (three meals and two snacks or interval feedings).

Although centralized service is increasingly relied upon, there has been a trend toward the use of small floor pantries in which microwave ovens are used to reheat meals which for various reasons cannot be served at the regular meal periods. Some new appliances have been devised to get hot food *hot* and cold food *cold* to the patient.

Management

In some hospitals the management of the kitchens and cafeterias, and the distribution of food to patients, have been assigned to the Kitchen Manager or Food-

Service Manager, usually a man with a commercial hotel or restaurant background. Dietitians are thus free to devote their efforts to therapeutic diets and to teaching student nurses and dietetic interns. In some instances the food-service manager reports to the chief dietitian and in others directly to the administrator or one of his assistants.

Milk cartons are individually labelled by dietary supervisor at the Sewickley Valley Hospital, Sewickley, Pa., for Meals on Wheels delivery to homes of elderly and handicapped. (Courtesy Saga Administrative Corporation, Menlo Park, Cal.)

Within recent years the use of food as a therapeutic agent has been increasingly recognized by members of the medical profession. In one large teaching hospital almost 70 percent of the patients were on special or therapeutic diets as of the Spring of 1972.

In some hospitals, the food services have been placed in the hands of outside caterers.

NURSING HOMES AND HEALTH CARE UNITS

In addition to the nursing homes which have long functioned to care for terminal cases, many new types of health care units have been developed. Some of these supply post-hospital or extended care at less cost to the patient. Others operate as clinics. In any event, these all require food service similar to that rendered in hospitals.

FOOD SERVICE IN SCHOOLS AND COLLEGES

Although schools were known in the ancient civilizations, there are scant records of their methods of food service. The Greek philosopher Plato is said to have entertained favorite students at dinner in his home following the dialogues at the Academy.

The universities which were established in Europe during the 12th century were not groups of buildings, but rather societies of teachers and students. The latter boarded with the townspeople and got their meals as best they could.

Oxford and Cambridge

At Oxford, founded in England in the latter part of the 12th Century, and at Cambridge, established in the following century, students lived in their quarters, and with the help of servants provided their own meals. Eventually dining halls were erected where the common evening meal was served with considerable ceremony, the dons (professors) occupying a high platform in front. These food-service customs have continued to the present day, although considerably altered by economic conditions.

English Public Schools

The English "Public Schools" such as Eton, Harrow, and Rugby, grew out of the religious institutions of the Middle Ages. Although called "public," they are essentially private boarding schools as we know them in this country. A hundred years ago the food served in many of these schools was poor by modern standards. It has been said that "Dotheboys Hall," the school described by Dickens in "Nicholas Nickleby," was no isolated example of either the administration or the food service of English boarding schools at the time. The prevailing feeling seemed to be that the enjoyment of food or other amenities by children was likely to stimulate them to evil.

American Secondary Schools

Nevertheless it was after the English "grammar" schools that the first secondary schools of the United States were modeled. The Boston Latin School, founded in 1634, and schools in other American colonies were patterned after the English schools in which their founders had been educated. An epoch-making act of the Massachusetts General Court (legislature) in 1647 made it necessary for any town having 100 or more households to set up a grammar school. This act marked the beginning of public education in the United States.

During the 19th Century many private schools were established under denominational or governmental auspices, or through private initiative or endowment. Early feeding of boys and girls in these private schools and academies was invariably in the form of table ser-

vice with student waiters or waitresses. This service has expanded into cafeterias and snack bars.

American Colleges and Universities

Food service has played an important part at Harvard, this country's oldest college, from its inception in 1638. In his book, "Diets and Riots," A. M. Bevis gives vivid and amusing accounts of the students' reactions over the centuries when food served did not suit their tastes.

Under President Lowell (1909-1933) a Department of Dining Halls was organized with capable leadership. Since 1931 members of the three upper classes of the college have lived in "houses" where table service is provided. In recent years, modern cafeterias have been provided for the various schools of the University—all operated by the Food-Service Department.

By 1776 ten universities had been established in the American colonies. In addition to Harvard there were William and Mary (1693), Yale (1701), Princeton (1746) Washington and Lee (1749), Pennsylvania (1751), Columbia (1754), Brown (1764), Rutgers (1766), and Dartmouth (1770). In each of these, various forms of food service have been provided from the beginning. This has been true of the State universities, beginning with North Carolina (1795) and Virginia (1825). Food service has also played an important part in the coeducational institutions, beginning with Oberlin (1833); and in the women's colleges, the first of which was Mount Holyoke (Seminary) (1837).

In addition, the Land Grant colleges were made possible by an Act of Congress in 1862, and now this group includes many of the subsequently established state universities. Many of our larger educational institutions, like Cornell, Johns Hopkins, and Stanford were endowed by private munificence. There were also smaller liberal arts institutions, originally founded, like the first colleges, under religious auspices. These, as well as the professional schools in the fields of theology, education, medicine, dentistry, business, and engineering, have grown rapidly during the present century.

In each of these, whether large or small, food service is provided. In most cases this was originally in the form of table service, but here again the cafeteria has come to be the popular method of mass-feeding.

Clubs and Fraternities

In schools where fraternities or clubs are permitted, meals are usually provided in the club or fraternity house in the form of table service. Usually this includes upper class members only.

Basic Foods Table. Dunster-Mather House, Harvard University. (Courtesy Mrs. Kay Lacoss, Dietitian, Harvard Food Service Department.)

Dining Room, Winthrop College, Rock Hill, South Carolina. (Courtesy Saga Administrative Corporation, Menlo Park, Calif.)

Increasing Enrollment

In recent years the tremendous increase in enrollments in schools, colleges, and universities, is taxing not only the teaching staffs but also the food services. Following are figures on enrollment in 1971 as compared with 1956 (figures for 1971 are estimated) as per the U.S. Department of Health, Education and Welfare:

School Enrollment 1956 vs. 1971 (000's omitted)

	1956	1971 (est.)
Elementary Schools	27,927	36,700
High Schools	8,543	15,100
Colleges	2,883	8,400

Fig. 1.7. School enrollment—1956 vs. 1971.

The School Lunch Movement

The feeding of needy school children was started in Germany in 1790 by American-born Count Rumford. France followed in 1849 with the institution of *cantines scolaires*. In 1865 Victor Hugo initiated school feeding in England, and the practice spread throughout Europe.

Boston was the site of the beginning of the school lunch program in this country. In 1894 the Boston School Committee granted management of their food service to the New England Kitchen, an organization started in 1890 to study food and nutrition for workingmen. In 1907 it was taken over by the Women's Educational and Industrial Union.

By 1913 many school lunch programs were developing throughout the country. In 1931 it was estimated that there were 64,500 school cafeterias, in addition to hot lunch facilities, provided in some 11,500 other schools. Today the cafeteria is an integral part of most elementary and high school plants. In 1971, of 116,307 public schools, some 80,000, or 68.8 percent were participating in the National School Lunch Program. However, of the approximately 52,200,000 children in elementary and secondary schools, only some 24,600,000 or 47.1 percent were being reached.

Federal Subsidies

An Act of Congress in 1935 made federal funds available to buy agricultural surplus foods for distribution to school children. This program was broadened by Congress in 1946 by grants-in-aid to states providing school lunches. The Child Nutrition Act of 1966 was designed to aid in meeting the nutritional needs of the nation's children. The Special Milk Program, which had been functioning since 1954, was made part of the Act, and a pilot breakfast program authorized. The Act also provided special funding assistance toward equipment. Conduct and supervision of Federal programs to assist schools in providing food service for children were transferred from other agencies and placed under the U.S. Department of Agriculture.

The original policy of the school lunch system was to provide free meals for children who could not afford to pay, and to make a nominal charge to those who could afford to pay.

Recognizing the increases in food cost and other operating expenses that have taken place, the Congress in 1972 passed legislation substantially increasing federal subsidies for school breakfasts and luncheons. They also made special provision for the feeding of needy school children.

Current Trends in School Lunch Programs

Breakfasts are now being provided as well as lunches in many schools. In some parts of the country central kitchens have been set up where food is prepared, cooked, and in some cases frozen, and then transported to the various schools where it is reheated and served. Obviously this eliminates the cost of cooking and other equipment. As plastic trays and disposable utensils are used, the dishwashing problem is minimized.

Type "A" Luncheons

The standard school luncheon, known as "Type A," consists of the following minimal nutritional requirements:

	Quantity
1. Milk, whole	½ pint
2. Protein-rich food consisting of any of the following or a combination thereof:	
Fresh or processed meat, poultry meat, cheese, cooked or canned fish	2 ozs.
Dry peas, beans or soybeans, cooked	½ cup
Peanut Butter	4 tbsps.
Eggs	1
3. Raw, cooked, or canned vegetables or fruits, or both	¾ cup
4. Bread, muffins, or hot bread made of whole grain cereal or enriched flour	1 portion
5. Butter or fortified margarine	2 tsp.

A "Type B" lunch was devised for schools not having adequate facilities for the preparation of the "Type A" lunch, as was a "Type C" lunch. Reimbursement to schools is based upon the type of meals served.

Fig. 1.8. Type "A" luncheon requirements.

Current Trends in College and University Feeding

Most private schools, colleges, and universities depend upon the cafeteria rather than table service for student feeding today. This is because of its lower

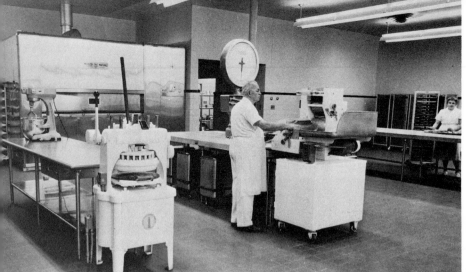

Kitchen, Polk State School, Polk, Pa. (Courtesy Middleby-Marshall Oven Co., Morton Grove, Ill.)

Ovens in Kitchen of Chattanooga High School, Chattanooga, Tenn. (Courtesy Middleby-Marshall Oven Co., Morton Grove, Ill.)

Rotary Oven at Illinois Institute of Technology, Chicago. (Courtesy Middleby-Marshall Oven Co., Morton Grove, Ill.)

Central Kitchen, Indianapolis, Indiana, School System. (Courtesy Middleby-Marshall Oven Co., Morton Grove, Ill.)

Kitchen, Edinboro State College, Pennsylvania. (Courtesy Middleby-Marshall Oven Co., Morton Grove, Ill.)

Grocery Warehouse, Los Angeles City School Districts. (Courtesy Flambert & Flambert, San Franciso, Cal.)

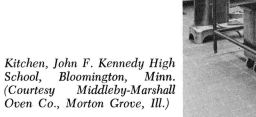

Kitchen, John F. Kennedy High School, Bloomington, Minn. (Courtesy Middleby-Marshall Oven Co., Morton Grove, Ill.)

cost and speedier service where large groups are to be fed. Student Unions in larger universities, such as the University of Minnesota, provide food service for "commuters," that is, students not living in the dormitories.

The "Hollow Square" or as it is called at Duke University, "the Free-Flow" type of cafeteria, has been introduced in many institutions and found not only efficient but psychologically advantageous in reducing the feelings of frustration which arise from waiting in conventional cafeteria lines.

Student demands for the so-called "basic foods" are being met on many campuses. In the Harvard University dining halls, for example, in addition to the regular cafeteria menus, the following items are available: rolled oats, wheat germ, peanut butter, cottage cheese, various flavors of Yogurt, honey, raisins, etc. Nutritionists feel that such diet fads may be harmful in lacking certain nutrients necessary to health and that they should be combined with conventional foods.

Students have long complained about board rates. As is well known, these rates are based upon the fact that all students will not eat 21 meals per week, even though entitled to them. If 15 meal contracts were issued and if students ate all of the 15 meals, it is likely that the cost would be little different from a 21 meal contract in which only 15 meals are eaten. Some colleges are issuing such short-term contracts. Yale still requires a basic 21-meal contract for resident undergraduates but has available a 10-meal and 5-luncheon contract for students living off campus. Princeton has a 20-meal contract (with "brunch" on Sundays); a 14-meal contract (breakfast-dinner or luncheon-dinner) for undergraduates, as well as a 7-meal dinner contract. At Duke University the 21-meal contract is offered as well as a 15-meal, 5-day (Monday through Friday) plan. As of the Fall of 1972, all mandatory meal plans at the Harvard Graduate School of Business Administration were abolished.

At Harvard, Yale, and many other universities students may have unlimited "seconds" on all except the main entrées and may have the option of eating in any dining hall.

College and university food-service directors have their own organization, The National Association of College and University Food Services, and meet regularly to discuss common problems.

Outside Contractors

In most of the school and college food services, management has been in the hands of the institutions. Recently there has been a substantial increase in the number of such food services operated by outside catering firms.

Sales and Purchase Statistics

Figure 1.9 gives the estimated sales total of foods and drinks and estimated purchase totals, plus percentages of each, for the various units making up Group II—industrial and institutional food services in 1970. Group I, Commercial Restaurants and Food Services, shows total estimated sales of $34,069,416, so that the combined total sales for Groups I and II are $41,405,809.

As indicated, sales figures are not shown for convents, seminaries, jails, and penal institutions as these institutions make no charge for food. However, the estimated purchases of these three groups total approximately $202,909. Extrapolating on the basis of a 40 percent of sales we could well add another $500,000 to the total sales of Group II as the sales equivalent of meals served in convents and seminaries, federal and state prisons and jails.

This Figure gives some idea of the extent and diversity of food services in industry and institutions.

THE IMPACT OF CHANGE

Heraclitus, the philosopher who lived in Asia Minor in the 5th Century B.C., is reported to have said, "Nothing is certain but change. You cannot step into the same river twice for new and newer waters are ever flowing by."

We are living in an era of great changes. The difference between our day and that of Heraclitus lies in the rapidity with which changes take place. Due to the applications of scientific research the pace of change has been accelerated. The late Professor Erwin Schell, of Massachusetts Institute of Technology, once illustrated this to the author's class at Boston University. He said that if the entire history of man on this earth—variously estimated at from 500,000 to 1,000,000 years—could be compressed within the past twenty-four hours, more scientific research would have taken place within the last ten seconds than in all previous time.

In the preceding pages, we have read of some of these changes which have taken place in the food-service industry over the years. Industrial and institutional food-service executives must be prepared for many more changes in the years ahead. We may not like them but we must adjust to them. To meet these changes successfully requires an open mind and a willingness to see the other fellow's point of view. Old patterns of thought and deep-seated prejudices must

Number of Units	Type of Establishment	Estimated F & D Sales (000 omitted)	Percent of F & D Sales	Estimated F & D Purchases (000 omitted)	Percent of F & D Purchases
Group II—Commercial, Educational, Government or Institutional Organizations Which Run Their Own Food-Service Operations					
4,000	Employee Feeding Industrial & Commercial Organizations	$ 560,806	1.35%	$ 280,403	1.85%
631	Sea-going Ships (1,000+ tons)	44,841	.11	26,905	.18
4,248	Inland Waterway Vessels	82,230	.20	49,338	.32
86,385	Public & Parochial Elementary & Secondary Schools (78,600 in National School Lunch Program)[3]	1,163,329	2.81	1,369,276	9.02
	Colleges & Universities[4]				
765	Public	654,996	1.58	372,511	2.45
1,354	Private	283,526	.68	163,574	1.08
	Transportation				
170	Ocean-going Passenger/Cargo Liners	40,648	.10	20,324	.13
22	Airlines	177,954	.43	80,080	.53
1	Railroad	20,741	.05	9,333	.06
10,448	Clubs	524,944	1.27	218,426	1.44
4,155	Voluntary & Proprietary Hospitals	1,868,396	4.51	747,348	4.92
1,704	State & Local Hospitals[5]	303,935	.73	203,182	1.34
856	Longterm General, TB and Nervous & Mental Hospitals	761,825	1.84	304,730	2.01
408	Federal Hospitals[5]	118,204	.29	103,254	.68
23,463	Institutions (Homes for Aged, Blind, Orphans, Mentally and Physically Handicapped)	623,138	1.50	496,173	3.27
3,746	Sporting & Recreational Camps	45,880	.11	27,528	.18
900	Community Centers	61,000	.15	27,450	.18
	Convents & Seminaries	***		70,767	.47
	Penal Institutions				
337	Federal & State Prisons	***		70,491	.46
4,037	Jails	***		61,651	.40
147,630	**TOTAL GROUP II**	$ 7,336,393	17.71%	$ 4,702,744	30.97%
	TOTAL GROUPS I & II	$41,405,809	100.00%	$15,185,787	100.00%

Group III—Government Feeding

	Defense Personnel			989,100	
	Commercial Employees			1,073,000	
	GRAND TOTAL			$17,247,887	

3. School lunch program commodities supplied under Sec 6, 32, 416 are worth $272,375,000. 2,721,658,000 half-pints of milk worth $126,974,610 additional supplied thru 94,000 outlets.
4. Colleges and universities which have food service whether contracted or not.
***The institutions make no charge for food served.

Fig. 1.9. Statistics of Industrial and Institutional Food Services, 1970. (Courtesy National Restaurant Association.)

be discarded. Only as we approach the future with objectivity and flexibility can we adequately deal with the changes it may bring. By cultivating such an outlook we can make our work more satisfying and worthwhile.

SUGGESTED READING

BEVIS, A. M. *Diets and Riots.* Boston: Marshall Jones Co., 1936.

BRYAN, MARY DE GARNO. *The School Cafeteria.* New York: F. S. Crafts Co., 1946.

CHEYNEY, E. P. *Industrial & Social History of England.* New York: The Macmillan Co., 1922.

COLEMAN, JOAN J. *Industrial Food Service Management.* Chicago: University of Chicago, 1954. (Dissertation for PhD. Degree—Microfilm)

CROTHERS, SAMUEL. *John H. Patterson.* New York: Garden City Publishing Co., 1926.

FOSTER, SIR WILLIAM. *John Company.* London: John Lane the Bodley Head Ltd., 1926.

GILMAN, N. P. *A Dividend to Labor.* Boston: Houghton, Mifflin Co., 1899.

GRAVES, FRANK P. *A History of Education.* New York: The Macmillan Co., 1918.

Greenslet, Ferris. *The Lowells and Their Seven Worlds.* Boston: Houghton, Mifflin Co., 1946.

Lundberg, Donald E. "The Hotel and Restaurant Business." Chicago: *Institutions Magazine,* 1970.

MacEachern, M. T. *Hospital Organization & Management.* Chicago: Physician's Record Co., 1935.

Meakin, Budgett. *Model Factories and Villages.* London: T. Fisher, 1905.

Morris, Helen. *Portrait of a Chef (Life of Alexis Soyer).* Cambridge, England: University Press, 1938.

Morrison, S. E. *The Rope Makers of Plymouth.* Boston: Houghton, Mifflin Co., 1950.

National Industrial Conference Board. *Industrial Lunch Rooms.* New York: 1928.

Norton, Arthur O. *Readings in the History of Education.* Cambridge, Mass.: Harvard University, 1909.

Stokes, John W. *How to Manage a Restaurant or Institutional Food Service.* Dubuque, Iowa: Wm. C. Brown Company Publishers, 1967.

U.S. Department of Agriculture, *The National School Lunch Program,* FNS 63, Washington, D. C.: U.S. Government Printing Office, 1971.

CHAPTER 2

Objectives and Policies in Industrial and Institutional Feeding

OBJECTIVES

Food services in industries differ in some respects from those in institutions. They also differ among themselves with respect to the size, location, physical structure, and policies of each individual establishment. Yet the industrial and institutional food services have many common objectives, such as to provide:

1. Food of good quality, properly cooked and prepared.
2. Prompt and courteous service.
3. Well-balanced, varied menus.
4. Reasonable prices consistent with service offered.
5. Adequate facilities.
6. High standards of cleanliness and sanitation.

Good Food

Successfully-operated food services have found it pays to use quality food products. On the other hand, the highest priced items are not necessarily the best suited to the purpose at hand. Lower-priced cuts of meat, for example, if properly prepared, cooked, and served, may afford nutritious, appetizing dishes. Food must not only be purchased right, but also properly stored, prepared, cooked, and served. Thus the successful operation of the food service depends upon the coordination of its various functions.

Prompt and Courteous Service

In industry as well as in institutions, meal periods are necessarily limited. Food must be served promptly. If food service is to play its part in the overall public relations program, it should be friendly and courteous.

Where large numbers are to be served in relatively short periods, the cafeteria or self-service lunch counter is most popular. Under other circumstances, table service is required. Canteens and food trucks are often employed to reach groups in remote locations.

In recent years, automatic vending machines have become increasingly in vogue.

Well-Balanced Menus

As industrial and institutional food services generally cater to the same patrons day after day, it is important that the menu be varied in order to maintain its appeal. Where students or patients are fed three meals daily, the need arises for providing a well-balanced menu from a nutritional standpoint.

Reasonable Prices

Food prices in employee feeding establishments vary, as has been noted from the previous chapter, from free meals to those covering part or all of the expenses involved. In some cases, prices are comparable to those charged by commercial restaurants.

Restaurant prices have been customarily based on the ratio of the "raw-food cost" to the sales dollar. In an earlier day, practically all food was purchased in a raw state and processed in the kitchen. Today such items as bread, rolls, pastries, ice-cream, and even entrees (so-called "convenience foods"), are purchased ready to serve. Many products are now being bought partially processed, ready for finishing. Nevertheless, the term "raw-food cost" is applied to all products delivered to the food service.

For many years restaurant practice has been to strive for a given food-cost percentage, that is, the ratio between the cost of the food and its sales value, 40% being a common goal, and to operate so that the combined food and labor costs did not exceed, say 70% to 75%. This left from 25% to 30% to cover rent and other overhead and a net profit. As labor costs have increased in recent years it has been necessary to lower the food-cost percentage to, say, 36% to 38%, and to keep other expenses under strict control in order to achieve a net profit after taxes.

Industrial and institutional food services are usually operated on a nonprofit or break-even basis. Nevertheless, they are expected, in some instances, to contribute to overhead expenses. For example, Figure 2.1, shows the percentages of a university food service.

Food	44.9%
Student Labor	8.9
Professional Labor	14.4
Supplies	8.8
University overhead	23.0
	100.0%

Fig. 2.1. Operating percentages of a University Food Service for year 1971.

Food Costs

With good management food costs depend almost entirely upon three factors:
1. The purchase cost.
2. The portion size.
3. The price charged the patron.

By adjusting these three factors, the food-cost percentage may be set at any desired figure. However, if it is set too low the patron receives insufficient food value for his money and consequently will be dissatisfied. If the food-cost percentage is set too high, there will be little left over to cover labor costs and other necessary expenses.

It is necessary for management to follow a middle course by which the food-cost percentage will be high enough to provide satisfactory food value to the patron, and yet not so high as to leave insufficient gross profit to cover other operating expenses.

Amount of Subsidization

What this food-cost objective will be depends upon management's policy and the extent of subsidization deemed advisable. Experience has shown that human beings do not generally appreciate what they get for nothing. Furthermore, if prices are too low it makes for invidious comparisons with prices charged by commercial eating places, and may reflect unfavorably from a public-relations standpoint.

Some industrial and institutional cafeterias are wholly subsidized. Others operate on a so-called nonprofit basis, where the food-cost percentage is set to cover all direct expenses such as food, labor, and supplies, but not utilities, space charges, nor administrative overhead. In some cases it is felt that the food prices should cover food and direct labor costs only, and still others are satisfied if merely the food cost is covered. Cafeterias operating on the nonprofit basis set their food costs between 45% and 55% depending upon policy. In setting food-cost objective, all factors, including wage rates paid, should be taken into consideration. Where higher wage rates are required, as under union contracts, the food-cost percentage may be reduced.

If a maximum food-cost goal of say 50% is set, the employees will be getting approximately 20% greater food value than they would in most commercial eating places. At the same time the worker's self-respect is enhanced, as he is paying a reasonable part of the cost of the service. Such an objective would seem fair to all concerned and should obviate outside criticism.

Patient Feeding

The feeding of patients in hospitals, involving as it does the problems of special diets and considerable service, is on a different basis. Raw-food cost per meal or per diem is the basic yard stick employed. The general objective is to conduct the food service so effectively that this cost and the overall unit Dietary costs are as reasonable as possible consistent with the patient's needs. The cost of food is, of course, part of the overall per-diem rate charged by the institution. Current inflationary pressures have been causing increases in hospital Dietary costs, as in other areas.

Adequate Facilities

Facilities both from the standpoint of space and equipment, should be adequate to provide for wholesome well-cooked food. As environment plays so important a part in the enjoyment of eating, the facilities should be clean and attractive. As will be seen in later chapters, much can be done in the original planning of the kitchen and service layout to make for simplicity in operation and to avoid excessive labor and overhead costs.

High Standards of Cleanliness

Good housekeeping is standard practice in any well-run business or institution. With respect to the handling of food, the utmost care should be taken. Not only should local, state, and federal health regulations be meticulously observed in the food service, but every effort should be made to enlist the whole-hearted co-operation of food-service employees and patrons in the interests of high standards of cleanliness and sanitation.

POLICY DETERMINATION

Major matters for policy determination with respect to food service on the part of management of a business or institution are:

1. Location, type of building, equipment
2. Style of service (cafeteria, counter, or table service, or a combination of one or more)
3. Operator—The institution itself or an outside contractor.

Outside Counsel Needed

Before planning a new food service, it is well to have the aid of an experienced, impartial, outside food consultant to make sure that all factors are being considered and that the new operation is properly designed and laid out for efficient operation. From his broad experience the consultant can also give sound advice on policy matters.

Physical Facilities

Physical facilities to be provided will depend upon the type of food service to be offered. (In Chapter 5 problems in connection with location, layout, and equipment are discussed.) The policy of management will determine the extent of the investment which may be allowed.

Extent of Self-Support

As outlined earlier in this chapter under the caption "Reasonable Prices," the extent to which the food service will be self-supporting will depend upon the pricing policy, size of portions, and the type and quality of food served. Operating costs, including labor and overhead items, will also be a factor.

Food Service Can Build Goodwill

Properly operated, the food service can be a means of building goodwill. This may take place among employees and staff members themselves as they eat in the cafeteria. Members of management should also make it a point whenever their schedules permit, to eat in the cafeteria. Thus they become familiar with the type of food and service offered. It will also afford opportunity for personal contacts which break down barriers between management and workers.

Friendly contacts on the part of food-service employees with patients in hospitals or students in educational institutions also is an important factor in building good public relations.

Patron's Questionnaire

In planning a new food service, management will usually give careful consideration to policy matters. A competent architect will be engaged to draw plans, and an experienced food-management consultant may be called upon for advice on layouts and operating methods. Frequently, however, little thought is given to the reactions of those who are to patronize the new food service. As a result, it may fail to meet the needs and desires of those who are expected to be its patrons.

A simple, yet effective way of securing this information is to send a questionnaire to the employees, students, patients, or others concerned. Answers to this questionnaire will aid in determining: potential patronage, whether for complete meals or for supplementary beverages and desserts; types of food preferred; and other salient facts.

By sending out the questionnaire well in advance, many facts may be obtained which will aid in policy determination. At the same time, the recognition accorded to the prospective patrons will build goodwill toward the food service from the start.

The letter and the accompanying questionnaire itself should be carefully worded to call forth objective answers. Usually patrons are asked not to sign their names to the questionnaire, and arrangements are often made to return the form to an impartial agency not connected with the establishment.

Figures 2.2 and 2.3 illustrate a letter and questionnaire sent to the employees of a New England hospital prior to the opening of a new cafeteria. In this case, of the 180 questionnaires issued, 152 (84%) were filled out and returned. All but twelve indicated their intention to patronize the new food service. Of the twelve, several were on special diets, and a few individuals ate their meals at home. Nearly one-half of those responding made specific suggestions, most of which were constructive.

OPERATION BY BUSINESS OR INSTITUTION

Business concerns usually operate their own employee food services under the supervision of the Personnel Department, although in some cases the responsibility may be assigned to some interested executive or to an employees' association.

In hospitals the food service is generally the responsibility of the Chief Dietitian and the Dietary Department, or of a Food-Service Manager.

January 6, 19

Dear Fellow Employee:

    Within a few weeks we expect that the new Cafeteria for employees will be ready. I am sure that you will be pleased with the splendid new equipment and the fine accommodations provided for us.

    Like other hospital cafeterias, the new Cafeteria will be operated on a non-profit, cash basis. The new plan means that you pay only for the meals you eat, and that you can purchase as little or as much as you wish. Payroll deductions for meals will be discontinued when the Cafeteria opens.

    In addition to serving food of the highest quality and providing prompt, friendly service, we want the new Cafeteria to meet the needs and desires of all employees to the fullest extent possible. For this reason we are enclosing a questionnaire which we would like you to fill out and return to guide us in our planning.

    You need not sign your name, but please give much thought to the questions and be quite frank and constructive in answering. In order that the questionnaire may be handled with the utmost fairness and impartiality, we are enclosing a stamped envelope addressed to John W. Stokes and Company, our food service consultants in Boston. Please mail your answers just as soon as possible, as we want to have the benefit of your ideas and suggestions, as well as those of all the other employees, in plenty of time before the new Cafeteria opens.

    Best wishes for the New Year during which we may look forward to many such improvements in our facilities which will make working at _____ Hospital more enjoyable.

Sincerely yours,

Administrator

jrs/jlm

Fig. 2.2.   Letter accompanying questionnaire.

SUBJECT: QUESTIONNAIRE RE CAFETERIA SERVICE

1. I expect to patronize the new Employees Cafeteria for the following meals and coffee breaks:

Breakfast _____   Morning Coffee Break   _____
Noon Meal _____   Evening Coffee Break   _____
Supper _____   Night (After midnite) Coffee Break _____
Midnight Meal_____

2. I do not expect to patronize the new Cafeteria because:

_____
_____

3. I would prefer the following main dishes for my daily meals: (List two or three which you like best of all)

Sunday_____

Monday_____

Tuesday_____

Wednesday_____

Thursday_____

Friday _____

Saturday_____

4. For desserts I like the following:
Ice Cream_____   Jello_____
Pie_____   Fruit_____
Puddings_____   Cake_____
            Other _____

5. I usually drink the following beverage:
Coffee_____   Milk _____
Tea_____   Hot Chocolate_____
            Chocolate Milk_____

6. I like Salads _____, especially_____Salad.
    I do not like Salads _____

7. I prefer to eat my heavy meal at:
            Noon _____
            Night _____

8. I would make the following suggestions regarding the new Employees Cafeteria:

_____
_____
_____
_____

Fig. 2.3. Employee questionnaire.

School and college food services are customarily operated by a manager who is under the direction of the Business Manager or the Treasurer.

Chief advantages claimed for self-operation are:

1. As the operation is directly under the control of the management, it is easier to maintain high standards of quality and service.

2. The food service renders other important services such as providing facilities for meetings, meals for executives, visitors, etc. It, therefore, should be under the same management.

3. Patients, students, employees, or the public may resent the idea of outsiders making a profit at their expense.

4. Operation by the institution or business itself is more economical, in that the fees paid to outside contractors are eliminated.

OUTSIDE OPERATION

Advantages cited for outside operation are:

1. Management is relieved of the responsibility of the food service and the "headaches" that go with it.

2. Because of the accumulated "know-how" of the contractor's organization, higher standards of quality and service can be offered.
3. Although the contractor must be paid a management fee, he can effect offsetting savings for the institution through his mass-purchasing power and tight control of food and labor costs.

Small Institutions

Outside feeding contractors generally will only take on food services that are large enough to be profitably operated. For industrial cafeterias, this means plants where more than 500 are employed, unless the management is willing to subsidize the operation to make it profitable. With respect to hospitals, experienced outside caterers generally do not feel that they can profitably operate an institution of less than 150 bed capacity. For schools, the size of the student body is also an important factor.

Formerly the small plant or institution had no alternative but to provide its own food facilities. Today, in many localities, new types of food service are offered. These include automatic food vending machines, mobile canteen units, and other methods.

Where outside services such as mobile canteens are sanctioned, management should see that food quality and sanitation comply with requirements, and that the outsiders are not allowed to disrupt the personnel or day-to-day routine.

Investigation Required

If outside contractors are being considered, a thorough investigation should be made of their standing and responsibility. Visits should be made to the contractor's operations in similar establishments to ascertain at first hand the quality of food and service offered.

CHAPTER 3

Management and Supervision

"A food service is as good as its management." This statement is generally accepted, for if any food service, industrial, institutional, or commercial, is to be successful, it must have sound management.

To manage is to direct and control. The food-service manager strives to direct and control the operation so that quality food is procured and prepared and served under high standards of sanitation at reasonable costs. The manager directs and controls the entire operation, delegating appropriate responsibility and authority to the supervisors for the departments under their charge. Because the supervisor is in close touch with the employees, his role is most important in accomplishing the objectives of the food service.

It was not until the turn of the century that management as a discipline, that is, an organized body of knowledge, began. At first, the emphasis was upon systems and incentives, the era of "scientific management." In the 1930s the emphasis shifted to the "human relations" approach in which the feelings of the workers were taken into account. Within the past decade the idea of "participative" management has developed in which the workers participate in decision-making. In addition, there have been many new approaches to the problems of management, suggested by students of industrial relations.

SCIENTIFIC MANAGEMENT

Frederick W. Taylor, known as "the father of scientific management," was born in Philadelphia in 1858 and graduated from Exeter Academy in New Hampshire. Because of a chronic eye ailment, he was unable to enter college. Instead he became a journeyman machinist and patternmaker. Sometime later he completed engineering studies.

Young Taylor was troubled by the soldiering, waste, and inefficiency he encountered in industry. He sought to determine what a "proper day's work" consisted of. This led to research, including time studies over a period of thirty years, out of which came the concept "scientific management," consisting of four principles:

1. The development by management of a body of knowledge, that is, the "science" of each particular task, with rigid rules for each motion of the worker and the perfection and standardization of tools, implements, and working conditions.
2. Careful selection and training of workers willing to adopt the best work methods.
3. Bringing the worker and the "science" of his work together through the constant help of management and through paying a liberal daily bonus for performing a proper day's work and following instructions.
4. Almost equal distribution of work and responsibility between the worker and the management, including planning, directing, and scheduling by management to give the worker every facility to perform his work.

The industry has been profoundly influenced by Taylor's work. Incentive systems, time study, and cost accounting reflect his ideas. Frank Gilbreth, a contractor and a friend of Taylor, became interested in scientific management and developed the study of *motion economy*. Time study and motion economy were carried on separately for a time, but are now used in combination. The method known as "Work Simplification" embodies both of these techniques and is based upon Taylor's methods of analysis as well as upon the studies in motion economy pioneered by Gilbreth and carried on by him after Taylor's death.

THE HUMAN RELATIONS EMPHASIS

While scientific management emphasized systems, the human relations approach emphasized people. In 1925, Dr. Elton Mayo, of the Harvard Business School, and colleagues began an intensive study of the workers in the Hawthorne plant of the Western Electric Company near Chicago. The results of this study, which lasted for several years, indicated that productivity depends upon the motivation and morale of the workers. Basically, the human relations approach stresses *the needs and desires* of the worker. The study also indicated that those working under incentive plans tended to restrict production to the levels which the workers felt were appropriate.

PARTICIPATIVE MANAGEMENT

Donald E. Lundberg and James P. Armatas, in their book *The Management of People in Hotels, Restau-*

rants and Clubs, point out that while a pure human relations program cannot be fully implemented in the food-service organization, as management needs to maintain its power to manage, however, the principles are valuable as an approach. Eight objectives are summarized in the book toward which food-service managers should devote their efforts:

1. Involve employees in decisions affecting their welfare.
2. Have concern for the welfare of employees.
3. Promote the maximum of job satisfaction.
4. Select workers for the jobs for which they are best suited.
5. Train and develop supervisory employees.
6. Provide realistic worker participation, making workers feel that they are a part of the organization.
7. Insure mental health.
8. Promote constructive goals so that workers may enjoy meaningful work experiences.

THE PRAGMATIC ATTITUDE

While all of these various approaches to management theory provide valuable insights for the food-service manager, he must have a *pragmatic* attitude, that is, from the various suggested ideas, he must pick out those he thinks *will work* in his situation and by testing, prove or disprove their validity.

Taylor believed that there is a "science" to every task. In 1899, for example, he was assistant general manager of the Bethlehem Steel Works, Bethlehem, Pennsylvania. He turned his attention to the "Yard," two miles long and a quarter mile wide, where several hundred laborers were unloading freight cars containing iron ore, coal, coke, limestone, sand, etc., each using his own shovel. He found that the weight of each shovelful, depending upon the material, varied from 3½ pounds to as much as 38 pounds. Through careful research, he determined that the optimum shovelful weight was 21½ pounds, and that a laborer could shovel that much weight throughout the day without undue fatigue. He then persuaded the company to furnish shovels for the men, large ones for light material and smaller ones for heavy matter, each holding exactly 21½ pounds of the material with which it was to be used.

He studied the "science" of shoveling and taught those who followed his instructions, and who were paid a substantial bonus, to use their arms, legs, and bodies to best advantage. In addition, he systematized the work of the Yard. At the end of two years, as a result of his efforts, the entire work load, which had required from 400 to 600 men to perform, was being accomplished easily by 140 men. Surely, if there is a "science" to shoveling, there must be methods of improving the numerous manual tasks required in the food service.

Many studies have been made of methods used by supervisors, some of whom are said to be "employer oriented," that is, authoritative, and others "employee oriented," concerned with the desires and feelings of workers. Results of these studies seem to show that both methods have their place. Both seem to work under certain circumstances. Some workers resent being "bossed" while others like to be told what to do.

No two individuals are alike. Each is actuated by many different motives. As Dr. Saul W. Gellerman points out in his book, *Motivation and Productivity*, each individual wishes to "be himself." He wishes to live in a manner appropriate to his preferred role; to be treated in a manner that corresponds to his preferred rank; and to be rewarded in a manner that reflects his estimate of his own abilities. The task of the food-service manager and his supervisors, therefore, is to make the work in the food service a more satisfying and fulfilling experience for his employees.

LEADERSHIP

How can the food-service manager get his or her employees to *want* to work for the best interests of the organization of which they are a part? This is a question that has been pondered over by many students of management theory. Essentially it is a matter of motivation.

Some psychologists believe that it is virtually impossible to "motivate" human behavior. The best that can be done, they say, is to create a climate in which employees motivate themselves.

On the other hand, history is replete with epics of military, political, and religious leaders who so motivated their followers to be willing to endure hardships, dangers, and even death for the sake of their leaders. A classic example of leadership is found in the story of the "Ten Thousand Greeks" as told in the *Anabasis*.

In the year 401 B.C., when the great Persian Empire dominated the Middle East, Darius, the young brother of the King, sought to usurp the throne. To aid in his task, he hired 10,000 mercenaries from Greece, where unemployment was rife at the time. A crucial battle was fought near Babylon, where the King's army was defeated, largely due to the courage and prowess of the Greeks. At the last minute, however, young Darius was killed. Thus, there was nothing left to fight for.

The Greek generals were summoned to a council by the Persian High Command, but on arrival all of the generals were slain. When the word of their assassination came to the Greeks in their camp, they were appalled. They had not been paid, they were far from home, surrounded by hordes of Persians who wished to annihilate them, and now they were without their leaders. However, there was among them a civilian named Xenophon, a writer, perhaps one of the first war correspondents. That night he had a vision and the next morning he called the remaining junior officers together. "Let us fight our way out," he urged, "We are Greeks—free men—while the Persians are slaves."

Impressed by his manner, the young officers called a meeting of the entire army. When the men cried out, "We have no generals," Xenophon replied, "You are all generals," and the march began. Xenophon reorganized the army, delegating authority and responsibility to those who merited it, with the result that the idealistic and independent Greeks became a disciplined unit. Living off the land, constantly harassed by the Persians from the rear, they forced their way up the valleys of the Tigris and Euphrates Rivers. They had been equipped for the desert but as they entered the mountain country winter fell upon them and they struggled through deep snow and ice-covered streams. They had to battle with the fierce tribes of the hill country. From September to January they marched some 2,000 miles, finally reaching the Black Sea and returning to their homeland.

What were the qualities of leadership that enabled Xenophon to guide the ten thousand men safely through their trials and tribulations?

1. He quickly inspired their confidence in his leadership.
2. He instilled self-confidence in his followers.
3. He *set an example* by undergoing the same hardships as his men.
4. He *listened* to complaints and suggestions, freely admitting his own mistakes when he made them. In the councils, when they had talked themselves out, he submitted his own plan of action, saying, "If anyone has a better plan, let him speak up. We only want to do what is best for all."

These principles are as applicable to management today as they were to the ten thousand Greeks nearly 2,400 years ago. Food-service managers would do well to emulate them.

Are Leaders Born or Made?

It is commonly held that leaders are born, not made, that one either has or doesn't have leadership qualities. Undoubtedly there have been outstanding leaders who seem to have inherited their talent for leadership. On the other hand, there have been obscure men who have risen to the opportunity and have become leaders like Xenophon, for example.

Between those who possess leadership qualities in a marked degree and those who lack them, there is a larger group who are gifted to some extent and who can, through study, self-discipline, and hard work, develop executive skills.

Among the successful food-service executives the author has known, practically everyone has achieved success because he has been willing to pay the price which leadership demands. Most of them worked a little harder, put in extra hours and gave up what others regarded as pleasures but which they looked upon as nonessential.

THE FOOD-SERVICE MANAGER*

In a food service, certain duties must be assigned to others. This gives rise to a series of steps known as the Functions of Management. These are:

1. *Planning:* The food-service manager must lay plans to *realize the objectives for which the food service has been instituted.* He must determine what these objectives are—in other words, what he wishes to accomplish. Physical facilities must be made available, equipment must be installed, food and supplies procured, stored, and prepared. Food quality, service, and decor must be such as to attract and satisfy patrons. Basically, the economic objective is to create a value in the goods and services offered which will induce patrons to pay more for them than what they cost so that a margin will remain to cover overhead expenses and administrative costs.

Simply defined, planning is *thinking ahead.* It requires imagination and the ability to forecast future contingencies based upon past experience. For the food-service manager there are tools which facilitate planning, such as budgets, staffing tables, and records of past operations. A new food service will have available plans, specifications, layouts, marketing studies, and the like.

2. *Organizing:* Once the objectives are established, the manager will *develop an organization.* Tasks which are related are combined into a job, or a series of jobs, to be performed by one individual. Supervisors are designated to direct groups of workers. These supervisors are accountable to assistant managers or they may report directly to the manager.

Organizing involves the delegation of responsibility and authority and determining accountability. It is easy to delegate responsibility, but some managers find it difficult to delegate authority. Yet, if a subordinate is to be given responsibility for the carrying out of a function, he must be given commensurate authority and be held accountable for the results.

This does not apply to "staff" functions as distinguished from "line" functions. Staff functions are indirect and advisory such as personnel, legal, accounting, medical, etc. The food-cost accountant will give no orders to kitchen employees when gathering data. If he uncovers problems he will report them to his superior who in turn will take them up with the chef or kitchen manager. In smaller organizations where relations between line and staff are more informal, these channels may be by-passed by mutual agreement.

It is essential, however, that any and all orders be given to an employee through his supervisor or department head, except under unusual circumstances, as in emergencies.

3. *Directing:* This involves *seeing that the objectives of the food service are carried out.* It may be subdivided into three heads:

a. *Supervising:* Seeing that plans, policies, and directives of management *are being carried out.*

b. *Controlling:* Seeing that the objectives are being carried out *in the manner prescribed by management.*

c. *Coordinating:* Seeing that the various departments *work together* in carrying out management's directives.

4. *Representing:* The manager must *represent* the food service to his many publics: the management of the institution which he serves; the employees, students or patients whom he feeds; his own staff, and perhaps others.

5. *Evaluating:* The manager must continually be evaluating his operation in terms of economic results and the satisfaction of patrons. Reports must reach his desk showing the results of his operations and complaints or suggestions from patrons. Through merit-rating plans he evaluates the effectiveness of his subordinates as they in turn evaluate those working under them.

Decision-Making

The food-service manager must constantly make decisions. Some executives pride themselves upon making quick decisions based upon "hunches" or intuition. Such decisions may sometimes be right, but when they

*These definitions are based upon an address given before the author's class at Boston University by Dr. John M. Welch of the University of Missouri and used with his permission.

are wrong the results can be disastrous. Right or wrong, decisions must be made. Here are some rules for decision-making which some food-service executives have found useful:

1. *Get all the facts, both pro and con.* Write down or have typed the points for or against a given proposal.

2. *Take time out to think through the implications of the decision.* Avoid making a commitment until you have had at least a few minutes of uninterrupted consideration. Don't let yourself be pushed into a snap judgment. Always be ready to ask, "Why does this have to be done immediately?"

3. *View the problem impartially and objectively.* Eliminate your own personal prejudices insofar as you can. Get the viewpoints of others who do not generally agree with you and try to understand why they feel as they do.

4. *Decide promptly without procrastination.* Based upon the facts you have assembled, rely upon your own judgment and make the decision called for without unnecessary delay.

Relations With Employees

The food-service manager must constantly practice self-discipline. He should dress neatly and observe the same standards of personal cleanliness he expects from his employees. He must set an example by being careful to observe the rules of the food service.

While the executive should be friendly with all employees, he will avoid undue familiarity which tends to lessen respect. He will be careful not to show favoritism. He will always listen to what an employee wishes to tell him but will avoid a direct answer by subsequently referring the matter to the employee's immediate supervisor. Above all, he will not give orders or make suggestions which might be construed as orders, to employees, but rather will work through channels by passing corrective suggestions to his subordinates. Only in this way can he build a well-functioning organization.

Relations With Subordinates

The successful manager will inspire confidence in his subordinates and make them aware that he has confidence in them. He will try to be *consistent* in his corrective measures, for nothing upsets workers more than a boss who is easy one day and hard the next. A tough boss is preferable to a vacillating one.

At times, when problems arise, the boss is tempted to take over. This undermines the confidence of the subordinate in charge, particularly if it is done in the presence of the employees. If the supervisor is capable, he should be allowed to work out his own problems. If he is incapable, he should be replaced. Above all, if he is to be admonished, it should be done privately and not in the presence of others.

Personal Problems

Like others, the executive has his moments of frustration and discouragement. It is difficult for him to discuss his problems with his subordinates. Although there may be times when he feels lonely and discouraged, he must constantly exhibit an attitude of confidence. He must make painful decisions. He can only take solace in the belief that what he is doing is for the best interests of the organization. He must have faith in himself and in the organization of which he is the head. If he is a religious man, he will be sustained by his spiritual convictions.

If the food-service executive is to do his work properly, he must maintain his health by means of proper diet, rest, exercise, and relaxation. He must find time to devote to his family and he must allocate time for reading, study, and constructive thinking. It is a large order to meet the demands of his job and in addition to keep up with the trade journals and attend association meetings and conventions. Yet it is quite true that the busy man is the one who gets the most things accomplished.

MODERN TOOLS OF MANAGEMENT

Systems Analysis

Increasing costs, the changing needs and demands of patrons, and other factors make it necessary that the food-service manager should constantly seek ways to increase the efficiency of his operation. The first step in any improvement program is to analyze the operation to see just how it is working. The use of tables, charts, graphs, and similar graphic presentations is helpful in enabling one to visualize the system or operation being studied.

Out of the scientific research during and follownig World War II has come many new analytical techniques. One that is much heard of these days is known as "Systems Analysis." As the name implies, it simply means the analysis of systems. In "Work Simplification," described in Chapter 12 of this book and in the "Work Flow Charts" illustrated in the same chapter, a single system is studied. Systems Analysis attempts to portray the many systems and subsystems which may be part of an organization, and to chart or diagram them so that their actions and reactions, impinging upon each other, may be seen simultaneously.

Now a food service is a system. It consists of many subsystems: a food procurement system; a storage system; a food preparation system; a service system; a cash control system; a sanitation system, and so on. Two Britishers, Gordon Cutcliffe and David Strank, of Eeling Technical College in London, have applied the principles of Systems Analysis or "Systems Design," as it is called in Britain, to the operation of food services.

In their book, *Analysing Catering Operations*, they have diagrammed the systems of a typical restaurant, which they say would also be similar to those of an industrial canteen or a college refectory. They have also analyzed the problems of queuing, staff selection procedures, menu-planning, batch cooking, waiter service, control and management.

Computers

Systems analysis makes widespread use of electronic data processing, that is, the use of computers. In many food services today computers are employed to process payroll data and issue paychecks, to compute inventories, to analyze menu requirements in hospitals where selective menus prevail, and so on. Yet, the computer remains a mystery to many food-service people.

In an interesting booklet, *Introducing The Computer*, published by International Business Machines Corporation, it is pointed out that many of the devices we see every day are really computers; for example, the dial telephone, the stop light on the street corner, and the automatic washing machine in the home. Each of these has the basic elements of the computer, namely, input, processing, and output.

For the washing machine, the input is dirty clothes, the processing consists of their washing, and the output is clean clothes. In your washing machine, you have several cycles to choose from. You can wash deli-

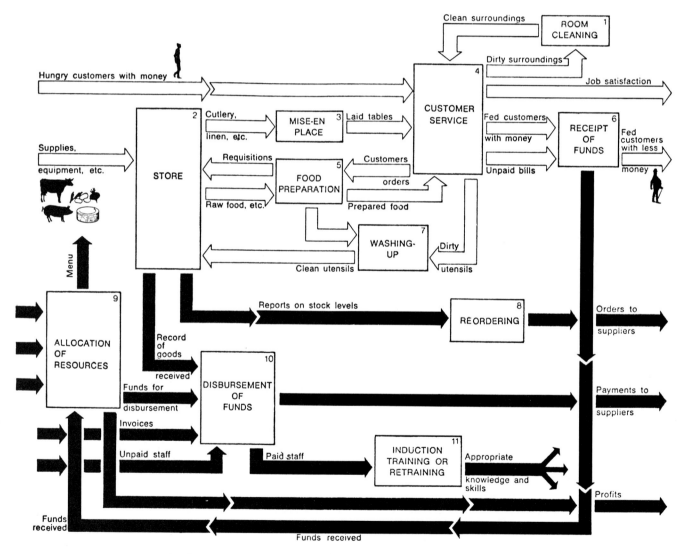

Diagram showing the different systems in a Food Service. Note that each of the boxes denotes the functions in which inputs and outputs take place. From Analysing Catering Operations by Gordon Cutcliffe and David Strank. Reproduced by permission of Edward Arnold (Publishers) Ltd., London, England.

cate items in a gentle cold-water cycle; you can wash shirts in a stronger warm-water cycle; or you can get soiled flannels sparkling clean in a heavy-duty hot-water cycle.

These cycles are like the "programs" of a computer. One cycle may give you cold water, easy washing action, several rinses, and a long spin. Another "program" or cycle may give you warm water, hard washing action, three rinses, and a long spin. When you use the washer you specify the "program" or cycle you want by simply turning a knob or pushing a button. Similarly, the computer goes through its various cycles in response to a program that is prepared in advance in accordance with the problem to be solved. It may direct the computer to add a number three times, multiply it twice, subtract it twice, or to do many other things.

Number Systems

It may help us to understand something of the workings of a computer if we consider the various number systems, particularly the "binary" system. Many of us are so accustomed to the decimal (10-digit) number system in ordinary use that we may be surprised to learn that there are systems based upon numbers other than ten. The binary system is based upon the number 2 and it has only two symbols: 0 and 1. In the early days of computers it was realized that the two symbols, 0 and 1, could represent not only numbers but also opposite conditions, such as negative and positive; minus and plus; off and on; no or yes; etc.

Let us take the number 468 for an example. In the decimal system these three digits represent:

Low-cost IBM System/3 Model 6, is designed for use by just about anyone who works in an office. With relatively little training at the computer's typewriter-like keyboard, a billing clerk can produce invoices, a manager can check the status of any customer account or inventory record, or an engineer can analyze a pipeline network. The data for these and many other applications are stored in high-capacity disk files that are an integral part of the system. Here, a manager looks over a sales report printed by the Model 6 from data entered through the keyboard. An optional television-like display unit (left) can be used to quickly answer a customer inquiry or to instantly display job results. (Courtesy International Business Machines Corporation, White Plains, N.Y.)

$$4 = 4 \times 10^2 = 400$$
$$6 = 6 \times 10^1 = 60$$
$$8 = 8 \times 10^0 = 8$$
$$\overline{468}$$

The exponents of a number indicate how many times that number is to be multiplied by itself. For example, $10^2 = 10 \times 10 = 100$. $10^3 = 10 \times 10 \times 10 = 1,000$. A number with a zero exponent is equal to 1, therefore $10^0 = 1$.

We can change this number 468 to a base 2 number by use of what is known as the "remainder method," as follows:

2/468	
2/234	remainder 0
2/117	" 0
2/ 58	" 1
2/ 29	" 0
2/14	" 1
2/ 7	" 0
2/ 3	" 1
2/ 1	" 1
0	" 1

Starting from the bottom up we read the binary number 111010100_2. We can change this back to 468 as follows:

$$1 = 1 \times 2^8 = 1 \times 256 = 256$$
$$1 = 1 \times 2^7 = 1 \times 128 = 128$$
$$1 = 1 \times 2^6 = 1 \times 64 = 64$$
$$0 = 0 \times 2^5 \pm 0 \times 32 = 0$$
$$1 = 1 \times 2^4 = 1 \times 16 = 16$$
$$0 = 0 \times 2^3 = 0 \times 8 = 0$$
$$1 = 1 \times 2^2 = 1 \times 4 = 4$$
$$0 = 0 \times 2^1 + 0 \times 2 = 0$$
$$0 = 0 \times 2^0 = 0 \times 1 = 0$$
$$\overline{468}$$

Other number systems may have bases of 3, 4, 5, 6, etc. The rule is that the largest digit in any number system is one less than the base number. Thus in the decimal system the largest digit is 9 and in the binary system the largest digit is 1. While the binary number 111010100_2 appears to be more cumbersome than the decimal number 468, the fact is that computers operate so rapidly that the nine digits are of little importance compared to the three. The important thing is that only two symbols are needed with binary numbers.

As this is not an arithmetical treatise, we will not go into the theory of exponents or the reasoning behind the "remainder method." If the reader has a child who has taken a course in the "New Mathematics" as taught in the schools today, he or she can probably answer such questions. Our purpose is merely to ex-plain the binary number system which has played an important part in the development of computers.

Just as you can order your washing machine to wash, rinse, or spin as required, so the programmer can instruct the computer to add, subtract, multiply, divide, or do a dozen other actions in any sequence desired.

There are four major reasons for the great efficiency of the computer. The first is its *speed*. The computer's lightning speed makes it possible for the first time to tackle problems that would be impossible to solve on an adding machine or ordinary calculator. For example, it would take an individual 100 days to do the adding that a computer can perform in ten seconds.

A second reason is *accuracy*. In the same ten seconds a computer can balance 10,000 checking accounts without making a mistake of even one cent.

In the third place, the efficiency of the computer is due to the *discipline* it imposes. In order to solve a problem with the computer you must clearly understand the problem and also program the computer to give you the right answer. To program a computer, for instance, to keep a record of a food-service inventory, you must know about inventory control and operations research techniques. You must also be aware of the basic policies of the food-service organization in question. The discipline, the insight, and the understanding—these are the indirect benefits resulting from problem-solving with a computer.

The fourth benefit of the computer is its *versatility*. It can do much more than add, subtract, multiply, and divide. A computer can sort data, straighten out data, and store it away for future reference. Any data in the computer can be printed as a form, punched in cards, written on a magnetic tape, shown on a TV-like display, or sent out in various other forms. This internal storage is known as the computer's "memory."

The programmer may use "branching" instructions to jump in and out on a program. A program is really a list of orders. Instead of having the computer follow the regular sequence of orders, if the programmer wishes it to jump to No. 15 after doing No. 10, he specifies this through the use of a "branching" or "transfer" instruction.

The computer cannot think, any more than a washing machine can think. What it does is to extend man's problem-solving abilities by performing many arithmetical, logic, branching, input/output instructions at a prodigious rate of speed. Basically the accuracy of the computer depends upon the accuracy of the programming. The programmer is, therefore, the key person. It is upon his knowledge and skill that the success of any computer depends. Consequently much time and effort is devoted by the various manufacturers to the training of programmers.

Because of the cost of the computer and the expense of operation, it is important that a computer be used, if possible, twenty-four hours a day. Many banks and other service organizations offer "shared time" of their computers to food services and other organizations to process payroll data, making the necessary deductions for taxes and other charges, and printing out the weekly pay checks.

Data terminals are in use in many large organizations where a communications terminal similar to an office typewriter is connected by wire to a computer perhaps many miles away. The user types the instructions to the computer, enters new data, and asks questions. The computer types out the answers and may ask for additional data. Even the ordinary telephone can serve as a temporary computer terminal in an audio response system. The user dials in a coded request for information. The audio response system returns the information from the computer, selects appropriate words or sounds from its vocabulary, compiles these into a message, and sends back a voice response over the telephone.

As recently as a dozen years ago, there were only about one thousand computers in the entire world. Today the number of computers exceeds 50,000 worldwide and the number of new computer applications is increasing rapidly. The myth of the "electronic brain" is disappearing, and instead, the computer is taking its place as a familiar tool in the plans and enterprises of imaginative business concerns, including food services and institutions.

For example, a computer was recently demonstrated at the Jester Center of the University of Texas in Austin, for use in monitoring and controlling college food-service operations on-line. Through the use of punched cards, punched badges, or magnetic strip badges, such violations as attempted duplicate usage or use of invalid (lost, stolen, cancelled, etc.) cards

Expanded communications capabilities and significantly improved performance are extended to users of medium-size and smaller IBM computers by the IBM System/370 Model 135. Shown as it might appear in an installation, this engineering design model has a three-disk 2319 drive and two-disk 2318 drive attached directly to the central processor. On the left is the IBM 3803/3420 magnetic tape system, and on the right the IBM 3211 printer, which can print 2,000 lines a minute. Two new punched card units are shown in the foreground. The IBM 3505 card reader (left) and the IBM 3525 card punch (right) provide fast, versatile handling of 80-column punched cards. The reader, IBM's fastest, can read 800 or 1,200 cards a minute. (Courtesy International Business Machines Corporation, White Plains, N. Y.)

can be detected. Statistics can be accumulated and printed after each meal and the computer programmed to create a billing, if desired.

This device is also used at the University of Pennsylvania in Philadelphia for meal ticket control. However, it can be programmed to compute food costs, inventories, etc.

Figure 7.1 (Chapter 7, Menu-Planning) shows selective menu sheets which are tabulated by a computer at the Massachusetts General Hospital in Boston.

The foregoing examples give evidence of the growing use of computers in schools, colleges, hospitals, and other institutional food services in the United States and Canada.

SUGGESTED READING

COPLEY, FRANK BARKLEY. *Frederick W. Taylor, Father of Scientific Management*. 2 volumes. New York: Harper & Bros., 1923.

CUTCLIFFE, GORDON, and STRANK, DAVID. *Analysing Catering Operations*. London: Edward Arnold, Ltd., 1971.

DRUCKER, PETER. *Managing for Results*. New York: Harper & Row, 1964.

GELLERMAN, SAUL W. *Motivation and Productivity*. New York: American Management Association, 1963.

INTERNATIONAL BUSINESS MACHINES CORPORATION, White Plains, N. Y. *Introducing the Computer* and other booklets.

LUNDBERG, DONALD E., and ARMATAS, JAMES P. *The Management of People in Hotels, Restaurants and Clubs*. Dubuque, Iowa: Wm. C. Brown Company Publishers, 1964.

MCGREGOR, DOUGLAS. *The Human Side of Enterprise*. New York: McGraw-Hill Book Co., 1960.

ROETHLISBERGER, F. J. *Management and Morale*. Cambridge: Harvard University Press, 1941.

STOKES, JOHN W. *How to Manage a Restaurant or Institutional Food Service*. Dubuque, Iowa: William C. Brown Company Publishers, 1967.

WHYTE, WM. FOOTE. *Human Relations in the Restaurant Industry*. New York: McGraw-Hill Book Co., 1948.

CHAPTER 4

The Food-Service Organization

FUNCTIONS OF THE FOOD-SERVICE ORGANIZATION

Whether in a business establishment, hospital, school, or other institution, there are certain functions in connection with the service of food which must be performed. These are: Administration, Purchasing, Receiving and Storing, Menu-Planning, Food Preparation and Cooking, Food Distribution and Service, Sanitation and Safety, Maintenance and Repairs, and Accounting.

Administration

In any food service there must be one individual who is responsible for all phases of its administration. This may be the Food-Service Manager or the Chief Dietitian. Regardless of the title, this person delegates the necessary authority and responsibility for the various phases of the operation to the members of the food-service staff, and holds these individuals accountable for the performance of their duties.

Essentially the function of the food-service manager is to get things done through others. This requires, in addition to technical food-service experience and know-how, a knowledge of management skills and techniques. It involves self-discipline, study, and analysis, keeping up with current developments in the food-service field and growth in the talents of leadership, as pointed out in Chapter 3.

Purchasing

Food and supplies are generally purchased by the food-service manager or one or more assistants designated to perform this function. In large establishments, certain supplies and contract food items may be purchased through the purchasing department with which the food-service manager maintains close liaison. In any event, perishable foods are generally purchased by the one in charge of the food service or an assistant.

Receiving and Storage

These functions are performed by the Receiving Clerk and the Storekeeper, respectively. In large organizations these may be representatives of the Purchasing or the General Stores Departments. In small organizations, receiving may be the function of a food-service employee who also performs other duties.

Menu-Planning

This may be done by the dietitian or the food-service manager. In some institutions, this function is performed on a team basis, with the assistant managers, dietitians, chefs, or other qualified individuals assisting the menu-maker.

Food Preparation and Cooking

This is the responsibility of the Kitchen Manager or Head Chef assisted by cooks, bakers, butchers, salad people, kitchen-preparation crew, porters, and cleaners, the number depending upon the size of the organization.

Food Distribution and Service

Food distribution starts in the kitchen and is then taken over by cafeteria supervisors, counter people, food-canteen crews, cashiers, and bus people. (If there is table service, this includes hostesses and waitresses and/or waiters.)

Service to patients in hospitals may be the responsibility of one of the dietitians or a food-service supervisor assisted by porters and floor kitchen workers. In some institutions, members of the Nursing and/or the Housekeeping Department also participate in service to patients.

Sanitation and Safety

Cleaning of dishes, utensils, and the premises is done by dishwashers, pot-washers, janitors, and cleaners. In some institutions, the Maintenance Department may cover some phases of rodent and vermin control, or outside exterminators may be retained for this purpose. Cleaning of coffee-making equipment and food-preparation machines is usually the responsibility of the employees who normally operate these appliances.

Safety may be part of the overall safety program of the institution. Usually some one of the food-service staff is assigned to this particular responsibility insofar as it affects the department.

Maintenance and Repairs

General maintenance and repairs are usually handled by the institution's Maintenance Department. Where a Preventive Maintenance program is in effect, food-service machinery and equipment, of course, should be included. Painting and decorating are usually scheduled by the institution's management.

Accounting and Clerical

This is the direct responsibility of cashiers, clerks, and food-cost accountants. Generally all records are tied in with the books of the institution's Accounting Department. Representatives of this department may participate in certain activities, such as taking of inventories.

Whether the operation is large or small, these functions must be carried out. However, in smaller organizations, one person may perform several duties.

PERSONNEL OF THE FOOD-SERVICE ORGANIZATION

The Food-Service Manager

While the manager need not be an expert chef, he or she must understand food preparation and cooking to a sufficient degree to command the respect of the cooks. This, of course, goes for all other phases of the operation. Yet the manager must be responsive to the needs and desires of those to whom the food is served. It is also essential that the manager maintain contact, through proper channels, with the management of the institution and with the heads of other departments cooperating with his own.

With the assistants, the manager is responsible for purchasing, knowledge of inventories, goes over advance menus, and watches food, labor, and overhead costs. Refrigerators, storerooms, kitchens, and serving areas must be checked daily. Equipment must be inspected, and high standards of cleanliness and sanitation maintained. Even the lowly garbage barrel (if a disposer is not in use) comes under the scrutiny of the alert manager. In addition to the routine administrative duties, the good manager is constantly aware of the importance of human relations. "She makes you feel that your job is the most important one here," was the comment of a cafeteria worker about a successful woman manager.

Assistant Managers

Assistant managers share administrative and supervisory duties with the manager. One, usually a dietitian, may be responsible for menu-planning. Another may act as the food-cost accountant and prepare daily, weekly, or monthly reports for the head of the department. Still others may be in charge of the kitchen, the cafeteria, distribution of food, etc.

In selecting assistant managers, it is important that at least one of the individuals is being trained as an understudy for the manager's post.

Cooks

Although some food services employ European trained chefs, the average industrial or institutional food service usually does not require that degree of training or versatility.

Menus in industrial and institutional food services are generally limited to one or two, or, at the most, three or four principal entrees daily. Where formulas are established and closely adhered to, it is possible to produce quality food with cooks who are reasonably experienced and competent. Many administrators like to train their own cooks. In some organizations, women cooks are preferred because of their knack in giving a "home-made" touch to the food they produce.

It is important that the head cook be experienced and capable. It is even more important that he be cooperative. The operation of a food service must be smooth and efficient during rush periods as well as in quieter moments. A good head cook can do much to prevent costly food waste in preparation and cooking, to maintain high standards of sanitation, and to inspire and train members of the kitchen crew.

Head Baker and Assistants

If a bakery is maintained, the Head Baker is responsible for the preparation of rolls, pastry, and baked desserts. (Bread is generally purchased from outside sources.)

The baker, whether a man or woman, should be experienced and competent. Here again the use of standard formulas will ensure uniform quality.

Dietitian

The trained dietitian is indispensable in hospital and institutional feeding where meals must be balanced nutritionally and where special (therapeutic) diets are required for patients. Accredited dietitians are also required for teaching student nurses and dietetic internes.

A dietitian or woman with home economics training can also contribute much in industrial food services to keep the menu well balanced, varied, and attractive. She may also be responsible for conducting tests to establish purchasing specifications, standard formulas, and portions, for developing new dishes, and maintaining food quality. It is desirable for such a woman to have had some practical experience in commercial restaurant work. In a large restaurant chain headed by the author, two graduate dietitians were employed to be in charge of menu preparation and testing of new dishes.

Other Employees

While the duties of other employees are important, they are of such nature that previous vocational experience is not essential. Selected individuals can be trained under experienced personnel.

Employment Procedures

Food-service workers are generally employed through the institution's Personnel or Employment Department in consultation with the Food-Service Manager.

Recruiting procedures will vary with the circumstances. In general, employees are recruited through such channels as:
1. Advertisements in newspapers or other media.
2. Employment agencies.
3. Placement departments of schools and colleges.
4. Friends or relatives of present employees.
5. Applicants seeking employment.

Induction of New Employees

New employees should be interviewed and selected by the head of the food-service department or a qualified assistant. At this time the duties and opportunities of the job are carefully explained. For this purpose descriptions of each job should be carefully prepared (See Figures 4.1 and 4.2) and kept available in the Manager's Operating Manual (See Figure 4.4.) During this interview, the importance of the job should be stressed and the advantages of employment in the particular institution pointed out.

Following the interview, the new employee should be shown through the food-service department and introduced to the supervisor and fellow employees with whom he or she is to work. A qualified older employee may be assigned as an instructor or "sponsor."

Training New Employees

It is not enough to turn the new recruit over to any supervisor or other employee for the orientation period. Experience reveals that many potentially valuable employees become discouraged and quit during these first days unless given close supervision and assistance.

In teaching new employees, it is essential that the instructor *know how to instruct*. For this purpose the job instruction principles of the "Training Within Industry" program, used so successfully during World War II, may well be adapted. Essentially there are four steps:

Chief Dietitian

"Serves in a Staff capacity as Head of the Dietary Service, under administrative supervision of the Superintendent of this Hospital, which Service is charged with the overall responsibility for the daily preparation and serving of both regular and therapeutic diets for approximately 650 patients; 300 employees; and many guests, from kitchens installed in separately located buildings.

"Actively participates in monthly hospital staff conferences; prepares the annual budget estimate for this Service including justifications for foodstuff costs - equipment - personnel and personally substantiates such estimates before the Superintendent; periodically analyses meals for nutritional values; prepares periodically, cost records of various types of meals as served; when necessary consults with both doctors and patients in planning new therapeutic diets; finally responsible for the adequacy of all advanced menus planned by subordinate dietitians; finally responsible for the preparation and serving of all meals in both buildings A and B; finally determines kind and quantities of food to be purchased; requisitions all supplies and equipment for this Service; conducts periodic inspections as to the overall care and sanitation of all equipment, work, storage, serving, diet kitchens and main kitchens, areas located in both buildings; prepares work orders for the repairs of all equipment; before submission to her superior, finally approves the monthly inventory reports on materials and equipment chargeable to this Service and maintains inventory of non-expendable supplies and equipment, etc.

"Has direct supervision over 2 Head Dietitians GS-9 and 1 Clerk-Typist GS-3 and maintains overall supervision of 132 employees in addition to approximately 7 patient employees; holds supervisor meetings periodically, regarding changes in procedures, hospital policies, etc.; holds monthly supervisor meetings to discuss both internal functional and personnel problems, etc.; conducts an overall continuing training program through supervisors; maintains a work evaluation program; before submission to her superior, finally reviews employee performance ratings, approves an overall schedule of hours for employees, and reviews and/or approves all leave for this Service; presents all disciplinary actions for the decision of her superior excepting minor infractions; interviews and selects applicants for employment; etc."

Fig. 4.1. Job description, Chief Dietitian position. (Actual description in use in governmental hospital.)

1. *Preparation:* Put the new employee at ease. Emphasize the importance of doing the job correctly, and endeavor to arouse his interest in learning.

2. *Presentation:* Explain and demonstrate how the job should be done properly. Point out the little knacks or key points that make the operation easier and quicker. By questioning make sure he is following you. Repeat points that may not be clear. Avoid proceeding too rapidly. Be patient. Remember you were a beginner once.

3. *Performance:* Let the new employee go through the procedure himself. Question him about key points and correct any errors. Let him repeat the performance until you are sure he understands it and can do it correctly.

4. *Check-up:* After he is on his own, assign someone to whom he can turn for help. Follow up frequently until he is able to stand on his own feet.

General Training

Training should be a continuous process. Certain individuals may be given on-the-job training, either by members of the staff or qualified outsiders. Others may be encouraged to take courses in food-service management offered by educational institutions, and to visit other food services and report on their observations. Current food-service trade journals, periodi-cals, and books dealing with food-service problems can be circulated among the staff.

Group Meetings

Staff meetings at which the manager and department heads discuss the progress being made and problems which have arisen may be held periodically. Occasional meetings may also be held with groups of employees to discuss problems in their areas and to ask for their suggestions.

Meetings of this kind can be successful in building teamwork if the following principles are observed:

1. Call meetings only when there is something of importance to discuss.
2. Plan the program carefully in advance.
3. Start on time. Close on schedule. Make the program brief. (Thirty minutes to an hour is usually long enough.)
4. The Chairman should state the problem briefly, then ask for suggestions. Keep the tone of the meeting serious, allow a little humor now and then, but try to keep on the subject. Don't let one or two do all the talking. Encourage the timid ones by asking them direct questions. A blackboard can be used to advantage.
5. Discuss only problems with which those present are familiar or can do something about. Limit the at-

Staff Position Description - Cafeteria Manager

I. Purpose of Position

To administer the function of the operation of the plant Cafeteria to include the purchase of food and supplies, observing current market trends taking advantage of seasonal price changes, the planning of daily menus, the control of monthly inventories and the scheduling of the required cafeteria personnel.

II. Duties and Responsibilities

A. Purchase of Materials and Supplies
1. Interviews suppliers' salesmen, and arranges for the purchase of all foodstuffs observing general market conditions to take advantage of volume buying and seasonal price fluctuations; purchase of foodstuffs similarly requires thorough knowledge of qualities and gradings of meats and vegetables, etc., whether canned or fresh or frozen.

2. Maintains proper inventories of materials and supplies properly to reflect the lowest possible cost of operation and to maintain an equitable ratio of food costs to sales.

B. Planning Daily Activities
1. Outlines menus to be followed, adjusting according to the season and as influenced by availability and price.

2. Supervises the preparation and service of all foods served in the Cafeteria, planning the specific volumes to be prepared calling upon past experience and present day-by-day sales volume.

C. Direct Supervision
1. Supervises activities of 25 Cafeteria Personnel (1 day foreman, 3 shift foremen, 1 cashier, 1 female supervisor, an assortment of 19 other employees including cooks, bakers, dishwashers, waitresses, and countermen).

D. Frequently called upon to prepare special dinners and luncheons for visiting groups as a part of the Company's Public Relations Program, serving from 12 to 300 in addition to the usual Cafeteria schedule.

E. Is expected to maintain a clean department and eliminate any unsafe working conditions.

III. Supervision: No. of people supervised directly? _25_ Indirectly? _____

IV. Contact with Others
1. Plant personnel from superintendents to hourly employees (Daily)
2. Suppliers' representatives for the purchase of foodstuffs, etc. (Daily)
3. With visiting company officials and visitors (Weekly)
4. Visiting groups of local and area organizations (Monthly)
5. State food inspectors (Infrequently)

V. Working Conditions
Satisfactory. Office well lighted and ventilated. 75% of time is spent in kitchen (which is quite hot) and dining room, and 25% of time is spent in serving areas and the office.

Fig. 4.2. Job description—Cafeteria Manager.

tendance to those concerned with the problem under discussion.

6. Make the program interesting. The use of "role playing" techniques in dramatizing right and wrong ways of performing food-service tasks is often effective.

With proper leadership and guidance such meetings can do much to develop goodwill and understanding. They can also bring about valuable suggestions and cooperation in eliminating waste and improving the efficiency of the entire organization.

Two Types of Meetings

A dramatic illustration of two kinds of meetings was brought out in a study of two coffee shops by Professor Thomas Farrell of Michigan State University and reported in the Cornell Hotel & Restaurant Administration Quarterly. The coffee shops were comparable in many respects and were studied in detail *during the absence of each manager.*

The woman manager of shop "A" holds weekly staff meetings one hour long. The first half hour is given over to demonstrations of techniques and explaining the functions of the group in relation to the overall objectives of management. During the final half hour the group discusses how they can operate best to allow each individual to obtain greatest satisfaction from his job and contribute most to the organization. Waitresses, bus boys, porters, and kitchen help all join in suggesting ideas and discussing how they can cooperate to better serve the customers.

The man who manages Coffee Shop "B" holds biweekly staff meetings for from 15 to 30 minutes. At these meetings he reviews the function of the eating place and lays down new policies and orders, tells of regulations which have been violated, presents cost figures to urge good operating methods and demonstrates proper techniques. Although profits have increased since he took over, he does not inform employees of the good results achieved through their efforts and his direction. Few suggestions other than complaints are offered by employees although each worker knows and performs his duties pleasantly and faithfully.

Both coffee shops are considered to be well managed. Both managers are meticulous about cleanliness, prompt service, and cost-saving techniques. Yet there was a startling contrast in the actions of the two groups of employees when the manager was absent (Shown in Figure 4.3).

Contrast of Group-directed and Manager-Controlled Formal Communication Systems in Two Coffee-Shops		
Operating Characteristics	A	B
When manager is not present (computed over 3 days)		
Increase in time before greeting customer at table	1%	90%
Increase in time taken to serve customer at table	5%	75%
Increase in number of watch off station	0%	20%
Increase in time off station	5%	80%
Increase in incomplete table set-ups	10%	50%
Increase in uncleared tables	10%	40%
Increase in unready station equipment	10%	60%
Increase in service errors	0%	70%
Increase in unreplaced equipment or unrestocked materials	10%	70%
General (all figures for year)		
Annual employee turnover	3%	50%
Annual lost time per employee	4 days	32 days
Customer complaints per day	3	15
Average number of grievances annually per employee	0.3	2.8
Percent of annual breakage of dishes (stock equals 100%)	15%	65%
Percent of down-time for repairing direct-serving equipment	3%	25%
Percent of food inventory not showing profit	1%	5%
Percent of small tool and equipment loss	1%	11%
Ratio of personnel costs to gross receipts	25%	33%
Quarterly profit increase or decrease	+24%	+15%
Quarterly increase or decrease in number of customers	+8%	+3%

Fig. 4.3. Contrast between operating results in two Coffee Shops (from Cornell Hotel and Restaurant Administration Quarterly, by permission).

Material

Many 16 mm. sound films, film strips, and slides on food-service subjects may be obtained free of charge, or at a small fee, from restaurant and trade associations, equipment manufacturers, food-processors, and state and federal governmental agencies. Such visual aids may be used to supplement programs for group meetings.

Food-Service Manual

It will be helpful to good administration if an operating manual is prepared setting forth various duties and responsibilities, schedules, wage rates, account-

ing procedures and forms, lists of equipment, layouts, prices, special service, job descriptions, etc.

Figure 4.4 shows the table of contents of such a manual. Copies are supplied to the manager and his assistants. The operation of any food service involves considerable detail, as it actually embraces both manufacturing and merchandising processes and routines. The adage "Pay attention to the pennies and the dollars will take care of themselves" is applicable to any phase of public feeding.

Successful operation involving so many details can best be accomplished by standardizing the correct procedures. Because of their variety, it is well to have these standard policies and procedures recorded in black and white. The manual does just this, and makes these records available in handy form.

When questions arise concerning policies, or when personnel changes take place, the manual can be of great value. A loose-leaf binder should be provided so that new pages may be inserted and the manual kept up to date.

CAFETERIA MANUAL Table of Contents	Page
Letter of Instruction	3
I. Locations and Hours Food Is Served	4
II. Equipment Inventory	5-12
III. Layouts of Kitchen and Cafeterias	13-16
IV. Menus and Formulas	17-18
V. Prices	19-26
VI. Purchasing and Receiving	27-30
VII. Payment for Food Purchases	31-32
VIII Cash Receipts	33-35
IX. Record Keeping	36-44
X. Schedule of Staff Hours and Duties	45-51
XI. Special Functions	52
XII. Food to be Taken Out	53
XIII. Food Trucks	54-55
XIV. Other Sales	56
XV. Payroll	57-60
XVI. Miscellaneous	61-62
XVII. Index	63-64

Fig. 4.4. Cafeteria manual.

Cooperation and Teamwork

How can one get human beings to *want* to do their best under varying circumstances? How can one obtain their whole-hearted cooperation at all times? These questions have perplexed parents, pedagogues, and philosophers throughout the ages. Basically they relate to the motives which underly the behavior of human beings. A century ago it was felt that the economic motive was the only urge that caused people to work. In recent years, studies in what has become known as the "science of human relations" prove that there are other motives besides a day's wages that actuate the worker. Some of these may be more important at times than his monetary compensation.

Motivation

What are these motives? Various schools of psychological thought stress, for example, such drives as sex, the inferiority complex, the effect of external stimuli, etc. Each of these, undoubtedly, has its place. However, we must remember that each personality is the result of many complex influences both of heredity and environment. The motives, urges, or drives that lead to action are many and varied.

There are numerous classifications of human motives. Among them is one by the late W. I. Thomas, a sociologist, which provides a valid and appropriate frame of reference for the food-service manager. Thomas classified all human motives under what he called "The Four Wishes":

1. Security
2. New experience
3. Response
4. Social recognition

Security

These include the desire for economic, emotional, and physical security, but they are really negative wishes or *fears*—fears of hunger, want, and lack of means. They are expressed in the desire to earn sufficient income to purchase the necessities of life and to provide for one's family and loved ones.

But there is another facet of these desires for security which the administrator should understand. Basic to the wish for security is *conservatism or resistance to change.*

In practical terms this means that care should be taken not to make changes that affect the worker without giving him adequate notice and explanation *in advance*. This applies to changes in job duties, in work location, equipment, rules, and other conditions of employment. When such advance notice is given and a reasonable explanation made, changes may generally be accomplished without difficulty.

In one institution, management decided to install air-conditioning in certain areas. This was done without notice to the workers. When the new system began to function, complaints were heard on every hand. Some thought it too cold, others objected that it was drafty.

No one seemed satisfied. Management had thought it would be a welcome improvement in working conditions. Had they taken the trouble to discuss it in *advance*, this change undoubtedly would have been more readily accepted.

New Experience

In every human being, to a greater or lesser degree, there are the desires for adventure, romance, for something different from the ordinary routine. This explains the fascination most people have for watching fire-fighters in action.

Many find satisfaction for their desires for new experience *vicariously*—in watching television, listening to the radio, going to movies or plays, reading detective stories or romantic fiction, or watching games and sport contests. They picture themselves in the role of the hero or heroine and thus satisfy the need for adventure and romance in their lives.

By bringing out the romance in the food-service field we may satisfy to some degree this group of desires. Consider our common foods, for example: tea from India or Ceylon; coffee from Brazil or Central America; the many kinds of spices, such as cinnamon from Saigon; curry from Java; sage from Dalmatia, to name but a few. Speakers or films may be secured from manufacturers or trade associations to portray the romance in the production and transportation of these foods, brought from the ends of the earth and handled every day by food-service workers.

The history of the establishment or institution with which the food service is connected may be replete with romance. If brought to the attention of the workers in an interesting manner, it will capture their imaginations. It will help them to realize that they too, are a part of the constantly unfolding drama.

Opportunities for creative tasks, such as developing a new menu item, or working out a more efficient method of handling some food-service problem may also satisfy the desire for new experience.

Response

These are desires for the sympathy and understanding of others. They have to do with the responses of family and friends. They find their culmination in romantic love and marriage. When the desires for response are not satisfied, feelings of loneliness arise. People who live alone often find companionship in a dog, cat, or other pet.

It should be remembered that food-service employees spend almost half of their waking hours, at least five days weekly, in the work place. Many workers make lasting friendships and even find their life-mates from among those with whom they work.

In one restaurant, Joe, the pot-washer and porter, was a good-natured, friendly fellow, liked by all. During the war he left to take a job as a truck driver at almost double the pay he had been earning. After six weeks, he returned and asked for his old job back. "I was pretty lonely driving that truck," he said. "I missed the boys and girls here in the cafeteria, and I decided that I'd be a lot happier here than working as a lonely truck driver, even though the pay was better."

Social Recognition

The desire for social recognition, that is, for the approval of those whom one esteems, is one of the strongest urges to action in human society. Who knows how many momentous battles have been won, inspiring books written, great pictures painted, soul-stirring musical compositions created, due in part at least to these compelling drives? Not a few of our outstanding business firms and numerous charitable institutions were founded by men who were largely motivated by the desire for social recognition. Many individuals find social recognition in lodges, clubs, and other organizations in which they play prominent parts; roles perhaps denied them in their work and family relationships.

These drives are related to what the sociologists call "status," the desire to be important, which often finds expression in modern life in "keeping up with the Jones." A food-service worker wants to feel that he is important, *as he is*, and that his job is important, *as it should be*, if he is justified in being on the payroll.

Satisfaction of these urges is often found in titles. A "dish-machine operator" has greater status than a mere "dishwasher." The title of "chef" is more important than "cook." A "custodian" feels that he is a step or so above a "janitor."

However, the mere bestowal of titles does not satisfy the desire for social recognition unless management makes clear the real significance of the designation. For example, if a "dish-machine operator" is impressed with the importance of his job, not merely in washing stacks of dirty dishes, but as *the guardian of the health* of the patrons who use the dishes, he will do a better job.

A group of women kitchen workers in a large food service went out on strike. For several cold, rainy weeks in early spring, they marched around the establishment in a picket line. After the walkout ended, a hitch occurred in the negotiations and strike threats were again made. The head of the business, remembering the discomforts of the picket line, couldn't be-

lieve that these older women meant what they said. But the Kitchen Manager, who knew the women, set him straight. "For the first time in years these women felt important. In their own eyes they were *heroines* on that picket line. They'd do it again if they could," he said.

Satisfying these desires involves something far more valid than trying to "kid the help" into believing they are something they are not. Fundamentally it means sincere respect for the dignity of each individual personality. Even a "Good Morning," or "Hello Bill!," or other greeting from the manager as he passes through the work areas will give recognition—if it is genuinely friendly and sincere.

Listening

Listening tactfully to worker's suggestions and even to his "gripes" is the mark of a good administrator. He will, at the conclusion, undoubtedly refer the matter to the worker's immediate superior in the interests of good organization policy. It is difficult to listen quietly and to refrain from comment. Nevertheless, it is a rewarding discipline. Often the mere recital to a sympathetic listener may, in itself, be sufficient to dispel a "gripe" or to solve a problem. After all, skillful listening to people's problems is the basis of modern psychiatric therapy.

The story is told of a food-service operator who became the Mayor of a small town. It was customary for the Mayor, following the monthly council meeting, to retire to his office to receive any citizens who might wish to see him One night, after a tiring day in the cafeteria and a long, contentious council meeting, the Mayor went to his office feeling completely worn out. Just as he seated himself at his desk, an irate woman taxpayer entered and began to pour forth her complaints in an almost hysterical manner. The harangue had hardly begun when the Mayor, despite his best efforts, fell into a doze. Suddenly he awoke with a start, realizing what had happened. He was about to apologize, when to his amazement he heard the woman say, "I want to thank you, Mr. Mayor, for listening to my story. My talk with you has helped me realize that perhaps I, too, have been in the wrong. You have solved my problem." And with that, she turned and left the room.

Suggestion Systems

As a result of listening to what the worker has to say, valuable suggestions may come to the food-service administrator. In many establishments, suggestion systems have been instituted, with monetary rewards provided for worthwhile suggestions.

Suggestion systems, *if properly operated and followed through,* can be profitable in brining about improved methods and actual savings. Essentially they are based on the desire for social recognition which is inherent in most human beings.

Mixed Motives

No two individuals are alike. In one, the desire for security will be dominant. In another, it may be the wishes for response, new experience, or social recognition that will play the leading role. Still others may be actuated by mixed motives.

The counter girl who is eager to earn money may be actuated by the desire for security. She may also wish to dress well so as to impress her boy friend (response) or to be thought well of by her group (recognition), or she may be saving for a trip to Florida (new experience). She may be actuated by some or all of these desires. Obviously, the individual who finds reasonable outlets for all four of these groups of wishes will have a well-balanced personality.

Informal Groups and Cliques

In every place where people work together day after day informal groups tend to form, and certain individuals, through sheer force of personality, assert themselves as leaders. These groups or cliques develop their own codes of behavior which may or may not be in the best interests of the enterprise in which they are employed. They have their counterpart in the "gangs" which are formed among adolescent youths.

The leaders of these groups are usually not of the submissive "yes-man" type. Because of their tendency to be outspoken and aggressive, they may have been overlooked in the past when supervisory jobs were assigned. Yet they are natural leaders, and their abilities and energies should and often can be diverted to constructive channels.

As an illustration, following a strike of kitchen workers in a large food service it was proposed by management that three young men, who had been leaders in the walkout, should be made supervisors. Despite objections, this was done and these men proved to be most effective in their leadership.

Developing Teamwork

The food-service administrator cannot be a psychologist or a psychiatrist. Yet many administrators have welded their organizations into smooth-working, effective teams through their insight and their understanding, often intuitive, of human motivation.

An illustration of this type of administrator came vividly to the author's attention some years ago while he was visiting The Clifton Cafeterias in Los Angeles. The head of the firm, Clifford Clinton, a leading food-service operator on the Pacific Coast, took pains to introduce to the author several long-service employees. Among them was one engaged in mopping the floors, another who was a dishwasher, and a third, the cafeteria manager. In each case Mr. Clinton said, "I want you to meet one of our associates, Mr. ----------." There were no "employees" in the Clifton organization. Every worker was an *associate*.

Monetary Incentives

Modern research in human relations, as pointed out earlier in this chapter, reveals that the desire for security is only one of the group of drives motivating the individual in the work situation.

Nevertheless, money *is* important. Provided other wishes are reasonably satisfied, monetary incentives are useful in developing teamwork and better supervision. In industry, much work is done on the basis of incentive systems, and in many businesses profit-sharing plans are in effect.

Suggestion systems, previously discussed in this text, are a means of employing monetary incentives. Food-service managers have also found bonus systems useful.

Bonus Systems

Many food services offer bonuses to supervisory employees who meet cost goals in areas under their control. For example, the kitchen manager and/or the chef may receive a monthly bonus provided the food-cost objective is attained. The same type of incentive may be offered with respect to labor costs and other expenses.

In setting up a bonus system it is essential that the award be offered only to those who can actually control the costs involved. One of the dangers is that supervisors may be tempted to shortcut or to sacrifice quality in their efforts to obtain the reward. This can be prevented by setting upper and lower limits within which the percentage requirements must remain. To illustrate, a cafeteria desiring to attain a 45% food-cost objective would stipulate that the actual cost must be no higher than 45%, but no lower than say 43.5%, if those responsible are to receive a bonus.

Bonus systems should be set up in simple terms so as to be readily understood by those sharing in them. The bonus should be based upon a short period so that interest will not lag. A monthly bonus is more effective than a quarterly or semi-annual payment for this reason. The bonus should be paid promptly, in cash or by separate check, and not included as part

Meat cutting demonstration: Boston University class in Food-Service Management. (Courtesy Irving Levitt Company, Boston, Mass.)

Professor at Zanmorano, Honduras, teaching student the harvesting of papayas. (Courtesy United Fruit Co.)

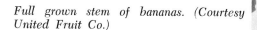

Full grown stem of bananas. (Courtesy United Fruit Co.)

Charles Banino, of Boston's Ritz-Carlton Hotel and a European-trained chef in his own right, demonstrates the art of fine cookery in the hotel kitchen to a Boston University class in Food-Service Management. The class was directed by John W. Stokes, the author, who is shown at Mr. Banino's right.

of the regular compensation. Withholding and social security taxes must be deducted, however.

Organization Charts

Organization charts can be helpful in graphically portraying the lines of authority and responsibility in an organization. However, such charts should be recognized for what they are worth. To attempt to delineate in a series of lines and rectangles on paper the complicated human relationships and interactions which exist in an organization can at the best be only symbolic. Personalities play such important roles in any organization that it is impossible to present a picture that is wholly true from a factual standpoint. After all, an organization is only as good as the people who man it.

Bill, the cafeteria porter, may be in the lowest echelon on the chart. Yet because of his leadership qualities and experience, he may be relied upon in times of stress by the food-service manager more than others on the upper levels. A young assistant who, because of his title, is placed high on the chart, may not yet have developed abilities requisite to the level on which his block appears.

These personal factors should be kept in mind in viewing any organization chart. If due allowance is made, the chart can be useful as an idealized sketch of the organization. It shows who reports to whom. It indicates responsibility for various functions, and how the lines of authority, responsibility, and accountability run. The cardinal principle is that an executive must have authority commensurate with his responsibilities.

Figures 4.5, 4.6, 4.7, 4.8 and 4.9 set forth Organization Charts of two employee food services, two hospital dietaries, and a college food service, respectively.

The Organization Chart in Figure 4.5 shows the organization of an employee food service in the head office of a large insurance company serving 4500 luncheons daily. Although the head of the organization is known as "Cafeteria Manager," he actually supervises several officers' dining rooms in addition to the cafeteria.

It will be noted that there are three "line" organizations headed by the Chef, Supervisor, and Head Baker, respectively. In addition, there is a "staff" organization under the Office Supervisor which essentially performs such staff functions as food-cost con-

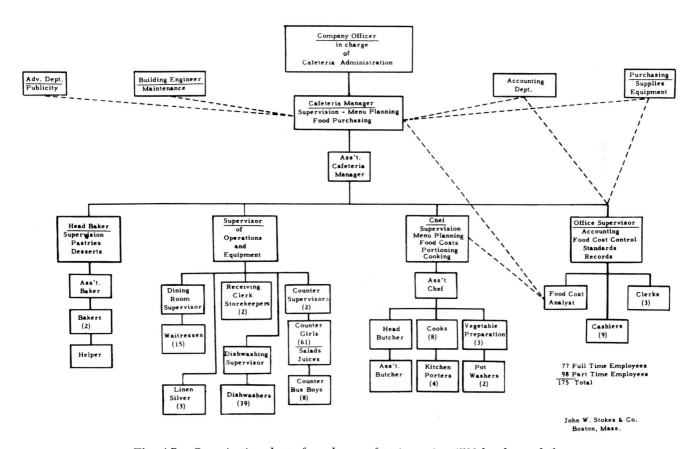

Fig. 4.5. Organization chart of employee cafeteria serving 4500 luncheons daily.

trol, and records and standards. The cashiers, however, who may be considered as "line" employees, come under the Office Supervisor.

"Staff" functions are also performed by the Company's Advertising, Maintenance, Accounting, and Purchasing Departments, as denoted by the dotted lines on the chart.

In this connection, it should be understood that the "line" departments are those which actually do the work of purchasing, receiving, storing, preparing, cooking, and serving the food to the patron. The "staff" departments aid with specialized services not directly concerned with the "line" functions. Both line and staff functions are, of course, necessary and important. It is well, however, to recognize the difference in each. For example, the Food-Cost Analyst works with the Chef on food-cost problems, as indicated by the dotted lines. However, the Analyst has no direct authority over the Chef or any of his employees. If a difference arises he must work through channels. That is, he must go to his superior, the Office Supervisor, who in turn takes the matter up with the Cafeteria

Manager, who may in turn discuss the matter directly with the Chef. Depending upon the relationships existing, this method of working strictly through channels may often be expedited by the Office Supervisor going directly to the Chef, who is on the same level of authority, as shown by the chart.

Figure 4.6 shows a small industrial cafeteria operation where the operation is headed by the Working Chef who also acts as the Manager. Here, however, similar line and staff functions are performed as in the organization portrayed in Figure 4.5. It will be noted that all departments, including Baking, Food-Cost Control, and Counter Service, report directly to the Chef-Manager.

Figure 4.7 shows the Dietary Department of a 300-bed general hospital. In this instance there is a Main Kitchen Manager (a man) who, in addition to being in charge of the kitchen, purchases meats and fresh vegetables. Other purchasing is done by the Chief Dietitian.

The Assistant Dietitian is directly in charge of the food preparation and service. She also functions in an

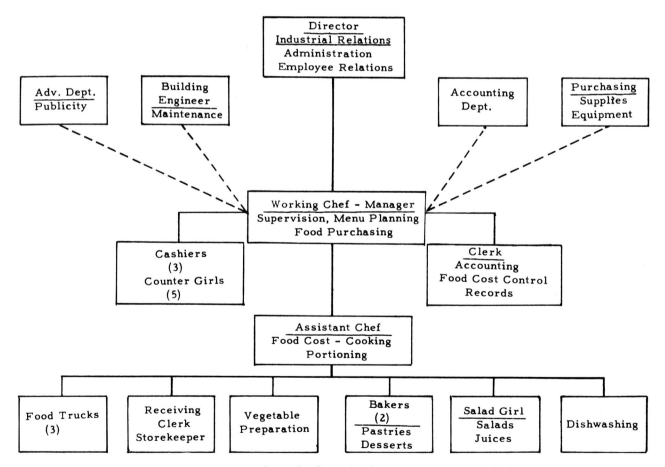

Fig. 4.6. Organization chart of industrial cafeteria serving 300 meals daily.

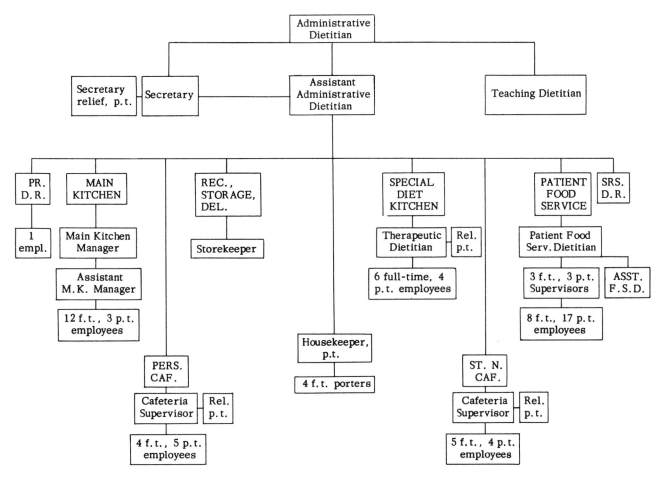

Fig. 4.7.   Organization chart of dietary department in a 300-bed general hospital.

administrative capacity in the absence of the Chief Dietitian.

Figure 4.8 shows the Food-Service Division of a 600-bed military hospital. Here the Food-Service Officer (Manager) is a man, and the Therapeutic Dietitian reports to him. In this hospital, ambulatory patients eat in the cafeteria, and tray service is provided for bed patients.

Figure 4.9, a line-chart, depicts the food-service organization in a college feeding some 2500 students and employees three meals daily. Under the Administrative Assistant to the Executive Dietitian, there are four Assistant Dietitians. One of these is in charge of three kitchens, the others in charge of two kitchens each, or nine in all. Each of the kitchens serves the dormi-

tory in which it is located, and in some cases a nearby smaller residence hall.

SUGGESTED READING

INSTITUTIONS MAGAZINE, "Personnel Management in Institutions" (An anthology including article by the author on Profit-Sharing) Domestic Engineering Co., Chicago, 1959.

LUNDBERG, DONALD E., and ARMATAS, JAMES P. *The Management of People in Hotels, Restaurants and Clubs.* Dubuque, Iowa: Wm. C. Brown Company Publishers, 1964.

STOKES, JOHN W. *How to Manage a Restaurant or Institutional Food Service.* Dubuque, Iowa: Wm. C. Brown Company Publishers, 1967.

WHYTE, WM. FOOTE. *Human Relations in the Restaurant Industry.* New York: McGraw-Hill Book Co., 1948.

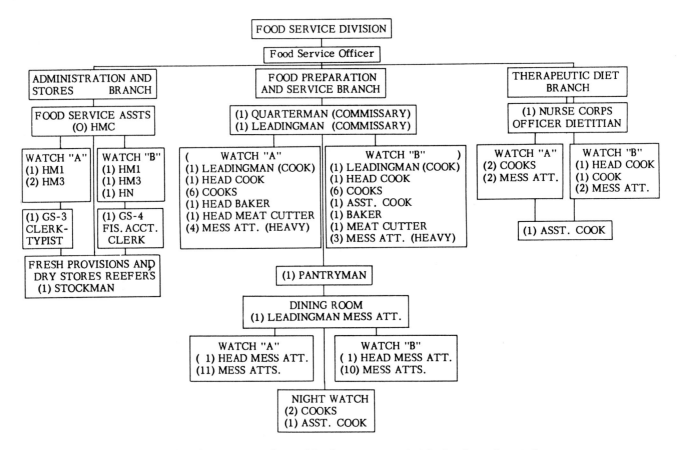

Fig. 4.8.   Organization chart of food service in a 600-bed military hospital.

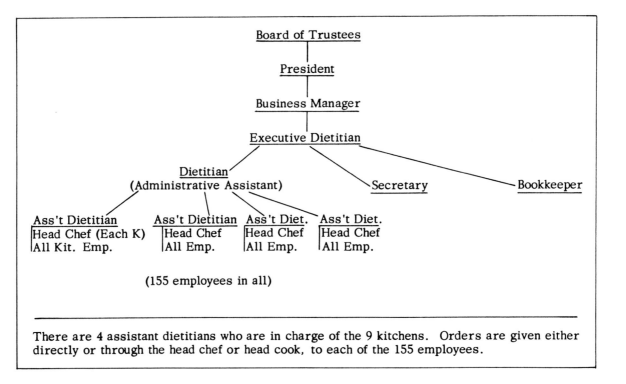

Fig. 4.9.   Organization chart of college dining halls.

CHAPTER 5

Food-Service Design and Equipment; Illumination, Preventive Maintenance

The design and layout of a food service has much to do with the success of its operation, not only from a cost standpoint but also with respect to the quality of the food and service. While the manager cannot be an expert on architecture, food facilities engineering, or interior decoration, he should be familiar with the principles of design and layout. He may be planning a new food service now or in the future and he should be constantly seeking to improve his operation. Changes in layout often offer opportunities for lowering operating costs and providing better service.

"DESIGN" AND "LAYOUT" DEFINED

The word "design" as used in this text has to do with the size, shape, style, and decoration of the building or areas used for food service and the relation of these areas, one to another. "Layout" more specifically refers to the detailed arrangement of the various areas within the food service and the location of the facilities and equipment in these areas.

Food-Service Designs Are Many

Designs and layouts vary considerably, depending upon the type of operation and the menu offered. Obviously, the menu and layout of a large deluxe table-service restaurant are quite different from that of a small counter-type eating place. Likewise, a hospital food service offers a different menu and requires facilities not found in a school lunchroom.

With the exception of some units of chain restaurant and franchise operations, no two food services are exactly alike. Each reflects the ideas of the operator and designer in achieving the purpose for which it is established.

As new kinds of processed foods, new methods of cooking, and new types of equipment are developed, designs and layouts change.

BASIC PRINCIPLES OF DESIGN AND LAYOUT

The underlying principles of design and layout are, however, essentially the same for all food services. Food and supplies are received and stored. Food is prepared, cooked, and served. Space and facilities must be provided for these functions. To accomplish this most effectively, the following principles should be observed:

1. *Provide Continuous Flow of Materials:* Materials such as food and supplies should proceed from the receiving entrance to the point of service or use in a continuous flow, without "back-tracking." Some of these, of course, will be placed in storerooms or refrigerators en route to await further use. These stor-

age areas should be arranged in the line of material flow. This is graphically portrayed in Figures 5.1 and 5.1A. In large food services and in commissaries, food production may be arranged in "work centers" for specialized production such as preparation, baking, or salad-making, or with cooking equipment such as ranges, steam kettles, steam cookers, and ovens grouped in batteries. These work centers are usually arranged at right angles to the general material flow, which includes the lateral movement in and out of these centers but which enables the materials to progress in a general forward direction toward the point of service.

2. *Have All Operations on the Same Floor Level:* Ideally, all operations of the food service should be on

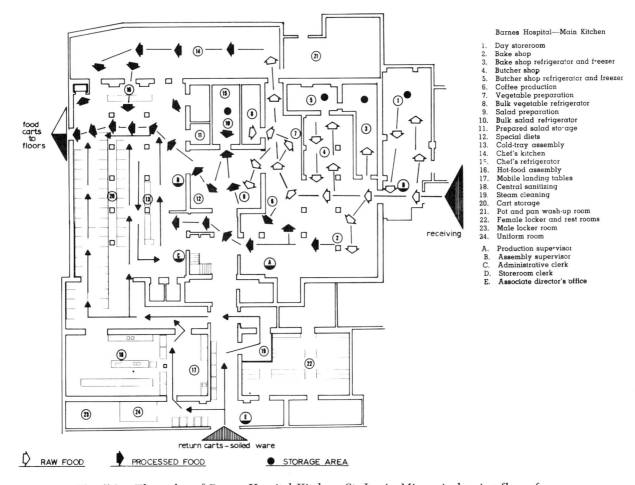

Barnes Hospital—Main Kitchen

1. Day storeroom
2. Bake shop
3. Bake shop refrigerator and freezer
4. Butcher shop
5. Butcher shop refrigerator and freezer
6. Coffee production
7. Vegetable preparation
8. Bulk vegetable refrigerator
9. Salad preparation
10. Bulk salad refrigerator
11. Prepared salad storage
12. Special diets
13. Cold-tray assembly
14. Chef's kitchen
15. Chef's refrigerator
16. Hot-food assembly
17. Mobile landing tables
18. Central sanitizing
19. Steam cleaning
20. Cart storage
21. Pot and pan wash-up room
22. Female locker and rest rooms
23. Male locker room
24. Uniform room

A. Production supervisor
B. Assembly supervisor
C. Administrative clerk
D. Storeroom clerk
E. Associate director's office

food carts to floors

receiving

return carts – soiled ware

▷ RAW FOOD   ◀ PROCESSED FOOD   ● STORAGE AREA

Fig. 5.1. Floor plan of Barnes Hospital Kitchen, St. Louis, Missouri, showing flow of raw food from receiving entrance to storerooms and of processed food through kitchen en route to floor galleys. Return routes of food carts and soiled dishes are also indicated, as well as the various supervisory centers. (Courtesy Barnes and Associated Hospitals, St. Louis.)

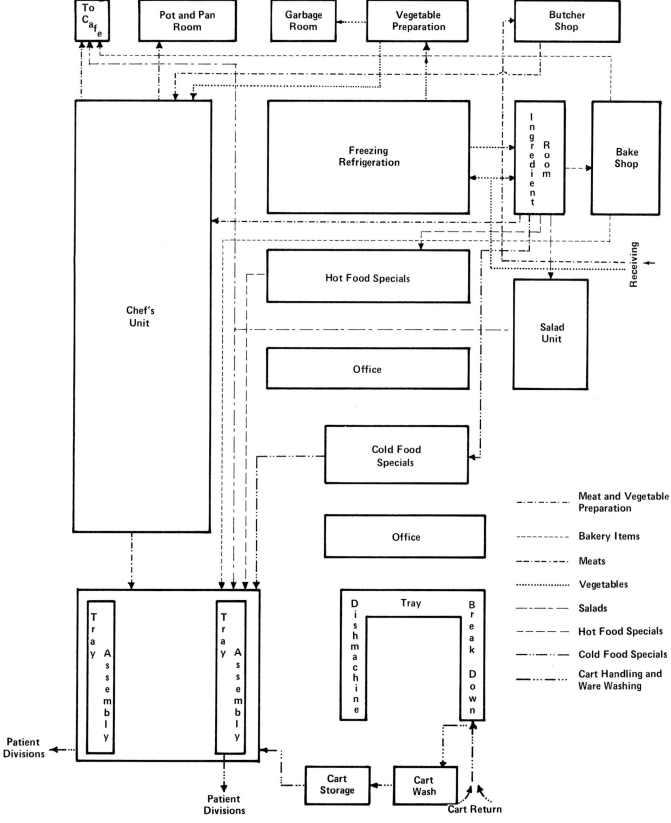

Fig. 5.1A. Flow of work diagram, showing movement of materials from receiving, through preparation, tray assembly and cleanup. (Courtesy Barnes Hospital, St. Louis, Mo.)

the same floor level. While this is not possible in some cases, such as in hotels and hospitals where food must be conveyed to different floors, vertical transportation involves many problems. In addition to cost, there are the difficulties of supervision and of getting hot and cold food to patrons at proper temperatures.

3. *Minimize the Distance Between the Kitchen and the Point of Service:* The distance between the location of the prepared food in the kitchen to the point where the farthest patron has to be served should be kept at a minimum. In a cafeteria, the serving counter usually adjoins the kitchen.

4. *Arrange Compact Work Centers in the Production Area:* The most effective arrangements of work areas in the production department or kitchen for food preparation, cooking, baking, salad-making, etc., are those where the worker is provided with all the necessary facilities within reach. In the large, old-fashioned kitchen, it was necessary for the cook to walk considerable distances during the day. In modern kitchens the refrigerator and principal cooking appliances are arranged within easy reach of the cook. Modular storage and preparation equipment is now available in which these facilities are combined in a single unit, this reducing the necessary walking to a minimum.

5. *Design for Efficient Traffic Flow, Delivery, and Pick-up:* Traffic in the kitchen and dining areas should be so arranged that moving lines of workers, patrons, or materials do not cross one another. With this free flow of traffic, pick-up and delivery operations should be arranged in sequence. To illustrate, patrons in a cafeteria leave the line and carry their trays to tables, and upon completing their meals, carry trays and soiled dishes to a window or conveyor without crossing the line of incoming patrons.

6. *Provide Working Conditions That Make for Productivity:* A food service should be designed so that work can be done without undue fatigue or discomfort which would lower the productivity of the workers. Productivity has to do with such factors as temperature, humidity, ventilation, illumination, wall, ceiling, and floor color, noise levels, aisle space, and the design of facilities in accord with the laws of motion economy. This involves what has been called "human engineering," that is, concern for the human element involved.

7. *Design for Sanitation and Safety:* The food service should be designed and equipment selected so that the highest standards of sanitation and safety can be maintained. Involved are such things as the elimination of openings and crevices which may harbor vermin or allow entrance of rodents, floor drains, and the installation of appliances that can be readily taken apart for cleaning. This is covered in more detail in Chapter 10 "Sanitation, Safety, and Fire Prevention."

FOOD SERVICE LAYOUT AND EQUIPMENT

Unfortunately, in the past, too little thought has been given to the planning of food-service facilities in industry and institutions from an operating standpoint. As labor and overhead rates have increased, it has become more important that the physical layout be such that it may be operated economically. Even more essential is the necessity of planning so that food may be conveyed quickly and at proper temperatures to the points of service. Food service plays such an important role in employee and public relations that adequate advance planning will pay dividends in lower operating costs and better food and service.

MAIN POINTS IN FOOD-SERVICE PLANNING

The main points in planning for the food service in an institution or in industry are:

1. Plan well in advance
2. Utilize competent counsel
3. Determine optimum location
4. Allow adequate space for present and future needs
5. Arrange layout for efficient production and distribution
6. Select well-engineered and durable equipment
7. Design for easy cleaning and sanitation

Plan Well in Advance

Aside from the initial investment, an industrial food service may involve an annual subsidy. In a hospital or similar institution, the food service may represent as much as 25% of the annual operating budget if overhead costs are realistically considered. These are *continuing costs!* It is logical, therefore, that the planning of the food service be an integral part of the overall planning at the very outset, rather than, as is often the case, a mere afterthought. Once utility lines and equipment are installed, changes are extremely costly. From every standpoint, careful advance planning will bring substantial rewards when the food service is in operation.

Utilize Competent Counsel

It is essential that competent architects and consulting engineers be employed to design the structure and functional facilities. No matter how qualified these experts may be, they cannot be expected to be fa-

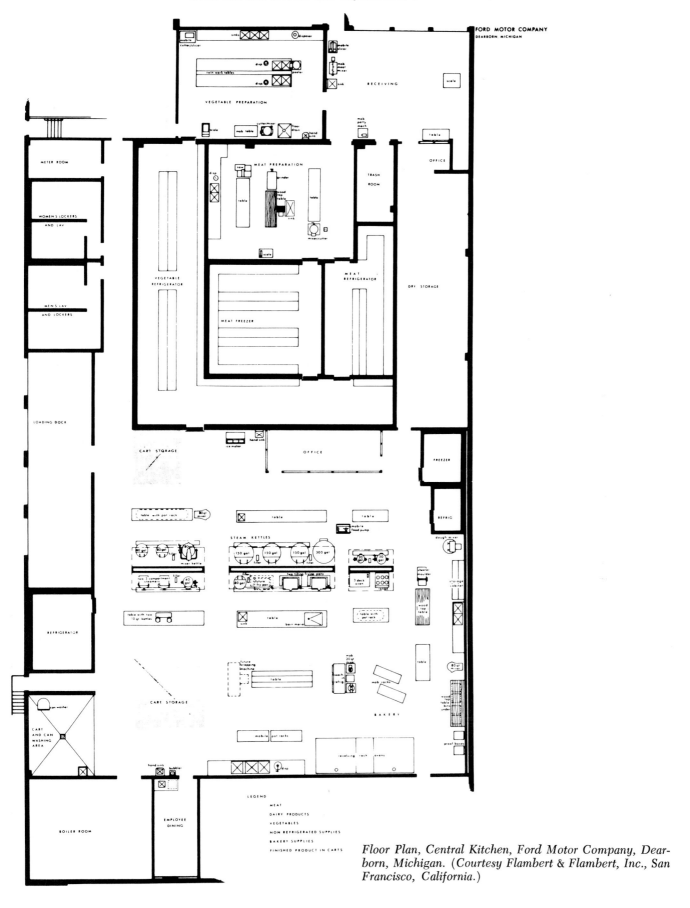

Floor Plan, Central Kitchen, Ford Motor Company, Dearborn, Michigan. (Courtesy Flambert & Flambert, Inc., San Francisco, California.)

miliar with all of the technical details of food-service operations. If the food service is to function economically and effectively, the layout and specifications should be impartially analyzed by an experienced food management consultant. This should be done before plans are finally approved so that desirable changes may be made. Needless to say, this individual should have no pecuniary interest in any equipment to be installed, but should be retained on a fee basis.

Determine Optimum Location

Here we use the word "optimum" in the sense of the most suitable under existing conditions. The best location for the food service with respect to service of meals would obviously be at the center of a circle encompassing the normal working locations of the patrons who are to use it. In a hospital it would be at the shortest distance, both vertically and horizontally, from the farthest patients' rooms.

However, such a central point might not be suitable from the standpoint of delivery facilities. It might not be desirable from environmental factors such as air, light, noise, and outside view. With respect to these factors the following points should be considered:

1. Availability to patrons
2. Facilities for delivery of food and supplies
3. Environmental factors

Availability to Patrons

Studies indicate that industrial workers generally will not walk more than approximately 1,000 feet from their work stations to a cafeteria. Therefore, in an industrial plant the ideal location of the food service would be at the center of a circle having a radius of say 1,000 feet within which the maximum number of employees work. In educational institutions having longer luncheon periods, this would not necessarily hold, yet the food service should be readily accessible to students and faculty. In hospitals, the growing emphasis upon the serving of food to patients at proper temperatures makes it necessary that the food preparation area be located at the shortest possible distance from the points of service.

Facilities for Delivery of Food and Supplies

The food service should be located so that it is easily accessible from the outside, so that the movement of vendors' trucks within the grounds may be limited. A separate entrance for deliveries is desirable if it can be arranged. Space should be provided for an adequate loading platform.

Environmental Factors

In locating the food service, consideration should be given to the psychological as well as the physical factors surrounding the preparation and dining areas. The location should provide plenty of light, air, and a space free from disagreeable odors, noxious fumes, and noise. If, in addition, there is a pleasant view from the windows, the appeal of the food will be enhanced.

Allow Adequate Space

The ideal arrangement is to provide space so that the entire operation may be accomplished on one floor, preferably at or near the ground level. This means that the Loading Platform, Receiving Area, Storerooms and Refrigerators, Food Preparation, Cooking, Serving, and Dining Areas will be laid out so that the materials (food and supplies) flow generally in one direction. "Back-tracking" will thus be minimized and labor cost reduced. (Figure 5.1 shows how this has been accomplished through the reconstruction of an existing hospital food service.)

Dining Space Required

It is well to start the space calculations with the Dining Area. Space required will depend upon:

1. The type of service to be employed. (Table Service, Self-Service, or a Combination of both.)
2. The menu to be served. (This may range from a complete meal, with few choices, served family style by waiters, to a number of entrees, displayed on a Cafeteria counter, with accompanying appetizers, desserts, and beverages.)
3. The number to be served. In a business establishment or institution, the number who will make use of the employees' cafeteria may range from 50% or less to 90% or more, depending upon:
   a. Length of meal period.
   b. Availability of other eating places, including homes of employees.
   c. Appeal of the food service: food quality, variety, prices charged, and the speed of service.

	Sq. Ft. Per Seat To Be Allowed	Turnover Per Seat Per Hour
Industrial Cafeterias°	12-16	2-3
Hospital Cafeterias°	12-16	2-3
School Cafeterias°	10-15	2-3
Table-service Dining Rooms	15-17	$\frac{1}{2}$-$1\frac{1}{4}$

°Not including serving counter

Fig. 5.2. Dining areas and turnover per seat, based upon data from "Commercial Kitchens." (Courtesy American Gas Association.)

Depending upon the menu, service, and layout, as many as twelve persons per minute may pass through a well-organized single cafeteria line offering a simple menu. Ten persons per minute is a reasonable maximum upon which to calculate. Normally, each cafeteria seat is occupied from 20 to 30 minutes so that the "turnover" (number of patrons using the seat) ranges from 2 to 3 per hour. The average time is somewhere between 22 and 25 minutes at the cafeteria dining table. Allowing for time to return tray and dishes to Dishwashing Area (if self-busing prevails), each patron spends about 30 minutes in the cafeteria dining room.

Theoretically, therefore, if 600 people pass through a single cafeteria line within an hour, 300 seats would be required. Actually the movement through the line is not constant, but irregular and spasmodic. Furthermore, the cafeteria periods may be staggered over two or more hours.

Figure 5.2 gives dining areas to be allowed and turnover per seat per hour for various types of cafeterias and a table-service dining room.

Planning the Dining Area

The number of seats required in a cafeteria dining room will depend upon customer load, the rate of movement through the line, and the seat turnover. The maximum load would occur during the busiest part of the noon or evening meal period. The rate of movement through the line will depend in part upon the menu offered and in part upon the arrangement of the line.

In a college cafeteria with a limited menu, the rate may run as high as 12 customers per minute. In commercial and industrial cafeterias with a wide variety of menu selections, the rate may run as low as 5 per minute. In one industrial cafeteria where the "hollow square" or "shopping center" type of service is employed, 7 customers per minute pass each cashier, so that by increasing the number of cashiers, more patrons can be accommodated.

In a single line, commercial cafeteria, where the rate of flow is 5 per minute or 300 per hour and the turnover is 1 1/2 per hour (that is, each patron occupies his seat an average of 40 minutes) it would be necessary to provide 200 seats (300 divided by 1.5). This can be expressed mathematically as

$$S = \frac{R \times N \times 60}{T} \text{ or in above case } \frac{5 \times 1 \times 60}{1.5} = 200$$

where S is the number of seats required, R the rate of movement per minute, N the number of cafeteria lines, T the turnover per seat, and 60 the number of minutes in an hour.

This is predicated upon a steady flow through the line at the hour of maximum patronage which would take place during busy meal periods. Under actual conditions, the flow is fluctuating and intermittent. It may also, in industrial and institutional cafeterias, be regulated by staggering the meal periods of various groups so as to spread the flow more evenly over the entire meal period. By thus balancing out the peaks and valleys of patronage, it is possible to achieve a more economical operation.

Building regulations in many localities set minimum standards for floor areas per seat and aisle widths in "places of public assembly" (usually defined as public rooms where 50 or more are gathered). These standards depend upon whether or not seats are fixed or movable. In general, the requirements vary from 8 to 18 square feet per seat in all types of eating establishments. A fast-moving, minimum menu type of service can do with as little as 8 square feet per patron seated, whereas a "plush" staff dining room would require as much as 18 square feet per seat.

Before planning the dining area, local and/or state building authorities should be consulted. In cafeterias generally, the minimum allowance for the dining area including tables, chairs, aisle, and counter space should be at least 12 square feet per seat. For institutional cafeterias, some authorities recommend that from 14 to 15 square feet per seat be allowed in order to avoid crowding.

It can be seen, therefore, that for 500 seats at 12 square feet per seat, a total of 6,000 square feet would be the minimum area required. This should be clear floor space, that is, over and above space taken by pillars, pilasters, and other fixed objects.

The most economical utilization of dining space comes through the use of tables 6, 8, and 10 feet long by 30 inches wide, seating, respectively, 3, 4, or 5 on each side, with no end seats. An aisle at least 3 feet wide should be allowed between the tables. Where square tables seating four each are used, more aisle space will be required proportionately.

In selecting chairs and tables, consideration should be given to appearance, weight, structural strength, lasting qualities, and ease of cleaning. Thus, while the use of 10 foot tables seating five on a side would result in greater seating capacity per given area, such tables are apt to be unwieldy. Lighter tables, seating 3 or 4 on a side (6 and 8 feet long, respectively), can be moved more readily for cleaning or other purposes. Square tables of the pedestal type, seating 4 each, are more appealing, but they are heavy and require more floor area per seat.

Hardwood table tops, such as maple, are most attractive and if coated with waterproof, stain-resistant varnishes can be easily cleaned. Maple tables, however, are heavy and expensive as to first cost. Most institutional food services use plastic materials, such as Formica, for table-tops. These are available in a variety of colors and are readily cleaned. The thin plastic top is bonded to a laminated wood base, and should be provided with a backing-sheet to prevent warping. A self-edge, made of the same material as the top and put on under pressure, is more serviceable than a metal edging which may be worked loose.

Folding metal tables with plastic tops are in use in many institutional dining rooms. Their use permits the room to be cleared quickly and easily for meetings and other purposes.

Chairs may be procured in many varieties made of wood, metals, or plastics. As it is customary to place the chairs on the tables while the floor is being mopped, weight is an important consideration. Colored plastic seats and backs on aluminum or chrome frames are often used to tie in with the color-scheme of the room. Here again, the factors of appearance, durability, and cost must be taken into account. When a considerable number of chairs are to be purchased, vendors will generally supply sample chairs to be viewed and tested. Chairs should be supplied with domes on the bottoms of the legs to prevent marring the floor.

Cardboard templates or cut-outs, cut to scale, are helpful in plotting out the actual seating arrangement on a blueprint of the proposed dining area. Thus allowance is made for structural obstructions, and the seating plan may be tested in advance.

In general, a rectangular area is best suited for the dining room, with the cafeteria line along the long side of the room adjoining the food preparation area. Experience would seem to dictate a ratio of 3 to 5 as being the optimum proportion. Six thousand feet of area then would be best provided by a 60 x 100 foot room.

Snack Bars

In large industrial or institutional cafeterias, there are those who will prefer to bring their own lunches from outside. Many of these supplement their lunches with beverages and/or desserts purchased at the cafeteria counter.

By providing a separate snack bar for the service of beverages and desserts, a speedy service can be provided for those wishing to purchase only these items. At the same time, pressure on the cafeteria line is relieved, affording better service to cafeteria patrons.

Kitchen Space Required

The size of the kitchen is influenced by a number of factors such as the type of operation, the menu offered, and the customer load. The extent to which prepared or partially prepared foods are used and whether or not a butcher shop and/or a bakery is to be provided should be considered. Inasmuch as so many food services are now buying prepared foods of all kinds, butcher shops are becoming a thing of the past. While full-fledged bakeries are also disappearing, and bread and pies are purchased outside, prepared mixes are widely used and most kitchens provide only a small section for baking. Due to the fact that compact kitchens save steps and thus increase efficiency, the trend is toward smaller compact kitchens.

The figures in Figure 5.3 show the number of square feet required both for the kitchen and the "back of the house." The kitchen area includes space for preparation, cooking, ware washing, baking, salad making, service, and the required work spaces and passageways. The back of the house includes the kitchen area and also the areas for receiving; storage (both dry and refrigerated) for food, supplies, rubbish and garbage; office facilities and employees' rest and locker rooms.

	Sq. Ft. of Kitchen Area Per Dining Room Seat	Total Back of House Area Per Dining Room Seat
Cafeteria	6-8	10-12
Table Service Dining Room	5-7	10-12
Lunch Room	4-6	8-10

Fig. 5.3. Approximate kitchen areas from "Commercial Kitchens." (Courtesy American Gas Association.)

Experienced designers may work on a percentage basis in determining space allocations. They may allow a space equal to from 50 to 60 percent of the dining area for the kitchen proper and another space equal to from 40 to 50 percent of the dining space to be allocated to receiving, storage, and the public and employees' areas required. Once these allocations are made, the designer lays out the equipment which has been selected. As this work proceeds, revisions may be made in the space allocations before final dimensions are determined.

FOOD PRODUCTION AREA

Space required for this area will depend upon the maximum number of meals served per hour and the menu offered. A complete Food Production Area would include:

1. Receiving and storage
2. Food preparation: Meats (butcher shop) and vegetables, (special diets in hospitals).
3. Cooking
4. Baking
5. Salad and dessert preparation
6. Dishwashing and potwashing
7. Office for food-service manager, dietitians, and clerical assistants.

Type of Food Purchased

If fabricated cuts of meat and baked goods are purchased outside, a butcher shop and complete bakery would not be needed. A simple service of sandwiches, beverages, and desserts, all purchased from outside sources, would further decrease the area required for preparation. If dishes, cups, and utensils of disposable material are used, the area needed for dishwashing would be minimized.

Loading Platform

An outside loading platform is required to facilitate the delivery of food. It should be located on the ground floor level near the service driveway and away from the entrance used by food-service patrons.

The platform should be at least 6 feet in depth. Its total area will depend upon the volume of deliveries, from a minimum of 60 square feet (6 x 10) where 300 meals are served daily to, say, 180 square feet where 1,000 or more meals are served.

It should be constructed of concrete, with slip-resistant, integral hardener, and be protected with a heavy steel angle iron along the edge and a bumper of wood or resilient material. It is essential that the platform be at the same level as the entrance to the inside receiving area. To protect goods from the weather, a roof covering the entire platform is recommended. The roof should be high enough to clear delivery trucks (at least 12 feet 6 inches in height). Steps with a handrail should be provided to the driveway level.

Receiving Area

The receiving area inside the building should be large enough to allow for counting, checking, and weighing of items delivered before they are placed in storage. Here again the area will depend upon the maximum volume of deliveries to be handled at a given time. At least 60 to 80 square feet should be provided. The area should be equipped with adequate platform scales and a beam scale, if meat is purchased in bulk. Dial platform scales are preferable. A heavy table and suitable hand or platform trucks should also be provided.

Dry Food Storage Area

It is essential that nonperishable foods be stored in a cool dry area and be protected against rodents and vermin. It is highly desirable that steam and water lines should not run through this area, but if this cannot be avoided they should be well insulated. It is well to install steel shelving so that the foodstuffs can be stored in orderly fashion, with air space around them and between the bottom shelf and floor level.

The use of prepared foods has changed the requirements for dry storage in food services. Prepared mixes have replaced flours; prepared, frozen or dehydrated potatoes are used in place of the fresh products; fruits and vegetables formerly bought in cans are now purchased in dehydrated or frozen form, to cite a few examples.

The space required will depend upon the purchasing policies of the institution, the time between deliveries, and upon the menu. Some food services store several months' supply of canned goods and staples. Others operate upon a delivery-to-delivery basis. It should be remembered that it costs money to maintain goods in a warehouse. The expense includes cost of handling in and out, interest on capital invested, and shrinkage due to various causes. Institutional purveyors figure that it costs approximately 1/2 of 1 per cent per month of total cost value to carry their warehouse inventories. Certainly there is justification for carrying at least a four days to a week's supply between deliveries and to carry over long week ends.

Areas required for dry storage depend upon (1) volume of dry storage per typical meal which will range from .025 to .050 cubic feet; (2) average height of storeroom space which is usable—from 4 to 7 feet; (3) maximum number of typical meals for which storage is required. This will range from three days to as long as several months in some cases; and (4) the average usable space in the storeroom after that taken up by aisles, shelves, etc. is subtracted. This ranges from 30 per cent to 60 per cent with 50 per cent as the usual factor. The space required can then be expressed in the following formula (From "Commercial Kitchens," American Gas Association, quoted by permission):

Dry Storage Area in Square feet equals:

$$\frac{\text{Volume (cu. ft.) per meal} \times \text{Number of Meals}}{\text{Average height (ft.)} \times \text{\% of floor area usable.}}$$

Steel shelving should be at least 18 inches in depth, with 14 inches between the upper shelves. This will allow for storage of #2 cans and two layers of #10 cans. If 36 inches is allowed below the bottom shelf, this will obviate bending, and the space may be utilized for the storage of drums or bagged items such as sugar, flour, and potatoes. These should be placed on raised platforms or, better yet, upon steel dollies mounted on casters for convenient access and cleaning.

Steel shelves above eye-level should be made of open wire or strap-metal and be tilted forward so that contents can easily be seen from a standing position on the floor. The highest shelf should be no more than 76 inches from the floor, most are not over 72 inches high. Storage of frequently-used items should be between 28 and 56 inches from the floor. Heavy items should be placed nearest the entrance.

Supply Storeroom

From a safety and sanitation standpoint it is important to provide a separate storeroom for supplies. This minimizes the dangerous possibility of mistaking soap powders, detergents, insecticides, and the like for food. It also protects foodstuffs from contamination by chemical odors, and provides better control of paper goods, cleaning utensils, and other supply items susceptible to pilferage. Space required for such a storeroom would range from a minimum of 40 square feet to a maximum of 1 square foot per 100 meals served. Here again much depends upon the operation and the type of supplies needed.

Storage of Perishable Foods

All perishable foods must be kept under controlled temperatures and humidities if they are to remain in good condition for appreciable periods of time. Even bananas and root or tuberous vegetables should be kept in cool, dry storage areas.

Frozen foods, meats, poultry, and seafood, dairy products, and fresh fruits and vegetables must be kept under refrigeration at the optimum temperatures for these various classes of foods. There is also the necessity of placing prepared foods such as salads, pastry dough, and pastry shells under refrigeration until they are to be served or further processed.

Garbage or Trash Storage

A garbage room and a room for the storage of trash should be provided near the loading platform. These rooms should be well screened, and it is desirable that the garbage room be refrigerated. However, if a garbage disposer connected with the sewage system is used, the garbage storage area will not be needed.

Incineration

Because of the valuable space taken up by wet and dry waste storage, many establishments have installed incinerators to dispose of all combustible waste, including garbage.

Walk-in Refrigerators

The conventional method of storing perishable foods has been through the use of built-in walk-in refrigerators. These generally are constructed of concrete and lined with cork or other insulating material. For economy of construction and greater insulating effect, these walk-in refrigerators are usually built in a block of four or more or in a row with one adjoining the other. In the older systems ammonia is used as the refrigerant. This in turn cools brine which circulates through the refrigerators. Often in large institutions, the refrigerating system includes a plant for the manufacturing of ice in large blocks.

With the use of freon and similar modern refrigerants, it is possible to decentralize refrigeration. Separate compressing units are recommended. Thus the possibility of a breakdown of the entire plant is precluded. New insulating materials make it possible to provide so-called sectional portable units, either in the walk-in or reach-in type. These may be located at the points most convenient for those who use them. Considerable labor-saving can thus result.

In planning a new food service, consideration should be given to the desirability of installing self-contained, portable units, erected from pre-built sections. The first cost is less than permanent construction, and the greater flexibility makes possible later rearrangement if required for expansion or other reasons.

Thermometers

Every refrigerator should be equipped with a thermometer so that temperatures can be checked constantly. In addition to the upright type of thermometer, it is desirable to provide a single-pen recording thermometer designed to record temperatures in walk-in boxes continuously on circular charts good for seven day revolution. These may be arranged for remote reading at one central point if desired.

Locks and Safety Provisions

All refrigerators should be capable of being locked to prevent pilferage. However, they should be provided with safety locks removable from the inside and alarm bells in case anyone should become locked within.

Service and Maintenance

As part of the purchase contract, provisions for service and maintenance should be scrutinized carefully. In many establishments, service is the responsibility of the maintenance staff.

Types of Walk-In Boxes and Optimum Temperatures

The following types of walk-in refrigerators are generally used, depending upon the volume, types of foodstuffs used, and methods of purchasing:

1. Deep Freeze
2. Meat Box
3. Dairy Box
4. Fruit and Vegetable Box
5. Fish Box

Deep Freeze (Temperature From −5° F. to −10° F.)

Where permanent walk-in refrigerators are installed, it is customary to build the deep freeze box within another box. The temperatures are usually maintained at from 40° to 50° F. in the outside or vestibule section.

With the increasing use of frozen foods it will often be found desirable to use upright frozen food storage cabinets. These are efficient, accessible, and flexible as to location. As one cubic foot stores approximately from 30 to 35 pounds, the capacity needed can be based upon estimated usage of frozen foods.

Meat Box (Temperatures From 34° to 36° F.)

Here the capacity required depends upon the type of meat purchased. Sufficient space should be provided to allow meats to be hung so that air can circulate freely. Removable wood or metal shelving is desirable for easy cleaning. Blowers should be provided for air circulation. Vermin-proof insulation on walls, floor, and ceiling is important; for the interior, glazed tile or stainless steel is preferable. Meat and poultry storage will normally require from 35 per cent to 40 per cent of the total refrigeration capacity.

Dairy Box (Temperatures Range From 35° to 40° F.)

This is used for storage of milk, cream, and other dairy products, usually purchased in 10 quart bulk cans. Capacity required will range from 20 per cent to 25 per cent of total refrigeration space.

Fruit and Vegetable Box (Temperatures Range From 35° to 40° F.)

Here will be stored fresh fruits and vegetables and other foodstuffs requiring moderate temperatures. In some food services, the outside section of the deep freeze will be used for this purpose. This box will require from 20 per cent to 25 per cent of the total refrigerated storage.

Fish Box (Temperatures Range From 31° to 40° F.)

Fresh fish and many types of sea food should be stored in cracked ice to avoid spoilage. Because of the odors emanating from sea food, this box should be placed in a location where contamination of other food can be avoided. Where frozen fish are used, as in sections of the country remote from the coasts, a deep-freeze box can be used. Capacity will depend upon quantities used.

Refrigeration Capacity Required

Total refrigeration capacity required in an institutional food service will depend upon the purchasing policies and frequency of deliveries. The increasing use of frozen foods necessitates more freezer space than was formerly allocated. Many food services freeze prepared or partially prepared foods, such as baked goods, on the premises. This makes lower freezer temperatures and increased freezer capacity a requirement.

The following data in Figure 5.4 taken from "Commercial Kitchens," published by the American Gas Association and quoted by permission, are useful in making calculations:

The figures in Figure 5.4 are given in cubic feet for meals served between deliveries. In general the higher figures apply to deluxe table-service restaurants, the average figures to hospitals and employee feeding operations, and the lower figures to schools.

Because of aisles, shelving, etc., much space in refrigerators is not usable for storage. The usable space in walk-in boxes may vary from 25 per cent to 55 per cent. In working with such tables as in Figure 5.4, 40 per cent is the factor commonly taken. Walk-in refrigerators are usually 7 feet in height. In designing food services it is necessary to consider also the space taken up by the outside walls of the boxes and their insulation as well as the inside walls.

Reach-In Refrigerators and Freezers

The current trend seems to be away from walk-in boxes and toward greater use of reach-in freezers and

	Refrigeration Capacity Required	(Averages)
Meats and Poultry	.010 to .030 cubic feet per meal.	(.020)
Dairy Products	.007 to .015 cubic feet per meal.	(.011)
Fruits and Vegetables	.020 to .040 cubic feet per meal.	(.030)

Fig. 5.4. Refrigeration capacity required.

refrigerators. Where fabricated cuts of meat, frozen vegetables, pastries, etc., are used, the reach-in type of refrigerator saves space, is more readily accessible, and makes working in freezing temperatures unnecessary.

DESIGN AND LAYOUT OF KITCHEN

In designing and laying out the kitchen area, three steps are necessary:

1. Determine the cooking load.
2. Decide upon the equipment required.
3. Lay out the equipment and facilities to afford maximum efficiency of operation.

The Cooking Load

To determine the cooking load we must consider the menu to be served, not only for one day or one week, but for a period of weeks through which a normal menu cycle operates.

For a simple illustration, let us take a single dinner menu in an institution such as a school, feeding 400 at each of three daily meals. The service is family style table service with student waiters carrying platters of food to 40 tables seating 10 at each table. Assume that the dinner menu consists of the following with no choices:

Soup	Salad
Meat or Seafood entree	Dessert
Potato and one other vegetable	Coffee

Multiplying the number to be fed by the portions of each menu item to be served, we obtain the maximum cooking load for each item. For example, if 400 portions of soup are required, and each portion is 8 ounces or 1/2 pint, 200 pints or 25 gallons of soup must be prepared, requiring about one hour's time.

In the same way, the cooking load may be figured for other menu items. If more than one daily menu choice is offered, the computation becomes more complicated. Nevertheless, the purpose of the estimate is to provide maximum kitchen facilities rather than exact requirements. It should not be difficult for one experienced in food management to work out a satisfactory balance, even given two or more choices.

Equipment Required

With the daily cooking load figured out over say a two week menu period, it is readily possible to prepare a list of necessary equipment.

For the soup previously mentioned, approximately 25 gallons would be needed daily. This would be prepared most conveniently in a 25-gallon stock pot (al-

though, of course, it could be cooked in pots on top of the range).

Thus as we go through the production essentials, we would find need for such general cooking equipment as:

Cook's work table and sink
Ranges (one or more of given types and sizes)[1]
Stock pots
Ovens (including convection ovens)
Steam cookers
Cook's refrigerator
Cooking utensils, storage racks, and shelves

Specialized equipment such as:

Deep fat fryers
Coffee makers
Toasters
Egg cookers

In the preparation area the following may be provided:

Potato peeler
Butcher's meat block, slicer, grinder, cubing machines, etc.
Vegetable choppers, dicers, slicers
Mixing machines
Juice extractors, blenders, etc.
Vegetable and salad work tables and sinks

If a special area is set aside for salad preparation, it should contain:

Work table
Refrigerator
Sink
Shelves for dishes and utensils

The baking area would require:

Work tables and sinks
Mixers and dividers
Ovens
Proof boxes
Refrigerator

Other specialized equipment, depending upon the extent of the bakery operation.

Maximum dishwashing facilities should include:

Prerinsing device
Dishwashing machine or 3 compartment sink for handwashing
Tables for soiled dishes
Sinks and racks for pot washing or pot washing machine
Garbage disposal unit

---

1. For large establishments, one or more heavy duty "hotel" ranges will be most suitable. For medium sized and smaller kitchens, the "restaurant-type" range will be most satisfactory.

Convection Oven. (Courtesy Vulcan-Hart Corporation, Louisville, Ky.)

Restaurant Range-Gas. (Courtesy Vulcan-Hart Corporation, Louisville, Ky.)

Thermionic Ovens (3 Bake and 2 Roast sections) at Manteno State Hospital, Manteno, Illinois. (Courtesy Vulcan-Hart Corporation, Louisville, Ky.)

Battery of Gas Ranges, 2 Fryers, and a Ceramic Broiler with Au Gratin Oven at Florida Atlantic University, Boca Raton, Florida. (Courtesy Vulcan-Hart Corporation, Louisville, Ky.)

10-31SFX Electric Super Fryer. (Courtesy Welbilt Corporation, Maspeth, N. Y.)

76-43 Continuous-Cleaning Gas Infra-Red Broiler. (Courtesy Welbilt Corporation, Maspeth, N. Y.)

11Y24 Continuous-Cleaning Gas Convection Oven. (Courtesy Welbilt Corporation, Maspeth, N. Y.)

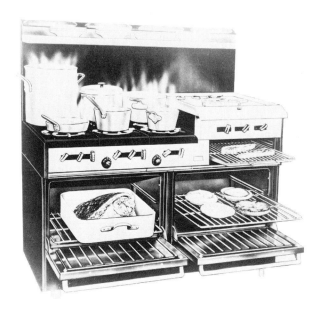

383 Continuous-Cleaning Gas Restaurant Range. (Courtesy Welbilt Corporation, Maspeth, N. Y.)

Continuous-Cleaning Garland Electric Restaurant Range. (Courtesy Welbilt Corporation, Maspeth, N. Y.)

Hobart Slicer with Chute Attachment. (Courtesy Hobart Mfg. Co., Troy, Ohio.)

Hobart Vertical Cutter Mixer. (Courtesy Hobart Mfg. Co., Troy, Ohio.)

Hobart Mixer. (Courtesy Hobart Mfg. Co., Troy, Ohio.)

Hobart Roast Beef Slicer. (Courtesy Hobart Mfg. Co., Troy, Ohio.)

Hobart Meat Slicer. (Courtesy Hobart Mfg. Co., Troy, Ohio.)

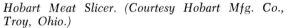

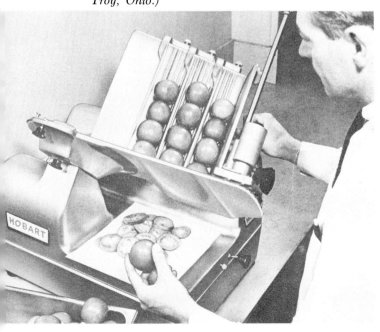

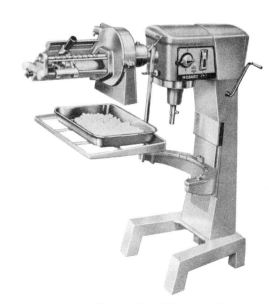

Hobart Food Cutter. (Courtesy Hobart Mfg. Co., Troy, Ohio.)

Additional Small Equipment

In addition to the preparation and cooking equipment previously mentioned, there are many smaller utensils required in food service. Figure 5.5 shows a list of such small utensils required in the preparation of various meals in school cafeterias. This provides an excellent checklist for any food service.

Other Labor-Saving Devices

The possibility of using conveyors, rollers, self-leveling devices for dishes, glasses, and cups, with heated and refrigerated cabinets and other labor-saving devices should be considered in larger operations. The slogan, "Put it on wheels!" should be kept constantly in mind.

Laying Out the Kitchen

By use of cardboard templates or, better yet, balsawood models of the various pieces of equipment mentioned previously, two purposes may be served in kitchen layout. First, the required area may be determined, and second, the equipment may be laid out and visualized so as to provide for the most efficient flow of materials and use of labor.

Labor cost in many cafeterias is the largest single item of expense. Care in kitchen layout will make work easier, service speedier, and labor costs lower. Sufficient time should be taken in advance to make sure that the layout is the most effective that can be devised. Once equipment is installed and the plumbing and electrical connections made, it is extremely costly to make alterations.

In the past, commodious kitchens with plenty of light and air space were considered ideal. Current labor costs and the advent of air conditioning, modern lighting, and new types of equipment have brought about many changes in kitchen planning. The current trend is to make kitchens compact and to reduce steps required.

It can be demonstrated that it costs at least 1 1/4 cents for a food service employee to walk 100 feet. This is true if the average wage is $2.00 per hour (not including fringe benefits) and the worker walks at an average rate of three miles per hour (15,840 feet). 200 divided by 158.4 = 1.26 or 1.26 cents per 100 feet. If we take into account the cost of fringe benefits, coffee breaks, trips to the rest room, etc., the actual cost is closer to 3 cents for each 100 feet traveled. By grouping equipment in the kitchen so that the most-used appliances are handiest to the workers using them, and arranging the layout so that the serving counter adjoins or is near the kitchen, many steps can be saved each working day. The daily saving of steps multiplies over the weeks and months to a substantial annual saving in labor cost.

Planning for Expansion

In laying out the kitchen, thought should be given to the possibility of future expansion. Floor space and the necessary utility connections can be provided in the layout for additional pieces of equipment that may be required or installed later. This foresight may save costly alterations at a later date.

Types of Equipment

Types of cooking equipment to be used will, of course, depend primarily on the type of fuel available. New and improved refrigeration, food preparation, cooking, and sanitation devices are constantly being developed. Many of these make possible better food products, and also minimize food waste and labor. Careful study needs to be given to the selection of equipment to make sure that each device will do the job expected of it, and to make certain that it will be more economical in the long run. The first cost of stainless steel, for instance, is greater than that of galvanized iron, yet it will prove more economical and satisfactory for permanent use. The use of aluminum and magnesium, by way of example, makes possible the reduction of weight with adequate structural strength in movable pieces of equipment.

Cleaning and Service

Careful consideration should be given to maintenance of food-service equipment. Cost of maintenance often has priority over the initial cost of equipment. Also a piece of equipment purchased at any price is not recommended if parts and service facilities are not readily available.

Other Service Equipment

Other specialized service equipment will be discussed in Chapter 9, "Distribution and Service of Food."

To Make or to Buy

With labor costs rising, many food services are dispensing with butcher shops and bakeries. They find that they can buy fabricated cuts of meat and baked goods at prices lower than the costs at which these items can be produced by the cafeteria itself, taking labor and overhead into consideration. In food services where less than 500 meals are served daily, it is generally more economical to buy pastries and fabricated meat cuts outside.

LIST OF UTENSILS FOR SCHOOL CAFETERIA

DESCRIPTION	Number to be served		
	150-250	250-350	350-500
Serving Trays -- plastic	14-22 Doz.	22-30 Doz.	30-42 Doz.
or			
Compartment serving tray	"	"	"
Soup Bowls, Plastic	"	"	"
Plates, 3 Partition, 10" Plastic	"	"	"
Salad Plates, 6"	"	"	"
Fruit Glasses, Plastic	"	"	"
Forks, Stainless Steel	"	"	"
Knives, " "	"	"	"
Teaspoons, " "	"	"	"
Soupspoons " "	"	"	"
Electric Mixer, Univex, 20 Qt.	1	1	1
Potato Peeler, Univex Model "D"	1	1	1
Coffee Maker, 40 cup Drip-O-Lator	1	1	1
Food Chopper, Universal No. 3	1	1	1
Butter Cutter	1	1	1
Greaser, Grater, Slicer, Shredder	1	1	1
Edlund Can-Opener, No. 2	1	2	2
Dial-A-Straw	2	3	4
Foley Food Mill 5 Qt. Size	1	2	2
Kurly Kate Metal Sponges	12	12	24
Menu Board w/letters	1	1	1
Kitchen Shears, Heavy Duty	2	4	6
S. S. Skimmer 4" Diam.	2	2	2
Aluminum Egg Slicer	1	1	1
1/4 to 1 Tablespoon, measuring spoons	2 sets	3 sets	3 sets
12" French Pastry Spoon, Maple	3	3	3
13" Serving Spoons, Solid	2	3	6
13" Serving Spoons, Slotted	2	2	3
17 1/2" Serving & Mixing Spoons, Solid	2	2	3
Tablespoons, Stainless	4	6	9
12" Wire Whip, Wooden Handle	1	1	1
#8-10-16-24 Disher Scoops	2 ea.	2 ea.	2 ea.
2 oz. Stainless Steel Ladles	2	2	4
8 oz. Stainless Steel Ladles	2	2	4
4 Compartment Silver Boxes (Metal)	3	4	6
9" Metal Tongs	2	3	3
10" French Knife	1	1	2
12" French Knife	1	1	1
10" Butcher	1	1	1
10" Meat Slicer	1	1	2
6" Boning Knife	2	2	2
12 1/2" Serving Fork	3	3	4
Breadknife, Serrated	1	1	2
Sandwich Spreader	2	4	6
12" Butcher's Steel	1	1	1
2 1/2" Paring Knives	3	6	12
Cleaver, Wooden Handle, 6" Blade	1	1	1
6" x 3" Dough Cutter	1	1	1
Large Rotary Beater, S. S. Blades	2	2	2
2" Maple Cutting Boards	2	2	2
Pastry Brush, Good Grade Bristle	2	2	4
Vegetable Brushes, White Fiber	6	6	12
Funnel Aluminum, 5 1/2"	1	1	1
Hand Grater	1	1	1
Can and Bottle Opener, Hand Type	2	3	3
Rolling Pin, Hard Wood	2	2	2

Fig. 5.5

DESCRIPTION	Number to be served		
	150-250	250-350	350-500
Kitchen Scales and Weights	1	1	1
Flour Sifter, Heavy Duty Double Screen	1	2	2
12 Qt. Double Boiler	1	1	1
20 Qt. Double Boiler	2	2	3
18-1/8 x 12 1/2 x 2 Bake Pan	12	12	18
23 x 12 1/2 x 2-3/4 Roast Pan	4	8	12
12 x 18 x 2 1/4 Utility Pan	12	18	24
20-3/8 x 17-3/8 x 7 Roaster	2	2	3
Cover of Above	1	2	3
1 Pint measures	2	2	3
1 Quart measures	2	2	3
2 Quart measures	2	2	3
4 Quart measures	1	1	1
4 Qt. Mixing Bowls	3	4	6
6 Qt. Mixing Bowls	3	4	6
11 Qt. Mixing Bowls	2	3	4
48 Qt. Mixing Bowls	1	1	1
18 x 26 x 1 Bun Pans	10	14	18
12 Cup Muffin Pans	18	24	36
Loaf Pans	12	12	18
9-3/4 x 1 1/2 Pie Pans	30	48	72
14" Fry Pan	1	1	1
1 Qt. Sauce Pan Household Wt.	2	2	3
2 Qt. Sauce Pan Household Wt.	2	2	
4 1/2 Qt. Sauce Pan Hotel Weights	1	1	2
7 Qt. Sauce Pan Hotel Weight	1	2	2
15 Qt. Brazier-Heavy Duty	1	2	
8 1/2 Qt. Sauce Pot-Heavy Duty	1	1	
26 Qt. Sauce Pot-Semi-Duty	1	2	2
3 Gal. Stock Pot-Semi-Heavy	2	2	3
5 Gal. Sauce Pot-Semi-Heavy	2	2	
6 Gal. Stock Pot-Semi-Heavy	2	2	3
10 Gal. Stock Pot-Semi-Heavy	1	1	2
15 Gal. Stock Pot-Semi-Heavy	1	1	1
10" Covers	2	2	2
12" Covers	4	4	4
14" Covers	1	1	2
5 Qt. China Cap	1	1	2
11 Qt. Colander	1	1	1
16 Qt. Colander	1	1	1
4 x 7 Flour Scoop	1	1	1
3 x 5 Sugar Scoop	1	1	2
3 1/4 Qt. Pitchers	3	3	
2-3/4" Diam. Salt-Pepper Shakers	12	12	18
12 x 16 1/4 Trays	15	20	25
Dishpan, 21 Qts.	2	2	2
16" Aluminum Sieve	1	1	2
5 Gal. Stock Pot, Semi-Heavy	2	3	4
3 x 5 Sugar Scoop	1	1	1
74 Qt. Mixing Bowl	1	1	1
Sauce Pot, Hotel Weight, 10 Qt.	1	1	1
18 Qt. Brazier	1	1	1
12 Qt. Sauce Pot	1	1	1
20 Qt. Sauce Pot	1	1	1
12" Covers	1	1	1
Refrigerator Containers w/cover	6	8	12
12 Qt. Water Pail	1	1	2

Fig. 5.5. (Continued)

Kitchen Arrangements

There are three typical patterns employed in arranging institutional kitchen equipment. These are:

1. Parallel
2. Straight Line
3. Work Centers

Parallel Arrangement

This is probably the most common pattern observed, with the ranges, broilers, and fryers in one line, and the steam kettles and steamers in another line back to back with the first, all under one large hood as shown in Figure 5.6.

Straight Line Arrangement

This is often found in hotel and large institutional kitchens where the work is divided among various cooks who perform specialized cooking functions, such as preparing sauces, broiling, frying, etc. Usually a serving counter with shelves separates the equipment from the waiters, and makes it convenient to serve them (as shown in Figure 5.7).

Work Centers

In large institutional kitchens, the equipment is often arranged in various sections, each constituting a separate work center. This has the advantage of keeping

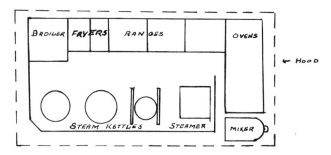

Fig. 5.6. Parallel cooking area (back to back under hood).

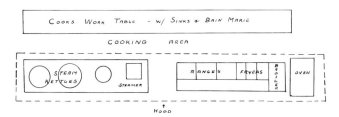

Fig. 5.7. Straight line cooking area.

traffic away from the work center and at the same time bringing the entire operation within reach of the serving area.

New Method of Arrangement Possible

One reason for the back-to-back arrangement shown in Figure 5.6 is to get all cooking equipment under the ventilating hood. Under new methods of ventilation, air is drawn through flues built in the backs of ranges and other appliances, rather than from overhead. This provides greater flexibility of arrangement. For example, the cooking equipment might well be placed in a semicircle with all appliances within easier reach of the cook's work table.

Layout of Hospital Kitchens

With respect to such functions as the receiving, storage, refrigeration, preparation, and cooking of food, the hospital kitchen should embody the layout principles found effective in modern commercial kitchens. Equipment in hospital kitchens is also similar to that used in other food services except, as previously noted, some use steam kettles, steam cookers, and ovens to replace the conventional hotel or restaurant range.

Food distribution is another matter however. Actually the hospital kitchen performs two functions. Cooked food is dispatched to:

1. Employees' cafeterias and staff dining rooms.
2. Patients, either in their rooms or, in some cases, in special dining rooms for ambulatory patients.

Within the past ten years many new methods of food distribution to patients have been developed. Formerly, most hospitals made use of the *decentralized* system of service. Under this plan, food is dispatched via bulk food trucks to floor kitchens where trays are prepared and carried to the patients in their rooms by members of the nursing, housekeeping, or dietary staffs.

Since World War II many hospitals have adopted the *centralized* method of food service. Essentially this means that all patients' trays are centrally prepared in the service section of the main kitchen. They are then conveyed to the patients' rooms usually without the intermediary of the floor kitchen. Various systems of centralized food service make use of highly specialized equipment. In addition to the new methods and appliances used in centralized services, there have also been many novel adaptations of decentralized service.

The layout of the service section of the hospital kitchen is dependent upon the system of food distribution in use. For this reason the entire subject of food distribution to patients will be treated in detail in Chapter 9 "Distribution and Service of Food," including the layout of the service section of the kitchen under different methods of distribution.

Ventilation and Air Conditioning

Advances in technology have brought about many changes in ventilation of kitchens and serving areas. Among these are the advent of air conditioning, the use of removable filters in kitchen exhaust systems, and the replacement of the conventional overhead ventilation hood by exhaust flues built in or on the appliances used for cooking. As previously suggested, these newer systems make for flexibility and more efficient arrangement of equipment in the cook's working area.

The accumulation of grease and other combustible matter in the exhaust flues of the overhead hood and connecting ventilating system frequently has been the cause of serious fires. In modern practice, filters are installed in overhead intake flues. They are also integrated in the construction of ventilating systems directly connected with ranges, deep-fat fryers, and similar cooking appliances. Frequently these filters are installed in the wall partitions directly in back of grills and hot plates, drawing smoke and fumes into the ventilating flues. As these filters can be removed and cleaned periodically, the fire menace is minimized.

Air conditioning has become widely accepted in commercial dining rooms, and is in use in many industrial and institutional cafeterias. It not only adds to the comfort of the patron, but also affects his appetite. Food services that are air conditioned generally report increased sales of entrees in warm weather—items which formerly sold only during the cool months. Where the air is filtered, humidified, and cooled before being recirculated, there is also less danger of air-borne contamination of food, and probably less likelihood of the spread of respiratory infections.

The introduction of air conditioning to kitchens and food preparation areas is also increasing, although by no means is its application so widespread as in cafeterias and dining rooms. There seems to be no doubt that air conditioning increases the productivity of kitchen workers.

In planning for ventilating and air conditioning facilities for new food services, or for installation in existing buildings, it is essential that competent engineering advice be sought. With this guidance those in charge should see that careful consideration is given to the many new types of ventilating and air conditioning equipment which make the food service more comfortable and healthful, both for patrons and workers.

Types of Fuel for Cooking

Gas, electricity, and oil are the principal types of cooking fuel used in industrial and institutional food services. However, the author on a visit some years ago to a 1500-bed hospital in one of the principal Latin American cities, found eight large wood-burning ranges in the main kitchen. Upon inquiring he learned that a wealthy local citizen had willed valuable forest land to the institution with the stipulation that the wood be used for fuel. Despite the use of what we North Americans might consider rather primitive equipment, an excellent food-service job was being done by the devoted Sisters of Charity in charge.

The question of electricity versus gas for fuel is a controversial one. Proponents of the former point out that electric cooking is cleaner, safer, more flexible, permits greater accuracy of control, and makes for less heat and consequently higher productivity on the part of kitchen workers. Arguments in favor of gas are based upon cost and reliability—freedom from interruption by storms. Advocates of gas-cooking feel that the gas burner can be readily regulated to give the intensity of heat required, and that new themostatic devices on gas appliances provide adequate control. They also point out that the extension of natural gas to wide areas of North America has brought about lower costs.

Cost of Gas vs. Electricity

As one kilowatt hour of electrical energy is equivalent to 3,412 Btu's[2] and one cubic foot of natural gas to 1,000 Btu's, it would not seem difficult to compare the cost of using one fuel versus the other for cooking. It is necessary, however, to take into account the relative efficiency of each fuel and of the equipment in which it is used as well as the rates charged for gas and electricity in the locality. These rates will depend upon the use of the fuel (special rates may be available for fuel used for cooking or heating or at different times of the day, etc.) and the quantity used, as rates per cubic foot of gas or kilowatt hour of electricity decrease as the quantity used increases.

The efficiency of prime cooking equipment depends upon its design and also upon its use. If the hot top of a gas range is fully covered with cooking utensils, it would have an efficiency of at least 50 per cent, as much of the heat is lost by radiation and convection from the sides and top of the range. Electric cooking equipment is more efficient in that heat losses are less.

2. A British Thermal Unit (BTU) represents the quantity of heat required to raise the temperature of one pound (about one pint) of water one degree Fahrenheit. The heat given off by a wholly burnt wooden match approximately equals 1 BTU.

Gaylord Model "A" Ventilator, Gonzaga University, Spokane, Washington. (Courtesy Gaylord Industries, Lake Oswego, Oregon.)

Gaylord Model "BD" Ventilator, Millard Fillmore Hospital, Buffalo, New York. (Courtesy Gaylord Industries, Lake Oswego, Oregon.)

Gaylord Model "E" Ventilator, Camp Curry, Yosemite Park, California. (Courtesy Gaylord Industries, Lake Oswego, Oregon.)

A Yardstick for Comparison

The food-service manager wants to know how to compare the costs of these two fuels. A relatively simple yardstick has been suggested by the American Gas Association, which they state takes into account the various efficiency factors. Known as the "Energy Ratio," it is based upon tests of cooking equipment under actual operating conditions. It indicates that 1 Btu of electrical energy is equivalent to 1.6 Btu's of natural gas.

As an illustration, if a food service uses 3,000 kilowatt hours for cooking during a given period, or 10,230,000 Btu's, it would require about 16,400,000 Btu's (1.6 times as much) or 16,400 cubic feet of natural gas to obtain the same result.

Assuming that electrical energy costs $.015 per kilowatt hour and gas costs $1.50 per 1,000 cubic feet, the comparison would be:

Comparative Costs Based on 1.6 Energy Ratio
Electricity: 3,000 kwh @ $.015 $45.00
Natural Gas: 16,400 cu. ft. @ $1.50 per M $24.60

The rates selected are arbitrary and used for illustration only. Actual rates would differ in different localities.

Other Types of Heat Energy

Steam is widely used in institutional and industrial cooking appliances. It may come as a by-product of the establishment's central power plant, or be generated in special boilers fired by gas, oil, coal, or electricity. Used at low pressure (generally 5 lbs.–10 lbs.) in steam cookers and steam kettle, it possesses many advantages in the preparation of soups and vegetables. Small table-model steamers, operating on principles similar to the home pressure cooker, at 15 lbs. per square inch, are being increasingly used in institutional kitchens. Steam has also been long used in the steam-table for keeping food warm before serving. The steam table has fallen into disrepute, as stated elsewhere in this text, not because of the steam, but because food has been allowed to remain in the table for excessively long periods.

So-called "bottled gas"—propane or butane gas—is employed for fuel purposes in some establishments remote from commercial gas lines.

Infrared incandescent lamps, long used in industrial drying ovens, have been introduced for cooking purposes in some commercial restaurants. Banks of infrared reflector lamps are widely used for keeping foods warm at the serving counter, and, in some cases, finishing the cooking of partially precooked roasts as they are sliced.

Microwave Cooking

The use of high-frequency electrical energy in cooking is a development growing out of the use of radar during World War II. Microwave cooking will be discussed in more detail later in the text.

COMPLETE KITCHEN LAYOUTS

In Figure 5.8 a complete industrial food service is shown. This includes a cafeteria dining area seating

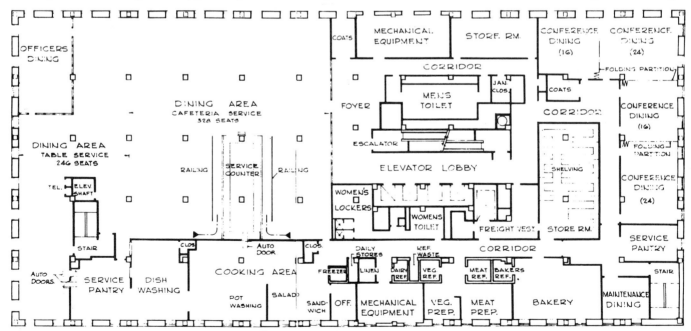

Fig. 5.8. A large industrial food service, Procter & Gamble Company, Cincinnati, Ohio. (Courtesy S. Blickman Inc.)

328, a table-service dining room with a seating capacity of 246, plus an officers dining room. There is a double cafeteria line. The various cooking and preparation areas are shown, not in detail, but in relation to the food service as a whole. The food-service layout of a university hospital is given in Figure 5.9. This includes the kitchen, a staff cafeteria, and the serving counter for the main cafeteria. Shown in dotted lines along the right wall of the kitchen are the storage positions of 14 food trucks used for distribution of food to patients.

COMPLETE HOSPITAL LAYOUT

In Figure 5.10 is shown a complete hospital food service layout (The Cleveland Clinic, Cleveland, Ohio, Hospital Unit #4). The service was designed to fill the needs of a 400 bed hospital plus an outpatient cafeteria and an employee staff cafeteria. A separate dining room is provided for doctors, although they use the cafeteria line.

All food is prepared in the kitchen for the entire food service. The kitchen is divided into separate work areas by arrangement of the equipment; no work area in the main kitchen is separated by walls. The bakery and ice cream rooms are separated by full height partitions with large glass panels—to allow supervision from any part of the kitchen. These rooms were separated for better temperature and humidity control.

The patients' tray service is a central tray system using a horizontal belt feeding into dumbwaiters. All diets are sent in room order from the same tray service. Special nourishments to be sent on trays are brought to the line from the small kitchen designated on the drawing. Between meals nourishments are routed to the floors on the food dumbwaiters.

The patients' tray service is arranged so that only the belt and the coffee urns are fixed. All other equipment is mobile and is moved up and down the line to fit the daily menu. Service can be changed from one side to the other, or from both sides at once, if desired. The heated food carts are wired with additional outlets for heated dispensers located adjacent

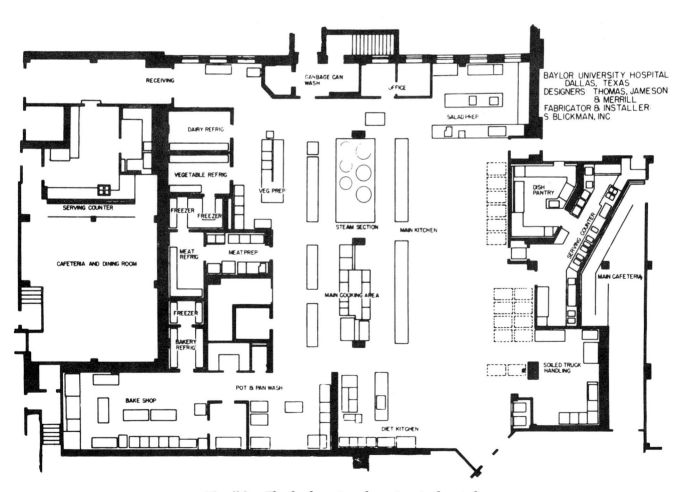

Fig. 5.9. The food service of a university hospital.

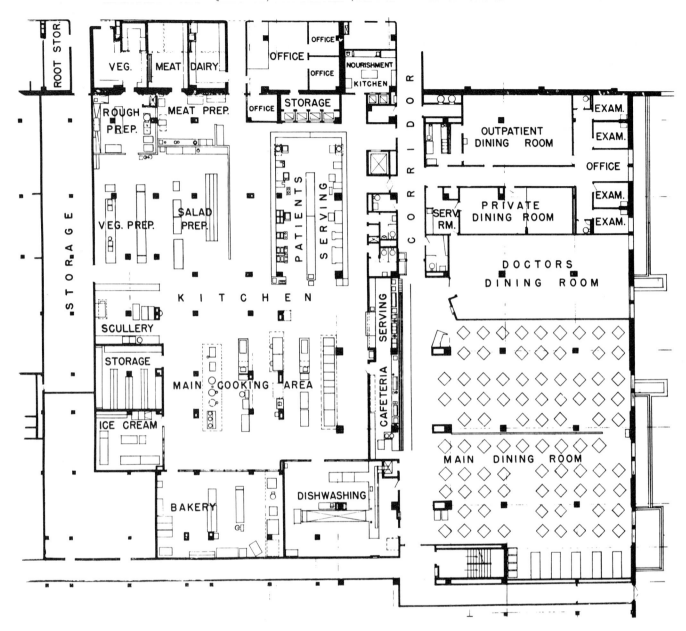

Fig. 5.10. Complete hospital food service layout, Cleveland Clinic Foundation, Hospital Unit #4, Cleveland, Ohio. (Designer, Ellerbe and Company; Superintendent, James G. Harding; Installation and Fabrication, Illinois Range Company.)

to them, when required. Each cart also has a heated base.

A double-service hot food and refrigerated unit form a portion of the center bar between two conveyor units. Refills are provided from this bar. The cafeteria receives all food from the main kitchen through the pass-through refrigerator and pass-through hot food unit. Portable dish dispenser and undercounter heated cabinets provide dish storage.

Soiled dishes are returned to the dish room by the bus boy. About half of the patients' trays are taken

care of by a second dish room in the old building. This room is located across the hall from the walk-in coolers indicated on the plan.

Since this institution is a clinic as well as a hospital, many outpatients receive special diets served from a special serving line in a small dining area. The food is prepared in the main kitchen.

The overall kitchen plan is arranged purposely with an oversize travel aisle, and the equipment has been arranged so that additional items may be added, as the census increases, without a major remodeling job.

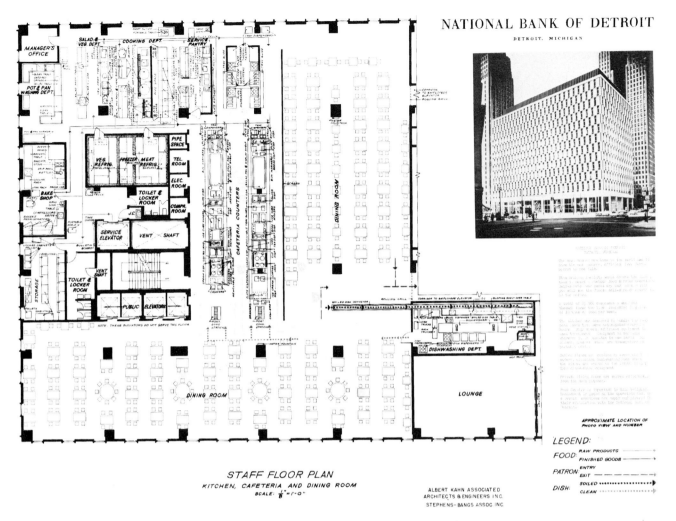

(Courtesy Stephens-Bangs Associates, Inc., Detroit.)

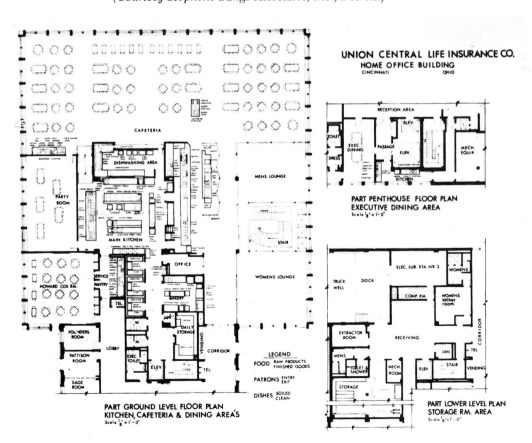

(Courtesy Stephens-Bangs Associates, Inc., Detroit.)

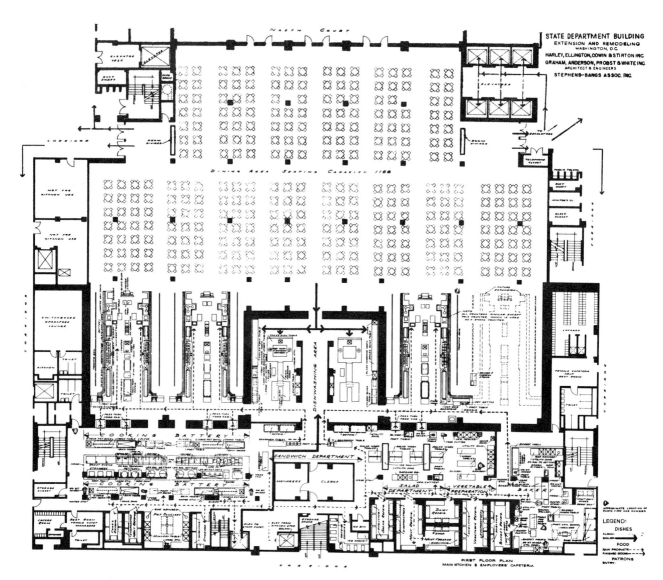

State Department Cafeteria, Washington, D. C. (Courtesy Stephens-Bangs Associates, Inc., Detroit.)

COMPLETE COLLEGE LAYOUT

The complete layout of a college food service is shown in Figure 5.11 (St. Joseph's Hall, College of St. Catherine, St. Paul, Minnesota).

Service was designed to provide food service for both boarding and day students. Average daily meals range at present from 1800 to 2000. Breakfast and lunch are served cafeteria style with self-bussing of dishes. The evening meal for boarding students and guests is served family style, using the cafeteria line as a pick-up station for many of the items being served.

In addition to regular service, special parties and dinners are given frequently. Many times these additional activities include groups of 300 to 400 on four or five consecutive evenings.

All food for the Sisters, who are served in a separate dining area, is also prepared in the kitchen.

Special features include wall hung-on island equipment mounted on pillar legs; all fabrication is stainless steel.

Visibility from the dietitian's office covers the entire kitchen. All equipment is low. The kitchen has no dividing walls or banks of equipment to separate areas.

The serving cafeteria line is separated from the dining area by a decorated wall to create a more comfortable dining area.

A small serving kitchen on the second floor, for afternoon or evening party service, is included. All food required is received by dumbwaiter from the main kitchen.

ILLUMINATION IN THE FOOD SERVICE

Effective illumination of food-service areas goes hand-in-hand with efficient layout and adequate equipment. Proper lighting of work centers makes for increased productivity, less fatigue, and safer working conditions. A well-lighted counter display makes food in the cafeteria more appealing. Commercial restaurants have found from experience that the right combinations of color and intensity in the lighting of dining rooms attracts customers.

An experienced illuminating engineer should participate in the initial planning of the food service. As a rule, the local electric company will make the services of such an expert available without charge.

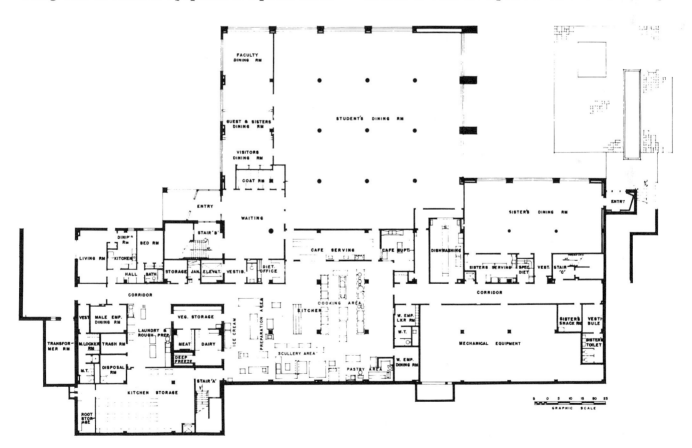

Fig. 5.11.   Complete college food service layout, St. Joseph's Hall, College of St. Catherine, St. Paul, Minn. (Designer, Ellerbe and Company; Director of Food Service, Sister Stella Marie; Installation and Fabrication, Illinois Range Company.)

In addition, the various manufacturers of electric lamps issue booklets giving valuable information on lighting. This can be used to advantage by those in charge of industrial and institutional feeding.

Measuring Illumination

The unit of illumination in common use is the "footcandle." This is defined as the direct illumination on a surface which is everywhere one foot distant from the light given by a standard source (the "international candle"). The footcandle may be considered the unit of *intensity*, while the equivalent unit of *quantity* of light given is the "lumen."

There has been a tendency, over the years, for the public to demand more and better light. Hence the footcandle levels set for homes, work areas, and public places have constantly increased. At the same time, the greater use of electricity and the tremendous increases in lamp efficiency have made these higher lighting standards available at no greater cost. It is said that a given area can be lighted to 100 footcandles today for the same or even less cost than that for which 5 footcandles could have been provided thirty years ago.

Levels of Illumination in Food Services

Some levels of illumination obtaining in present day practice in food services are as follows:

Table II   Levels of Footcandles

Area	Footcandles maintained in service
Corridors	5
Dining Area	20 to 100
Kitchen	50
Food Displays	100
Elevators and Stairways	20
Locker rooms	20
Shipping and Receiving	30
Storage and Stock Rooms	20
Toilets and Washrooms	20
Parking Areas	5

Some people require more light than others. For example, from visibility tests it has been found that the average worker in the 50-65 age group requires about twice the illumination needed by the average 20 year old. These same measurements also show that some individuals may require as much as 10 times as many footcandles as others to achieve a specified visibility level. In other words, individual differences should be taken into account when specifying footcandle levels.

Supplementary Lighting

While high levels of lighting have reduced the need of numerous localized lights, many conditions in the food service make supplementary lighting desirable. In the Receiving Room; in the Food Preparation, Salad, Baking, and Cooking sections there are areas where multiple rows of fluorescent lights may well be used to provide extra illumination.

Color

It is well known that the full beauty of color cannot be seen unless the light source itself contains all of the colors of the spectrum. Although the *Standard* fluorescent lamp radiates all of the colors to some extent, yellow-green and orange are dominant, and red and green weak. The Standard type of lamp is excellent for black and white seeing tasks. For such work it gives higher light output and, consequently, better visibility. For work where discrimination between colors is essential, and for use in areas where it is desirable to emphasize the beauty and richness of color, the new *Deluxe* fluorescent lamps are preferred.

Deluxe lamps are obtainable which give two tints of white light: The Deluxe Cool and the Deluxe Warm (this latter is now being sold by different manufacturers under the name "Home-Line.") The former type closely simulates the cool, natural, out-of-doors daylight. The latter suggests the warmer light sources found indoors and approximates the color of the incandescent lamp. In places where food is displayed. Deluxe Cool is the type that should be used, since it gives the best overall color rendition.

Fluorescent versus Incandescent Lamps

The difference in operating costs between fluorescent and incandescent lamps in constant use is considerable. Where lights are on 24 hours a day—as in some washrooms, for example—it may cost three times as much to obtain equal footcandles of illumination with incandescent as with flourescent lamps. Any comparison between the cost of the two lamps would depend upon the type of lamps used, as well as upon the rates charged for electricity. It is safe to say that where an area is to be illuminated for from 25 to 30 hours per week or more, the fluorescent lamp is more economical per foot candle. In a closet, for example, where light is needed only a few minutes at a time, several times a day only, the incandescent lamp would be much cheaper. Tables are available from lamp manufacturers giving actual cost comparisons under given conditions.

CARE OF EQUIPMENT AND PREVENTIVE MAINTENANCE

Food-Service Equipment

With the application of labor-saving machinery and equipment, the modern food-service operation has become mechanized to a considerable degree. However, too little attention has often been given to training employees in the use and care of equipment. Although in some cases outside maintenance service is provided, the organization's own maintenance department is generally called upon for maintenance and repairs of kitchen and cafeteria equipment. In all of this work there is need to standardize methods of inspection and to clearly define the responsibilities involved. This means establishing a system of *preventive maintenance*, the object of which is to keep equipment in good shape by correcting deficiencies before they result in breakdowns.

Proper maintenance of equipment is important from many standpoints, such as:

1. Food Quality and Service
2. Sanitation
3. Safety
4. Fire Prevention
5. Capital Investment and Operating Expense

Food Quality and Service

Modern methods of food preparation and cooking depend upon control of temperatures and cooking times. Thermometers, thermostats, and other timing and regulating devices must be in constant working order. Dull cutting edges in slicing and grinding machines, or maladjustments in mixers, for example, may well affect the quality of the food prepared in these devices. Breakdowns in kitchen machinery inevitably slow up service.

Sanitation

Failures of mechanical refrigeration may allow the development of harmful bacteria. Improper functioning of dishwashing machines may result in contaminated dishes and utensils. Neglect in the cleansing of slicers, grinders, choppers, mixers, and other food preparation machinery as previously mentioned, is also a dangerous and unsanitary practice.

Safety

Statistics compiled by insurance companies show that a large proportion of food-service accidents occur in the kitchen. Training of employees in the use of machinery and proper inspection and maintenance procedures will pay dividends in reducing kitchen accidents.

Fire Protection

Kitchen exhaust flues and hoods, if not kept clean, present a potential fire hazard. Frequent inspection of hoods and flues leading from ranges, ovens, and deep-fat fryers, and the subsequent removal of accumulated grease and dirt will reduce the danger of kitchen fires. Fire extinguishers should be provided. Special apparatus for smothering fire with chemical foam is used in large food services.

Capital Investment and Operating Expense

The capital investment in cafeteria and kitchen equipment will run to many thousands of dollars. By prolonging the life of such equipment, preventive maintenance will pay for itself many times over. From the standpoint of operating expense, neglect in inspecting and maintaining food-service machinery and equipment will prove costly in wasted food and supplies, as well as in reducing operating efficiency of cafeteria workers.

Responsibility for Maintenance

Responsibility for proper maintenance procedures is twofold:

1. It is the responsibility of the food-service manager to see that workers are instructed in the proper use of machinery and equipment, and that any deficiencies are reported promptly to the maintenance department.

2. It is the responsibility of the plant engineer or maintenance head to see that emergency repairs are made promptly and efficiently, and also that regular inspections of equipment are made periodically as part of the system of preventive maintenance.

The User's Inspection

The user or operator of kitchen equipment is the most important single factor in preventive maintenance. He or she must be thoroughly familiar with the equipment, and with proper methods of operation, inspection, and preventive maintenance. Efficiency, length of service, and operating costs depend largely on the way in which the equipment users do their work. If daily maintenance services are faithfully performed as a matter of routine, major repairs and overhaul can often be avoided. These daily services include preventing abuse of equipment, performing checks and inspections as outlined below, and reporting defects to the plant engineer.

The user's general inspection and servicing include the following checks of each item and its supporting members or connections:

1. An external visual inspection to determine that the unit is in good condition and is not being used beyond the safe operating limits.
2. An external visual inspection to determine whether or not the unit is efficiently fulfilling its intended use.
3. An external inspection for loose brackets, lock washers, locknuts, valves, steam, gas and electrical connections, etc.

Users' Instruction Sheet: Mixing Machine

1. Place mixing bowl in proper position on rim of mixer, with pins of bowl support set into holes in ears on sides of bowl. Lock bowl in position with bowl locks on each side of bowl rim.
2. Select proper beater for ingredients to be mixed: flat paddle beater for creaming butter and mixing muffins and cakes; wire whip for whipping cream and light icing and beating egg whites; or dough hook for mixing bread dough.
3. Throw machine in gear by throwing clutch lever in. To change speed, throw clutch lever in again. If machine has no clutch lever, stop motor between speed changes.
4. Raise and lower bowl by turning large hand-wheel. A set screw acts as a stop and adjusts height of bowl in relation to beater. For operations such as mashing potatoes or creaming butter, start beating with bowl in its lowest position, and raise bowl gradually to working position as food breaks up. Do not spin wheel rapidly; slow it down toward end of its travel so bowl support comes against set screw stop gently. Do not operate beaters at high speed on heavy loads.
5. The attachment drive operates at three speeds. Attachments include meat chopper, vegetable slicer, shredder, juice extractor, coffee mill, tool grinder, peanut butter mixer, and pulley for driving freezer. Most of these operate at No. 1 speed.
6. Do not put hands, spoons, or utensils in bowl while machine is in motion.
7. Use long-handled spoon or spatula to stir mixture from bottom. Use rubber scraper to scrape down sides of bowl after machine is stopped.
8. Wash bowl and beater immediately after using to prevent food from drying on surface. If egg mixtures or flour batters are used apply cold water before washing with hot water. Dry beaters thoroughly and hang them up to prevent bending or breaking.
9. Dry bowl thoroughly to prevent rust.
10. Never drag bowl across floor.
11. Wash body of machine with warm water and mild soap. Clean beater shaft.

Fig. 5.12. Users' instruction sheet: mixing machine.

4. An examination of unit and parts to discover wear which may cause failure if replacement is not made.

Users' Instruction Sheets

To instruct cafeteria workers in care and use of kitchen equipment it is well to prepare an Instruction Sheet for each principal piece of equipment. These sheets may be compiled from information furnished by the manufacturer, or by the food-service manager in cooperation with the plant engineer or maintenance head. By way of illustration, an instruction sheet for a Mixing Machine is given:

Similar sheets may be prepared for other pieces of equipment. In order to dramatize these points, it may be well to stage demonstrations by workers in the use and care of various pieces of machinery at employees' meetings from time to time.

Work Sheets for Preventive Maintenance

Work sheets may be prepared by the plant engineer or maintenance head in order to standardize and systematize the preventive maintenance carried on by members of his department.

The work sheets list the steps in inspecting and servicing all kitchen equipment, except toasters which are cared for by the electrician. Steps are numbered and arranged in a sequence which provide maximum economy of action for the inspector. Alongside each item is a rectangular check space for noting work done. Frequencies of performance are indicated by location of check space in the time schedule columns.

Plant engineer personnel prepare work sheets and check off work done as follows:

1. Record at top of form the date of inspection, building, and serial number of each piece of equipment inspected. All equipment should have an identifying number in a conspicuous place. If two or more like pieces of equipment are inspected in a single kitchen, use additional work sheets.
2. As each item is inspected, mark its check space with one of the following:
   a. "V" if item is satisfactory
   b. "X" if adjustment is required
   c. "XX" if repair or replacement is required.
3. After completing the inspection, sign the work sheet and give it to the mechanic who is to make the adjustments or repairs indicated by X or XX. The mechanic circles the X or XX to indicate that correction has been made. If the mechanic is unable to make the repair, or if the repair is to be done by contract maintenance, he explains the work required on a separate sheet of paper at-

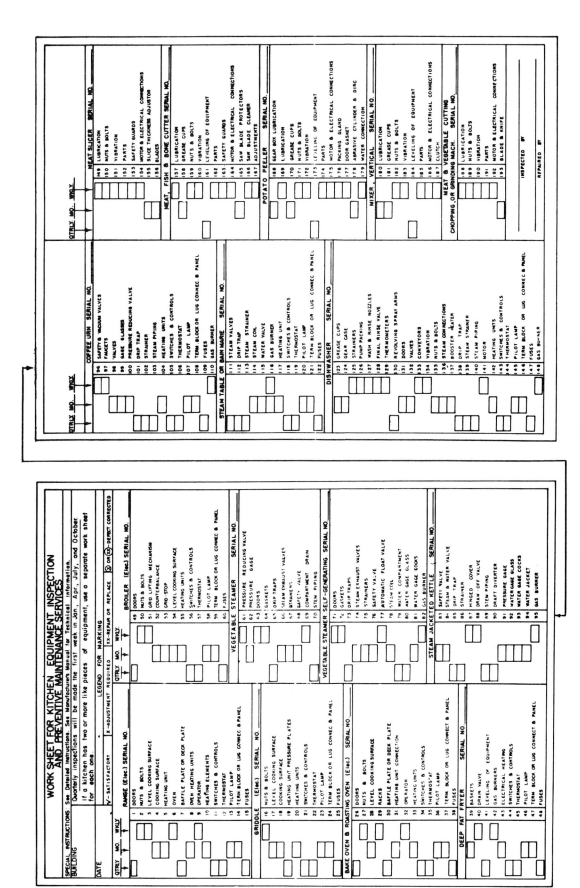

Fig. 5.13. Work sheet for preventive maintenance of kitchen equipment.

81

tached to the work sheet, identifying the items involved by item number.

Figure 5.13 illustrates such a work sheet for preventive maintenance of kitchen equpiment.

Inspection Procedures

Detailed procedures should be worked out for the maintenance department personnel with respect to the various items of kitchen equipment. These include detailed instructions as to the type of inspection required, and also a time schedule showing periods at which these various pieces of equipment are to be inspected.

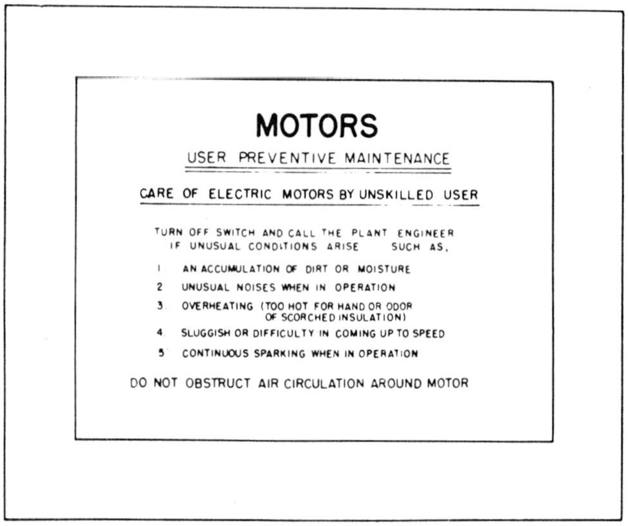

Fig. 5.14. Placard for care and use of motors.

Refrigerating, Electrical, Ventilating, and Air-Conditioning Equipment

A similar program can be set up for refrigerating, electrical, ventilating, and air-conditioning equipment including work sheets and inspection procedures. A placard for care of motors is shown in Figure 5.14.

Care of Refrigerators

It is essential that food-service personnel be instructed in the care and use of refrigerating equipment. This is important for sanitation and to minimize food waste.

Figure 5.15 shows a placard which may be placed on or near all refrigerators giving suggestions as to proper use and care.

SUGGESTED READING

Dana, Arthur W. *Kitchen Planning.* New York: Harper & Brothers, 1945.

General Electric Company, Large Lamp Dep't. *Footcandles in Modern Lighting Practice.* Cleveland, Ohio.

Kotschevar, L. H., and Terrell, M. E. *Food Service Planning, Layout and Equipment.* New York: John Wiley & Sons, 1961.

Stokes, John W. *How to Manage a Restaurant or Institutional Food Service.* Dubuque, Iowa: Wm. C. Brown Company Publishers, 1967.

Thomas, Orpha Mae. *Scientific Basis for Design of Institutional Kitchens.* New York: Teachers College, Columbia University, 1947.

U.S. Department of Agriculture, *A Guide for Planning and Equipping School Lunchrooms.* Washington, D. C.: Superintendent of Documents, U.S. Government Printing Office.

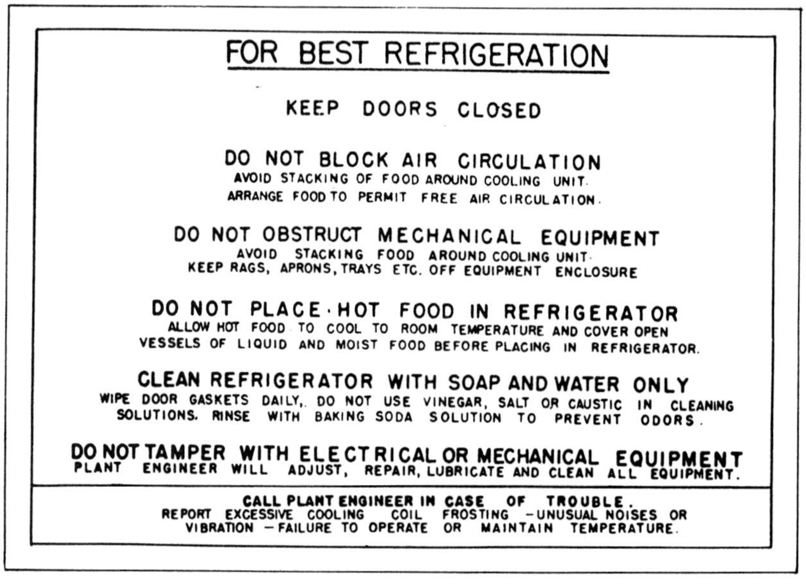

Fig. 5.15. Refrigeration placard.

CHAPTER 6

Purchasing, Receiving, and Storage

PURCHASING

Purchasing of food and supplies is one of the most important functions of the food service. The *prices paid* for food determine, to a large extent, the *prices that will have to be charged* the patron. The *quality* of the food served will depend upon the grade, type, and characteristics of the food that is purchased.

It is essential that the food buyer have experience in the food business. He should know the basic cuts of meat, and how fresh fruits and vegetables, and canned and frozen foods, are graded and packed. He must have a general knowledge of markets, and be posted on crop conditions and current trends. Needless to say, he must be familiar with the menu requirements and the food preparation facilities of the institution for which he works. Familiarity on the part of the buyer with methods of cooking will enable him to select types of food best suited to the needs of the food service for which he buys.

Yield

The basic standard in food purchasing is not the lowest price or the greatest quantity for the money. Rather it is the "yield" or quantity of cooked, edible food produced or yielded from a given quantity of raw food purchased.

For example, a cut of beef, such as a rib roast, from which the bones have been removed, may yield servings at a lower unit cost than a lower-priced cut of beef which includes waste in bones and trimmings. A higher-priced food item may often yield more servings of a better quality than a similar item on which the purchase price is lower. See Figures 6.1 and 6.2, "Yield-Tests."

Specification Buying

For these reasons, the principles of "specification buying" have been widely adopted in well-managed

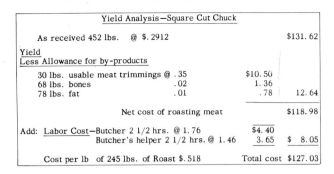

Yield Analysis—Square Cut Chuck			
As received 452 lbs. @ $.2912			$131.62
Yield			
Less Allowance for by-products			
30 lbs. usable meat trimmings @ .35		$10.50	
68 lbs. bones	.02	1.36	
78 lbs. fat	.01	.78	12.64
Net cost of roasting meat			$118.98
Add: Labor Cost—Butcher 2 1/2 hrs. @ 1.76		$4.40	
Butcher's helper 2 1/2 hrs. @ 1.46		3.65	$ 8.05
Cost per lb of 245 lbs. of Roast $.518		Total cost	$127.03

Fig. 6.1. Yield analysis—square cut chuck.

Yield Test—U.S. Grade Good Round			
Raw Weight 82 1/2 lbs. @ .43 Cost			$35.48
Labor Cost for Boning, 1 hour			2.03
Total Cost			$37.51
Credit for By-Products			
Usable trim (for hamburgers)	8	@ .40	$ 3.20
Bones (for soups, stock)	14 1/2 lbs. @ .03		.44
Waste	4 1/2 lbs. @ .00		.00
Shank Meat (for stews, hamburger)	10 1/2 lbs. @ .40		4.20
Total	37 1/2 lbs. ———		$ 7.84
New Cost of Boned Round			$29.67
Yield: Bottom Round 26 lbs.		@ .65	$16.90
Top Round 19 lbs.		@ .672	12.77
Total: 45 lbs. of Boned Round			$29.67

Fig. 6.2. Yield test—U.S. Grade Good round.

food services. Essentially specification buying involves four steps:

1. By means of tests, the grades, qualities, types, unit quantities, etc. of the food items *best suited to the use of the particular food service* are determined.

2. This data is recorded and specifications are written out for each food item tested. (See Figure 6.3. Example of Meat Specifications; also Figure 6.10, Specifications for Canned Sliced Apples.)

3. When a given item is purchased, the specifications are given to the vendor and the buyer endeavors to obtain the specified item at the lowest possible price.

4. When the item is delivered, it is carefully checked to see that it meets the specifications given. (See Receiving—later in this chapter.)

Prepared Food Items

Labor cost is a vital factor today. For example, frozen vegetables generally cost more than fresh vegetables, but require little labor in preparation. Savings in labor and uniformity, as well as superior quality in "off-seasons," may more than offset the additional cost involved. Other food items, formerly purchased in bulk or in the raw state, are now available partially prepared or prepackaged. These include such products as: individual portions of soluble coffee, hot-chocolate, milk, buttermilk, ice cream, jellies, catsup, mus-

tard, and other condiments, as well as individual cans of soups, chowders, and prepared foods. Potatoes and apples may be purchased ready-peeled or sliced in various shapes. Meats are available in fabricated cuts. Pies, rolls, muffins, and pastries may be obtained in finished or frozen form, or mixed and shaped ready for baking. Prepared cake and breading mixes, icings, puddings, gelatin desserts, and soup bases are widely used.

The buyer must have in mind not only the yield, but also the net overall unit food and labor costs of such items—as compared with those ready for conventional methods of cooking. Thus he may be able to effect further savings.

Groups of Purchases

Food purchases may be broken down into three groups:

1. *Perishable foods*—meats, poultry, seafood, fruits, vegetables, butter, eggs, etc.
2. *Staple foods*—groceries and canned goods.
3. *Contract items*—coffee, milk, ice cream, bread, rolls, etc., which are usually purchased on a contract basis.

Perishables

These are generally bought by the manager of the food service or by a qualified assistant who is assigned to purchasing. In some cases the buyer visits the markets regularly, checks the daily offerings, and places orders accordingly. Where markets are at some distance, or between trips to the markets, the buyer will check prices with two or more vendors by telephone, and select the most favorable offerings. In this case, the merchandise must be carefully inspected upon receipt to ensure that specifications are met.

In some localities, perishables, such as fruits and vegetables, may be purchased from nearby growers who bring their products in for inspection. Perishables should be bought to meet menu requirements only.

Staple Foods

Staple foods, such as flour, sugar, spices, condiments, and other grocery items, are usually purchased on a weekly basis either by telephone or from salesmen who call regularly on the buyer. Usually staples are purchased from wholesale grocers or jobbers who specialize in institutional products. Some national food manufacturers sell direct or through distributors to the institutional trade. Institutional products are specially packaged, generally in larger units than for retail trade.

PURCHASE SPECIFICATIONS

General: All merchandise to be U. S. Govt. Inspected. Where grades are specified, they refer to U. S. Govt. Grading.

BEEF

Strip   (Strip loin or shell - Bone in) -- Top Prime

1. Shell to measure, flat, not more than 1 1/2 inches from the meat on the hip end and not more than 2 1/2 inches from the principal muscle meat on the rib end.

2. Square cut on the ends, no pin bone.

   a. On the hip end, last blade to be split and the cut made perpendicular to the line of the backbone and square with the plane of the cutting table.

3. Good conformation on the back and the fat trimmed to no more than 1/2 inch of covering.

4. To weigh not less than 15 pounds and not more than 17 1/2 pounds.

5. It is desirable that the strips be as long as possible, preferably selected to 16 inches or more.

6. Strips should be aged not less than 2 1/2 weeks nor more than 4 weeks.

Strip   (Strip or Shell - Bone in) -- Top Choice
         Same as above except for grade.

Trimmed Short Loin -- Prime

1. Square cut on the ends, no pin bone.

2. Flank to measure 2 1/2" from eye on rib end and 2 1/2" from the meat on hip end. (Suet and pin bone tissue may have to be sliced off to establish this point).

3. Good conformation on the back and the fat trimmed to no more than 1/2 inch of covering.

4. Trim suet from tenderloin to no more than 1 inch of fat covering and remove surplus suet from under flank.

5. To weigh no more than 27 pounds.

6. Loins should be aged from 2 1/2 weeks to no more than 4 weeks.

Fig. 6.3.   Example of meat specifications. (Courtesy Sonesta Hotels.)

Contract Items

Certain items requiring daily or weekly delivery, such as milk, ice cream, bread, and coffee, are usually purchased from a single supplier on the basis of a negotiated contract. In some cases, the price is based on a sliding scale depending upon the total yearly volume.

Governmental institutions are generally required by law to purchase food and supply items on a sealed bid basis. Requests for quotations are sent to vendors, and sealed formal bids are opened on a specified date. Bonds or deposits are often required to guarantee the vendor's performance.

Prepared and Convenience Products

Many products are now sold to the institutional trade in prepared or semiprepared form. Fruits and vegetables may be fresh, canned, frozen, or dehydrated. Meats are available in fabricated cuts rather than only in quarters, sides or whole carcasses as formerly. Poultry can be brought in the form of breasts, thighs, drumsticks, etc. Seafood can be purchased frozen, ready cut or prepared form, such as fish fillets, fish sticks, lobster tails, lobster meat, crab meat, and deveined shrimps. New methods of food preservation such as "freeze-dry" and "dehydrofreeze" make possible the purchase of prepared foods which occupy less storage space and, in the case of freeze-dry products, can be stored without refrigeration.

Schools, colleges, hospitals, and industrial caterers are making use of complete entrees, prepared and frozen by various manufacturers. When reheated, these can be individualized through the use of garnishes and different kinds of vegetables. The cost is usually greater than entrees prepared "from scratch" in the kitchen. However, where labor costs are high and help difficult to obtain, such "convenience" entrees are worth considering. In using such entrees tests should be made in advance. In a large Eastern university samples of entrees submitted by manufacturers are tested by a panel composed of representatives of the faculty, students, and the food service. In a recent test, for example, only 19 out of 80 samples were found to be acceptable to the high standards of the panel.

In addition there are many "convenience" foods pre-packaged in individual portions such as jellies, condiments, sugar, salad dressing, soluble tea and coffee, hot chocolate mixes, cereals, soups, and coffee whiteners. These products save preparation labor and facilitate portion control and costing.

There are also many prepared foods in bulk packages for restaurant and institutional use, such as mixes for cake, piecrust, muffin, doughnut, breading, roll and custard; whipped toppings and icings; prepared gelatin desserts and puddings; fillings for pies and tarts and soup bases.

Labor cost is increasing and the use of these prepared foods reduces preparation labor in food service kitchens. Frozen vegetables, for example, may cost more than the fresh variety, but require no preparation labor. They are of uniform quality and are available the year around. These factors may more than offset the additional purchase cost.

In considering the use of these prepared foods, the buyer must have in mind not only the quality and yield but also the unit food and labor costs involved, as compared with foods prepared "from scratch" in the kitchen. By careful analysis of such factors, he may be able to effect savings in overall costs.

FEDERAL STANDARDS

For more than fifty years the United States Government, through the Department of Agriculture, has established standards and grading procedures for meats, dairy products, and processed foods. With respect to meat products, the government maintains an inspection service of slaughter houses. Such federal inspection is required for meats shipped across state lines. Federal inspection stamps appear on inspected carcasses that are to be shipped interstate. These federal services make for uniformity as well as safety. The experienced buyer makes use of the standards as a sound basis for comparison, knowing that he can rely upon the designated grades. There are, however, variations in qualities and yields within the grades.

The food buyers must take this into account in seeking the best buys.

Meat Grades

Meats are graded by federal graders in accordance with three basic characteristics:

1. *Conformation*: The general form and structure of the carcass. This involves ratio of bone to total weight.
2. *Finish:* Color, type, and distribution of the fat throughout the carcass. "Marbling" is one of the characteristics that is evidenced in the fine lines of fat running through the meat.
3. *Quality:* This is an overall appraisal of the carcass, taking into account its potential tenderness and palatability when cooked.

Grades of meet purchased for restaurants and institutional food services are usually from the following, listed in order of desirability (and price)

Beef	*Veal and Lamb*	*Mutton*	*Pork*
Prime	Prime	Choice	U.S. #1
Choice	Choice	Good	U.S. #2
Good	Good	Commercial	U.S. #3
Standard	Commercial		
Commercial			

Grades below Commercial, known as Utility, Cutters, and Canners, or in lamb, veal, and mutton known as "culls," are not generally available to the institutional trade, but are used by the packers in preparing processed meat products.

Packers' Brand Names

Packers offer "selected grades" of their own which usually approximate the federal grades. Sometimes these meats are upgraded because, although technically unable to make the higher grade, their general quality is felt to justify a somewhat higher price. Here again the experienced meat buyer must use his own judgment.

Standards have not been as widely accepted for pork as for other meats. Consequently most pork products are sold under the packers' own brands as "selected grades."

Beef (See Chart—Figure 6.4)

Formerly "prime beef" constituted only about 1/2 of 1 per cent of the total beef available. Today, about 6 per cent of the beef that is graded falls into U.S. Prime. Within recent years the "prime" grade has been combined with the upper range of what was formerly known as "choice." Similar changes have been made in the other lower grades. Most popular-price food

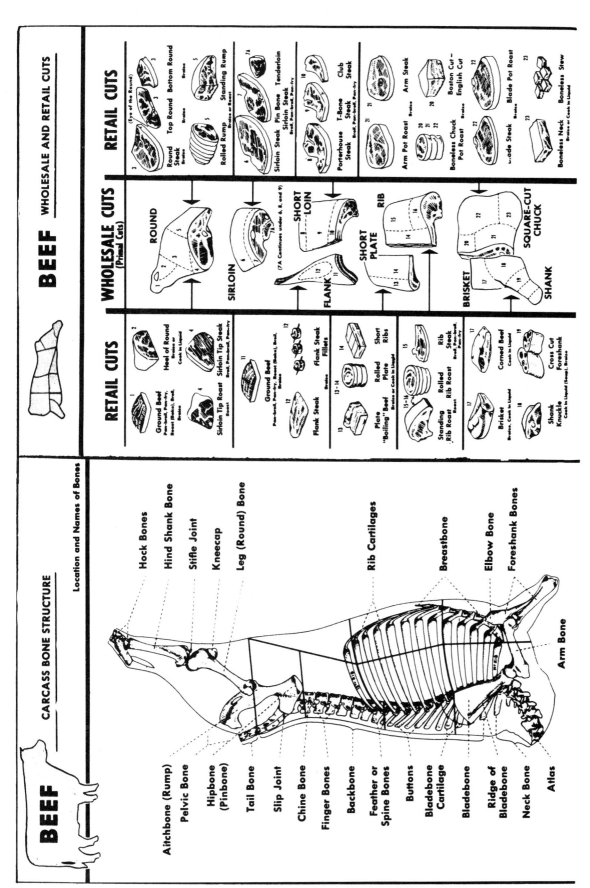

Fig. 6.4. Beef carcass and cuts of beef. (Courtesy Swift & Co.)

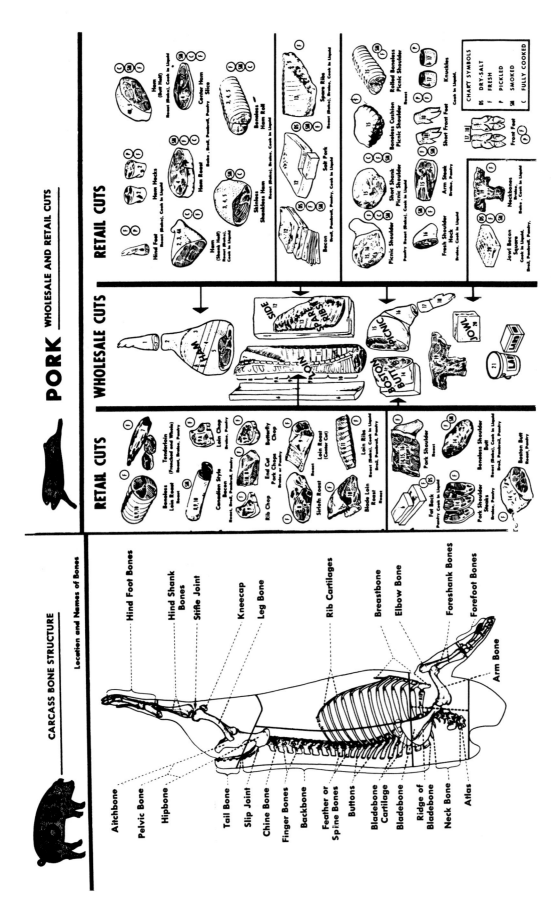

Fig. 6.5. Pork carcass and cuts of pork. (Courtesy Swift & Co.)

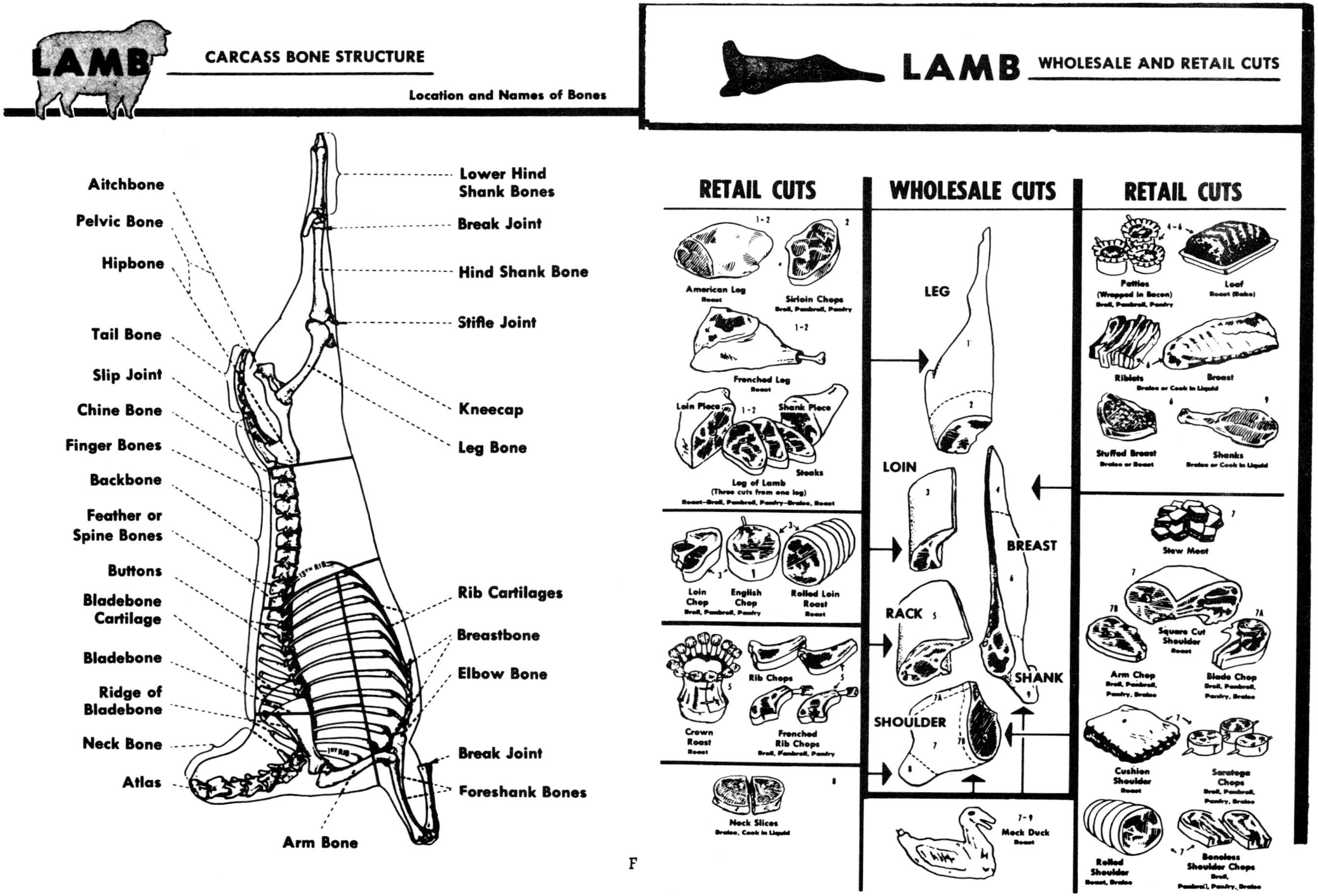

LAMB

WHOLESALE AND RETAIL CUTS

RETAIL CUTS

Patties (Wrapped in Bacon) Broil, Panbroil, Panfry

Loaf Roast, Bake

Riblets Braise or Cook in Liquid

Breast Braise or Cook in Liquid

Stuffed Breast Braise or Roast

Shanks Braise or Cook in Liquid

Stew Meat

Square Cut Shoulder Roast

Blade Chop Broil, Panbroil, Panfry, Braise

Arm Chop Broil, Panbroil, Panfry, Braise

Cushion Shoulder Roast

Saratoga Chops Broil, Panbroil, Panfry, Braise

Boneless Shoulder Chops Broil, Panbroil, Panfry, Braise

Rolled Shoulder Roast, Braise

WHOLESALE CUTS

LEG

LOIN

BREAST

RACK 5

SHANK

SHOULDER

Neck Duck Roast

RETAIL CUTS

American Leg Roast

Sirloin Chops Broil, Panbroil, Panfry

Frenched Leg Roast

Shank Piece Braise

Steaks Broil, Panbroil, Panfry, Braise, Roast

Leg Piece

Leg of Lamb (Three cuts from one leg) Roast—Broil, Panbroil, Panfry—Braise, Roast

Rolled Loin Roast Roast

English Chop Broil, Panbroil, Panfry

Loin Chop Broil, Panbroil, Panfry, Braise

Crown Roast Roast

Frenched Rib Chops Broil, Panbroil, Panfry

Rib Chops Broil, Panbroil, Panfry

Neck Slices Braise, Cook in Liquid

F

CARCASS BONE STRUCTURE

Location and Names of Bones

LAMB

Lower Hind Shank Bones

Break Joint

Hind Shank Bone

Stifle Joint

Kneecap

Leg Bone

Rib Cartilages

Breastbone

Elbow Bone

Break Joint

Foreshank Bones

Aitchbone

Pelvic Bone

Hipbone

Tail Bone

Slip Joint

Chine Bone

Finger Bones

Backbone

Feather or Spine Bones

Buttons

Bladebone Cartilage

Bladebone

Ridge of Bladebone

Neck Bone

Atlas

Arm Bone

Fig. 6.6.   Lamb carcass and cuts of lamb. (Courtesy Swift & Co.)

89

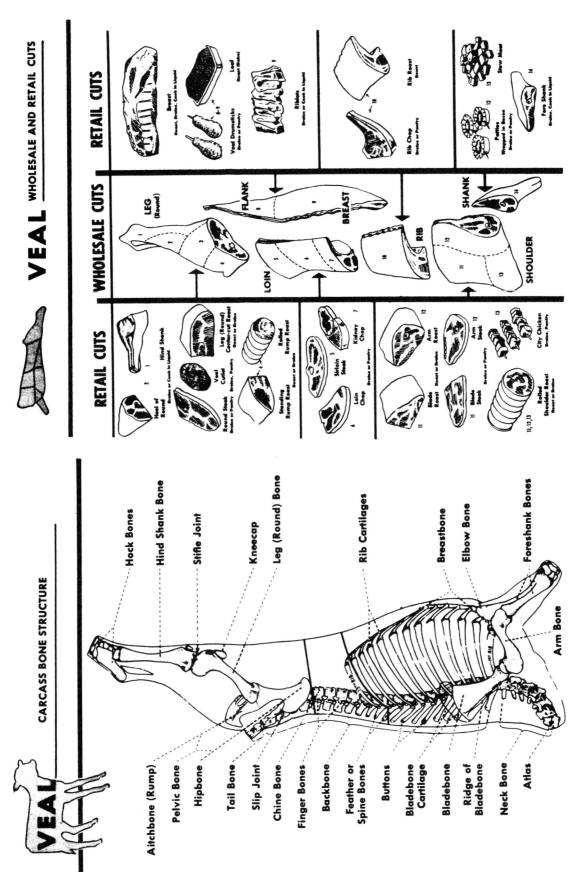

Fig. 6.7. Veal carcass and cuts of veal. (Courtesy Swift & Co.)

services now use "choice" grades for roasting and broiling and "good" or "commercial" grades for ground meat dishes, stews, and other uses.

It should be remembered that ordinarily the difference between the highest rated meats in one grade and the lowest in the grade above is slight. The experienced buyer who is a competent judge of meats can often get better value by noting the characteristics of the carcasses available.

Meats are graded upon request but all meat shipped across state lines is inspected for wholesomeness. The round purple stamp indicates that it was found to be wholesome when inspected. Meats not shipped across state lines are often graded by state inspectors but their services are not generally as thorough as those of the U.S. Department of Agriculture.

Methods of cutting the carcass vary in different areas but it is important to specify the style, unit weight, measurements, trim, fat content, amount of bone, etc.

Beef can be bought in carcasses, as sides, quarters, primal or wholesale cuts or portion cuts. These latter are similar to the retail cuts shown in the Beef Chart, Figure 6.4.

Fat content is important in buying ground meat. Good hamburger should have a fat content of from 15 to 20 per cent. Cheaper hamburger may run as high as 35 per cent fat. The higher the fat content, the greater the shrinkage in cooking. Ground meat, unless frozen, should be used within 24 hours. Figures 6.1 and 6.2 indicate the yield on various beef cuts.

Aging of Beef

Ribs and loins of high grade beef are aged to improve flavor and tenderness. This is accomplished by hanging these cuts from 3 to 6 weeks at 34° to 38° F. at high humidity.

Frozen Beef

Many portion cuts of frozen beef and pork are now on the market. Hamburger in bulk or in preshaped, preportioned patties, separated by wax papers, is used in many food services. There are also steaks, pepper steaks, cheeseburgers, and precooked frozen entrees in a variety of styles.

Chief reliance in buying these products must be placed upon the processor and the package label, as federal stamps or grade marks are not given.

Lamb and Mutton (See Chart—Figure 6.6)

Lamb is the meat of young sheep from six weeks to eight months old. "Spring lamb" is lamb under six months of age. A sheep one year of age or older is classed as mutton. Best mutton comes from "wethers" —castrated rams having thick flesh well covered with fat.

In general, the heavier the lamb, the greater the proportion of meat to bony structure. Age is an important criterion as younger lambs are generally of better quality. A "spring lamb" has five tooth-like points at the ends of the knee-joints. These points wear off and decrease to two as the animal grows older.

Fresh lamb is available most of the year. Prefabricated, frozen cuts are also on the market. Frozen lamb chops and stuffed breasts are among the items available. Here again the package label and the processor must be depended upon for quality.

Veal (See Chart—Figure 6.7)

A young calf, butchered at the time of weaning when from 2 to 3 months old, is known as veal. Best veal is from milk-fed baby calves although grass-fed veal from calves butchered at from 3 to 6 months is on the market. The flesh of milk-fed veals is creamy white of even texture with small amounts of fat marbling.

Frozen veal cutlets, breaded or unbreaded, are available under various packers' labels.

Pork (See Chart—Figure 6.5)

The official grades of pork—U.S. No. 1; U.S. No. 2; U.S. No. 3, and Cull—are further divided into meat type, fat type, packing, or sow. The same principles of grading are used as with other meats but as market hogs do not vary greatly, the grading standards are not widely used.

About 75 per cent of pork is cured and sold as smoked ham or bacon, boiled, and pressed ham, sausage and pickled pigs' feet. The other 25 per cent is fresh pork. Lard is fat trimmed from the carcass or rendered leaf fat.

Hams

Uncooked hams come smoked, mildly cured, or regular. Scotch ham is cured but not smoked. Fresh ham is a cut of fresh pork, neither smoked nor cured.

Fully-cooked ham is cured, smoked, and processed so that it is ready to serve heated or cold. Through processing, much of the shrinkage has already taken place.

The various styles of hams, either uncooked or fully cooked, are:

Bone in hams weighing 8 pounds or more.
Skinless, shankless hams with the shank bone removed and skinned and trimmed of excess fat.

Semi-boneless hams with the aitch bone removed (some may have the shank bone removed as well). *Round boneless hams* are boned, skinned and formed into cylindrical shape. They weigh from 6 to 14 pounds.

Boneless hams, fully cooked, are boned, skinned, and closely trimmed but retain the natural ham shape. They weigh from 8 to 12 pounds.

Country style or Virginia hams are aged and more heavily cured and smoked than other types. They can be obtained as bone-in, fully cooked, skinless, defatted hams, or boneless, fully cooked hams.

Bacon

Bacon is made from fat bellies and is both cured and smoked. It is available as slab, stick, or sliced bacon. Slices are of various thicknesses and are often designated by the number of slices to the pound.

Canadian bacon is a boneless cut from the back and is also cured and smoked. It can be procured fully cooked and is available in canned form.

Poultry

Broilers, fryers, roasters, and turkeys are graded as follows by the U.S. Department of Agriculture:

Poultry

U.S. Special or U.S. Grade A. A.
U.S. Prime or U.S. Grade A.
U.S. Choice or U.S. Grade B.
U.S. Commercial or U.S. Grade C.

Most food services use U.S. Grades A or B. The practice now is to mark the grade names on tags sealed to each bird. The boxes in which the poultry is packed are also stamped with the U.S. Grade.

Chicken

Fresh chicken can be bought as broilers (or broiler-fryers), roasters, capons, and stewing chickens. *Broiler-fryers* are usually marketed when 8 weeks old and weigh between 1 1/2 and 3 1/2 pounds. A fryer is similar but generally slightly larger.

Roasters are tender chickens weighing from 3 1/2 to 5 pounds and are marketed when about 12 weeks old. *Capons* are castrated male chickens weighing from 4 to 7 pounds. *Stewing chickens* are mature hens with meat less tender than that of broilers or roasters.

Federal grading and inspection applies only to chickens shipped in interstate commerce and not necessarily to chickens sold within the state in which they are processed. Inspection is for wholesomeness with the inspection mark found on the giblet bag, wing-tip, or carton.

Fresh, ready-to-cook chickens can be procured whole, split in halves without the backbone, or split into quarters. Whole legs, thighs, drumsticks, breasts, backs, wings and giblets are also available as parts or portion-controlled. Boned chicken breasts and boned half-breasts can also be purchased.

Frozen, ready-to-cook whole chicken parts are on the market. Precooked chicken products are also available. These include breaded, preportioned chicken; breaded chicken fillets (patties of light and dark meat); boned chicken roll; and other chicken specialties such as breaded Chicken Kiev.

Turkey

Government grading and inspection of turkeys is similar to that of chickens. The four classes of turkeys are:

1. *Young hens:* Females usually 7 1/2 months old.
2. *Young toms:* Males less than 1 year of age. Both young hens and young toms are soft-meated, with flexible breast bones.
3. *Old hens:* Females over a year old.
4. *Old toms:* Males over a year old.

Both old hens and old toms have toughened flesh and hardened breastbones.

Weights of turkeys range from the small fryer-roaster with an oven weight of 3 to 9 pounds to large birds weighing 30 pounds or more.

Fresh or "dressed turkeys" are feather-dressed with head, feet, and viscera intact. *Ready-to-cook turkeys are drawn*, ready for cooking. These are also available as turkey parts, either as run of the mill or graded for size, including wings, drumsticks and boned turkey breasts.

Many types of frozen turkey meat are available as boneless uncooked roasts or in turkey rolls which are precooked, either with white or dark meat or a combination of both.

Duck

U.S. Standards for dressed duck are:
U.S. Grade A, Young,
U.S. Grade B, Young,
U.S. Grade A, Old,
U.S. Grade B, Old,
U.S. Grade C.

Young ducks are immature birds of either sex, usually from 10 to 12 weeks old and with soft meat flesh. Old ducks are mature birds of either sex with dark and toughened flesh. For roasting, a young bird is recommended.

Eggs

Size is usually the criterion in purchasing eggs. The various size classifications and minimum weights (in 30 dozen crates) are as follows:

Egg Sizes and Weights

Size	Minimum Net Weight (lbs.)
Jumbo	52
Extra Large	48 1/2
Large	45
Medium	40
Small	34

As a rule if large eggs are more than 15 per cent higher in price than medium eggs it is more economical to buy medium eggs. In the Fall, when medium eggs are in large supply, this sized egg is generally a better buy.

Frozen eggs have been used for many years for bakery purposes. They come in 30 pound containers as whites, sugar yolks, or whole eggs.

Dried eggs, known as whole-egg solids, egg white solids, or egg yolk solids, are also on the market.

Butter

Butter is graded by the "score," based on 100 points for perfection. The score given depends upon color, flavor, body, salt content, and freshness. Actually, butter with score of 93 to 95 is the best obtainable in the market. In general, butter used for table purposes is 92 score or better, while 90 score butter is used for cooking purposes.

Margarine

Margarine is made from vegetable oils and may contain in addition, butter, salt, flavoring, artificial coloring, emulsifying agents, and preservatives. Vitamins "A" and "D" are usually added. Margarine is graded like butter, has about the same keeping qualities but is less likely to absorb odors. It is packaged in quarter pound cubes, 1 and 5 pound, prints, pats for table use and in 24 and 32 pound cubes.

Cheese

There are many varieties of cheese, most of which are made from cow's milk, or its whey. Some cheeses are made from goat's or sheep's milk. Natural cheeses are aged by the manufacturer. Process cheeses are made by a heat process with an emulsifying agent added. Process cheeses melt uniformly. Figure 6.8 lists some of the commonly used cheeses and their uses.

There are almost as many types of packaging as there are varieties of cheese: wheels, such as for American and Swiss cheese; sausage-shaped cylinders in which Italian cheeses come; and the loaf in which cream and processed cheeses are packaged, are some of the most common types. Cheeses such as American and Parmesan come shredded or grated.

Kind	Principal Uses
American	Cookery Table service Processing
Blue (Bleu)	Salads Canapes Table service Dessert
Camembert	Cheese trays Table service Dessert
Cottage	Salads Table service
Cream	Salads Sandwiches Table service Desserts
Gruyere	Cheese trays Table service Desserts Processing
Mozzarella	Pizza Cookery
Parmesan	Grating Cookery
*Roquefort	Salads Table service Dessert
Swiss	Sandwiches Table service Processing

* (The name Roquefort is protected by law, and is reserved for genuine Roquefort, that cheese which is aged in the caves of Combalou in Roquefort, France.)

Fig. 6.8. Some cheeses and their uses. (Courtesy Volume Feeding Management.)

Milk and Cream

Milk can be purchased as whole fresh; butter-milk; skimmed; canned evaporated; sweetened condensed; and dry or powdered.

Fresh whole milk is purchased by food services in half-pints, 1/3 quarts, quarts, half-gallons, and 5 gallon cans. For dispensers it is available in special 5 and 10 gallon containers. Canned evaporated milk comes in No. 1 (14 oz.) and No. 10 cans (103.7 oz.). Condensed milk is also available in No. 1 cans. Dry whole milk is available in 1 and 5 pound cans while nonfat dry milk comes in 1, 5, 25, and 50 pound bags.

Cream must contain at least 18 per cent butterfat. Coffee cream usually contains 18 to 22 per cent; light whipping cream 30 to 36 per cent; and heavy whipping cream 36 per cent or more butterfat.

Many products are on the market today in powder, paste, or liquid form for use as substitutes for milk and cream. Mixtures of this type are made from non-milk fats and milk solids. Some, containing sugar and flavoring, are dispensed from containers having a gas that aerates the product, giving it the appearance of whipped cream. There are also a number of nondairy products in powder or liquid form known as "coffee whiteners" that can be used entire or mixed with water or milk to produce substitutes for milk and whipped cream.

Ice Cream

In most states, ice cream must have a minimum butterfat content of 10 per cent for vanilla and somewhat less for chocolate and other fruit and nut flavors. High quality ice cream will range from 14 to 18 per cent or more in butterfat content. *Sherbet* is a frozen dessert made from milk flavored with fruit juices or other flavorings. It may contain egg whites and a stabilizer. *Water ice* is made from water and sugar with flavorings.

Ice cream and sherbet come in 2 1/2 or 3 gallon containers. Ice cream can also be had in individual portions or in quart bricks cut into portions.

Soft ice cream, usually 4 to 5 per cent butterfat content, is produced in some food services in a special freezer, using a purchased mix.

Fresh Fruits and Vegetables

While federal grading has not been applied as widely to fresh fruits and vegetables as to other products, it is rapidly coming into use. Most fruits are graded U.S. Fancy or U.S. No. 1; or U.S. No. 1 and No. 2 Most vegetables are graded U.S. No. 1.

Purchasing fresh fruits and vegetables presents many problems, even to the experienced buyer, for the following reasons:

1. The fact that the market is subject to constant fluctuations between supply and demand due to weather, crop conditions, and other factors.
2. The perishable nature of fruits and vegetables.
3. The many variations in market practices, grading, and the produce itself.

Because of these factors, it is essential to emphasize quality rather than price in buying produce. A safe method is to purchase fresh fruits and vegetables by brand names which are usually consistent in quality.

One university food service placed the buying of fruits and vegetables in the hands of a produce merchant with whom they had a long and satisfactory experience and in whom they had confidence. He buys all fruits and vegetables and is compensated by a small mark-up on the products he purchases. Checks are made from time to time by the university food purchasing agent to make sure that competitive prices are being paid. This arrangement has been in effect for several years and has worked out satisfactorily.

Because fresh produce is graded at the shipping point, it should be inspected for quality when it is purchased and delivered. Make sure that it is reasonably clean, free from damaging cuts, bruises, and insects, and not overripe. Some fruits such as peaches and cantaloupes will not ripen satisfactorily if picked prematurely. Others, like pears and bananas, are better if picked green and allowed to ripen. Tomatoes, for example, will not ripen properly if exposed to temperatures under 50° F. for appreciable periods.

Produce should be bought by weight whenever possible. The terms "lug," "flat," "crate," "hamper," etc., mean little unless the exact size of the container is known. Packs should be examined to make sure that the layers underneath are of the same quality as those on top.

Because of the many varieties of fruits and vegetables (there are some 8,000 varieties of apples, for example) the buyer should have detailed information available on these various types and kinds, characteristics, methods of packaging, etc. Sources for such information are given in the reading list at the end of this chapter.

Canned Fruits and Vegetables

Government grades for canned fruits and vegetables are as follows:

Canned Fruits

Grade A or Fancy
Grade B or Choice
Grade C or Standard
Below Standard in Quality

Canned Vegetables

Grade A or Fancy
Grade B or Extra Standard
Grade C or Standard
Below Standard in Quality

Many packers grade their own products; however, if terms such as "Grade A," "Grade B," etc., are used, the products must come up to the government standards. Many canners subscribe to continuous governmental inspection. Where private brands are used and have been found satisfactory, many buyers will depend upon these labels. When brands not previously used are offered, it is wise to make tests of the various quality characteristics and the drained weight.

Methods of canning have improved since 1809, when Nicholas Appert, a Parisian confectioner, won an award from the French government for demonstrating that food could be preserved by subjecting it to heat in sealed containers. Under modern conditions, fruits and vegetables for commercial canning are selected crops of high quality, harvested at the proper stage of maturity and sealed in cans usually within hours after picking. Methods of canning in use today tend to preserve color, flavor, and nutritive value.

Labelling

Most canners do not label their own canned goods, although they code the tops of the cans with identifying letters and numbers. The cans are labelled with the distributor's brand or sold "bright," that is, un-labelled.

Federal regulations require that certain information appear on the label. This includes the name and address of the distributor or canner; style of pack; net contents, names of ingredients if not standard foods; variety; use of artificial or imitation flavors. If the product is below standard quality or fill, it must be indicated. In addition, some distributors provide information as to portions, net weights, etc. An example of a descriptive label of this type is shown in Figure 6.9.

Cutting Tests

Canned fruits and vegetables are products of nature and despite the care exercised by growers, canners, and graders, there is always the possibility of variations between different packs of even the same label and grade. Experienced buyers therefore make it a practice to test canned goods periodically by "cutting"

or opening selected cans and inspecting the contents. The following steps are usually taken in such tests:

1. The appearance of the sample can is observed to make sure that there are no dents or bulges. In some cases a vacuum gauge is used to determine the vacuum. The gauge should register at least one inch of vacuum although three inches denotes a good vacuum.

Can Sizes, Volume and Number Per Case of Canned Fruits and Vegetables				
Can Size	Diameter	Height	Volume (oz.)	Number in Case
6Z	2- 1/8"	3- 1/2"	5.8	48
8Z (tall)	2-11/16"	3- 1/4"	8.3	48
300	3"	4- 7/16"	14.6	48
303	3- 3/16"	4- 3/8"	16.2	24
2	3- 7/16"	4- 9/16"	19.7	24
2 cylinder	3- 7/16"	5- 3/4"	25.3	24
2-1/2	4- 1/16"	4-11/16"	28.55	24
3 cylinder	4- 1/4"	7"	49.6	12
5	5- 1/8"	5- 5/8"	56	12
10	6- 3/16"	7"	105.1	6

Note: Volumes given represent total water capacity of can. Actual volume of pack will be somewhat less depending upon head space in can. Weights of pack will vary according to density of product. Various other sizes of cans are used for juices, meats, fish, poultry.

Fig. 6.10. Can sizes. Volume and number per case. (Courtesy Natl. Canners Assn.)

2. The information on the label is recorded on a form provided for this purpose and the can is opened.

3. The distance between the product and the top of the can is measured to determine the degree of fill. This varies with different products but the National Canners' Association recommends that cans be filled as full as possible without impairment to products and within the following distances from the top of the can:

No. 2 Cans	19/32 inches
No. 2 1/2 cans	20/32 inches
No. 10 cans	27/32 inches

Fig. 6.9. Descriptive label on canned peas. (Courtesy National Institutional Food Distributor Associates, Inc., Atlanta, Ga.)

If the fill is from 1/2 to 3/4 inches from the top of the can it is not considered excessive.

4. The "drained weight" is then measured by draining the contents of the can through a screen of specified size and mesh for two minutes.

5. The number of pieces, if indicated on the label, is determined and the product inspected for flavor, color, uniformity, odor, and absence of defects.

Syrup Density

Although the density of the syrup is not a factor in grading, federal regulations require that the type of packing be stated on the label. Syrups may be water or juice, plain or slightly sweetened; light syrup; medium syrup; heavy or extra heavy syrup.

The density of syrup is measured by a Brix hydrometer. Normally for every degree Brix, the product is estimated to have 1 per cent sugar content. As sugar strengthens the cellulose of fruits and berries, fragile products packed in heavy syrups are desirable. If the syrup cannot be utilized by the food service, however, it is more economical to purchase fruits in lighter syrups at lower prices if the quality is acceptable.

Testing of Canned and Frozen Fruits and Vegetables

Factors to be considered in the testing of canned and frozen fruits and vegetables are listed in Figure 6.17 at the end of this chapter.

Frozen Foods

Frozen fruits and vegetables are being increasingly used by restaurants and institutions. They are grown and packed under the same controlled conditions as canned produce. Improved methods of freezing are bringing many new types of frozen foods on the market.

Although federal grades for frozen foods are similar to those for canned goods, packers have been slow to adopt federal standards. They prefer to sell by brand names and descriptive labelling.

Frozen fruits may be packed in 10 or 30 pound cans. Frozen orange juice comes in 32 ounce cans packed 12 to the case. Fruits may be frozen unsweetened or packed 5 to 1 (5 pounds of fruit to 1 pound of sugar) 4 to 1, or at other ratios.

Most frozen vegetables are packed in block form but some, such as peas and lima beans, are frozen loose. Various styles are offered; for example, broccoli and asparagus are packed as spears and cuts. Frozen vegetables come in 2, 2 1/4, and 2 1/2 pound packages or in 20 pound cases. Frozen French fries are in 5 pound bags, six to the case, corn on the cob in cases of 48 ears.

Many precooked frozen foods, put up in entrée form for institutional use, are on the market. This makes possible a wide menu variety with a minimum of waste.

Some precooked and frozen entrées recently listed:

Seafood Newburg	Crabmeat Tetrazzini
Chicken a la King	Pot Roast au Jus
Coq au Vin	Welsh Rarebit
Beef Stroganoff	Roast Beef Hash
Sirloin Tips in Gravy	Shrimp Curry
Swiss Steak	Shrimp Fried Rice
Crab meat Soufflé	Macaroni & Cheese
Sliced Turkey Supreme	Hot Dutch Potato Salad

These foods are completely seasoned, cooked, then frozen. Preparation requires only reheating.

These are available in a variety of sizes, from individual packs (12 to a case) to 5 pound packages.

Canned entrées run to such dishes as spaghetti and meat balls, ravioli, macaroni and cheese, beef goulash, beef stew, and baked beans. Most canned entrées are packaged in No. 3 cylinder (46 fluid ounces) or No. 10 cans. Many are also available in 8 to 9 ounce cans for individual service.

Frozen cakes and pies have also made great inroads in the volume feeding industry. A partial cake list includes cheese, fudge, coconut, apple, spice, and devil's food. Frozen pies include fruit, cream, and custard in a variety of flavors.

Most of the items require only defrosting. Some pies, however, notably the fruit and custard varieties, require baking after defrosting.

Frozen cakes and pies are sold as whole units. Most commonly, cakes come four to the case; pies come six to the case.

Prepared soups include canned soups, dehydrated soups, and soup bases. Canned soups usually come in a No. 3 cylinder can, holding about 46 fluid ounces. Dehydrated soups consist of all the ingredients needed. All that is necessary is to add water and cook. Most commonly dehydrated soups come in No. 10 cans, though other types of packaging are available. Some companies market a line of powdered bouillon mixes which require only the addition of hot water to make soup. They are available in single service packets, 1,000 to the case, and also come 48 1-gallon packages to the case.

Which Type to Buy

The purchasing agent is often concerned with the desirability of buying a fresh, canned, dehydrated, or frozen fruit or vegetable. Frequently this depends upon the use to which the product is to be put. If, for example, a fruit cocktail is to be served in a high class restaurant, fresh or frozen fruits would ordinarily be used. If fruits are to be used in a gelatin dessert, however, the canned product would be acceptable. Much depends upon the menu and the type of food service. Cost is another factor.

To Make or to Buy?

In determining whether to make certain items from "scratch" or to buy them partially or fully prepared, it is necessary to take into account the kitchen labor involved in addition to the material cost. This is discussed in Chapter 12 "Controlling Labor Costs."

Dried and Dehydrated Vegetables

Dried vegetables include many varieties of beans, green and yellow split peas and lentils packed in 100 pound bags.

Dehydrated potatoes are widely used for mashed potatoes. They come in either flake or granule form. Some operators feel that the flakes possess advantages over the granules. They are also available diced or sliced. Dehydrated potatoes are packed in No. 10 cans or 5 pound bags, six to the case. Powdered sweet potatoes is another dehydrated product that has grown in popularity.

Freeze-Dry and Dehydro-Freeze Products

Through the combination of freezing and dehydration two new forms of food processing have been developed. In Dehydro-freezing, the product is first dehydrated and then frozen. The resulting product takes up half the space required by the original product but must be kept under refrigeration. Freeze-drying is a reversal of the process; the food is first frozen and then dried by a process known as "sublimation" by which the ice particles are changed to a vapor without passing through the liquid stage. The resulting product is not only reduced in bulk but can be stored without refrigeration. Only a few freeze dry items have been placed on the market as the process is at present an expensive one. These include mushrooms, crab meat, shrimp, chives, shallots, and red sweetball peppers. The freeze-dry process is costly but other products are being added as techniques of this method of processing are being perfected. Freeze-dried coffee has become widely accepted.

Fish

Fish can be purchased fresh, frosted, frozen, canned, mild-cured, pickled, dry-salted, and smoked. Most fresh fish is bought in the following forms:

Whole or Round: As taken from the water.
Drawn whole: With only the entrails removed.
Dressed or pan-dressed: Ready to cook.
Fillets: Sides of fish cut lengthwise away from the backbone.
Steaks: Cross section slices of large fish (such as halibut or swordfish).

Whole fresh fish should have full, clear eyes, bright skin, tight scales, bright red gills, firm elastic flesh which sticks closely to the bones, and a fresh odor, both inside and at the gills.

Canned fish is bought by the case, the size of the can dictated by menu requirements. Smaller varieties include:

Anchovies: Packed in 2, 13, and 28 oz. cans.
Caviar: in 3 1/2, 4, 7, and 14 oz. cans.

Sardines: In oblong cans of 3 1/2, 8, and 11 oz., or the 15 oz. oval can.

Salmon can be purchased in 3 3/4, 16, or 64 oz. cans. There are five varieties of salmon as shown in Figure 6-11.

1.	King, Chinook or Spring: A large fish averaging 22 pounds. Color: salmon red to pinkish white. Used for salads and recipes requiring large pieces.
2.	Red, Sockeye or Blueback: Averages 7 pounds. Color: deep red. Texture firm. Used chilled in salads or in hot dishes.
3.	Coho or River: Averages 8 to 9 pounds. Red color but lighter than Sockeye. For salads, sandwiches and cooked dishes.
4.	Pink or Humpback: Average weight 4 pounds. Color light to deep pink. For casseroles and sandwiches.
5.	Chum or Keta: Averages 9 pounds. Lacks color. Used in cooked dishes.

Fig. 6.11. Varieties of canned salmon.

Tuna is packed in oil or brine and comes in four grades:

1. Fancy—choice large pieces of white tuna meat.
2. Standard—used in salads.
3. Grated—used in casseroles or creamed tuna dishes.
4. Flakes—used for creamed tuna.

Packaging is in 6 to 7, 12, and 66 1/2 oz. cans.
Frozen Fish is available in whole or dressed form and as steaks and fillets. It also comes in sticks, squares, rectangles, and fillet shapes, cut from frozen blocks. These may be breaded and ready to cook, or breaded and precooked, ready to heat.

Shellfish

Clams can be purchased live in the shell, shucked fresh or frozen, or canned. Clams are canned whole or minced, for food-service use in No. 5 and No. 10 cans; for clam chowder in No. 5 and No. 10 cans; and in glass jars, No. 5 and No. 10 cans for clam broth and juice.

Crabs can be purchased live by the dozen; cooked in the shell; as crab meat; and as canned crab meat in 7 1/2 oz. cans. "Soft shell" crabs are blue crabs taken after shedding their shells while moulting. The *Alaska King Crab*, a different species, weighs up to 15 pounds. Only the legs and claws are used and are frequently frozen in the shells without precooking.

Lobsters are now shipped alive to all parts of the country. Picked cooked lobster meat is packed in 6 and 14 oz. and No. 5 and No. 10 cans. *African lobster tails* come from a variety of crayfish shipped frozen to this country and sold in 10 and 20 pound cases. Split lobster tails are packed 20 to 28 to a 20 pound box for food-service use.

Oysters can be purchased live, in the shell; shucked, fresh and frozen; and canned. Fresh shucked oysters are packed in metal containers or waxed cartons and sold by the gallon, according to size ranging from 160 or less to over 500 per gallon. Smaller oysters usually are a better buy for dishes in which size is not essential. *Canned cove* oysters are packed in 4 3/4 oz. cans and *smoked oysters* in 3 1/2 oz. cans.

Scallops are the shell muscles of this bivalve. *Bay or cape scallops* are taken from inshore waters, are smaller and considered a greater delicacy than *sea scallops*. The latter are taken from the offshore banks and are more plentiful. On the Boston market, bay scallops are listed in sizes from 500 to 800 and sea scallops from 110 to 170 per gallon. On the New York market they are listed as "large," "medium," and "small." Scallops can be purchased natural, breaded raw, or precooked. Half-ounce, portion-controlled breaded scallops are also on the market.

Shrimp. Unless otherwise designated, the term refers to the tail of the shrimp, fresh, cooked, or frozen. Uncooked shrimp is known as "raw" or "green" shrimp. On the Chicago market shrimp are graded by count, ranging from extra jumbo (less than 15 per pound); jumbo (15 to 20 per pound); small (43 to 65 per pound), and bait (over 60 per pound). In the New York market, shrimp are sold by count and grade designations are not used. Canned shrimp come in 4 1/2, 7, and 38 oz. cans. Frozen shrimp are available in various forms such as shell on; head removed; raw, peeled, cleaned and breaded; or breaded precooked, ready to heat.

Bread and Rolls

Bread for sandwiches should be wrapped. Standard slices are 3/8 inches thick, but may be up to 5/8 inches thick if desired and approximately 4 1/2 inches square. Rolls come in a variety of styles but as they are short-lived, particularly the hard variety, they should be bought for immediate use.

Coffee

Coffee is usually purchased by brand name based upon individual preference, price and service. Most brands are blends of Brazilian coffees with a mixture of "milds," or high altitude coffee, to give body and to add flavor. Most restaurants and institutions purchase ground coffee delivered weekly or oftener in glassine-lined bags to preserve the aroma. Some operators, however, prefer to buy coffee in the bean and grind it themselves. Color of the brew is determined largely by the degree of roasting to which the beans are subjected. Preference to the degree of roast varies in different sections of the country.

Coffee is ground in various degrees of fineness, depending upon the type of coffee maker used. In general there are three grinds, namely coarse or "steel cut" for percolators and paper filter devices; regular or urn-grind for urns and dripolators; and fine or "glass maker" grind for vacuum and automatic coffee makers. For these latter it is packaged in 2 1/2, 2 2/3, 3 or 4 oz. bags, each designed for use with a 10 to 12 cup glass bowl. For urns it is packed in 8 oz, 14 oz., 1 and 5 pound bags, (ground or in the bean). For ships it comes in 2 pound vacuum cans, 12 to the case. Special grinds and packs are available for vending machines.

Soluble coffee is packaged in individual envelopes, in .74 oz. bags for glass coffee bowls, and in 4.5 oz. bags to make 50 to 60 cups of brew. Soluble *decaffeinated coffee* is also packed in individual envelopes, 100 to the box. *Coffee break kits* containing individual envelopes of soluble coffee, sugar, coffee whitener and a wooden stirrer, are also on the market.

Tea

Teas are of three types: (1) fermented or black; (2) unfermented or green; (3) semifermented or oolong. Most institutional blends are black teas. Terms such as pekoe, orange pekoe, and souchang refer to size of the leaves rather than to quality.

Tea for hot tea is packed in paper tea bags 200 or 250 to the pound and in boxes of 100 tea bags, ten to the case. For iced tea, it comes in 1 oz. bags, 24 or 48 to the carton. Tea also comes in 100 pound chests. Instant tea for institutional use is packed in jars for use with dispensers.

Cereals

Breakfast cereals may be cooked, semicooked, or ready to serve. Dry cereals are packed in individual packages, each containing a single serving, 50 or 100 to the case and for camp use 200 to the case. Some are packed with plastic bowls for use in lieu of china.

Mayonnaise and Salad Dressings

These are packed in 1 gallon jars or 1 to 5 gallon cans. A new package in a 1 gallon unbreakable polyethylene container is now on the market.

Jams and Jellies

These come in No. 10 cans and in individual, single-service packages.

Catsup and Chili Sauce

These are purchased in No. 10 cans and bottles of 10, 12, and 14 oz. size for catsup and also 11 oz. for chili sauce. Catsup also comes in single-service packets.

Syrups

Pure maple syrup is available in 10 and 12 oz. bottles and in quart or gallon cans. Cane and maple syrup is sold in 8, 12, and 14 oz. bottles and also in cans. Imitation maple syrup comes in 1 and 5 gallon cans and in individual single-service packages.

Sugar

Both cane and beet sugar can be purchased as granulated, powdered or confectioner's sugar, and in cube form. Individual single-service envelopes are also available in varying weights, packed in boxes of 100 to 1,000. Bulk sugar is sold in 5 to 10 pound bags and also in 100 pound sacks.

Flour

Because so many food services buy bread, rolls, and pastries ready-baked or use prepared mixes, relatively little flour is purchased today. For dusting foods, thickening gravies or sauces, the less expensive pastry flour is often used.

Bread Flour is made from hard wheat with high gluten content which gives structural support to the products.

Pastry Flour is made from soft wheat with lower gluten content but able to carry high ratios of sugar, fats, and other ingredients. *Cake flour* is similar but more highly refined.

All purpose flour is suited to most kinds of baking and can be used for thickening purposes.

Self-rising flour contains salt and a leavening agent. Flour is sold by the barrel (196 pounds) or 98 pound sacks (1/2 barrel) or it may be sold by eighths (24 or 24 1/2 pounds) or quarters of a barrel (48 or 49

pounds). Some specialty flours are sold in 100 pound sacks. Buyers should check to see whether prices are for 98 pounds or 100 pounds.

Pasta Products (Macaroni, Spaghetti, Noodles, Etc.)

These come in various shapes and sizes. The best macaroni products are made from 100 per cent semolina, a derivative of hard durum wheat. When this is in short supply it is combined with farina, from non-durum wheats. If the farina is of high quality, the product will not be inferior but will not have the yellow color of semolina. Pasta products come in boxes of 10, 20, and 25 pounds.

Spices

Current trends toward variety in food flavors have increased the use of spices and herbs. Among the many on the market, some of the most common are shown in Figure 6.12.

Whole and powdered spices are usually packed in 1 and 5 pound cans. As they lose flavor over extended periods, they should be purchased in small quantities as needed.

Common Spices and Their Uses
Allspice, which combines the flavor of nutmeg, cinnamon and cloves and is used ground in puddings, pies and cookies. Whole allspice is used for stocks, sauces and gravies.
Chili Powder, a blend of ground chili peppers, oregano, garlic and cumin. Commonly used in chili con carne, chili beans, meat loaves and stews.
Cinnamon is used whole in pickling, preserving and sometimes in coffee and chocolate. Ground cinnamon is used in pies and puddings.
Cloves are used whole in baked ham and other preparations.
Curry Powder is a blend of many spices and is used on shrimp, chicken, lamb, and other meat dishes, and in salads.
Ginger is the flavoring ingredient in gingerbread and cookies and can be used ground on fresh fruit cups and cantaloupes.
Mace is the outer covering of the nutmeg but is less pungent. Used in cakes, stewed cherries, etc.
Mustard is used whole for pickles and beets; ground with sauces and gravies; and prepared (in 1/2 and 1 gallon jars and individual packages) for use with meats such as frankfurters and corned beef.
Nutmeg is used whole for grating as for eggnog, and ground in apple pies, puddings, custards and doughnuts.
Paprika is used largely for coloring baked items and as a garnish for salads, cottage cheese and similar items.
Pepper: Whole peppercorns are used in stock. Ground pepper, both black and white, is used as a seasoning in cooking and on the table. Black and white pepper come from the same plant.
Cayenne pepper is a hot spice of a different variety used in curry powder and other dishes.

Fig. 6.12. Some commonly used spices.

Shortenings

These are of two basic types: (1) those made from animal fats, such as lard, beef fat and butter; and (2) those made from vegetable oils, such as margarine and hydrogenated shortenings. Fully hydrogenated shortenings can be used for deep frying, baking and icings. For deep frying, shortenings should have a high smoke point. Smoke points for hydrogenated shortenings are: standard shortenings: 400° F.; all-purpose fully hydrogenated shortenings: 460° F.; and special deep frying shortenings: 500° F.

Shortenings are generally sold in 50 pound fiber containers or in 50 and 100 pound tins.

Other Prepared Foods

Sauce bases eliminate the greater part of preparation for a variety of entree items. You can buy all-purpose sauce base, a la king sauce, newburg sauce, curry sauce, and tomato sauce, just to name a few. Packaging varies with the type of sauce and with the manufacturer. Most frequently, sauce bases come in a package with the yield marked on it.

Soup bases are seasonings in paste form that can be used as bases for soups and gravies. Turning a base into a soup or gravy requires preparation, as only the stock has been supplied.

Most manufacturers package soup bases in jars, which vary from 1 to 4 pounds. One company puts them in 16 ounce cans with resealable plastic tops. They also come in 30 to 50 pound drums.

Prepared mixes open a whole new world of menu possibilities. They literally take the work out of assembling and measuring ingredients. Among those available are cake mixes, muffin mixes, doughnut mixes, hot roll mixes, and cookie mixes. One company even markets a cheese souffle mix.

Again, packaging varies, but the most prevalent is a 5 pound bag. Look into these mixes. You'll be surprised how much time, money, and labor they can save you.

Prepared breading mixes for deep frying are also used in many food services. They are said to absorb about 25 per cent less fat than bread crumbs and to result in a more palatable finished product.

Soy Analogs or Spun Proteins

These are spun products of the soybean which are so similar to beef, chicken, or ham that it is difficult to tell the difference. They are high in proteins and low in fats. A number of universities and other institutions are using them because they are acceptable to vegetarians and also because they provide high nutritive value at a somewhat lower cost. They are available in products analogous to Chicken, Beef, Corned Beef, Turkey, Ham, and Sausage. They come in 72 ounce rolls except for the sausage analog which comes in 1 lb. packages. Their use is rapidly increasing in institutional food services.

Irradiated Foods

Foods preserved by irradiation will be available to food services in the near future. When properly packaged to prevent recontamination, these foods can be stored for extended periods without refrigeration.

For a number of years the U.S. Army Laboratories at Natick, Massachusetts, has been conducting research in the treatment of food with ionizing radiation. In 1961 a six-year program in radiation preservation of foods was launched. Recent tests by the Army Surgeon General have indicated that irradiated foods are as wholesome as nonirradiated foods. Acceptance tests of a number of food items in garrison mess halls show that irradiated foods are favorably received. Among the products evaluated were bacon, ham, pork, pork sausage, chicken, beef, shrimp, and haddock.

The U. S. Food and Drug Administration has approved canned bacon sterilized with ionizing radiation for human consumption. The Natick Laboratories prepared a limited production purchase price description on which the first commercial production tests of irradiated bacon will be made. The FDA has also approved the disinfestation of wheat and wheat products and the sprout inhibition of potatoes with gamma radiation at prescribed energy levels.

The Container Division of the Natick Laboratories is also conducting research in the use of packaging materials for freeze-dry and other food products. Some are designed to dissolve when the product is cooked. Others are of edible material. The prospect thus looms that future diners may be able to eat the package as well as the food it contains.

A similar research program with respect to prolonging the shelf life of sea food is being carried on by the Bureau of Fisheries of the U.S. Department of Interior at Gloucester, Massachusetts.

Yield Tests

In setting up specifications for purchasing, and in compiling formulas and cost cards, it is advisable to make quality and yield tests. These tests may be made by the cooks, assisted by one of the dietitians, or by the butcher or baker, or other employee. It is essential that someone be assigned to observe the tests and record results.

Figures 6.1 and 6.2 show actual yield tests made of different cuts of beef. In each case it is seen that the actual cost of the cooked, edible meat is much higher per pound than the cost of the raw meat as purchased.

It will be seen from Figure 6.2 that the final cost of the Round averages around 66 cents per lb. This is somewhat higher than the price at which the same finished product could have been purchased at the time.

Similar tests might be made of poultry, canned goods, etc. In testing canned goods, the contents of a can are run through a standard sieve and the "drained weight" measured, and an appraisal made of other quality characteristics. The drained weight gives the actual quantity of solid fruit or vegetable content in the can.

Factors to be considered in the testing of canned fruits and vegetables are given in Figure 6.17 at the end of this chapter.

Data on Standards and Grades

Full information may be obtained from the Superintendent of Documents, U.S. Government Printing Office, Washington, D. C., 20402, regarding printed matter available on federal grading of food products. There are also numerous handbooks and buyers' guides.

Market Data

The U.S. Department of Agriculture publishes bulletins giving information on commodity prices, foods in plentiful supply, and other information which can be obtained by contacting the Department. Commodity prices are quoted daily in the financial pages of the newspapers and over the radio. In addition there are available market bulletins from private sources.

STEWARD'S MARKET QUOTATION LIST ____19__

WM. ALLEN & CO. N. Y. STOCK FORM 6082 REVISED-PRINTED IN U. S. A.

Each article column has the headings: ON HAND | ARTICLE | WANTED | QUOTATIONS

ARTICLE	ARTICLE	ARTICLE	ARTICLE	ARTICLE
BEEF	**Provisions (Cont'd)**	**FISH (Cont'd)**	**Vegetables (Cont'd)**	**FRUIT (Cont'd)**
Corned Beef	Pig's Knuckles, Fresh	Carp	Estragon	Dates
Corned Beef Brisket	Pig's Knuckles, Corned	Codfish, Live	Egg Plant	Figs
Corned Beef Rump	Pig, Suckling	Codfish, Salt Boneless	Garlic	Gooseberries
Corned Beef Hash	Pork, Fresh Loin	Codfish, Salt Flake	Horseradish Roots	Grapes
Beef Chipped	Pork, Larding	Eels	Kale	Grapes
Beef Breads	Pork, Spare Ribs	Finnan Haddie	Kohlrabi	Grapes, Concord
Butts	Pork, Salt Strip	Flounders	Lettuce	Grapes, Malaga
Chuck	Pork, Tenderloin	Flounders	Lettuce, Ice Berg	Grapes, Tokay
Fillets	Sausages, Country	Flounders, Fillet	Lettuce, Plain	Grapefruit
Hip Short	Sausages, Frankfurter	Fluke	Leeks	Grapefruit
Hip Full	Sausages, Meat	Haddock	Mint	Guavas
Kidneys	Shoulders, Fresh	Haddock, Fillet	Mushrooms	Lemons
Livers	Shoulders, Smoked	Haddock, Smoked	Mushrooms, Fresh	Lemons
Loin, Short	Shoulders, Corned	Halibut	Okra	Limes
Strip	Tongue	Halibut, Chicken	Onions	Limes, Florida
Shell Strip	Tongues, Beef Smoked	Herring	Onions, Yellow	Limes, Persian
Ribs Beef	Tongues, Fresh	Herring, Smoked	Onions, Bermuda	Muskmelons
Shins	Tongues, Lambs	Herring, Kippered	Onions, Spanish	Oranges
Suet, Beef	Tripe	Kingfish	Onions, White	Oranges
Tails, Ox	**POULTRY**	Mackerel, Fresh	Onions, Scallions	Oranges
VEAL	Chickens	Mackerel, Salt	Oyster Plant	Peaches
Breast	Chickens, Roast	Mackerel, Spanish	Parsley	Peaches
Brains	Chickens, Broilers	Mackerel, Smoked	Parsnip	Pears
Feet	Chickens, Broilers	Perch	Peppermint	Pears
Fore Quarters	Chickens, Supreme	Pickerel	Peas, Green	Pears, Alligators
Hind Quarters	Cocks	Pike	Peas	Pineapples
Head	Capons	Porgies	Peas	Plums
Kidneys	Ducks	Pompano	Peppers, Green	Plums
Legs	Ducklings	Redsnapper	Peppers, Red	Pomegranates
Liver	Fowl	Salmon, Fresh	Potatoes	Quinces
Loins	Geese	Salmon, Smoked	Potatoes, Bermuda	Raspberries
Racks	Goslings	Salmon, Nova Scotia	Potatoes, Idaho	Strawberries
Saddles	Guinea Hens	Scrod	Potatoes, Idaho	Strawberries
Shoulder	Guinea Squabs	Shad	Potatoes, Sweet	Tangerines
Sweet Breads	Pigeons	Shad Roes	Potatoes, New	Watermelons
MUTTON	Poussins	Smelts	Potatoes, Yams	Watermelons
Fore Quarters	Squabs	Sole, English	Pumpkins	**BUTTER**
Kidneys	Turkeys, Roasting	Sole, Boston	Romaine	Print
Legs	Turkeys, Boiling	Sole, Lemon	Radishes	Cooking
Racks	Turkeys, Spring	Sturgeon	Rhubarb, Fresh	Sweet
Saddles	**GAME**	Trout, Brook	Rhubarb, Hot House	**EGGS**
Saddles, Hind	Birds	Trout, Lake	Sage	White
Shoulder	Partridge	Trout, Salmon	Shallots	Brown
Suet	Pheasant, English	Weakfish	Sorrel	Mixed Colors
LAMB	Rabbits	Whitebait	Sauerkraut	Pullets
Breast	Quail	Whitefish	Spinach	**CHEESE**
Fore Quarters	Venison, Saddles	Whitefish, Smoked	Squash Crooked Neck	American, Kraft
Feet	**SHELL FISH**	**VEGETABLES**	Squash Hubbard	American, Young
Frils	Clams, Chowder	Artichokes	Tarragon	Bel Paese
Kidneys	Clams, Cherrystone	Asparagus	Thyme	Camembert
Loins	Clams, Little Neck	Asparagus	Tomatoes, New	Camembert
Legs	Clams, Soft	Asparagus, Tips	Tomatoes, Hot House	Cheddar
Lamb, Spring	Crabs, Hard	Asparagus, Fancy	Turnips, White	Cottage
Racks, Double	Crabs, Meat	Beans	Turnips, Yellow	Cream
Racks, Spring	Crabs, Oyster	Beans, Lima	Turnips, New	Cream, Phila.
Saddles	Crabs, Soft Shell	Beans, String	Watercress	Cream, Phila.
Shoulder	Crabs, Soft Shell Prime	Beans, Wax	**FRUIT**	Edam
PROVISIONS	Lobsters, Meat	Beets	Apples, Cooking	Gorgonzola
Bacon	Lobsters, Tails	Beets, Tops	Apples, Baking	Liederkranz
Bologna	Lobsters, Chicken	Broccoli	Apples, Crab	Parmesan, Grated
Bologna	Lobsters, Medium	Brussels Sprouts	Apples, Table	Roquefort
Crepinette	Lobsters, Large	Cabbage	Apricots	Roquefort
Salami	Oysters, Box	Cabbage, Red	Bananas	Roquefort, Broken
Hams, Corned	Oysters, Blue Points	Cabbage, New	Blackberries	Stilton
Hams, Fresh	Oysters	Carrots	Blueberries	Store
Hams, Polish	Scallops	Carrots	Blueberries	Swiss
Hams, Smoked	Shrimps	Cauliflower	Blueberries	Swiss, Gruyere
Hams, Virginia	Turtle	Celery	Cantaloupes	Swiss, Gruyere
Hams, Westphalia	**FISH**	Celery Knobs	Cantaloupes	**Miscellaneous**
Head Cheese	Bass, Black	Chicory	Honey Balls	
Lard	Bass, Sea	Chives	Melons, Casaba	
Lyon Sausage	Bass, Striped	Corn	Melons, Honeydew	
Phil. Scrapple	Blackfish	Corn	Melons, Persian	
Smoked Butts	Bluefish	Chervil	Melons, Spanish	
Pig's Feet	Bloaters	Cranberries	Cherries	
Pig's Heads, Corned	Butterfish	Cucumbers	Cherries	
		Dandelion	Cherries	
		Escarole	Chestnuts	
		Endive	Currants	

Fig. 6.13. Market quotation list. (Courtesy William Allen & Co.)

Market Quotation Sheet

Food buyers generally make use of a daily quotation sheet listing the various items regularly purchased, the quantity needed that particular day, and four columns for listing the prices quoted by different vendors. Quotations are usually received by telephone, and the lowest bid circled for placing the order. Figure 6.13 shows a form of market quotation sheet used by restaurant and hotel buyers. For smaller operations the same general form may be used listing only the items desired.

Where such quotation sheets are used, the specifications involved are clearly understood by both parties through established practice.

Purchase Orders

It is the usual practice to issue purchase orders for equipment, supplies, and food items to be delivered at a later date. Generally, written purchase orders are not issued for foods delivered on the day of purchase. In such cases informal orders are issued giving the

necessary information to personnel involved in receiving and quality control.

The purchase order should show: the date issued, name and address of vendor, quantities, descriptions, and unit prices of the goods ordered, and delivery conditions required. Each purchase order bears a consecutive number which is referred to when the invoice is prepared. Purchase orders may be prepared in duplicate or triplicate, with one copy remaining in the Purchasing Department's records, one copy going to the vendor, and a third copy going to the Food Service Department (where the purchasing is done through a general Purchasing Department).

The purchase order provides a complete record of the transaction for the guidance of the purveyor as well as for the institution. It also gives accurate information to the Receiving Clerk in checking quantities and prices of goods delivered. Where deliveries are delayed or back-ordered, it is useful for tracing purposes. Figure 6.14 illustrates one form of Purchase Order. The form shown in the Figure is made up in

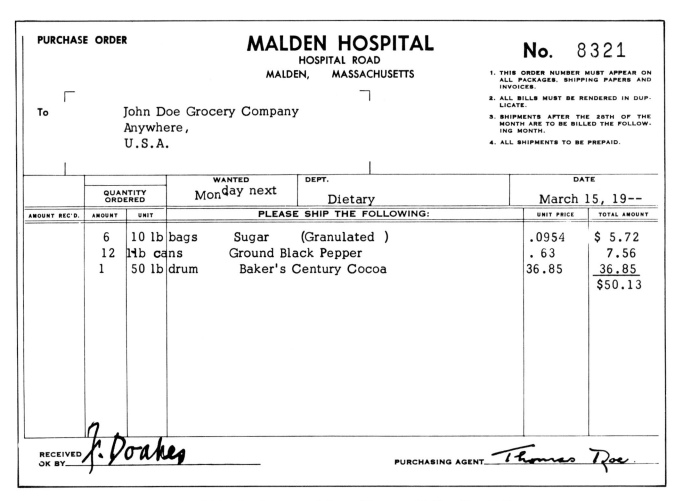

Fig. 6.14.   Purchase record form. (Courtesy Malden Hospital.)

quadruplicate, with the white original going to the Vendor, the yellow second copy to the Receiving Department, the pink third copy to the Purchasing Department, and the gold fourth copy to the Accounting Department. These forms are made up with snap-out carbons which are thrown away after the form is filled out.

Purchase Price Record and Specification Card

A card showing prices paid in the past for a given commodity, particularly the most recent price, is useful to the buyer. It saves the time required to look up previous invoices, and shows at a glance the price trend of that particular item.

Figure 6.15 shows a form of Purchase Price Record card. This contains spaces for the days and months. By making each year's entries with a different colored pencil or ink, this card can be used for many years. It will be noted that the bottom of the card is used to record the specifications. In this case, the specifications for Canned Sliced Apples are given.

Cash Discounts on Purchases

Although bills are usually paid through the Accounting Department with the exception of petty cash items, the Food Service Department can help the establishment take advantage of cash discounts offered by promptly checking and approving invoices for payment.

From an accounting standpoint, the income from purchase discounts is a *financial* and not an *operating* transaction. It is not considered in actually costing and pricing food items. Nevertheless, a substantial annual saving in overall food-service costs can be realized by taking advantage of cash discounts offered by vendors.

Relations With Vendors

Maintenance of friendly relations with vendors is a good policy. This was demonstrated during the last war when friendly vendors were able to keep many industrial and institutional food services supplied in times of general scarcity.

It is also a rewarding policy to treat vendors' salesmen with courtesy. Consideration shown by the buyer

Date	1	2	3	4	5	6	7	8	9	10	11	12	13	14	15	16	17	18	19	20	21	22	23	24	25	26	27	28	29	30	31
Sep.	94																														
Oct.																										84					
Nov.																															
Dec.																															
Jan.																	84														
Feb.																															
Mar.																															
Apr.																												96			
May																															
Jun.	84																														
Jul.																															
Aug.																															

SPECIFICATIONS: Sliced Apples — Canned

Grade "A" or U. S. Fancy, sliced in segments not larger than quarters; uniform size not less than 2″ in length; good bright color; texture, firm but tender; normal apple flavor; slight amount of sugar added. Score 85 or higher. Drained weight 102 ounces to #10 can. Packed 6 #10 cans to carton. Price per #10 can given above.

Fig. 6.15. Purchase price and specification record.

in not keeping the salesman waiting longer than necessary will be appreciated. The salesman will often be the bearer of new ideas, and not infrequently keeps the buyer posted on important market trends and conditions.

On the other hand, this relationship should not be carried too far. The buyer, of necessity, must limit the time he can spend with salesmen. In most food services, interviews with salesmen are limited to definite hours each week. The acceptance by the buyers of gifts or gratuities from salesmen with whom he does business is forbidden by many organizations. Relations with vendors, if they are to result in mutual satisfaction, must be a "two-way street." Claims as to quantities and qualities must be based upon fact, not mere opinion. To illustrate: When a cook complains that a given dish was unsatisfactory because of poor qualities of the ingredients as received (e.g., meat), this should be carefully investigated. The facts should be established before making a complaint to the supplier. It may be that the fault lay in the methods of preparation. In any event, if proper methods of quality control were in effect, the unsatisfactory merchandise would not have been accepted in the first place.

RECEIVING

It is one thing for the buyer to order food or supplies. It is equally important to make sure that the food service receives exactly what has been ordered. Errors frequently occur, and unless a careful check is made of count or weight (or both, if required) and quality as well, substantial losses can take place.

The Receiving Clerk

Definite responsibility for receiving should be placed upon one individual who is usually designated as Receiving Clerk. In smaller food services this individual may be responsible for other duties as well.

The Receiving Clerk must be mentally alert, accurate, and should have some food knowledge. Above all he must be trustworthy. His principal function is to count and/or weigh the various items delivered and accurately record their receipt. Where the Receiving Clerk is well informed about food, he may check the quality as well as the quantity received. Ordinarily, however, the check for quality is usually made by the manager, an assistant manager, or one of the cooks.

Weighing Deliveries

A set of platform scales should be available in the Receiving Area, located so they may readily be used.

Platform scales built into the floor save lifting. In any event, the scales should have a large full-face dial so that the weight may be seen by the delivery man, as well as the Receiving Clerk, to prevent argument. Beam scales may also be provided for weighing of meats purchased in bulk.

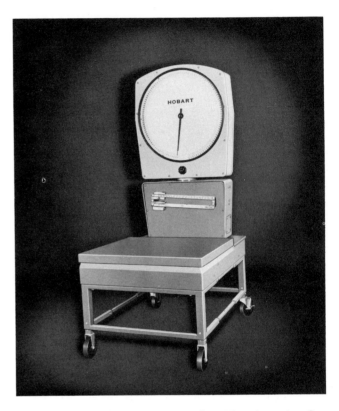

Hobart Bench Scale. (Courtesy Hobart Manufacturing Co., Troy, Ohio.)

Scales should be checked regularly by the local official sealer to make sure they are in good working order.

Each different item should be weighed separately. Even if the total weight agrees with the total shown on the delivery ticket, it is possible for some high-priced items to be short and some low-priced items over in weight so as to make up the required total.

Blind Receiving

There are two methods of receiving generally in use. In the conventional method, the Receiving Clerk is informed of the goods expected through duplicate purchase orders or other means. He then checks to see that these are delivered.

In "Blind Receiving," the Receiving Clerk is given no information. Vendors may even be asked to omit prices and quantities from their delivery tickets. The

Receiving Clerk must count or weigh every item delivered, and make an appropriate entry in the Receiving Record. This latter method is often employed when carelessness is suspected. It is used to *compel* the Receiving Clerk *to count and/or weigh each item,* and not merely copy the information from the delivery tickets.

Receiving Records

Some sort of record is usually provided in which the Receiving Clerk enters the date, name of vendor, description of items, and the quantities or weights received. This may be merely a blank book with penciled columns. In large establishments, a Receiving Sheet with sufficient spaces to record a day's deliveries is used. In others, a Receiving Ticket is made out for the items covered by each invoice. Normally these are used when merchandise is received without an accompanying invoice. A form of Receiving Report is shown in Figure 6.16. This form is used in conjunction with the Purchase Order form (Figure 6.14), a copy of which is sent to the Receiving Clerk when the Purchase Order is issued. It will be seen that this Receiving Report form covers the merchandise received from a single vendor. A separate form is made out for each supplier.

Inspection for Quality

Normally the inspection of merchandise received from a quality standpoint is the responsibility of the food-service manager, chef, dietitian, or someone with the requisite food knowledge.

Some food services arrange with the local office of the U.S. Department of Agriculture to have one of their representatives make periodical spot checks of such food items as eggs, milk, cheese, or canned goods. This is usually done without advance notice to the food-service personnel and the inspector takes random samples from goods received. Eggs, for example, are candled. A nominal fee is charged by the department for this service, and such inspections are made approximately eight times each year.

Marking Merchandise Received

Incoming merchandise of a perishable nature should be marked or tagged immediately upon receipt. The following data should be recorded on the tag or marked on the outside of the case or package:

1. Date of receipt.
2. Name of Vendor.
3. Description of Merchandise.
4. Weight or count when received.

Such marking accomplishes several purposes. It gives a weight or count which may be checked at any later time to test the accuracy of the original receipt. In the case of items such as ground coffee which should be used in order of receipt to preclude staleness, it identifies and dates each package. Where the same item is to be reissued to the kitchen or preparation areas in the same form as purchased, it gives the purchase weight or count for use in computing unit costs, and avoids duplication. It also makes possible the accurate measurement of shrinkage which may take place during storage, as in the case of meats, for example.

Return of Merchandise

When merchandise is unsatisfactory, it should be returned to the Vendor immediately. The Receiving Clerk should be instructed in the procedure to be followed in notifying the vendor and issuing the necessary credit memorandum. This will vary in different establishments.

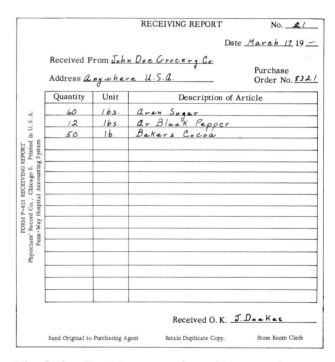

Fig. 6.16. Receiving report form. (Courtesy Physicians Record Co.)

STORAGE

All foods should be placed in storage as soon as possible following delivery unless they are to be processed immediately. Dry groceries, canned goods, and staples should be placed in the Dry Storeroom. Perishable foods, of course, should be placed under refrigeration promptly.

The Dry Storeroom

As previously pointed out in Chapter 5, "Design and Equipment," the Storeroom should be located near the Receiving Entrance and the Main Kitchen. Food and supplies should move in the shortest possible line from the Receiving Area to the Storeroom, and thence to the processing areas (see Figure 5.1).

The Storeroom should be kept at a temperature of from 50° to 55° F. Recent experiments in food technology at one of the leading universities indicate that canned goods tend to lose valuable nutrients if kept at room temperatures for considerable periods of time. This loss can take place even though there is no noticeable change in the appearance of the containers such as swelling. This means that steam and hot water pipes should not run through the storage area. If, through oversight or lack of proper planning, it seems necessary to run such pipes through the Storeroom—and the author can scarcely recall a storeroom where such is not the case—they should be effectively insulated. The floor should be of quarry tile or concrete and arranged so as to slope to a central drain so that it can be flushed regularly. Steel shelves with perforated steel uprights should be installed so that the height of the shelves may be adjusted to take two layers of #10 cans, or three layers of #2 or #2½ cans. Shelves should not exceed 18 inches in depth to permit convenient access.

The lowest shelf should be at least 30 inches above the floor so that the space underneath may be used for storage of bagged items such as sugar, flour, or potatoes. These should be placed on metal dollies or skids with legs so that the platforms are at least 6 inches above the floor. This makes it possible to move the skids with a truck-jack, and to wheel the dollies out so that the floor may be easily cleansed. On the other hand, a separate storage area for bulky merchandise of this sort will make possible even greater opportunities for cleanliness.

A movable platform scale and a metal work table equipped with a table scale should be at hand in the storeroom. Where such scales are equipped with visible dials, time will be saved and errors minimized.

Four Essentials

There are four essentials to be observed in the care and control of the Dry Storeroom:

1. It should be dry and cool (50° to 55° F.) to prevent swelling of canned goods and to prevent spoilage.
2. Housekeeping is important. It must be kept clean, free from rodents and vermin. This means that all wall, ceiling, and floor openings should be sealed or otherwise protected. A drain for flushing is desirable.
3. Goods should be arranged so that "first-in" items will be "first out."
4. Food and supplies should be kept under lock and key to prevent pilferage. One individual should be responsible for the key during the hours he is on duty. Food storerooms are often equipped with recording time-locks which register on a chart each time the door is opened.

Control Essential

Control of all of the places where food is stored is an important step in the control of food costs. This means that only authorized persons enter the storerooms, that records be kept of items moved in and out, and all foods be protected against pilferage.

Housekeeping in Refrigerators

In a previous section we have discussed the storage of perishable foods and the various refrigerators and freezers and their functions. Good housekeeping is as essential in refrigerators and walk-in boxes as in dry storerooms. Meats should be hung or placed so that the cool air may circulate around all surfaces. Butter, milk, and cream should be separated from foods having strong odors. Eggs should not be subjected to freezing temperatures, and, as the shells are porous, should be kept from odoriferous foods.

Beef improves in flavor and tenderness as the result of ageing. It can be safely kept for several months at about 34 degrees F. On the other hand, pork, lamb, mutton, and veal should be kept only for short periods, as they are subject to rapid deterioration.

Fresh fish should be packed in ice in a fish box and kept at from 30-33 degrees F. away from other foods which may take on its odor.

Refrigeration coils should be defrosted regularly. When boxes are being defrosted, all foods should be moved to another box or covered so as to be kept dry while the box is being cleaned.

As with dry storage, all refrigeration units should be kept under lock and key when not in use. Safety locks should be provided on walk-in boxes so that they can be readily opened from the inside in case anyone becomes locked in by mistake. In addition, push buttons may be provided connected with alarm bells. Employees using walk-in boxes should be instructed in the use of these safety devices.

Temperatures will vary as the doors are opened allowing warmer air to enter. For this reason it is

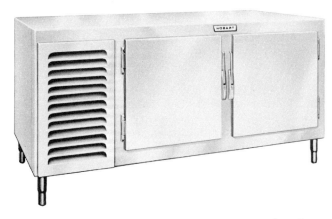

Hobart 2-section Refrigerator and Frozen Food Cabinet. (Courtesy Hobart Mfg. Co., Troy, Ohio.)

Hobart Reach-In Refrigerators. (Courtesy Hobart Mfg. Co., Troy, Ohio.)

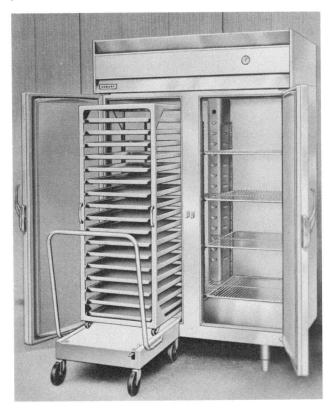

Hobart Roll-In Refrigerator. (Courtesy Hobart Mfg. Co., Troy, Ohio.)

Hobart Walk-In Refrigerator. (Courtesy Hobart Mfg. Co., Troy, Ohio.)

advisable to shut the door behind one upon entering a walk-in box.

Upright Freezers

With the increasing use of frozen foods in institutions, upright deep-freeze units have come into wide use. These units make for efficiency, as they can be located where needed and their large doors and shelves make for convenient access. Furthermore, the kitchen personnel are not subjected to the health hazards of

exposure to varying low and high temperatures found in working with walk-in deep-freeze units.

Other Refrigeration Units

In addition to the walk-in boxes, other refrigerators are needed. The cooks require a box in which to store leftovers. The baker, if one is employed, also needs a refrigerator, although he often makes use of one of the walk-in boxes. The salad makers must have a place to store and chill salads and cold desserts. These

New Victory Refrigerator with Operational Indicator Panel, Enclosed Condensate Evaporator and Insulated Compartments and Pilaster Strips. (Courtesy Victory Metal Mfg. Corp., Plymouth Meeting, Pa.)

needs are generally met by upright reach-in refrigerators. In fact, the current trend seems to be toward reach-in rather than walk-in refrigerators because of greater flexibility afforded through the use of the former.

Other refrigeration units are installed in the counter line, in floor-kitchens, and in serving pantries. Milk is served from refrigerated dispensers, or from counter refrigerators holding individual containers. Similar counter refrigerators are used for individual cartons of ice cream. Cold "bainmaries" are provided on the counter for salads and cold desserts, and for butter-chips. There are also refrigerated water coolers, self-levelling devices, and refrigerated food trucks and conveyors.

Cooling units used in the distribution and service of food will be discussed further in Chapter 9, "Distribution and Service of Food."

Pass-Through Refrigerators

Pass-through refrigerators are widely used between the kitchen and the serving area. Salads, for example, are made up in the salad preparation area and placed in the pass-through refrigerator through the door opening into the salad room. The serving people, when salads are required to replenish the counter supply, merely open the door on their side of the box and

Juices and Dessert Display (Pass-Through Refrigerator) at Cafeteria Place de Justice (Court House), Montreal, view from patrons' side. (Courtesy Bernard et Associés, Montreal P. Q. Canada.)

Pass-Through Refrigerator for display of juices and desserts at Place de Justice (Court House) Cafeteria, Montreal, view from kitchen side. Glass is one-way so that attendant may see food but patrons cannot see into serving area. To retain freshness, pies are cut only as taken by patrons. (Courtesy Bernard et Associés, Montreal P. Q. Canada.)

FACTORS TO BE CONSIDERED IN THE TESTING OF CANNED AND FROZEN FRUITS AND VEGETABLES

CANNED FRUITS

Apples
Taste, color uniformity of size, general appearance, count, tenderness, and drained weight. Avoid apples with brown bruises, insect or similar injuries.

Apple Sauce
Taste, color, general appearance, consistency, absence of defects, and texture. Avoid apple sauce with a poor, dull, variable color, off flavor, thin and watery, coarse and lumpy, contains excessive objectionable substances such as particles of seeds, peel, and flecks.

Apricots
Flavor, taste, general appearance, color, uniformity of size, count, absence of defects, firmness, tenderness, syrup density, clearness of syrup, and drained weight. Avoid apricots with a variable color such as pale yellow or brown, excessive variations in size and thickness, and fruit with blemishes, worm holes, insect damage, bruises or spots from improper processing, crushed or broken pieces.

Cherries (R.S.P.)
Flavor, color, firmness, syrup density, absence of defects, and drained weight. Avoid cherries that are soft or tough, with poor or brownish color, bird or insect injuries, limb injuries and mutilated fruit.

Fruit Cocktail
Taste, general appearance, color, uniformity of size, absence of defects, firmness, syrup density, and drained weight. Avoid fruit cocktail that shows excessive presence of defects such as seed, peel, discolored areas in the pieces of fruit, spotted, discolored, broken or crushed grapes, grapes with cap stems attached, crushed or spotted cherries, or insect damage in any of the fruit. The syrup should not be cloudy.

Grapefruit
Taste, general appearance, color, wholeness, absence of defects, firmness, tenderness, texture, syrup density, and drained weight. Avoid grapefruit that shows a dullness or variable color, also that has considerable amount of particles of seeds.

Peaches
Taste, general appearance, color, type, uniformity of size, symmetry, count, absence of defects, firmness, tenderness, clearness of syrup, syrup density, and drained weight. Avoid peaches that are off color or have a wide color variation, excessive stems or leaves, peel, pits, pieces of pits, insect blemished units such as discoloration, dark spots, worm holes or other insect damage, abnormal shape fruit and crushed or broken units. The fruit should not be mushy, under-ripe or hard.

Pears
General appearance, color, taste, uniformity of size, symmetry, count, absence of defects, firmness, tenderness, clearness of syrup, syrup density, and drained weight. Avoid pears that are off-color, variation in size, poor trimming, uneven halves, blemished, hard, mushy fruit.

Pineapple
Taste, color, general appearance, flavor, uniformity of size, count, symmetry, absence of defects, texture, firmness, tenderness, consistency, syrup density, and drained weight. Avoid fruit of dull color and excessive variation in thickness, size, and shape.

CANNED VEGETABLES

Asparagus
Taste, color, type, uniformity of size, flavor, count, absence of defects, general character, tenderness, clearness of liquor, firmness, cut, and drained weight. Avoid asparagus that has excessive grit or open heads, broken heads, small pieces, poorly cut units, units damaged by spots, stained, and insect or other injury, sediment of particles in liquor, color, and very soft or mushy units.

Green Beans
Taste, color, type, flavor, uniformity of size, sieve size, absence of defects, maturity, texture, firmness, tenderness, clearness of liquor, cut, wholeness, and drained weight. Avoid green beans that have an excessive presence of loose seed and pieces of seed, split units and small pieces of pod. Watch for beans that are off color.

Fig. 6.17. (Courtesy Sonesta Hotels.)

Beets	Taste, color, uniformity of size, count, symmetry, flavor, absence of defects, maturity, tenderness, and drained weight. Avoid beets that are coarse or tough, have stringiness of fiber, noticeably soft or mushy, lack of uniformity of color, lack internal discoloration, poor peeling or trimming, crushed units, and insect injury.
Corn	Taste, color, tenderness, general appearance, and drained weight. Avoid corn that has a poor or objectionable flavor, that has been excessively slated or sweetened, tough, or undeveloped grains, noticeable presence of silks, particles of cob, worm eaten kernels, or distinctly bad color.
Okra	Taste, color, uniformity of size, general appearance, absence of defects, maturity, tenderness, clearness of liquor, and drained weight. Avoid okra that shows a great variation of color, cloudy or discolored liquor; irregular in size; split pods; tough unedible ends; poorly trimmed pods; discolored spots on the pods; and poor flavor.
Peas	Taste, color, type, sieve size, uniformity of size, absence of defects, tenderness, clearness of liquor, and drained weight. Avoid peas that have a variation in color, cloudy liquor, excessive sediment, broken peas, spotted or otherwise discolored peas, mushy or hard peas.
Tomatoes	Taste, color, general character, wholeness, absence of defects, and drained weight. Avoid tomatoes that show a drained weight or less than 50% of the capacity of the container, and are excessively broken up, lack of predominant red color, and excessive amounts of skin.
Tomato Catsup	Taste, color, general appearance, absence of defects, consistency. Avoid tomato catsup that shows excessive particles of seed, tomato peels, and core material, off color, unripe or bitter flavor, objectionable odors of any kind.
Tomato Paste	Taste, color, general appearance, absence of defects, texture, percentage of concentration. Avoid tomato paste that has a scorched, bitter flavor, or objectionable odor, excessive particles of seed, tomato peel, core material, or off color.
Tomato Puree	Taste, color, general character, absence of defects, percentage of concentration, texture, and specific gravity. Avoid tomato paste which has a bitter flavor or objectionable odor; prominent presence of seeds, particles of seeds, tomato peels, off color, or particles of core.

CANNED JUICES

All fruit juices should be checked for taste, color, style, absence of defects, flavor, and sweetness.

Apple Juice	Look for flavor, then color when you buy apple juice. Avoid apple juice that is cloudy, dull, or off color; that has excessive amounts of particles of apple pulp, seeds, and other residue.
Grape Juice	Avoid grape juice that has an off color or off flavor; that contains excessive sediments or particles of skin, seed, or pulp.
Grapefruit Juice	Avoid grapefruit juice that is off flavored, dull or off color; that containes excessive particles of core, skin, seed particles, membrane, or has other defects.
Orange Juice	Avoid orange juice that has an off flavor or that is dull or amber in color; that contains excessive particles of membrane, core, skin, or seed particles.
Pineapple Juice	Avoid juice that has an off flavor, is off color, dull, and contains excessive particles of core or seed or pulp.
Tomato Juice	Avoid tomato juice that is reddish brown in color or that has color that ranges orange to yellow; that has the presence of particles of seeds, skins, objectionable flavor; juice having poor consistency, being either too heavy or too thin; juice that separates rapidly, leaving practically clear liquid at the top.

Fig. 6.17. (Continued)

Apples — Taste, color, general appearance, uniformity of size, type, texture, firmness, tenderness, absence of defects, sugar or syrup ratio. Avoid apples that are brown or gray, soft, hard, mushy, excessive peels, bruises, blemishes of any kind, and damaged fruit.

Asparagus — Taste, color, type, size, uniformity, tenderness, cut, and absence of defects. Avoid asparagus that has a pronounced variation in color, poorly formed spears stocks, poorly cut units, open heads and small pieces, presence of grit or other foreign material, variance in size, and insect injury.

Lima Beans — Taste, color, type, size, tenderness, general appearance, and absence of defects. Avoid lima beans that are off color, shriveled and spotted, presence of excessive extraneous material.

Beans — Taste, color, general appearance, type, style, size, tenderness, texture, maturity, and absence of defects. Avoid beans that do not have the typical green color, excessive extraneous vegetable material, spotted or blemished pieces, small pieces, split ends, or ragged cut units, and firm or hard units.

Broccoli — Taste, color, uniformity of size, texture, firmness, general appearance, and absence of defects. Avoid broccoli that shows variation in color, defects or formation such as shattered heads, poorly trimmed units, grit and foreign material, units damaged by spots, variation of size, and insect injury.

Brussel Sprouts — Taste, color, count, size, general appearance, texture, firmness, tenderness, and absence of defects. Avoid brussel sprouts that have a pronounced yellow color, or smells definitely off color for any reason. Look for excessive grit, and other foreign matter, poorly cut and poorly trimmed heads, surface blemishes such as spots, stains, and insect damage.

Cauliflower — Taste, color, style, texture, firmness, tenderness, general appearance, maturity, and absence of defects. Avoid cauliflower with a marked green or bluish tint, or pronounced gray color, excessive extraneous vegetable material, small clusters, leafy clusters, and insect injury.

Peas — Taste, color, type, sieve size, texture, tenderness, general appearance, and absence of defects. Avoid peas that are definitely off color, and have a pronounced quantity of extraneous vegetable material, such as broken peas or loose skin, pea pods, and stems.

Spinach — Taste, color, tenderness, general appearance, drained weight, and absence of defects. Avoid spinach that is definitely off color, or has an excessive variation in color, grit, sand, seed heads, grass and weeds, crowns of root stubs, coarse or tough leaves and stems, shredded or ragged leaves and stems, or portions of leaves and stems.

Blueberries — Taste, color, uniformity, general appearance, firmness, absence of defects, and sugar or syrup ratio. Avoid blueberries that have a red purple color or a dull color, excessive amount of extraneous material, such as leaves and stems, green berries, undeveloped berries, or berries damaged by insects, crushed, mushy, or broken berries.

Peaches — Taste, color, type, size, symmetry, count, style, texture, tenderness, firmness, sugar or syrup ratio, and absence of defects. Avoid peaches that are materially darkened and noticeably variable in color, excessive variation in size and thickness, misshapen, prominent presence of extraneous material such as leaves or stems, peel, whole pits or pieces of pit, and damaged from mechanical or insect injury, very soft and mushy or excessively firm fruit.

Strawberries — Taste, color, type, size, count, maturity, firmness, tenderness, general appearance, sugar or syrup ratio, and absence of defects. Avoid strawberries that are off color, hard or deformed, soft and mushy, excessive extraneous material such as weeds, grass, leaves, caps, and portions thereof.

Fig. 6.17. (Continued)

obtain such items as they need. The pass-through type of refrigerator makes it possible to place food under refrigeration promptly, and to keep it there without exposure to room temperatures until it is needed. At the same time, it saves steps on the part of both the preparation and serving personnel—so important in these days of high labor costs.

Care of Refrigerating Equipment

All refrigerators should be provided with thermometers and temperature readings should be taken at least daily as a matter of routine. Walk-in boxes are often provided with recording-thermometers which register on circular charts the temperatures throughout a 24-hour period.

Failure of refrigeration, particularly during warm weather, can cause spoilage of food. This not only adds to food cost, but may lead to food-poisoning. Walk-in boxes may be equipped with alarm bells or signals that operate when the refrigeration is not functioning. In one large hospital, the alarm system for the various walk-in boxes is connected to a signal-board near the station of the night telephone operator. Thus, the failure of refrigeration during the hours when the main kitchen is closed can be immediately reported.

Trained refrigeration mechanics are generally employed in institutions having their own maintenance departments. In such establishments, the preventive maintenance program includes inspection of all refrigerating equipment, and regular schedules for defrost-ing and cleaning, (see Chapter 5, section on Preventive Maintenance; also Figure 5.15, "Refrigeration Placard").

SUGGESTED READING

AMERICAN CAN CO. *Purchase & Use of Canned Foods.* New York, 1957.

AMERICAN HOSPITAL ASSOCIATION. *Food Purchasing Guide.* Chicago, 1953.

CORNELL UNIVERSITY. *Fresh Vegetable and Fruit Purchasing.* Ithaca, N. Y.

DEFENSE DEPARTMENT, *U.S. Army Manual on Food Purchasing and Storage,* Washington, D. C.

KOTSCHEVAR, LENDEL H. *Quantity Food Purchasing.* New York: John Wiley & Sons, Inc., 1961.

LUKOWSKI, ROBERT F. *Receiving Practices in Food Service Establishments,* University of Massachusetts, Amherst, Mass., 1960.

NATIONAL ASSOCIATION OF HOTEL AND RESTAURANT MEAT PURVEYORS. *Meat Buyer's Guide to Standardized Meat Cuts.* Chicago, 1961.

NATIONAL LIVESTOCK AND MEAT BOARD. *Meat Manual.* Chicago, 1956.

STOKES, JOHN W. *How to Manage a Restaurant or Institutional Food Service.* Dubuque, Iowa: Wm. C. Brown Company Publishers, 1967.

TODOROFF, ALEXANDER. *Food Buyer's Information Book.* Chicago: Grocery Trade Publishing House, 1946.

UNITED FRESH FRUIT AND VEGETABLE ASSOCIATION. *Specifications.* Washington, D. C.

U.S. DEPARTMENT OF AGRICULTURE. *A Fruit and Vegetable Buying Guide for Consumers.* Washington, D. C.

U.S. DEPARTMENT OF JUSTICE, Bureau of Prisons. *Operating a Culinary Department.* Washington, D. C., 1950.

WENZEL, GEORGE L. *Wenzel's Menu Maker.* Austin, Texas.

CHAPTER 7

Menu-Planning

Menu-planning, or menu-making as it is sometimes termed, involves making up in advance the menus that are to be served. As the menu-planner selects the dishes to be offered, it is his or her function to see that patrons are satisfied and their continued patronage assured. This is not an easy task in the institutional or industrial food service where the same patrons appear day after day. Variety and eye appeal must be constantly kept in mind, as well as limiting factors such as food costs and availability of foods and equipment. In hospitals there is also the problem of special or therapeutic diets.

Although menu-planning is sometimes considered a routine procedure, it offers opportunities for the exercise of imagination and ingenuity. It also plays an important role in the success of the food service, both from a dollars and cents standpoint and in building the goodwill of patrons, employees, and the public.

TEAMWORK IN MENU-PLANNING

Generally menu-planning is the responsibility of one individual—the Chef, the Manager, or Assistant Manager, and in hospitals, of the Chief Dietitian or her assistant. In some institutions the dietitians share this responsibility on a rotating basis.

A recent trend is to appoint a committee or team to plan the menus, the committee headed by an experienced menu-maker. Members serve for one or more months in rotation. Thus the ideas of various staff members are given expression. If properly organized and given the right leadership, such a committee aids in bringing about teamwork on the part of the staff. Group planning is also a safeguard against repetition and lack of variety.

To avoid the complications of large committees, the menu-planning group should consist of three, or at the most five, members serving at a time.

CONSIDERATIONS IN MENU-PLANNING

In planning the menu several considerations should be kept in mind, such as:

1. Needs and desires of patrons
2. Variety
3. Menu appeal
4. Seasonal factors
5. Foods available
6. Physical equipment
7. Nutritional balance
8. Price structure

Needs and Desires of Patrons

Obviously, an industrial food service patronized by women office workers would not offer the same menu as a cafeteria serving male employees who do heavy physical work. In the office cafeteria, sandwiches, salads, soups, and light entrees are preferred as compared with the heavier dishes relished by the men workers. The menu-maker must be aware of the needs and preferences of the patrons in planning the menu.

From observation of institutional feeding in different sections of the United States and other countries, one finds that eating habits play a larger part in menu selection than actual physical needs. These habits depend upon racial and social backgrounds, climatic and geographical conditions, economic considerations, and individual differences.

In many sections of the South, green vegetables are cooked with bacon or pork strips, while along the Mexican border dishes seasoned with hot peppers are in demand. In New England and along the coasts, sea food is popular. Fish and egg dishes are usually found on the menu, especially on Fridays and fast days, and in some places Kosher food is provided.

Industrial cafeterias have done much to introduce new dishes and to change the eating habits of industrial workers. As previously mentioned, the author has referred to these employee food services as "epicurean melting pots." Intriguing old country entrees have been popularized along with native American dishes. Not only has this broadened the eating habits of the patrons but it has also given the menu-makers a wider range in their search for variety.

In hospital food service, patients are not offered rich, heavy dishes lest these provoke digestive upsets. Certain patients, whose conditions require it, are limited to special or therapeutic diets, such as soft, liquid, bland, low-calorie, low-sodium, salt-free and sugarfree. Advances in nutritional science have stimulated the use of special diets as an integral part of therapy in recent years. Whereas it was customary when visiting a hospital Dietary to find perhaps 10% of the patients on special diets, this ratio has increased to 25% or higher in many institutions. In a large general hospital noted for its research work, we found 65% of the patients on special diets. This, of course, reflects the greater recognition accorded nutritional therapy and the increased emphasis being placed upon nutritional research. In any event, this trend means greater responsibility and effort on the part of the therapeutic dietitian and the Dietary Department.

Variety

Formerly hospital patients generally received a set meal, but today they are being offered greater freedom of choice with what is known as the "Selective Menu." Under this plan, the patients on regular diets select, usually the day before, their preferences for the following day's meals. This usually includes choices as to entree, vegetables, dessert, and beverage. This freedom of choice, while adding to the menu-maker's problems, has resulted in increased satisfaction on the part of patients wherever the selective menu has been introduced, and notwithstanding fears to the contrary, there has been no additional cost—in fact, less waste of food, as with a set menu, patients often rejected what was set before them.

A sample selective menu sheet is shown in Figure 7.1. This sheet is divided into three sections: Breakfast, Noon, and Night, and instructions for its use appear on the reverse side. As these menu selections are tallied by a computer, the patients are asked to use a #2 pencil in checking off the items of their choice. Different colors of ink are used to denote the different classes of patients and the diets assigned to them. Figure 7.6A shows a college menu.

Menu Appeal

The individual dishes can be varied and made appealing by contrasts in:

1. Color
2. Form
3. Texture
4. Flavor
5. Temperature

Color Contrasts: A plate consisting say of a white fish, potatoes, and cauliflower, all white or nearly so in color, is drab and uninteresting in appearance. The introduction of color through the additions of red beets, yellow carrots, or a green vegetable will make this dish more appealing. The same effect may be achieved with garnishes: a sprig of parsley, a piece of lemon, a slice of orange, or a sprinkling of paprika. Every meal should contain at least one colorful food.

NAME ______
ROOM ______ DIET ______

BREAKFAST: Sun., Day 20

LOCATION

CENSUS

Half Grapefruit

Frozen Orange Juice

Shredded Wheat (L)

Rice Krispies

Oatmeal

Farina

Gelatin

Scrambled Egg (L-P)

Hard Cooked Egg

Unbuttered English Muffin

English Muffin

Grape Jelly

COFFEE CREAM MILK
TEA CREAM MILK LEMON
SANKA CREAM MILK

WHOLE MILK LARGE SMALL
SKIM MILK LARGE SMALL
CEREAL CREAM

TOAST: WHITE GRAHAM L
CORN OIL MARGARINE L

NO COFFEE NO TEA NO SALT
NO PEPPER NO SUGAR

PLEASE SEE INSTRUCTIONS ON BACK

Massachusetts General Hospital

PS 6941 BBS (4842)

NAME ______
ROOM ______ DIET ______

NOON: Sun., Cycle I, Day 20

L Broth

Clear Mushroom Soup

Roast Turkey (L) with Orange Dressing and Gravy

Gravy (L-P)

Cranberry Jelly

M Diced Turkey (L)

P Flavored Yogurt

L Whipped Potatoes

Brussels Sprouts (L)

S Carrot Coins (L-P)

Lettuce

Banana

D Canned Royal Anne Cherries

L Cookies (P)

Claret Sundae (P)

Vanilla Ice Cream (P)

D GELATIN
L CUSTARD

FRENCH L
OIL & VINEGAR
SALAD DRESSING
LOW CALORIE

COFFEE CREAM MILK
TEA CREAM MILK LEMON
SANKA CREAM MILK

WHOLE MILK LARGE SMALL
SKIM MILK LARGE SMALL

BREAD: WHITE GRAHAM L
CORN OIL MARGARINE L

NO COFFEE NO TEA NO SALT
NO PEPPER NO SUGAR

NAME ______
ROOM ______ DIET ______

NIGHT: Sun., Cycle I, Day 20

L Special Cream Soup

L Broth

French Potato Soup with Leeks

L Cheese Fondue (P) with Grape Jelly

Hot Roast Beef (L) Sandwich with Brown Gravy

Gravy (L-P)

M Diced Beef (L)

Baked Potato

L Succotash

L Stewed Tomatoes

L Strained Stewed Tomatoes

Sunshine Salad

Lettuce

Pound Cake (P)

D Applesauce

Vanilla Ice Cream (P)

Lemon Water Ice (L-P)

D GELATIN
L CUSTARD

FRENCH L
OIL & VINEGAR
SALAD DRESSING
LOW CALORIE

COFFEE CREAM MILK
TEA CREAM MILK LEMON
SANKA CREAM MILK

WHOLE MILK LARGE SMALL
SKIM MILK LARGE SMALL

BREAD: WHITE GRAHAM L
CORN OIL MARGARINE L

NO COFFEE NO TEA NO SALT
NO PEPPER NO SUGAR

GOOD MORNING!

This is your menu for tomorrow. The Food that you order will be tallied by a computer so PLEASE MARK YOUR MENU CAREFULLY.

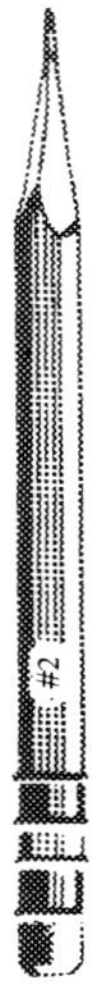

1. Use only a #2 soft-leaded pencil.
2. Fill in the box in front of the food item you choose.
3. Mark only in the boxes – make marks dark and definite.

Example:		Spec.	Reg.	
	B	▯	▯	Beef Pattie
	L	▯	▯	Mashed Potato
	S	▯	▯	Carrots (L-P)
	D	▯	▯	Peaches

A properly filled in box looks like this ▮

NOT like these

4. Erase completely any marks you change.
5. A representative of the Dietary Department will pick up your menu by 10:30 a.m. and will be happy to assist you in making your selection.
6. You will be served only the items selected.

Key for symbols

L	Low Sodium (Low Salt)	N	No Dressing
P	Plain	S	Strained
D	Dietetic	B	Bread-Free - Low Sodium (Low Salt)
		M	Minced

PLEASE DO NOT BEND, FOLD, TEAR, DAMPEN OR MUTILATE YOUR MENU

DO NOT WRITE BELOW THIS LINE

B.T.N.	P.M.	A.M.

PS 6941 A BBS (4842)

Bay State Systems, Inc.

Fig. 7.1. Selective menu. (Courtesy Miss Louise Hatch, Chief Dietitian, Massachusetts General Hospital, Boston, Mass.)

When several colors are used, care should be taken to see that they blend harmoniously. (See Figure 7.2.)

Form and Texture. Diversity in shape may be obtained by dicing, shredding, slicing, cutting, molding into balls, wedges, blocks, strips, or other interesting forms. Potatoes, for example, may be served whole: (baked, boiled, oven-browned) or in various shapes such as diced, mashed, or in different geometrical forms as in croquettes, potato-patties, french-fried, sliced potatoes, etc. Other vegetables such as raw carrots lend themselves to similar treatment. Various shapes on the plate add to eye appeal. Gelatin desserts and salads may show contrasting colors, and may be molded in various shapes, diced, shredded, or whipped. *Texture* provides contrast also. Soft, creamy entrees may be accompanied by crisp, chewy vegetables, for instance, the smoothness of mashed potatoes and the crispness of parsnips, the softness of a melon ball and the firmness of a diced apple. In a Chef's Salad, for example, the variety of textures lends zest to the dish—turkey, ham, cheese, tomato slices and mixed greens—each with a texture of its own. Chinese food, with its sliced almonds and fried water chestnuts, is a good example of the use of contrast in textures.

Twenty-five Commonly Used Garnishes	
1. Apples	13. Grapes
2. Bananas	14. Green or Red Peppers
3. Beets	15. Melon Balls
4. Berries	16. Nuts
5. Carrots	17. Olives
6. Cherries	18. Parsley
7. Cheeses	19. Pickles
8. Citrus Fruits	20. Pimientos
9. Cream (Sour or whipped)	21. Pineapple
10. Croutons (With soup)	22. Prunes
11. Cucumbers	23. Radishes
12. Eggs (Hard-cooked)	24. Tomatoes
25. Water cress	

Note: Some of the above may be used in fresh, dried or canned form and in many different shapes.

Fig. 7.2. Twenty-five commonly used garnishes.

Flavor provides an amazing number of opportunities for achieving variety. Often confused with "taste," flavor is really a complex of three types of sensory stimuli: tastes, aromas, and tactile or feeling factors. The "taste buds" on the tongue and in the mouth detect only four tastes: *sweet, salty, sour,* and *bitter.* The feeling detectors in the mouth tell us whether a food is *cooling,* like peppermint; *astringent,* like an unripe persimmon; *biting,* as in pepper; *numbing,* like cloves;

or *tooth-coating,* like rhubarb. The nose also detects feelings such as the *pungency* of raw onions.

Through the "olfactory patches" high up in the nose, aroma plays a more important part in flavor perception than either taste or feeling. Flavor chemists state that the normal human being can differentiate more than 200,000 odors. While many of these are derived from chemicals other than food, it can be seen that through contrasts in flavor a myriad of varieties are available to the ingenious menu-planner.

Flavor contrasts are found in the plated dish as well as in the succession of dishes in a complete meal. A fatty meat like pork, served with an acidy relish like applesauce; turkey and cranberry sauce; baked ham with pineapple rings, are illustrations of the use of contrasting flavors. Sweet and sour are often set in apposition, as with sweet cookies and a tart lime or lemon sherbet. A salad containing pears, bland in flavor, may precede a highly flavored dessert.

Temperature contrasts are often found between the different dishes of a complete meal. A chilled juice, perhaps topped by a colorful sherbet, may precede a hot entree. At the same time, the entree may be accompanied by a cool salad. Ice cream and coffee is another cold and hot combination often ordered at the end of a meal.

Seasonal Factors

While hot dishes are generally relished more during cold weather, and lighter meals, such as salads and cold plates, featured in the warm months, air-conditioning has tended to free the menu from an absolute dependence upon weather conditions. Modern transportation facilities have made fresh fruits and vegetables available from Southern markets for longer periods of the year. The advent of frozen foods now makes it possible to serve many dishes which used to be seasonal—such as strawberry shortcake—throughout the year. Nevertheless the menu-planner still finds opportunities for change and variety as the seasons roll around.

As fresh fruits and vegetables are in plentiful supply from nearby sources in the Spring and Summer months, they can be featured profitably. Seafoods such as fresh lobster, smelts, and shad roe and other fishes and shellfish, for example, are available in quantity and hence at reasonable prices during their seasons.

Holidays, both religious and secular, with which traditional foods and decorations are associated, can be appropriately tied in with the menu. New Year's Day, Lincoln's and Washington's Birthdays, Valentine's Day, Easter, Memorial Day, Fourth of July, Labor Day, Hallowe'en, Veterans Day, Thanksgiving, and Christmas are some of the major holidays to be celebrated in the food service with special menus, traditional foods, and decorations.

In addition there are many holidays with their local time-honored customs. In New England, for example, the traditional meal for the Fourth of July is fresh salmon and new peas. Jewish people eat matzoth (unleavened biscuit) at their Passover celebration. Turkey and cranberry sauce are a Thanksgiving Day standby.

These occasions enable the ingenious menu-planner to feature special foods appropriate to the celebration and to dress up ordinary dishes in holiday attire.

The "Weight Watchers"

Because overweight seems to increase one's susceptibility to certain diseases, particularly those of the circulatory system, widespread interest in the caloric content of foods has been aroused in the general public. The trim figure has become fashionable and the United States has become a nation of "weight watchers." From the standpoint of public health this is commendable. It does, however, have its effect upon the food-service menu.

On the theory, "If you can't fight 'em, join 'em," food manufacturers have been alert to this trend and have come out with many new "low calorie" foods and beverages. Institutional food-service operators are also featuring low-calorie dishes on their menus.

The "calorie" is the unit of the metric system which denotes the quantity of heat required to raise the temperature of one gram of water one degree Centigrade. The unit used in nutrition is the "Calorie" (capital "C") which is the quantity of heat required to raise the temperature of one *kilogram* (1,000 grams or about 2.2 lbs.) of water one degree Centigrade. Thus the number of Calories in a given portion of food is a measure of its heat or energy content. If one "burns up" through physical exertions more calories than he consumes, he will lose weight. If, on the other hand, he consumes more calories than he utilizes, the excess will be stored up in body fat and he will gain weight.

Figure 7.3 lists the Caloric content of some common foods. This is taken from the latest statistics of the U.S. Department of Agriculture and is based upon one pound portions, mostly of raw food.

Nutritional Factors

In schools, colleges, hospitals, and other institutions where most or all of the daily meals are served to the same people week after week, every effort is made to plan the menu so that a balanced diet is available. In the school lunch program special attention is given

Calories in Edible Portions of One Pound of Common Foods, As Purchased	
Apples (raw, good quality various types)	242
Bacon (raw-sliced)	3016
Bananas (raw-good quality)	262
Beans (white, canned with pork & tomato sauce)	553
Lima Beans (baby limas-frozen)	553
Beef Rib (choice-without bone: 64% lean 36% fat)	1,673
Cantaloupes (refuse: rind, cavity contents)	68
Club Steak (choice-with bone: 54% lean, 46% fat)	1,443
Coffee (brewed-black)	18
Hamburger (raw-regular grind)	1,216
Bread-White (enriched, made with 5%-6% nonfat drymilk)	1,247
Broccoli (frozen-spears)	127
Butter	3,248
Cheese (cheddar type-known as "American")	1,805
Chicken (fryers-drumsticks)	313
Codfish (raw-flesh only)	354
Corn (canned-cream style)	372
Eggs (chicken-whole, fresh all sizes. Refuse: shells)	658
Cream (light coffee or table cream)	957
Frankfurters (raw)	1,402
Fruit Cocktail (canned-water pack)	168
Gelatin Desserts (made with water-fruit added)	304
Grapefruit (all varieties-pink, red, white)	91
Haddock (raw-flesh only)	358
Ice Cream (approximately 12% fat)	939
Lamb Legs (choice-separable lean meat)	612
Lettuce (raw-all varieties)	44-56
Liver-Beef or Calves (raw)	635
Lobster (northern-meat only)	413
Macaroni (enriched or unenriched)	1,674
Margarine	3,206
Mayonnaise	3,257
Milk (whole-3.5% fat)	295
Oranges (raw-all commercial varieties. Refuse: skin, seeds)	162
Peaches (raw. Peeled fruit. Refuse: thin skin, pits)	150
Peas, frozen	331
Pie, Apple (baked, crust made with unenriched flour)	1,161
Pork Loin (medium fat class, without bone, 80% lean)	1,352
Potatoes-Raw (refuse: parings and trimmings)	279
Rice (white-polished, enriched, common consumer types)	1,647
Tomatoes (ripe-raw. Whole fruit)	100
Turkey, Raw (all classes. Ready to cook. Refuse: bones)	722

Fig. 7.3. Calories per pound in edible portions of common foods from "Composition of Foods"—U.S. Dept. of Agriculture.

to children whose nutritional needs are not being met by the food they get at home.

The need for nutritional balance in these institutions places an added and not always appreciated burden upon the menu-makers. As the food-service director of a well-known women's college recently stated, "These girls will turn their noses up at the potatoes on their plates and then go out after the meal to gorge themselves on gooey chocolate sundaes at the Snack Bar."

Classes of Foods

Foods are generally divided into five classes: proteins, carbohydrates, fats, minerals, and water.

Proteins function to maintain the growth and repair of the body cells. They also supply energy to the body if there is lack of sufficient carbohydrates and fats in the diet. Chemically, proteins consist of "amino-acids" and are found in such foods as milk, eggs, fish, meats, and to a lesser degree in wheat, corn, rice, and nuts.

Carbohydrates are compounds containing carbon, hydrogen, and oxygen. They supply heat and energy to the body. Carbohydrates are primarily of plant origin and their chief sources in food are rice, potatoes, cereals and flour products, legumes, and other vegetables.

Fats are the most concentrated source of energy the diet can provide. They also add palatability to the diet. Fats are found in vegetable oils such as cottonseed, corn, peanut, soybean, olive, and sesame and in butter, margarine, milk, cheese, eggs, fish, meat, and nuts. Fat is stored in many areas of the body. In addition to being a reservoir of energy it serves as insulation against cold, protection against shocks and bruises, and a packing and support for some of the body organs.

Generally speaking, if the substance is liquid at room temperature it is called an "oil"; if solid, a "fat." According to their chemical structure, fats are divided into three groups: (1) saturated; (2) unsaturated; and (3) polyunsaturated fats. Saturated fats are primarily the hard animal fats such as suet or lard. Unsaturated fats are derived principally from vegetable oils.

When certain vegetable oils are subjected to a stream of hydrogen they become solidified and result in the "hydrogenated shortenings" widely used in restaurant baking and cooking. When used in frying, they do not break down into fatty acids as quickly as do the nonhydrogenated fats. They also have superior keeping qualities.

Minerals, together with water and vitamins, are known as "body-regulators." They are the substances which regulate the functions of the blood cells, muscles, nerves, and glands so that the food can be used most effectively to produce energy and body-building.

There are thirteen different minerals known to be required in the human body and all must be derived from the diet. In addition there are other minerals in the body the functions of which, at present, are unknown. Compared with other classes of foods, minerals are required in relatively small amounts. The supply of only three is likely to be critical in bodily health. These are calcium, iron, and iodine.

Ninety per cent of the *calcium* in the body is present in the bones and teeth. Lack of calcium may cause bone malformations and dental caries. Good sources of calcium in foods are milk and most dairy products; shellfish, egg yolks, canned salmon and sardines (with bones); soybeans and green vegetables.

Iron plays an important part in the maintenance of red blood cells. Its deficiency may cause a reduction in the oxygen-carrying capacity of the blood, a condition known as *hypochromatic anemia.* Iron is supplied by such foods as liver, heart, kidney, lean meats, shellfish, egg yolks, dried beans and other legumes, dried fruits, nuts, whole grain and enriched cereals and dark molasses.

Iodine is essential to the diet. A lack of iodine causes swelling of the thyroid glands and the disease known as "goiter." Among natural foods the best sources of iodine are seafoods and vegetables grown in areas where the soil is rich in iodine. Where such food is unobtainable, the best source is iodized salt.

Water

Water not only serves as an essential nutrient but is also the body's means of transportation of the various food and chemical elements carried by the body fluids. The sensation of thirst, caused by the dryness of the inside of the mouth, is nature's warning against the danger of bodily dehydration. Nutritionists recommend a daily intake of about 2.5 quarts of water, including drinking water, fluids and the water in solid foods. Most solid foods have a large water content.

Oxygen

Oxygen is not usually thought of as a food, but it plays an indispensable role in the transformation of food into bodily heat and energy. In breathing, oxygen is carried to the lungs where it passes to the blood stream, replacing the carbon dioxide which is exhaled. The oxygen is carried to the various body cells where it acts to generate energy.

Vitamins

Vitamins constitute a group of organic compounds which in small quantities are essential to health. They are not manufactured in the body as are the secretions of the bodily glands, but must be obtained from the diet. Most foods contain a variety of vitamins but no one food contains all of them in sufficient quantity for the satisfaction of normal requirements. Vitamins are needed for normal bodily functions. In addition, they act as *"catalysts,"* that is they stimulate the action of the *"enzymes"* which are so important in the digestive processes. Modern nutritional research has made it possible to identify many of the vitamins and has also led to the manufacture of these compounds synthetically.

There are two kinds of vitamins, namely, those that are "fat-soluble" and those that are "water-soluble." The fat-soluble vitamins are absorbed with the dietary fats and tend to be stored in the body in moderate quantities. Given this resource, man is not so dependent upon their day-to-day supply in the diet. Water-soluble vitamins are not stored in the body in appreciable amounts and a constant dietary supply is advisable to avoid their depletion. Care must be taken in cooking food containing water-soluble vitamins lest they be leached out through the use of too much water or through overcooking.

A list of the principal vitamins is shown in Figure 7.4 with their properties and principal food sources. In addition to those listed in this figure there are several other vitamins about which complete data has not yet been established, such as *pantothenic acid*, which has to do with the adrenal gland, *biotin* and *folic acid*.

A WELL-BALANCED DIET

The average adult, if left to himself, will ordinarily consume sufficient food and beverages to meet his normal energy and fluid requirements. However, he or she may not choose a diet that is *well-balanced* from the standpoint of nutritional needs. Shown in Figure 7.5 is a plan for a daily balanced diet for adults developed by the U.S. Department of Agriculture and organized around four basic food groups.

NEW DISHES

The menu-planner is constantly on the lookout for new and intriguing dishes. For years restaurants have borrowed or adapted foreign dishes to brighten up their menus. The excellence of the French cuisine has made French terms, such as "table d'hôte, à la carte, hors d'oeuvres" and a host of others, familiar to the American public. Many French dishes have become well known in this country. The same has been true

Principal Vitamins, Their Properties and Sources in Foods		
Fat-Soluble Vitamins		
Name	Properties	Sources in Diet
Vitamin A	Growth and repair of body cells and normal vision. Lack causes "night blindness."	Liver, egg yolks, dark green leafy and deep yellow vegetables, tomato products, butter fortified margarine, cheese from whole milk.
Vitamin D	Utilization of calcium and phosphorus. Deficiency causes bone malformation.	Most foods contain negligible amounts. Best source artificially enriched milk, butter and margarine.
Vitamin E	Not well known.	Seed oils, liver and eggs.
Vitamin K	Through the liver, it controls clotting of blood.	Leafy green vegetables. Intestinal "flora" normal supply.
Water-Soluble Vitamins		
Thiamine	Enables body cells to function normally. Lack causes "beri-beri."	Richest sources: pork, "organ meats" (liver, kidney, heart), yeast, lean meat, eggs, green leafy vegetables, whole or enriched cereals, berries, nuts and legumes.
Riboflavin	Deficiency causes "stomatitis" (inflammation of mouth), skin and eye disorders.	Organ meats, liver sausage, milk, cheese, meat, eggs, green leafy vegetables, whole grains and legumes.
Niacin	Deficiency in areas where corn is principal diet causes "pellagra."	Liver, meats, fish, whole grain, and enriched bread and cereals, dried peas and beans, nuts and peanut butter.
Vitamin B-12 (Only vitamin combining mineral element-cobalt).	Failure of intestinal linings to absorb B-12 causes "pernicious anemia."	Exclusively in animal foods: liver and kidney best sources. Also in muscle meats, fish and whole milk.
Vitamin C or Ascorbic Acid.	Aids bone and tooth formation and healing of burns and wounds. Lack of it causes "scurvy."	Citrus fruits and juices, strawberries, cantaloupes, raw or minimally cooked vegetables, fruit, potatoes and tomatoes.
Pyridoxine	Lack of this vitamin causes inflammation of skin about eyes, ears, nose and mouth.	Liver, meats, whole grain cereals, soybeans, peanuts, corn and other vegetables.

Fig. 7.4. Vitamins: their properties and sources in foods.

A Daily Balanced Diet For Adults
1. Milk Group—two or more cups daily.
2. Meat Group—two or more servings.
3. Vegetable & Fruit Group—four or more servings.
4. Bread-Cereal Group—four or more servings.
In Group 1, ice cream or cheese could replace milk. In Group 3, a dark green or deep yellow vegetable should be included every other day (for Vitamin A) and citrus or other fruit daily (for Vitamin C). Bread or cereals in Group 4 should be whole grain, enriched and restored.

Fig. 7.5. Daily balanced diet for adults. U.S. Dept. of Agriculture.

to a lesser degree of Italian and German cooking terms and foods.

More recently the American menu has taken on an international aspect. Dishes such as Chinese chow mein, Mexican chili con carne, Spanish arroz con pollo, Italian pizza, German sauerbraten, Russian borscht, Scotch broth, English muffins, and Hungarian goulash, to mention a few, are as well known in this country as in their places of origin.

In Scandinavian countries the open-face sandwiches are popular. Single slices of different kinds of bread topped, for example, with fried eggs, a variety of meats, cheese or anchovies, colorfully garnished, make an unusual display. In some restaurants, these open-face sandwiches are available through vending machines even after the eating places have closed. In the cities they are also sold from mobile carts to people on their way home from work.

Sources of new ideas may be found in the food service literature available. The restaurant and institutional trade journals publish many articles about food and the food manufacturers' advertisements present beautifully colored reproductions of exotic new dishes. Visits to other similar food services also bring new ideas to the menu-planner.

PLATE ARRANGEMENT

The arrangement of the food on the plate has much to do with its appeal. A plate that is overloaded is distasteful to the fastidious diner, although desirable to others. Proper spacing should be allowed for the entrée, vegetables, sauces, or garnishes.

A simple matter such as the placement of a piece of pie upon a plate may make it appear generous or skimpy. Many restaurants assure proper plate arrangement by preparing diagrams showing exact location of the various items on the plate, as shown in Figure 7.6.

entrée

Fig. 7.6. Plate arrangement. (Courtesy Fast Food Magazine.)

MECHANICS OF MENU PLANNING

A large sheet of paper, ruled with vertical spaces for the days of the week and with horizontal spaces for the meal periods, will provide space for a week's menu. If coffee breaks or snacks, or in the case of institutions, nourishments, are served between meals, additional horizontal spaces will be needed.

The breakfast menu is the simplest to prepare. It will be easy to pencil in the fruits or juices; the cereals, pastries, or pancakes; the breads and toasts and the egg or meat dishes that may be offered. Individually packaged cereals and such convenience items as honey, syrup, jams, jellies, and condiments are widely used these days. They save labor and eliminate waste and at the same time give a wide variety to the patron. Being preportioned, they carry a known and exact unit food cost.

Planning for the noon and evening meals will call into play the skill and know-how of the menu-maker. First of all, the main entrees for the various days and meals are selected. Appropriate vegetables are added to each entree. With the main entrees selected, juices, soups, appetizers, and desserts can be added. Beverages are usually the same, day to day.

As the menu for the coming week is prepared, it is well to have the records of the previous weeks on hand to note the numbers of the various dishes sold when last appearing on the menu. The previous week's menu should also be available. During the planning of the menu the various factors such as patrons' preferences, profitability, foods available, limitations of equipment, variety, and if called for, nutritional balance will be kept in mind by the planners.

The Cyclical Menu

Many food services use a cyclical or master menu where the principal entrees are worked out for a definite period of anywhere from two to six weeks or more. At the end of the period, the cycle is repeated.

The U.S. Army, for example, draws up a Master Menu for each month in the year, seven months in advance, for more than 2,000 mess halls in continental United States. On any given day, the many enlisted men scattered over the country will be served the same breakfast, luncheon, and dinner. Cyclical menus are used by many restaurant chains and institutions.

The Cyclical Master Menu is a useful guide, even though it may not always be possible to carry it out exactly due to weather or market conditions.

Advisory Councils

Sound nutritional habits may be brought about through education and the proper organizational set-up. In a long-term governmental hospital we recently met with the Patients' Council, made up of representatives of each of the wards and presided over by the administrator. Part of the program was devoted

WELLESLEY COLLEGE MENU

April 3-9   This Menu Subject to Change Without Notice

	Breakfast	Luncheon	Dinner
Monday 3	Orange Juice Grapefruit Sections Fried Eggs Boiled Eggs Matzos	Hearty Beef Soup-Crackers Tunafish Salad-Lettuce Pecan Rolls-Butter Peach Halves Matzos	Broiled Chicken Rice Pilaf Italian Green Beans Cranberry Sauce Wellesley Fudge Cake Matzos
Tuesday 4	Orange Juice Boiled Eggs Popovers Matzos	Chicken Rice Soup-Crackers Grilled Frankfurts Bermuda Salad Bowl Potato Chips Frankfurt Rolls-Butter Fresh Apples Matzos	Italian Meat Loaf-Gravy Whipped Potatoes Carrot Pennies Grape Jelly Strawberry Whirl Ice Cream Cookies Matzos
Wednesday 5	Orange Juice Prunes Scrambled Eggs Marmalade Coffee Cake Matzos	Pea Soup-Croutons Sukiyaki-Chow Mein Noodles Lettuce Salad Assorted Dressings Onion Rolls Jello-Cream Matzos	Fried Fillet of Haddock (ALT: French Fried Potatoes Beets Lemon-Tartar Sauce Banana Strawberry Cup Matzos
Thursday 6	Orange Juice Grapefruit Sections Boiled Eggs French Toast-Syrup Matzos	Clam Chowder-Crackers Spanish Omelet Vegetable Salad Homemade Bread Fresh Grapefruit Matzos	Swiss Steak Summer Squash Broccoli Pickles Buttercrunch Ice Cream Vanilla Ice Cream Matzos
Friday 7	Orange Juice Scrambled Eggs Nantucket Blueberry Bread	Chicken Consomme'-Croutons Italian Spaghetti Meat Balls in Sauce Cabbage-Carrot Slaw Grated Cheese Italian Bread Apple Macaroon Crunch	Baked Ham-Grilled Pineapple (ALT: Candied Sweet Potatoes Spinach Mustard Cherry Cobbler-Topping
Saturday 8	Orange Juice Fried Eggs Boiled Eggs Pineapple Coconut Muffins	Washington Chowder Grilled Cheese Sandwich Bacon Lettuce Salad Fresh Melon	Braised Beef Noodles Whole Kernel Corn Celery Sticks-Carrot Curls Brownies
Sunday 9	Orange Juice Prunes Scrambled Eggs Sausage Danish Pastry	Pineapple Juice Tahitian Chicken Rice Garden Peas Cranberry Sauce Peach Shortcake Whipped Cream	Chuck Wagon Chowder-Crackers Hos Pastrami Beef Rolls Mixed Greens (Radish, Cukes) Russian Dressing Dill Pickles Pear Halves

Figure 7.6A. A College Menu.

to a discussion of menus and food-service problems. Similar organizations exist in other institutions. For example, the food-service manager of a well-known women's college meets monthly with an advisory council of students to discuss common problems. Many industrial cafeterias have joint committees of management and employees to work with the cafeteria manager.

Through the cooperation of these groups, sound nutritional programs may be publicized. There is also the opportunity to display posters and other material stressing proper nutritional practices.

Dietitions and food-service managers may well take advantage of the current popular interest in nutrition by giving talks and conducting discussions on this interesting subject.

Price Structure

In commercial restaurant menu-planning, the over-all food-cost objective is constantly kept in mind. The food-cost percentage of each dish is carefully figured, and its effect on food cost considered before it is placed on the menu. If the raw-food cost of a given dish is out of line, the menu price may be changed, the portion size adjusted, or the item left off the menu until conditions become favorable for its reappearance.

Not only is the cost of every dish considered, but also the effect of each menu item upon the others. For these calculations, careful records are kept of the sales of each dish every time it appears on the menu. With this data are recorded the conditions existing on the date the item was offered, such as weather, special sales in department stores, parades or conventions in town, and other pertinent factors.

In a restaurant operated by the author, a sudden storm at noon hour might cut the number of customers by 50%, no light matter when preparations have been made to serve several thousand luncheons.

While such detailed menu forecasting is not ordinarily necessary in the institutional or industrial food service, the price structure must be kept in mind. If a definite food-cost objective is to be attained, the costs of the various menu items should be compiled in advance. Records of previous sales are valuable in indicating the popularity of a given item and in determining its effect on the food cost. If a dish does not sell, the reasons for its unpopularity should be sought. It may be found wise to discard it, or to change it some way so as to increase its appeal. These problems will be further discussed in Chapter 11, "Control of Food Cost."

MERCHANDISING THE MENU

Even though industrial and institutional food services are generally conducted on a nonprofit basis, there is no reason why food merchandising techniques should not be employed. Some of these have been discussed under the sections on Variety and Appeal. Others worthy of consideration are:

1. Odd-cent pricing
2. Descriptive titles

Odd-Cent Pricing

In many cafeterias, menu items are priced in five cent steps with figures ending in 5 or 0 (25c, 30c, 35c, 40c, etc.) Yet astute retail merchandisers have found that there is a definite appeal in odd-cent pricing.

Where this principle has been applied to menu-pricing, it seems to work. A dish priced at 39¢ appears to be much less expensive than one at 40¢. In nonprofit food operations there is ample justification for odd-cent pricing. It facilitates the principle of determining prices based on raw food costs and gives the patron more for his money. If, for example, based upon its unit cost and the objective desired, the price of a given item turns out to be say $.3056, the actual price, under the conventional five-cent step method, would be set at 35¢. By use of the odd-cent pricing method the price could be set at 31¢, and the proper food cost ratio would be maintained.

It may be argued that it is easier for the cashier to add up the customer's check if it is in five cent steps. Furthermore, odd-cent pricing requires a cash register that will record in odd cents (some registers are designed only for five cent steps). Yet, advocates of odd-cent pricing believe that is is in accord with sound merchandising principles and that the extra trouble required is more than offset by added customer satisfaction and increased sales. Figure 7.7 shows a luncheon menu of an industrial cafeteria illustrating the use of odd-cent pricing.

Descriptive Menu Titles

Another way to add to the appeal of menu items is by the use of descriptive wordings. "Creamy Whipped Potatoes" sounds more appealing than just "Mashed Potatoes," and "Chopped Tenderloin Tips" more interesting than mere "Hamburg." "New England Clam Chowder" or "Manhattan Clam Chowder" means more to the patron who reads the menu than just "Clam Chowder."

There is no end to the interest and appeal that may be added by using descriptive adjectives, names of localities, brands, or other titles to the names of dishes

COMPANY - FOOD SERVICE				
Luncheon Menu - Week Beginning February 7,				
Monday	Tuesday	Wednesday	Thursday	Friday
Tomato Juice .04	Grapefruit Juice .04	Tomato Juice .04	Prune Juice .06	Apple Juice .04
Orange Juice .07	Prune Juice .06	Orange Juice .07	Tomato Juice .04	Tomato Juice .04
Grapefruit Juice .04	Tomato Juice .04	Apple Juice .05	Orange, Grape-	Orange, Grape-
			fruit Juice .06	fruit Juice .06
Vegetable Soup	Chicken Soup, Bowl .10	Split Pea Soup,		
(bowl) .10	Frankforts .18	Bowl .10	Lamb Broth, Bowl .10	Fish Chowder,
Slice Ham Sand-	Minute Steak .30	Boiled Ham .28	Toasted Cheese	Bowl .21
wich .15	Broiled Pork Chop .35	Beef Croquettes .20	Sandwich .12	Tunafish Salad
Grilled Hamburg		Baked Beans,	Cheese and Olive	Sandwich .15
steak .28	Green Beans .07	Brown Bread .17	Sandwich .12	Baked Stuffed
Broiled Pork	Carrots .05	Chopped Ham	Italian Spaghetti .22	Haddock .26
Chop .35	Scalloped Potato .05	Sandwich .15	Roast Stuffed Lamb .28	Roast Rump of
	Mashed Potato .04	Baked Beans,		Beef .30
Green Beans .07		Small Order .07	Green Peas .05	
Sauerkraut .05	Green Salad .05	Baked Macaroni .08	Scalloped Corn .10	Sliced Beets .05
Mashed Potato .04	Tomato Salad .16	Stewed Corn .10	Mashed Potato .04	Peas & Carrots .05
Boiled Potato .04		Mashed Potato .04	Boiled Potato .04	Mashed Potato .04
	Spanish Cream .12			Boiled Potato .04
Pineapple Salad .15	Nut Tea Cookies .03	Peach Salad .17	Vegetable Salad .12	
Green Salad .05	Fruit Cup .08	Green Salad .05	Green Salad .05	Banana Salad .17
	Apple Pie .08			Vegetable Salad .12
Apple Pie .08		Fruit Compote .09	Banana Cream Pie .08	Green Salad .05
Lemon Pie .08		Apple Pie .08	Apple Pie .08	
Fruit Cup .08		Boston Cream Pie .12	Fruit Cup .08	Mince Pie .08
Stewed Prunes .06		Coffee Jello,	Tapioca Pudding,	Apple Pie .08
Rice Pudding		Whipped Cream .12	Whipped Cream .12	Fruit Cup .08
Whipped Cream .12				Chocolate Pud-
				ding, Whipped
				Cream .12

Fig. 7.7. Menu of a small industrial cafeteria serving luncheons only.

offered. Care must be taken, however, when "Chopped Tenderloin Tips" are offered that they are really made from tenderloin tips, or when "New England Clam Chowder" appears it is made with cream and not with tomatoes. Patrons must know that they can rely on the descriptions given.

Where patrons, such as hospital patients, order from a written menu, the descriptive titles should help them to form an idea of what the dish is like. Recently we worked in a hospital when "Welsh Rabbit" was listed on the selective menu. Some of the less-sophisticated patients apparently expected a dish of rabbit meat. Great was their disappointment upon receiving a concoction of melted cheese and toast.

Descriptive titles are widely used in commercial menus, and can also be of value in institutional and industrial food services. Just one additional imagination-kindling word on the cafeteria signboard can add much to the appeal of the dish.

Flexibility

Although menus are generally planned several days or a week in advance, flexibility should always be maintained. A sudden change in weather, the arrival of supplies of fresh fruits or vegetables in the market, or a drop in meat prices may make it profitable to change the menu accordingly. While the menu is a helpful guide, it should not be allowed to become a straitjacket.

The Shorter Menu

In a Virginia industrial cafeteria we found four or five hot entrees and seven vegetables listed on the menu daily. As a result these items had to be repeated frequently. Two or three hot entrees and three or four vegetables would have been ample. Food costs were high because of the quantity of food left over, some of which went into the garbage. Preparation of many items also increased labor costs.

In these days of high food and labor costs, commercial restaurants have found it advisable to shorten their menus. Institutional food services generally have not erred in trying to serve too many items. In many schools and other institutions, only one entree may be served at a meal. While the current trend in hospitals is to make menus selective, it is wise to limit the number of cafeteria entrees in the interests of economical operation—one or two hot soups, two or three hot entrees, and three vegetables. Salads, which are handmade, can be produced in variety from a single basic pattern. Desserts may consist of one cake, two pies, one pudding, and one fresh or stewed fruit. Ice cream, of course, is always available, and keeps from day to day in its frozen state. Where there is a separate snack bar, a variety of sandwiches can be made to order, and beverages and frozen desserts served without excessive leftover food. At such a snack-bar, egg dishes and other short orders may be served which could not be handled on the cafeteria counter without slowing up the line.

Getting Patron Reaction

It is most helpful to the menu-maker to get the reactions of patrons on food and service. One way of doing this is to seek answers to direct questions. This is often done by the dietitians in their rounds among the patients in a hospital. However, most people are hesitant about making verbal complaints, so that their answers to the question "How do you like the food?" may often be a polite but not wholly frank, "It's fine!"

Another method often practiced by managers of commercial restaurants is to circulate around the dining room during meal hours and listen to comments made. One large industrial catering service makes it a rule that all offices must be locked during meal hours so that the managers and their assistants will be in the cafeteria to observe and listen.

It is good practice to train waitresses, counter people, bus boys, and other serving personnel to report any customer reactions they may hear regarding menus, food, and service.

The success of the proprietor of a famous New York restaurant is reputed to be based upon his habit of watching the food returned to the kitchen during meal periods. He made it his business to find out why some dishes were returned practically untouched. Then he improved the unpopular item or removed it from the menu.

Patrons' Questionnaire. Because of the human reluctance to voice unfavorable comments, many food-service managers have urged patrons to send in their "gripes" in written form, without signing their names.

In many commercial cafeterias we noted suggestion cards on each table, asking that customers give their comments and suggestions on the food and service.

On the menu shown in Figure 7.8, this procedure is followed. The food-service officer in this military hospital reports that comments are frequently noted. Many are favorable, some unfavorable. All, he states, are most constructive in helping him to satisfy his patients.

In our work in hospitals, we have often found it helpful to distribute simple questionnaires and allow patients to indicate their reactions without signing their names. This is done in cooperation with the dietitian, and often results in the discovering of ways to improve the menu. A form of such a patient questionnaire is shown in Figure 7.9.

SUGGESTED READING

ATKINSON, ALTA B., and BLAIR, EULALIA C. *Volume Feeding Menu Selector.* Institutions/Volume Feeding, Chicago, 1971.

DAHL, CRETE, *Food and Menu Dictionary.* Chicago: Institutions/Volume Feeding Magazine, 1972.

FOWLER, SINA F.; WEST, BESSIE B.; and SHUGART, GRACE S. *Food for Fifty.* 4th ed. New York: John Wiley & Sons, 1961.

HEINZ, H. J. Co. *The Heinz Handbook of Nutrition.* New York: McGraw-Hill Book Co., 1959.

MONTAGNE', PROSPER. *Larousse Gastronomique.* New York: Crown Publishers, 1961.

STARE, FREDERICK J., M.D. *Eating for Good Health.* Garden City, New York: Doubleday & Co., Inc., 1964.

STOKES, JOHN W. *How to Manage a Restaurant or Institutional Food Service.* Dubuque, Iowa: Wm. C. Brown Company Publishers, 1967.

U.S. DEP'T OF AGRICULTURE, *Composition of Foods,* Agricultural Handbook No. 8, U.S. Gov't Printing Office, Washington D.C. 20402.

U.S. DEP'T OF AGRICULTURE, *Food, Yearbook for 1959,* U.S. Gov't Printing Office, Washington, D.C. 20402.

WENZEL, GEORGE L. *Wenzel's Menu Maker.* Austin, Texas, 1947.

BREAKFAST MENU

PLEASE NOTE:
COMPLETED MENUS FOR EACH PATIENT BEING SERVED ON THE WARD WILL BE IN THE FOOD SERVICE DIVISION PRIOR TO 1400 HOURS (1) DAY IN ADVANCE OF THE SERVING DATE. FOR ANY ASSISTANCE CALL EXTENSION 214.

BREAKFAST MENU TUESDAY 21 JANUARY
NAME _____ WARD _____
MESS CARD CODE NO. _____

PLEASE CIRCLE DESIRED ITEMS

FRUIT JUICES: ORANGE - APPLE - TOMATO GRAPEFRUIT - PINEAPPLE

CHILLED PRUNES OR FIGS - GRAPEFRUIT SEGMENTS

ASSORTED DRY CEREAL - COOKED FARINA

MESS HALL: } EGGS TO ORDER (ANY STYLE)
ON WARDS: }

GRILLED SAUSAGE - BROILED BACON
FRENCH TOAST W/MAPLE SYRUP

HOT TOAST-BUTTER-ASSORTED JAM & JELLY ASSORTED DOUGHNUTS

BEVERAGES:
COFFEE - MILK - HOT COCOA
INDICATE PORTION: LIGHT-MEDIUM-HEAVY

REMARKS:
PLEASE PUT THE FOLLOWING REMARKS ON BACK OF SLIP AND RETURN TO FOOD SERVICE OFFICER AFTER EACH MEAL.: WAS FOOD HOT? ANY MISSING ITEMS? ANY SUGGESTIONS? DID YOU ENJOY FOOD?

DINNER MENU

DINNER MENU TUESDAY 21 JANUARY
NAME _____ WARD _____
MESS CARD CODE NO. _____

SOUP AND CRACKERS

ENTREES: CIRCLE DESIRED ENTREE

SALISBURY STEAK
HOT FRENCH DIP BEEF SANDWICH
BAR-B-Q BEEF ON A BUN
FILLET OF FISH W/LEMON WEDGES & TARTAR SAUCE

VEGETABLES: CIRCLE DESIRED ITEMS
MASHED POTATOES W/GRAVY
SHOESTRING POTATOES

FF BUTTERED LIMA BEANS
FF BUTTERED SPINACH (GARNISHED)

SALAD - CATSUP - MUSTARD

DESSERTS: CIRCLE DESIRED DESSERT
TAPIOCA PUDDING
CHILLED TINNED PEACHES

BREAD - BUTTER - JELLY

BEVERAGES:
LEMON LIME-COFFEE-MILK-TEA-BUTTERMILK
INDICATE PORTION: LIGHT-MEDIUM-HEAVY

REMARKS:
PLEASE PUT THE FOLLOWING REMARKS ON BACK OF SLIP AND RETURN TO FOOD SERVICE OFFICER AFTER EACH MEAL.: WAS FOOD HOT? ANY MISSING ITEMS? ANY SUGGESTIONS? DID YOU ENJOY FOOD?

SUPPER MENU

SUPPER MENU TUESDAY 21 JANUARY
NAME _____ WARD _____
MESS CARD CODE NO. _____

SOUP AND CRACKERS

ENTREES: CIRCLE DESIRED ENTREE
ROAST BEEF W/HORSERADISH SAUCE
GRILLED PORK CHOPS W/SPICED APPLESAUCE
BEEF & PORK CHOP SUEY W/FLUFFY RICE
PEACH HAM LOAF
ITALIAN PIZZA
FILLET OF FISH W/LEMON WEDGES & TARTAR SAUCE

VEGETABLES: CIRCLE DESIRED ITEMS
MASHED POTATOES
SHOESTRING POTATOES

FF BUTTERED STRING BEANS
FF BUTTERED BRUSSEL SPROUTS

SALAD - CATSUP - MUSTARD

DESSERTS: CIRCLE DESIRED DESSERT
MARBLE CAKE
PUMPKIN PIE

HOT DINNER ROLLS-BREAD-BUTTER-JELLY

BEVERAGES:
LEMON LIME-COFFEE-MILK-TEA-BUTTERMILK
INDICATE PORTION: LIGHT-MEDIUM-HEAVY

REMARKS:
PLEASE PUT THE FOLLOWING REMARKS ON BACK OF SLIP AND RETURN TO FOOD SERVICE OFFICER AFTER EACH MEAL.: WAS FOOD HOT? ANY MISSING ITEMS? ANY SUGGESTIONS? DID YOU ENJOY FOOD?

Fig. 7.8. Selective menu sheet. (Courtesy U.S. Naval Hospital, Chelsea, Mass.)

Dear Patient:

May we ask you to help us by answering the following questions. Please feel free to make any comments you wish, and please be frank! By doing so you will help us be of greater service to all.

1. What is your opinion of the quality of the food served in this hospital?

2. How do you rate the appearance of the food?

3. Are hot dishes served <u>hot</u> and cold ones <u>cold</u>?

4. Which is your favorite beverage: Coffee _____?
                                           Tea _____?
                                           Milk _____?

5. Has a dietitian talked with you about food?

6. Did you ever have to wait for food when you were hungry?

7. Do you have any special wishes?   Yes _____No _____

    If so, have they been satisfied?   Yes _____ No _____

8. Additional Comments:

It is not necessary for you to sign your name to this questionnaire.

Thank you!

Dietary Department _____ Hospital

Fig. 7.9.   Patient's questionnaire.

CHAPTER 8

Food Preparation and Cooking

Food preparation involves the cleaning and removal of waste or inedible portions; the cutting, piercing, chopping, grinding, or mashing, and the shaping or molding and other processes that must take place to ready the food for the cooking process.

Proper preparation of food is important not only from a culinary and dietetic standpoint, but also because of the operating costs involved. The major portion of kitchen labor is engaged in preparation, that is, getting the food ready to be cooked. It is in this area that food waste must be closely watched.

Anyone who has tried to peel a potato by hand for the first time understands how waste can be caused by indiscriminate trimming. This applies to meats, fish, and poultry as well as to fruits and vegetables.

Modern research in nutrition has brought home the necessity of proper methods of preparation. In the mashing of potatoes, for example, excessive loss of valuable vitamins may be prevented to some extent by the introduction of milk, cream, or butter to cover surfaces exposed to the air.

LABOR SAVING MACHINERY

Because of the labor involved in quantity preparation of food, machinery has been devised for all phases of the process. These machines not only save labor, but do a more uniform and cleaner job of food preparation.

Machines commonly used in industrial and institutional kitchens are: meat grinder, slicer, patty maker, cuber, tenderizer, power saw, vertical cutter-mixer, slicer, dicer and grater, juice extractor, mixing machine, pie-roller, bread slicer, and doughnut machine; in the bakery there are dividers, pie-crust-rollers, crimping machines, etc. Many institutions are equipped with machines for producing soft ice cream.

It is not enough to have the machines installed. They should be used. While making a survey of a Southern industrial cafeteria not long ago, we noticed that one of the cooks laboriously cut potatoes into tiny cubes. Not far away was a dicing machine, the use of which would have made this task quicker and easier, and would have produced a uniform product. In this case the fault was equally with supervision. This man should have been trained to use labor saving devices.

Some machines, including the mixer, have attachments for performing other jobs such as stirring, whipping, and grinding. The same machine may be used by the chef for mashing potatoes as well as by the baker in mixing dough.

Food preparation machinery should be carefully selected, both as to its construction and its suitability for the particular kitchen operation in mind. Service and repair parts should be available, as emphasized in Chapter 5, "Design and Equipment."

Location is also important if steps are to be saved and kitchen labor conserved. The various pieces of machinery should be positioned with respect to the flow of food through the work centers and convenient to the workers who are to use them. Thus the chopping block, meat grinder, and slicer will be located near the refrigerator where meat is stored; the mixing machine in the baking section of the kitchen; and the vertical cutter-mixer convenient to the vegtable preparation area. Pass-through refrigerators, if strategically placed between preparation areas and points of service, also reduce walking and transport time.

The importance of proper location of equipment was pointed up recently when the author visited a splendidly-equipped cafeteria in Minnesota. Upon inspecting the kitchen it was found that the salad preparation area had been located near the walk-in box for meats; the meat preparation area, on the other hand, was located near the salad refrigerator, resulting in considerable cross traffic.

COOKING IN QUANTITY

Institutional and industrial food services generally do not go in for fancy dishes. With the menu limited, and rapid service a prime necessity, simple wholesome dishes of wide appeal are usually featured. It is essential, however, that these dishes be properly cooked and well flavored.

The outstanding quality of good home-cooked meals is due not only to the cook, her recipes, methods of cooking and seasoning, but also to the fact that such meals are cooked in small quantities and served almost immediately.

Quantity cooking is different from home cooking. Because of the effects of various ingredients upon each other in large batches, it is not generally possible to merely multiply a recipe for five by twenty in order to provide servings for 100. Conversely, one cannot reduce a large batch menu mathematically and expect to obtain the same quality and flavor in the smaller portion.

COOKING IN SMALL QUANTITIES

While the main entree may have to be prepared in advance of the start of the meal period, vegetables may be cooked in several smaller batches. Many fine restaurants have achieved their reputation for fine food

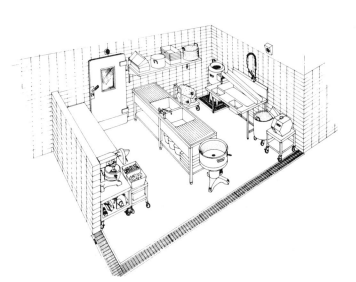

Illustration of a Labor-Saving Vegetable Preparation Department. (Courtesy Hobart Mfg. Co., World Headquarters, Troy, Ohio.)

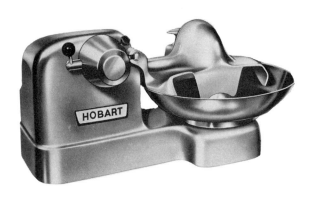

Hobart Food Cutter. (Courtesy Hobart Mfg. Co., Troy, Ohio.)

Hobart Meat Chopper. (Courtesy Hobart Mfg. Co., Troy, Ohio.)

Hobart Tenderizer. (Courtesy Hobart Mfg. Co., Troy Ohio.)

Hobart Meat Saw. (Courtesy Hobart Mfg. Co., Troy, Ohio.)

Hobart Fat Percentage Measuring Kit. (Courtesy Hobart Mfg. Co., Troy, Ohio.)

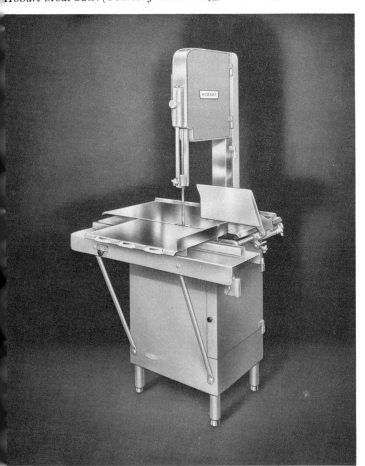

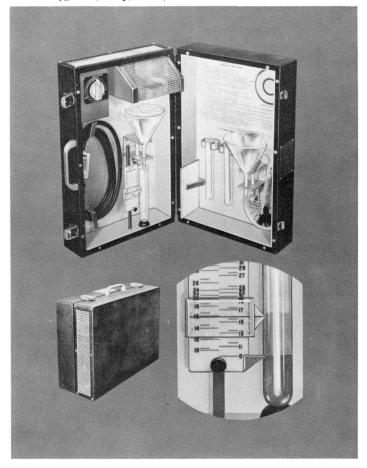

Market Forge Modular Tilting Skillet with adjoining sink. (Courtesy Market Forge, Everett, Mass.)

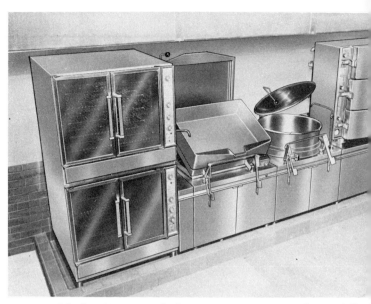

Market Forge stacked Convection Ovens, Tilting Skillet 40 gallon Tilting Kettle, 3 Compartment Steam Cooker Hillside Junior High School, Salt Lake City, Utah. (Courtesy Market Forge, Everett, Mass.)

Market Forge Modular cooking equipment. Matching modular base cabinets housing various appliances may be combined in any desired arrangement. (Courtesy Market Forge, Everett, Mass.)

Counter Char-Broiler. (Courtesy General Electric Co., Chicago Heights, Illinois.)

No. 45 Butter Cutter. (Courtesy Bloomfield Industries, Inc, Chicago, Illinois.)

by attention to details such as cooking the vegetables in small batches.

REDUCING THE TIME INTERVAL

In one food service studied, the virtues of the cook were extolled, particularly his early hours. Arriving punctually at 5:30 A.M. daily, he began his morning's work immediately. Upon investigation it was found that many of the main entrees were cooked by ten o'clock, only to remain in a steam table until serving time, several hours later. When changes were made in the schedule so that cooking of meat and vegetables was finished shortly before serving, a noticeable improvement in food quality was noticed. What had been considered a virtue was in fact a serious fault. Obviously, the time interval between cooking and serving should be reduced to a minimum.

Food left on the steam table will not only be overcooked and lose nutrients in the process, but will shrink appreciably, thus increasing food costs.

THE PHYSICS OF COOKING

From a physical standpoint, heat is transferred from its source to the food to be cooked in three ways:

1. Convection
2. Conduction
3. Radiation

Without delving too deeply into the principles of physics involved, it is known that certain metals, such as aluminum and copper, for example, possess greater "conductivity" than other metals and nonmetallic substances. An aluminum vessel placed over a burner *conducts* the heat to the contents within it. If it contains water, the heated water rises upward and *convects* the heat throughout the vessel. *Radiation* is the heat that is transferred or *radiated* by light or heat waves in a straight line through the air (a nonconductor) to the object to be heated. To illustrate: Radiant heat is sent out by the broiler to the steak being broiled on it. Heat is also radiated from infrared lamps placed over a counter to warm or finish cooking the food placed under it. Food is also a conductor of heat.

Microwave cooking relies upon the principle of radiation. This will be discussed more fully later in this chapter.

In connection with conventional cooking methods, it should be remembered that although water boils at 212° Fahrenheit (at sea level), it does not boil immediately upon reaching that temperature. A considerable amount of heat must be added to bring 212° water to the boiling point. This is known as "latent heat."

Conversely, while water freezes at 32° Fahrenheit (at sea level), a considerable quantity of latent heat must be added to bring ice at 32° F. to 32° water.

METHODS OF COOKING

The method of cooking to be employed will depend primarily upon the characteristics of the food to be cooked. Either dry heat or moist heat is used. Baking in an oven subjects the food to dry heat, as does broiling. Boiling, stewing, or braising in water makes use of moist heat. The principal methods of cooking used in institutional food services are:

Baking

In baking, the food is cooked by dry heat in an oven at the proper temperatures. Baked foods include breads, pastry, rolls, fish, vegetables, fruits, macaroni, and baked desserts. (Note: In baking certain types of bread and rolls, steam is injected into the oven during the baking process to produce a crisp, shiny crust.)

Boiling

To boil is to cook in water or other liquid at a temperature at which bubbles constantly rise and break at the surface. (The temperature depends upon the altitude or atmospheric pressure, and the type and quantity of solids being cooked.) Many foods, including most meats and vegetables, as well as cereals and eggs, can be cooked by boiling.

Braising

In braising, the meat or vegetables are browned in a small quantity of hot fat, then allowed to simmer (cook slowly) in a small amount of water in a covered pan until done. Beef pot roast, fricassees, Swiss steak, braised beef with vegetables, braised lamb, and braised pork chops are examples of foods cooked by this method.

Broiling

Broiling is done by subjecting the food to direct heat consisting of radiated and convected energy. The food is usually placed on a grill below or between fires or heated surfaces. Meats, poultry, seafood, many vegetables, and some fruits are prepared by broiling. The toasting of bread comes under this category.

Frying

In panfrying or panbroiling, the food is cooked in a shallow pan with just enough fat to prevent the food from sticking to the pan. This method is com-

General Electric Range with Convection Oven. (Courtesy General Electric Co., Chicago Heights, Ill.)

General Electric Model CB421 Single Section Heavy Duty Electric Broiler with Convection Oven Base. (Courtesy General Electric Co., Chicago Heights, Ill.)

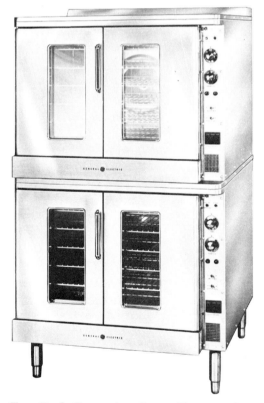

Two Deck Convection Oven. (Courtesy General Electric Co., Chicago Heights, Ill.)

Counter Model Instamatic Convection Oven. (Courtesy Crescent Metal Products, Inc., Cleveland, Ohio.)

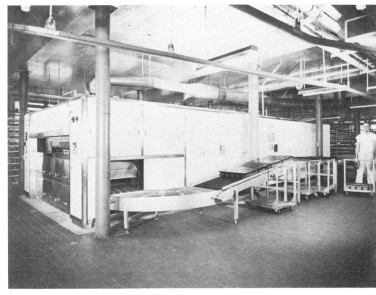

Traveling Oven, Walter E. Fernald State School, Waltham, Mass. (Courtesy Middleby-Marshall Oven Co., Morton Grove, Illinois.)

Market Forge 40 gallon Tilting Kettle and Convection Oven. Generator supplying steam to kettle is located in base cabinet beneath oven. (Courtesy Market Forge, Everett, Mass.)

Kitchen, Clear Creek School, Denver, Colorado, showing (left) Electric Double-Deck Convection Oven, Electric Heavy Duty Range Battery, and (foreground) Milk Cooler. (Courtesy Vulcan-Hart Corporation, Louisville, Ky.)

Market Forge Modular Cooking Equipment; Left to Right: 5 gal. Trunnion Kettle; 2-40 gal. Tilting Kettles; 2 compartment Steam Cooker. (Steam generator in base cabinet.) (Courtesy Market Forge, Everett, Mass.)

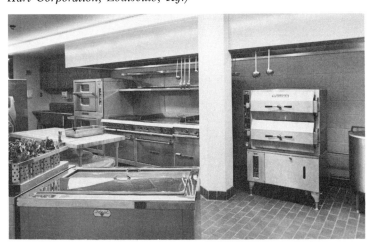

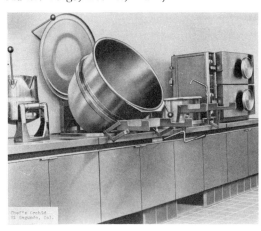

monly used with seafoods, vegetables, meat balls, eggs, etc. (Grilling of meats, hamburgs, pancakes, etc., is similar to frying.)

In sautéing the food is cooked in a pan with a small amount of fat (butter is often used), and is turned and browned on each side as it cooks. This method is used with seafood, poultry, and some meats.

In deep fat frying, the food is wholly immersed in hot fat, the temperature of which ranges from 300 to 400 degrees Fahrenheit. Various types of potatoes, seafood, meat, poultry, nuts, doughnuts, fritters, noodles, onion rings, and even fruits, such as bananas, sliced apples, and grapes, can be fried in deep fat.

Many of these foods are first dipped in a batter and "breaded," or coated, with bread crumbs or a prepared mix. Prepared breading mixes are now in wide use, and are said to absorb 25% less fat than bread crumbs, and to produce a lighter and less greasy product.

Roasting

Roasting is essentially the same as baking, in that the food is cooked by dry heat in an oven. However, the term roasting applies generally to meat and poultry such as roast beef, lamb, pork, and fowl. Roasts are generally "basted" by dipping spoonfuls of the juices over them from time to time as they are cooked.

Steaming

Steaming, or steam cooking, is accomplished by placing the food to be cooked in an enclosed vessel known as a "steamer" in which low pressure (from 3 to 10 pounds per square inch) steam is present. This steam may be generated from water within the vessel, or from an outside source.

Steam cooking is generally used for vegetables, but may also be employed in cooking meats, poultry, seafoods, fruits, cereals, eggs, and puddings. In some cases, food may be started in the steamer and finished in a hot oven. Small table type steam cookers are used in many institutional kitchens.

Excessive steaming may cause considerable shrinkage. In one hospital kitchen we watched baked ham being cooked by steaming. Realizing that the steaming was being overdone, we had the cook boil and roast a similar quantity of ham. The shrinkage was 8¼% less than by the former method. Based on the quantities of meats processed in the steamer in this manner, it was estimated that excessive steaming was costing this institution more than $3,000 annually through undue shrinkage.

Steam Cooking Area, Dining Commons Kitchen, University of Alaska, College, Alaska. Vegetable Preparation is to the right. Behind and under the hood are the fryer, range, two-deck broiler and two-deck ovens. (Courtesy Flambert & Flambert, San Francisco, Cal. Credit to Edwin Crittenden Architects and Associates.)

Stewing

In stewing, the food is boiled slowly or simmered in a small quantity of liquid, usually in a covered vessel. Meats, poultry, vegetables, seafoods, and combinations of these in chowders or stews are typical of this type of cooking. Soups are prepared from a base or stock of bones and meat which has been allowed to simmer in this manner for a long time. Many fruits are also cooked by stewing.

SHRINKAGE IN MEAT COOKERY

The modern emphasis on low-temperature cooking of meats is important from the standpoint of cost as well as of flavor and tenderness. Research has demonstrated that a ten-pound standing rib of beef, for example, cooked for approximately two and one-half hours at 450 degrees F. will shrink about 36%, while a similar roast cooked four and three-quarter hours at 300 degrees will shrink only 22%. The latter method

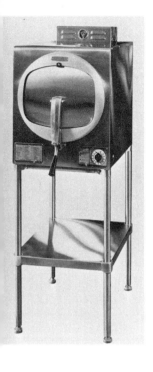

Market Forge Steam-It 15 P. S. I. Pressure Cooker, (may be gas or electrically operated.) (Courtesy Market Forge, Everett, Mass.)

Market Forge 2-compartment Steam Cooker on modular base containing steam generator. (Courtesy Market Forge, Everett, Mass.)

Hobart Vischer Steam Cooker. (Courtesy Hobart Mfg. Co., Troy, Ohio.)

Hobart-Vischer Counter Model Steam Cooker. (Courtesy Hobart Mfg. Co., Troy, Ohio.)

The Recon-Plus, which stores from 100 to 1500 frozen portions at 0°F. until needed, then by turning dial reheats them to serving temperature in minutes. (Courtesy Foster Refrigerator Corporation, Hudson, N. Y.)

B-311. Preparing Bacon, Texas A & M College, College Station, Texas. (Courtesy Middleby-Marshall Oven Co., Morton Grove, Ill.)

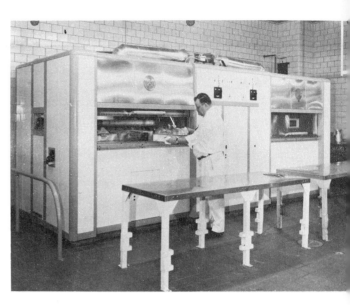

Rotary Oven at Maryland State Penitentiary—B-305. (Courtesy Middleby-Marshall Oven Co., Morton Grove, Illinois.)

"Compact" or Revolving Oven at Illinois Youth Center, Joliet, Illinois. (Courtesy Middleby-Marshall Oven Co., Morton Grove, Illinois.)

Friomat Continuous Automatic Fryer. (Courtesy Crescent Metal Products, Inc., Cleveland, Ohio.) (No. DCK-70-726)

DC-71-1020 Gas Tilt Fryer. (Courtesy Crescent Metal Products, Inc., Cleveland, Ohio.)

will yield one pound, 6 ounces more of cooked meat, and will produce jucier, more tender, better-flavored meat.

Because of the longer time required, some cooks have been reluctant to adopt low-temperature cooking methods. Not only is training required, but it is important the cafeteria supervisor check the temperatures at which meats are cooked.

"Delayed Cooking"

A new method, developed by Swift & Company, known as "Delayed Cooking" makes possible greatly reduced shrinkage with improved acceptability. Under this method a 20 pound rib roast can be browned satisfactorily in one and a half hours at 350° F., then held for three hours at 140° F., at which time the center will have reached the same temperature. The roast can be held at 140° up to 24 hours during which time acceptability is said to improve and it can be held for 48 hours without reduction of acceptability. It is stated that under this method the flavor, tenderness, and juiciness are enhanced. Shrinkage on a 20 pound rib roast is said to be held to 15 per cent, a low figure for dry heat cooking.

Delayed cooking can be applied to ham, turkey, and other meats, using the prescribed temperatures for the different products. It cannot be used with ground or chopped meats nor should meat once held in a 140° F. oven be removed and reheated.

A disadvantage of the delayed cooking method is the time taken and the oven space tied up. In some food services, however, the cooking is done at night at such low temperatures that basting is not needed. Thus the ovens are not tied up during the busy day periods.

Carry-Over Cooking

This is the cooking which continues in heavy foods after they have been removed from a cooking appliance.

For rare beef done to 140° F. using a 300° oven, the roast should be removed from the oven when the internal temperature reaches 130° F. The meat will continue to cook, however, until it reaches 140° F. For medium doneness, the internal temperature should finally read 160° F. and for well done 170° F. This applies to beef, veal, and lamb.

Pork should be roasted at 350° F. to an internal temperature of 185° F. so as to kill any trichinae (parasitic worms) which may be present and also to crisp the surface fat to make the product tasty.

COFFEE MAKING

Coffee is undoubtedly America's most popular beverage. On the other hand, it is probably the most abused. Astute restaurateurs have found that "a good cup of coffee" will bring repeat customers and build business. Yet the temptation to "water coffee," and the lack of training and carelessness on the part of employees responsible for coffee making often make it difficult for the patron to get a satisfactory cup of the beverage.

Coffee in the home is made in small quantities and consumed almost immediately. For mass-feeding operations, the coffee must have *body*, as well as flavor and aroma, so that it will be acceptable for drinking many minutes after it is brewed. Hotel and restaurant blends of coffee, used in institutional feeding, are designed to provide that body or keeping quality. To the green coffee beans from Brazil, which provide the bulk of our coffee, are added "milds" from the highlands of Columbia or Central America, or coffees from other parts of the world according to the roaster's formula.

Roasting brings out the flavor and aroma, and also plays an important part in coloration. The "heavier" the roast, in general, the darker will be the resulting brew. Racial backgrounds and regional differences govern color preferences. Some groups prefer heavily roasted dark coffee; others a lighter roast and color. New Yorkers prefer darker coffee than Bostonians. Most institutional coffee is given a medium roast.

Next comes the grinding. For vacuum coffee makers, known as "glass-maker," the fine grind is used. For urns, a less fine "regular" or "urn-grind" is appropriate. For paper filters, coarser or "steel-cut" grind is necessary. Special grinds are used in automatic coffee makers. Proper grinding requires that the knives of the grinder be kept constantly sharp. Otherwise the coffee will be bruised rather than cut. This allows the aroma to escape, and shortens the period of freshness. For this reason it is usually better to purchase **coffee ground** by the roaster who has the facilities for keeping the grinding knives in good condition. Grinders used in institutions are apt to lack proper care in this respect. Reputable roasters provide service at least weekly in most areas of the country, delivering ground coffee in specially-lined bags or containers within a short time after roasting and grinding.

Coffee for institutional purposes is generally made in an urn or a vacuum coffee maker. In the urn, the ground coffee is placed in a cloth or paper bag or metal container through which boiling water flows or is poured either by hand or automatically. The brew

Disposable Decanter (with replaceable Bowl features). (Courtesy Bloomfield Industries, Inc., Chicago, Ill.)

Bunn-Omatic Model OT. (Courtesy Bunn-O-Matic Corp., Springfield, Ill.)

Koffee-King® Automatic. (Courtesy Bloomfield Industries, Inc., Chicago, Ill.)

Five Warmer Unit, Model RT. (Courtesy Bunn-O-Matic Corp., Springfield, Ill.)

Koffee-King® Supreme Coffeemaker. (Courtesy Bloomfield Industries, Inc., Chicago, Ill.)

Bunn Pour-Omatic® Model VPR Brewer. Courtesy Bunn-O-Matic Corp., Springfield, Ill.)

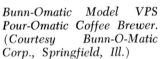

Bunn-Omatic Model VPS Pour-Omatic Coffee Brewer. (Courtesy Bunn-O-Matic Corp., Springfield, Ill.)

Step-Up Two Burner Coffee Range. (Courtesy Bloomfield Industries, Inc., Chicago, Ill.)

Bunn-Omatic® Model U3 Twin 3-Gallon Urn. (Courtesy Bunn-O-Matic Corp., Springfield, Ill.)

Silex Slim-Line Warmers. (Courtesy Bloomfield Industries, Inc., Chicago, Ill.)

Modular construction Filpax Vaculator. (Courtesy Vaculator Division, Hill-Shaw Co., Chicago, Ill.)

Cory Solid State Coffee Brewing System C701. (Courtesy Cory Corp., Chicago, Ill.)

Single unit Vaculator. (Courtesy Vaculator Division, Hill-Shaw Co., Chicago, Ill.)

Cory Solid State Coffee Brewing System C703. (Courtesy Cory Corp., Chicago. Ill.)

Filpax Vaculator automatic coffee brewer. (Courtesy Vaculator Division, Hill-Shaw Co., Chicago, Ill.)

Cory Solid State Coffee Brewing System C705. (Courtesy Cory Corp., Chicago, Ill.)

Papermatic Vaculator. (Courtesy Vaculator Division, Hill-Shaw Co., Chicago, Ill.)

Cory, Model C704, makes up to 300 cups per hour. (Courtesy Cory Corp., Chicago, Ill.)

Urn Measure. (Courtesy Bloomfield Industries, Inc., Chicago, Ill.)

Cory, Model CCR, Automatic Electric Creamer. (Courtesy Cory Corp., Chicago, Ill.)

drips down into a receptacle from which it may be drawn for serving. This receptacle (in the urn) is generally jacketed by hot water and should be kept at a uniform temperature (from 185° to 190° F.)

It is standard practice to use one pound of ground coffee to two or two and one-half gallons of water. Usually about one half of the brew is repoured back through the urn. This should not be done until after the urn bag containing the grounds is removed. An interval of ten minutes should be allowed for the coffee to "set" before being served.

In the vacuum coffee maker, holding from 10 to 12 cups or 1/2 gallon, the water is brought to a boil in the lower bowl, then it expands and ascends to the upper bowl containing the coffee. It is essential that the rubber gasket connecting the two bowls be air-tight, so that the vacuum formed in the lower bowl will draw the brew back through the cloth or metal filter when the heat is shut off. Coffee for glass makers is finely ground and prepackaged in quantities of $2\frac{1}{2}$, 2 2/3, 2 3/4, 3, or 4 ounces depending upon the quality of the coffee used and the strength of brew de-desired.

Good coffee results when the following steps are followed:

Brewing Urn Coffee

1. *Accurately measure* the ground coffee.
2. *Spread coffee evenly* on the filter to ensure uniform extraction.
3. *Use fresh boiling water.* Fresh water from the cold water line is essential. (As an illustration, the Ritz-Carlton Hotel of Boston, to be sure of fresh cold water, has had a special pipe connected with the city water main in the street so that the water used for coffee would not be warmed through contact with steampipes in the basement.) When water contains elements affecting its taste, filters should be used.
4. *Pour water in slow, circular motion.* Make sure you wet all the grounds evenly. Total exposure time should be completed within *from 4 to 6 minutes* when using urn or drip grind.
5. *Remove grounds immediately.* As soon as water has dripped through.
6. *Mix brew.* Draw off heavy coffee from bottom of batch and pour back into brew (after grounds have been removed) to assure uniform mixing.
7. *Hold coffee at 185° to 190° F.* Never allow it to boil!
8. *Serve fresh coffee.* Make coffee fresh at frequent intervals.

Brewing in a Vacuum Coffee Maker

1. *Make sure of accurate measurement.* Coffee for vacuum makers can be purchased in preportioned sealed packages or, if coffee is purchased in bulk, a dispensing machine can be used to give proper measure.
2. *Fill lower bowl* with cold, fresh water to water-level mark. If bowl is unmarked, leave at least an inch at top for expansion of water.
3. *Adjust clean filter* in upper bowl. If cloth filter is used, rinse in cold water and store in cold water.
4. *Put correct amount of coffee* in upper bowl.
5. *When water is boiling* briskly in lower bowl, set upper bowl on lower bowl. Be sure that gasket fits snugly to effect vacuum. If metal upper bowl is used, make sure that it contains no dents that will prevent proper sealing.
6. *Stir water in upper bowl 30 seconds.* Total exposure time *2 to 4 minutes* with fine or vacuum grind.
7. *Turn off heat.*
8. *Remove lower bowl.*
9. *Rinse upper bowl and filter.*

Daily Cleaning and Care of Urns

1. Always clean urn immediately after each use. Add small quantity of hot water, brush sides, and rinse with hot water until it runs clean. Urn is now ready for next batch.
2. At the end of each day clean and brush several times. Then rinse with hot water. Remove clean-out cap at end of coffee faucet (or take apart faucets which have no caps) and scrub pipe leading to center of urn. Scrub and rinse spigot with hot water. Rinse urn with hot water.
3. Place several gallons of fresh water in urn, and leave cover partly open until next use.
4. Always empty and rinse urn with boiling water before using again.

Semiweekly Cleaning of Urns

1. Be sure outer jacket is 3/4 full of water.
2. Turn on heat and fill urn jar 3/4 full of water; use only urn-cleaning compounds. Following manufacturer's directions, mix thoroughly and let stand about 30 minutes.
3. Clean gauge glasses, faucet pipe, plugs, etc., using long thin brush. Use urn-cleaning compound for scrubbing. Take faucet valve apart and clean thoroughly. Clean all tubes well.
4. Scrub inside and outside of cover with long handled brush.
5. Rinse inside of urn three or four times with hot water, scrubbing each time. Also rinse the parts well.

Touch 'n Brew Twin Automatic Undercounter Urn. (Courtesy S. Blickman, Inc., Weehawken, N. J.)

Mini-Brew Twin Automatic Urn—1973 Model. (Courtesy S. Blickman, Inc., Weehawken, N. J.)

Lo-Line Twin Urn—1973 Model. (Courtesy S. Blickman, Inc., Weehawken, N. J.)

1973 Touch 'n Brew Twin Automatic Urn with Built-in Agitation. (Courtesy S. Blickman, Inc., Weehawken, N. J.)

Lo-Line 600 series Single Urn. (Courtesy S. Blickman, Inc., Weehawkin, N. J.)

1973 Touch 'n Brew Single Automatic Urn with Built-In Agitation. (Courtesy S. Blickman, Inc., Weehawkin, N. J.)

Mini-Brew Single Automatic Urn, 1973 Model. (Courtesy S. Blickman, Inc., Weehawken, N. J.)

Repeat until all traces of foreign odor and cleaning solution are removed.

6. Leave a few gallons of fresh water in urn with cover partly open until next use. If cold water is used, allow urn to cool to prevent cracking liner.

7. If urn baskets are used, they should be scoured with scouring powder or stiff brush and urn cleaner. Rinse thoroughly and let dry. *Never* use steel wool. Spray heads on automatic urns should be checked to see that all holes are open. If any are clogged, use stiff wire to open. Coffee dealers usually supply urn bags, urn cleaner, and the necessary brushes to their institutional customers.

GENERAL HINTS ON COFFEE MAKING

1. *Coffee.* A good blend of coffee of uniform quality with requisite flavor, strength, and aroma should be used. Care should be taken in storage so that ground coffee is used on a "first-in first-out" basis. Store ground coffee in a cool, dry place. Heat and moisture cause rapid deterioration. Coffee picks up outside odors quickly.

2. Use the proper grind for the coffee maker. Too fine a grind for the equipment used is the chief cause of bitter and astringent coffee. Too coarse a grind produces weak, flavorless coffee.

3. Make sure that the urn bag does not come in contact with the brew. Several devices are on the market to prevent this. One is a collar that raises the urn ring. Another is a riser coffee basket with metal grids on which the urn bag rests. Some urns are equipped with metal baskets with which filter paper is used. With these a coarse grind of coffee such as "steel-cut" should be used. Exposure time should be from 6 to 8 minutes, at the maximum, for such filters.

4. Rinse urn with boiling water after each batch to remove the film of old coffee that coats all exposed surfaces, thus preventing it from affecting the next brew.

5. Rinse urn bags and cloth filters in hot water to remove old coffee deposits. Do not use soaps, bleaches, or detergents as they will affect the flavor of subsequent brews.

6. Store cloth filters in cold water when not in use to prevent sourness, rancidity, or the picking up of food odors. Replace urn bags at least once each week. Use the correct size urn bag. If the bag is too large, it may hang in the brew and cause the coffee to lie in a ball rather than in an even layer. This interferes with proper extraction.

7. With vacuum makers do not set upper bowl on the lower bowl until water in latter is boiling. Doing so may start the water into the upper bowl before it is hot enough to brew good coffee.

8. *Proportion.* Research by the coffee industry indicates that the ideal proportion is two gallons of water per pound of coffee. Many food services use 2 1/2 gallons per pound. During the rise in coffee prices a few years ago, many operators succumbed to the temptation to increase the water content and in some instances 3, 3 1/2 or even 4 gallons of water were used per pound of coffee. Actually the difference in cost per cup between using 2 1/2 and 4 gallons of water, at current coffee prices, for, say, 4 1/2 ounces of coffee in a 6 ounce cup, is less than one-half cent for the coffee alone. It is "penny-wise and pound-foolish" to risk dissatisfaction and loss of patronage to gain so little.

9. *Temperatures.* In the coffee maker the coffee should be kept at a temperature of from 185° to 190° F. and should not be allowed to reach the boiling point. When served it should be at 165° F.

10. *Frequent Batches.* Coffee should not remain too long in the coffee maker. It is preferable to make more fequent batches.

11. *Exposure or Brewing Times.* When the boiling water contacts the ground coffee in the coffee maker, it first extracts the oils and solids which produce body aroma and flavor. If allowed to drain too long, or if the brew is poured back through the grounds, astringent materials are extracted which give coffee a bitter flavor. Although previously stated it is well to repeat the following:

Maximum Exposure Times

Vacuum makers	2 to 4 minutes
Urns or drip makers	4 to 6 minutes
Paper filters	6 to 8 minutes

12. *Cream.* The quality of the cream has much to do with the quality of the coffee. In order to reduce costs so that coffee with cream can be sold at a low price, some cafeterias use a mixture of homogenized milk and canned evaporated milk. However, a good grade of coffee cream (at least 18% to 22% butter fat) will make the most satisfactory cup of coffee with cream.

Automatic Coffee Makers

New types of automatic coffee urns are now on the market. These claim economical use of coffee through greater extraction, uniformity, and labor-saving advantage.

SOLUBLE COFFEE

Tremendous gains have been noted within recent years in consumer acceptance of soluble or "instant" coffee. Although manufacturing methods vary in detail, the process of producing soluble coffee is essentially that of brewing coffee in strong solution under controlled conditions, and then evaporating it.

In may areas of the United States and Canada instant coffee is used in a large proportion of households. Since the introduction of "hotel and restaurant" blends of instant coffee in 1953, soluble coffee has become widely used in industrial and institutional food services. In addition to the speed and convenience with which it can be prepared, the following advantages have been cited:

1. *Uniformity.* It requires little training on the part of employees to produce a consistent brew.

2. *Economy.* Although comparable in first cost to ground coffee, it affords a food-cost saving of approximately 10 per cent, in that there is no loss of brew absorbed in the grounds. Use of soluble coffee also eliminates the necessity for urn bags, filters, and expensive coffee-making equipment.

3. *Labor-Saving.* Coffee preparation time is said to be reduced by 75 per cent. In addition, labor required for disposing of coffee grounds and cleaning of equipment is eliminated.

How to Use Soluble Coffee

In using instant coffee, care must be taken to keep the brew hot. Boiling water should be used in making instant coffee, and the brew should be kept at or slightly above 180° F. until served. Manufacturers' directions as to quantity should be carefully followed.

Machines are now available in which soluble coffee is dispensed and hot water added when the brew is drawn off either for cup service or in serving decanters. These are in use in a number of institutional cafeterias where patrons serve themselves by merely pushing a button.

For making iced coffee, instant hotel and restaurant blends of soluble coffee are said to be superior to ground coffee in many respects. New blends of instant coffee are now on the market which are said to give off the full-bodied aroma of ground coffee.

Instant coffee for industrial and institutional use is packed in metal foil envelopes and will keep indefinitely. These envelopes are available in one cup, twelve-cup (1/2 gallon or glass coffee-maker bowl size) and fifty cup (2 1/2 gallon or urn-size) quantities.

Many food services use the small envelopes to supplement regular coffee service during periods when volume is low. This saves making up a larger amount and helps reduce food cost. In hospitals and similar institutions, the one-cup envelopes are useful in providing coffee for night nurses and employees, and for individual service to patients after the kitchen is closed. The new Freeze-Dry soluble coffee for institutional use comes in 4 ounce and 8 ounce bags.

TEA

Tea has always been a popular beverage in North America, even from the early colonial days predating the "Boston Tea Party." Years ago while making canoe trips in the Quetico Forest of Western Ontario, the author found tea the indispensable beverage of the woodsmen, forest rangers, and other voyagers in the North Woods. Occupying little bulk and light in weight, a pot of tea was easily brewed over an open fire. After a hard day of paddling and carries over the portages, a pot of hot tea proved to be a great restorative. Even the "timber-cruisers," who spent their days in the forests, carried only tea, never coffee. Although these rough and ready stalwarts turned to whiskey on their infrequent visits to town, tea was their mainstay while in the woods.

As in all parts of the British Commonwealth, tea is widely used in Canada, although the preference seems to be for a darker and stronger brew than that used in the United States.

Chinese restaurants have popularized the use of tea as a beverage. In the Southern states, iced tea is popular throughout the year, whereas in the Northern States, it is served only during warm weather.

Individual tea bags with or without tags, usually weighing 200 to the pound, are popular in institutional services. In making tea, it is essential that water be at or close to the boiling point when it is poured over the tea bag, that the teapot or teacup be hot, and that the tea be allowed to steep no longer than three or five minutes. Oversteeping extracts the tannic acid and produces a bitter taste.

Iced Tea

Iced tea for institutional use is usually prepared with one-ounce tea bags immersed in water which has been brought to the boiling point, in the proportion of two 1 oz. bags to a gallon of water. It should steep the required three or five minutes, and then be poured over a glass filled with ice cubes. Where this is not practicable in large scale production, the tea is precooled, and ice added to the glasses when serving. Because of the diluting effect of the ice, iced tea is prepared in stronger solution than for the hot beverage, usually at double strength.

HOT CHOCOLATE

Hot chocolate or cocoa is served in many institutions, particularly in schools for children, in place of coffee. It is also popular with adults, as sales in dinettes indicate. Many institutions use a hot chocolate mix containing cocoa, powdered milk, and sugar. This may be obtained in individual envelopes (making one-cup), in 2 lb. bags (one gallon), or in 25, 50, or 100 lb. drums for quantity use.

POULTRY COOKERY

Young chickens from 1 1/2 to 3 1/2 pounds can be fried in deep fat at 350° F. for about 15 minutes or they can be roasted. Under either method, a temperature of 185° F. should be reached all the way to the bone. Older and tougher birds should be simmered, steamed, or stewed.

Turkeys should be roasted at 300 to 350° F. with the back up, as many of the fat glands are in the back and in this position the fat melts and flows over the bird, basting it during the roasting period. For sandwiches, many food services boil turkeys so as to reduce shrinkage and thus increase the percentage of usable meat.

FISH COOKERY

Methods of preparation and cooking of fish depend upon the structure, shape, texture, and other qualities of the different varieties. As most fish have little connective tissue they require short cooking times.

Fat content helps determine the cooking method best suited to a given species of fish. Lean fish do not usually lend themselves to dry heat cooking methods unless a fat or moistening agent is added. Fish that are high in fat are best broiled or baked so that the excess oil is extracted. Moist heat cooking is used for nearly all varieties of fish, not for tenderizing but to provide variety. Excessive cooking of any kind will toughen and tend to disintegrate fish.

Fish are often baked in a sauce or small quantity of liquid to prevent drying. Baking is frequently combined with other methods, such as steaming, to produce "au gratin" dishes. "Gratin," meaning crusted, refers to food covered with a sauce, ordinarily cheese, sprinkled with crumbs and browned.

Broiling is well suited to fatty fishes but it is also used with lean where the fat is brushed on before broiling. Fish can be floured, crumbed, or plain, but should always be buttered or preferably oiled before broiling. Butter burns quickly under the intense heat of the broiler. Shellfish are often dipped in a batter then breaded before cooking.

VEGETABLE COOKERY

Vegetables are valuable in the maintenance of alkaline reserves in the body, for the vitamins and minerals they contain, and for their bulk and laxative properties. As their generally low food cost helps offset the higher cost items, vegetables should be presented attractively on the menu.

Cooking changes the flavor, breaks down the cellulose, and reduces the water content of vegetables. It should also improve their digestibility, flavor, and appeal. Overcooking decomposes vegetables, destroys their flavor, and impairs their appearance. This is particularly true of sulphurous vegetables such as broccoli, brussels sprouts, cauliflower, cabbage, and turnips. Overcooking of green vegetables such as peas, string beans, and leaf greens causes discoloration and loss of vitamins and other nutrients.

The modern trend is toward cooking vegetables in small quantities at frequent intervals. In many food services frozen vegetables in 2 1/2 pound containers are reheated in steam pressure cookers as needed.

EGG COOKERY

Eggs are a complete protein food and also contain important vitamins. Egg yolks are high in fat and iron. They are excellent meat substitutes for luncheon and dinner in addition to their popularity as breakfast items. They are also low in food cost.

In addition to table service, eggs are useful in other ways: as a clarifying agent such as in consommés; a binder in meat loaves and breadings; as an emulsifying agent in mayonnaise; as a thickening agent in custards; and as a leavening for cakes.

Eggs should never be boiled; rather they should be soft-cooked in the shell by simmering in water between 185° and 195° F. The timing for soft cooked eggs should be 3 to 5 minutes; for medium cooked, 7 to 8 minutes; and for hard cooked, about 15 minutes. After they are cooked they should be plunged into cold water to stop the cooking and to prevent formation of a green ring around the outside of the yolk, which results from the combination of the sulphur in the white with the iron in the yolk.

Egg shells are porous and despite cleaning processes dirt and fecal matter from the nests may find their way under the shell. While the egg itself is protected by the thin membrane under the shell, the shells should not be used in cooking processes. Cooking removes the danger of infection from the egg itself.

While white-shelled eggs are preferred over brown-shelled eggs in some areas and vice versa, research has proved that the color of the shell has no bearing upon the quality or nutritive value of the egg within.

The most popular methods of egg cookery are simmering (not boiling), poaching, frying, country style, and as omelets. Cooking times and temperatures will vary according to the size and number of the eggs, their temperatures, and the water temperature. Simmering temperatures should be checked with a thermometer.

SOUP COOKERY

Soups may be classified as (1) *Clear,* including broths, bouillons, consommés and vegetable soup; (2) *Thick,* such as cream soups, purées, chowders and bisques; and (3) *Special and national,* both clear and thick, such as Minestrone (Italian); Olla Podrida (Spanish); Oxtail, (English); Scotch Broth (Scottish); Pot au Feu (French), and many others.

In the past, soups were made from *soup stocks,* the liquids in which meat or meat bones, fish or fish bones, or vegetable tops and cuttings are simmered to extract their flavors and essences. As few food services do their own butchering today they do not have the bones to make the stock and the stock pot has fallen into disuse. To take its place, many restaurants and institutional food services make use of manufactured *soup bases,* which are made from rendered complete stock with seasonings, in either paste or granular form. Canned and dehydrated soups are also used in many food services.

SAUCE COOKERY

European chefs are famous for their sauces which enhance, but do not smother, the flavors of food. As a base for sauces, gravies, and soups they prepare a thickening agent known as roux (pronounced roo) made from bread flour and a fat, such as butter, margarine, shortening, chicken fat, oil, or rendered meat drippings. When cooked just enough to dissipate the taste of the raw starch it becomes white or pale roux and is used in white sauces. When cooked longer so that it becomes brown in color it is known as brown roux and is used in brown sauces.

Thickening agents other than roux are used such as cornstarch, oatmeal, rice, and products like raw potatoes in puree soups. *Buerre manie,* (pronounced burr mah nee) is made by mixing 4 oz. of softened butter with 3 oz. of sifted flour and kneading until well combined. It is then used for thickening sauces by pinching off pea-sized balls and dropping them into the sauce when it is near the boiling point, and mixing them smooth.

Sauces may be warm or cold. The warm sauces, which comprise the largest number, are derived from five basic "mother sauces." These are:

1. *Espagñole (Spanish) or brown sauce:* Made from onions, celery, carrots, butter, flour and a brown roux and used in various meat and poultry dishes.
2. *Bèchamel or cream sauce:* Pronounced (bay shah-mel). Originally prepared from veal stock, the term is now applied to cream sauce. It is made from milk and/or cream with white roux and is used with vegetables and cream dishes.
3. *Tomato sauce:* Prepared from tomato products, stock, seasonings, and roux. It is used with many meat, poultry, fish, vegetable, and pasta dishes.
4. *Velouté sauce:* (Pronounced va-lou-tay) Made from either chicken or fish stock with a light roux. Used with the product (chicken or fish) from which it is made.
5. *Hollandaise sauce:* A yellow sauce made from egg yolk, butter, lemon juice, and "gastric" (a mixture of white wine or vinegar, crushed pepper, shallots, and spices). It is used with fish, vegetables, and eggs. Because of its egg and butter content it should not be subjected to high temperatures. Since it provides an excellent host for bacteria, it should not be held over from one meal to another.

DEEP FRYING

Foods may be deep-fried in oils, compounds, vegetable shortenings, lard, or rendered meat fat. Most deep frying in food services is done with hydrogenated vegetable fats. The primary object, regardless of the medium used, is to provide fast heat transfer, to impart a crisp surface, and to enhance the flavor of the product.

Foods to be fried are usually dipped in a batter and/or breaded. The sudden contact with the hot fat changes the coating into a protective crust. The fat must be hot enough to develop this protective coating or the product will become saturated with fat and loose particles of food may fall into the fat and burn, thus increasing the rate of its decomposition.

Hydrogenated vegetable shortenings do not break down as readily as other fats. They also have a higher "smoke point" (i.e., the temperature at which fats begin to smoke).

INFRARED COOKING

Infrared rays are a form of radiation which are a little longer than the light waves which are seen as red and shorter than radio waves or microwaves. Their

Market Forge Modular Deep Fat Fryer, Gas Operated. (Courtesy Market Forge, Everett, Mass.)

Saucier-Mat, for sauce and gravy production. (Courtesy Crescent Metal Products, Inc., Cleveland, Ohio.)

wave lengths are expressed in "microns" (millionths of an inch).

Broilers using dry heat are excellent for cooking fish, meat, and other tender items. Some of the heat is carried to the food by convection, the rest by radiation in the form of infrared rays. Infrared waves from 1.4 to 5 microns in length are most effective in cooking food as they pass through the water vapors created around food when it is heated.

The amount of energy which reaches food from an infrared source varies geometrically with the distance from the source. Thus a steak placed 2 inches from the heat source will cook four times as fast as if it were placed 4 inches away.

Infrared energy may be produced in either gas or electric appliances. A recent invention, the gas-fired "Ultra-Ray" broiler, produces almost 100 per cent infrared radiation. It consists of three layers of Incaloy metal screens sandwiched together. Air and gas pass readily through the screens and produce a blanket of flame about 3/8" thick. Temperatures vary from 1150° to about 1,500° F. The device reaches maximum capacity within 6 seconds.

Infrared lamps are also used to keep food hot and to give it color on the buffet table or cafeteria counter. Infrared lamps transmit heat instantaneously to the food exposed to them and make the food appear more red or brown in color.

MICROWAVE COOKING

Microwave energy is a type of high-frequency radio energy similar to that which carries radio and television programs from a broadcasting station to the receiver. The energy coming from a broadcasting station may, for example, vibrate 550,000 times in a second, while the microwave energy used in cooking will vibrate almost *two and one-half million times per sec-*

ond. It is this difference in frequency which gives microwave energy its peculiar characteristics.

Microwave heating grew out of the production of the first successful radar set just before the beginning of World War II. Radar sets produce microwave energy, send it out as a searching beam, and pick it up as it bounces back with target information.

The development of the "magnetron," a type of tube which produces microwave energy in practical quantities, was the invention which made radar possible. Following the war, the advent of new types of these tubes, particularly the continuous-wave magnetron, opened the door to microwave heating.

When microwave energy comes into contact with a substance, any one, or a combination of three things can happen (see Figure 8.1).

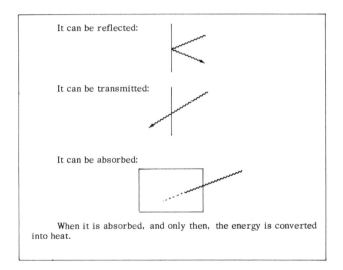

Fig. 8.1. Microwave energy. (Courtesy Raytheon Mfg. Co., Lexington, Mass.)

Whether a substance reflects, transmits, or absorbs microwave energy depends upon its molecular structure. Raw, precooked, refrigerated, or frozen foods and water *absorb* the microwave energy and become hot. Air, and many (but not all) glass, china, and paper products *transmit the energy.* In these cases, since there is no absorption, there is no heating. Metal, on the other hand, *reflects* the microwaves, and again, since there is no absorption, remains cool. The net result is the opportunity to cook or heat food in an oven and on utensils which remain at room temperature, except for such heat as they may pick up from the food being processed.

Many plastic utensils have been used to advantage in microwave cooking. On the other hand, some plastic materials absorb heat and give off objectionable odors and tastes as they become excessively hot. A simple test is to place the given plastic vessel in the oven (along with a glass of water to protect the magnetrons if the utensil does not absorb the energy) for about one minute. If the utensil remains cool, it has not absorbed the energy, and vice versa.

The magnetron produces energy at a fixed rate, according to its size, between 800 and 2,000 watts. Thus if one item requires, say, 3 minutes to cook, two items of the same size would require 6 minutes. For this reason the microwave oven of the usual size is not useful as a heavy production appliance but is used primarily to cook food to order, to defrost small items, and to reheat foods quickly. In most food service kitchens the microwave oven performs an important function as a supporting piece of equipment.

Because of their water content, most foods do not become hotter than 212° F. in the microwave oven.

Litton Menumaster Systems Microwave Oven (70-50) for high volume, heavy duty applications in schools, hospitals and industrial cafeterias. (Courtesy Atherton Division, Litton Industries, Minneapolis, Minn.)

Hobart Microwave Oven. (Courtesy Hobart Mfg. Co., Troy, Ohio.)

7200 Microwave Oven. (Courtesy Market Forge, Everett, Mass.)

One advantage of the microwave oven is that no wild heat is given off. All of the microwaves are contained within the oven and no heat escapes outside. In this respect, the microwave oven is highly efficient.

Since heat is applied within as well as on the surface of the food in a microwave oven, control of cooking times is more important than with other cooking devices. This is done usually automatically by timer mechanisms on the oven.

Microwave Energy Heats Quickly

It is fascinating to watch food items being cooked in a matter of *seconds* in a microwave oven—a process which would take many *minutes* under conventional cooking methods. The table shown in Figure 8.2 gives microwave cooking times for various well-known items.

While the microwave oven is an excellent device for heating food portions rapidly, some food technologists feel that as a prime cooker, the intense heat it gives off tends to toughen proteins, especially those in seafoods.

Surface browning thus is delayed or does not take place with small food items. If a piece of meat is large enough, browning will take place. When a brown, crusted surface is required, for example, as on meats, it can be achieved by browning the meat in a conventional broiler, either before or after cooking it in the microwave oven.

SALAD MAKING

A salad is any cold dish of meat, poultry, seafood, fruit, vegetables, or dairy products, served singly or in combination, as a rule with some type of dressing. Salads are usually prepared in a department of the kitchen sometimes called the "salad pantry," where they are plated, ready for service. They are then refrigerated until needed.

		Typical Processing Times					
Process	Quantity	Item	Time	Process	Quantity	Item	Time
Roasting	1	Beef, standing rib, 22 lbs.	45 min.	Reheating	1	6 oz. slice roast beef	25 sec.
Roasting	1	Beef, boned and rolled, 9 lbs.	20 min.	Reheating	1	8 oz. casserole	1 min.
Roasting	1	3 lb. chicken	9 min.	Reheating	1	#10 can green beans	6 min.
Cooking	1	5 oz. fish fillet	30 sec.	Reheating		4 lbs. mashed potatoes	4 min.
Cooking	15	5 oz. fish fillets	6 min.	Reheating	1	8 oz. baked potato	40 sec.
Cooking	1	1 lb. lobster	3 min.	Reheating	1	Apple pie (six portions)	50 sec.
Cooking	1	6 oz. baked potato	2 min.	Reheating	14	1 oz. Swedish meat balls	1 1/2 min.
Cooking	12	6 oz. baked potatoes	15 min.	Reheating		1 portion spaghetti	15 sec.
Cooking	2	Scrambled eggs	30 sec.	Reheating	1	4 oz. portion meat loaf	30 sec.
Cooking	1	Western sandwich	30 sec.	Reheating	1	3 oz. slice ready cooked ham	20 sec.
Cooking	12	5 oz. baked apples	4 min.	Defrosting	2	3 oz. lamb chops	20 sec.
Cooking		1 lb. link sausages	4 min.	Defrosting	1	Commercial pack fresh frozen green peas	2 min.
Cooking		1 lb. bacon	4 min.				

All reheating is based on an initial temperature of 40° F.

Fig. 8.2. Microwave cooking times. (Courtesy Raytheon Mfg. Co. Lexington, Mass.)

Salads add variety and color to the meal and allow the salad maker to express artistic and creative ability. They add essential nutrients to the diet and as they are low in calories will appeal to the "weight-watchers." They can also be sold profitably.

Four types of salads are generally offered:

1. *Appetizers:* These include shrimp, lobster, and crabmeat cocktails; fruits; pickled herring and chopped chicken livers. Such salads should be light so as to stimulate, rather than to satisfy the appetite.

2. *Accompaniments:* These include mixed green or chef's salads, hearts of lettuce, pear and cottage cheese, and pickled beets. These are served as side dishes with the dinner, in moderate portions. Such salads should contrast with the accompanying food and preferably not be so sweet as to jade the appetite.

3. *Main course salads:* These constitute the whole meal, such as various combinations of meat, poultry, seafood, fruits, vegetables, dairy, gelatin, or macaroni products. Examples are chicken salad with celery and pineapple; fruit salad; tomato stuffed with tuna salad; and stuffed green peppers.

4. *Dessert salads:* These include various flavored gelatin molds, aspics, and mousses. They are often sweet in flavor and composed of fruits, nuts, dairy products, and gelatins.

Salads should be kept chilled until ready for service. Dressings should not be added until just before service; if they are, the salad may become limp.

RECIPES OR FORMULAS

In a restaurant where fancy dishes are prepared to order, as in a large hotel, the individuality of the chef plays a prominent part.

For most food services, however, the important factors are quality and uniformity of food and speed of service. To insure uniform quality, it is well to establish a definite recipe or formula for each dish, and to insist that this formula be followed day by day. If changes or improvements are to be made, they should, if approved, be incorporated on the written formula record.

The rigid adherence to written formulas is important not only from the standpoint of uniformity but also from a cost standpoint. Cost records are based on the ingredients and quantities set forth in the formula, and any change in a formula has its consequent effect on cost. A form of formula or recipe card is shown in Figure 8.3.

Cooking is essentially a manufacturing process in which raw material is processed into finished goods ready for delivery to the customer. In any manufacturing process formulas are carefully followed. There is no reason why the same method should not apply in the kitchen.

Formula or Recipe Cards

Formulas are recorded in many forms including on cards for files or visible record holders (usually 4 x 6 inches or larger), loose-leaf sheets (various sizes), and in ordinary notebooks. There should be a master file of formulas for the person in charge of the kitchen —covering kitchen, bakery, salad preparation, and other departments if any. A card or visible record file is preferred for this purpose. For use of cooks, bakers, and salad people a loose-leaf book which can be referred to in the work area is desirable. Either of these affords an opportunity for inserting additional formulas and for keeping the formulas in alphabetical order for ready reference.

In the midst of a busy morning's work, the cook may hesitate to consult the recipe file lest he soil it with greasy hands. In Pope's Cafeterias in St. Louis, mimeographed copies of the day's recipes are provided so that each employee responsible for food production will have the recipes at hand when he needs to refer to them.

Formulas can be combined with other records for handy reference. For example, under some systems they are recorded on the reverse side of the food cost card. In Figure 8.3 is shown a formula for fish chowder, together with the serving instructions.

In making up a formula or recipe card, the heading should show the item, the yield in quantity, the

---

FISH CHOWDER

Yield: 6 gallons; 100 portions.   Portion: 8 ounces.

Ingredients	Quantities or Weights	Service Instructions
Salt pork: diced	1 lb. 8 oz.	Use two #10 dippers filling 10 ounce bowl to line. Make sure fish and potatoes are about equal in amount. Stir container frequently while serving so that solids do not concentrate on bottom.
Onions: sliced	2 lbs.	
Potatoes: diced	6 lbs. 8 oz.	
Water: at boil	2 1/4 gal.	
Haddock: skinned and boned	15 lbs.	
Milk: homogenized	2 gal.	
Salt	4 oz.	
Pepper	1 1/2 tspns.	

Steps:

1. Fry salt pork until crisp. Remove from fat and drain.
2. Fry onions in pork fat until browned. Add onions and potatoes to water. Bring to boil. Cook about 10 minutes.
3. Add fish and cook until fish breaks up in pieces.
4. Stir in salt, pepper and milk. Simmer 15 minutes.
5. Add pork pieces before serving.
6. Note: if haddock is running soft use cusk if obtainable.

Fig. 8.3. Formula for fish chowder.

number of portions, and the standard portion size. Next the ingredients are listed, preferably in the order that they are processed. Finally, the steps in the process are listed in order, with specific key points such as cooking times, etc., noted.

Tables of weights and measures and equivalents are also useful in connection with the preparation of formulas. These are given in detail in most good cookbooks.

ORDERING OF FOOD TO BE COOKED

An estimate must be made each day of the quantity of food to be prepared and cooked. In small food services, this is done on an informal basis—as the chef, by scanning the menu and referring to quantities sold or used on previous occasions, can readily estimate the quantity to be prepared. In larger food services, careful forecasts based on previous sales records must be made, and formal orders prepared and given to the cooks. This is sometimes noted on the typed or mimeographed menu sheets.

The great fear of the average cook is that he will be "caught short," that is, not have enough food cooked for a given meal. As a result he is tempted to overproduce. If more food is cooked than sold, it must be utilized at a later date or thrown into the garbage. Even if the cook is imaginative and resourceful and uses up leftover food, it must be remembered that this food carries a double labor cost.

The modern trend is to eliminate leftovers by accurately forecasting the amount to be produced for a given meal period. This is not easy in view of the many variables such as changing customer preferences, vagaries of the weather, and the pulling power of one menu item against another.

It is far better to run short of an item toward the close of a meal than to run over. Preparing food in smaller quantities at frequent intervals is also helpful in keeping down leftovers. The use of partially-cooked items, such as French fries ready-blanched, chicken pies frozen or partially baked, or other frozen entrées which can be quickly reheated, provides reserve foods which can be utilized when menu items run out.

In hospitals and similar institutions where there are selective menus and where the number of patients on regular diets may vary considerably from day to day, careful computation is usually made. Menu sheets filled out by the patients are separated into breakfast, luncheon, and dinner selections, and the selections tabulated. Often this tallying is done on a denominator or similar counting machine.

Two order sheets are generally prepared, one for hot foods, known as the "hot sheet," and one for cold foods, the "cold sheet." On these sheets the totals are entered from the different patient floors and wards, and an estimate made of food required for the cafeterias and dining rooms. These are totalled and a copy of the hot sheet given to the kitchen supervisor or the chef. The cold sheet goes to the supervisor in charge of salad preparation.

At the J. Hillis Miller Health Center of the University of Florida at Gainesville, experiments have been successfully conducted in the application of data-processing machines to the daily tabulation of patients' diets. Some 380 patients are fed in the Center hospital and 65 per cent are on therapeutic diets. About one-third of these change each day. As there are 47 different selective diets, it can be seen that the number of variables is considerable and that the use of the computer saves much time and effort.

THE KITCHEN A PRODUCTION CENTER

The kitchen is the production center of the food service. In recent years the trend has been to reduce the tasks of the production department by the use of prepared or precooked foods. Some restaurateurs believe that the day will come when all preparation of the food may be done outside. This, they feel, will enable the food service to concentrate, to its profit, upon the service function.

Effective management of the kitchen or production department entails definite scheduling of the food to be cooked to make sure that all needed items are actually produced. This is done by means of a *production schedule,* which is discussed in Chapter 13.

This is also important from the standpoint of labor utilization, also explained in Chapter 13.

The Kitchen Manager or Chef

Upon the kitchen manager, chef, head cook, or whoever is in charge of the kitchen, will fall the responsibility for the success or failure of the food preparation and cooking. While it is essential to have an individual who has had experience in quantity cookery and mass-feeding, it is even more important that the one in charge of the kitchen have executive ability.

He or she must be able to weld the kitchen employees into a smoothly working unit, and to cooperate with other members of the staff. The kitchen head should also be cost conscious with respect to both food control and the utilization of labor. While cooks do not always possess all of these qualifications at the start, much can be done through proper training to develop latent talents along these lines.

Charles L. Banino of the Ritz Carlton Hotel, Boston, one of the nation's outstanding chefs, with his assistants demonstrates fine points of the culinary art to members of the author's Boston University class in Food-Service Management, in the hotel kitchen.

TOOLS AND UTENSILS

Having the right tools and utensils is essential to good food preparation and cooking. To the chef, his knives are important. A good cook purchases his own set of knives, keeps them sharpened and takes care of them. A check list of knives and other tools and utensils used in cooking is shown in Figure 8.4.

Measuring devices of various kinds are used in cooking. These include:

Measures: Round lipped, graduated containers with side handles in pint, quart, half-gallon, and gallon sizes. One gallon *coffee measures* are used in repouring brew for mixing coffee in urns.

Measuring cups: Small, accurately graduated cups holding 1/2 pint.

Measuring spoons: Set, usually five, calibrated spoons, linked together, accurately measuring 1/8, 1/4, 1/2 and 1 teaspoon and 1 tablespoon.

Scoops or dippers: Of accurate capacity, often with rotating member for emptying, used to measure and shape contents. Sizes are shown in Figure 8.5.

SUGGESTED READING

AMENDOLA, JOSEPH, and BERRINI, JAMES M. *Practical Cooking and Baking for Schools and Institutions.* New York: Ahrens Publishing Company, 1971.

BUREAU OF SUPPLIES AND ACCOUNTS. *The Cook Book of the U.S. Navy.* Washington, D. C.: U.S. Government Printing Office, 1949. (Free)

CULINARY INSTITUTE OF AMERICA. "The Professional Chef," *Institutions Magazine,* Chicago, Ill., 1962.

HART, CONSTANCE C. *Recipes for School, Institutional, and Commercial Food Services.* New York: Appleton-Century-Crofts, Inc., 1942.

A Check List of Tools and Utensils Used in Cooking

Knives Most Commonly Used:

French knife, with wide curving and pointed blade, usually 12" long. Used for slicing, chopping and mincing.

Roast beef slicer, with long 14" blade that will slice completely across the roast.

Chef's slicer: 12" long with pointed blade to dissect around bones or to slice cooked meats.

Butcher knife: Heavy bladed and pointed, used in sectioning raw meat or to chop through small bones or cartilage.

Steak knife or scimitar: A curved, pointed blade knife used in making accurate cuts of meat.

Boning knife: A short, 6" bladed knife used in filleting fish or separating meat from the bone.

Fruit or salad knife: A short 6" knife in various shapes used for preparation of salad fruits and vegetables.

Paring knife: With very short (2 1/2" to 3 1/2") blade for paring fruits and vegetables.

Cleaver: Heavy, square-nosed knife used to chop through bones and cartilage.

Other knives include pie and cake knife, oyster knife, clam knife, spatulas, and pancake or meat turners.

Pots and Pans

Stock pots: Large, round, high-walled pots with loop handles, for boiling and simmering. May have draw-off valve or strainer. Sizes: 2 1/2 to 40 gallon capacity. (Steam kettles are usually used for this purpose.)

Sauce pots: Large, round pots of medium depth with loop handles. Used for stove-top cooking where stirring or whipping is required. From 8 1/2 to 80 quarts.

Braziers: Large, heavy, shallow-walled pots with loop handles. For searing, braising and stewing. Sizes: 12 to 28 quarts.

Sauce pans: Small, shallow pans with single long handle and cover. For range-top cooking of smaller quantities. From 3" to 6" deep, 1 1/2 to 11 1/2 quart capacity.

Sauté pans: Large, round, shallow, heavy, straight-walled pans with long handles. (Larger sizes have loop handles.) For sautéing or shallow-fat cooking. Sizes: 2 1/2" to 4" deep and from 10" to 20" inside diameter.

Sautoirs: Smaller, round, shallow pans with sloping sides for quick frying with small amounts of fat. One long handle. Inside bottom diameter, 5" to 11".

Skillets: Heavy iron pans for frying or pan-broiling. Various sizes.

Frying pans: For light frying. In various sizes.

Double boilers: In two sections with water in bottom section and food in upper covered section. For cooking foods that may be scorched by direct contact. Upper section from 4 to 40 quart capacity.

Roasting pans: Large, rectangular, medium-walled pans. Sizes to fit range or roasting ovens. With or without covers.

Bake pans: Large, rectangular, shallow pans without covers. Various sizes to fit ovens.

Sheet pans: Rectangular, shallow (1") pans of various sizes used for baking.

Counter or service pans: Shallow, wide-rimmed pans designed to fit a standard steam table opening. Usually 12" X 20", but may be 1/2, 1/3, 1/4 or 1/8 sizes as inserts with adapters. Usual depth, about 2 1/2".

Strainers and Sieves

Strainers: Various sized perforated metal bowls with long handle and hook for hanging across pot. Used for draining and straining.

Colanders: Perforated metal bowls with feet and loop handles for draining salad ingredients after washing, etc.

China caps: Perforated metal strainers with round tops tapering to points, like inverted cones, with long handles and hooks. Used to strain semisolids which are forced through perforations with wooden roller.

Sieves: Round metal frames with mesh bottoms of various gauges. Used to sift dry ingredients like flour, and in making tests of canned goods.

Other Utensils include scoops, whips, spoons, tongs, pie and cake markers, dough cutters, wooden paddles, skimmers, brushes, block scrapers and pot hooks.

Measuring Spoons: Set, usually five, calibrated spoons, linked together, accurately measuring 1/8, 1/4, 1/2 and 1 teaspoon and 1 tablespoon.

Scoops or Dippers: Of accurate capacity, often with rotating member for emptying, used to measure and shape contents. Sizes are shown in Figure 8.5.

Ladles: Metal cups of known capacity on long handles with hooks at end. Used to measure and also to dip, stir or mix.

Meat Thermometers: For measuring interior temperatures of meats being cooked.

Fig. 8.4. Check list of tools and equipment used in cooking.

Scoop Sizes		
Number	Capacity	Approximate Weight
30	2 tablespoons	1 to 1 1/4 ounces
24	2 2/3 tablespoons	1 1/2 to 1 3/4 ounces
20	3 tablespoons	1 3/4 to 2 ounces
16	4 tablespoons	2 to 2 1/4 ounces
12	5 tablespoons	2 1/2 to 3 ounces
10	6 tablespoons	4 to 5 ounces
6	10 tablespoons	6 ounces

Fig. 8.5.   Scoop Sizes.

KOTSCHEVAR, LENDEL H. *Quantity Food Production.* Berkeley, Calif.: McCutchan Publishing Corp., 1964.

LUNDBERG, DONALD E., and AMENDOLA, JOSEPH. Understanding Baking." *Institutions Magazine,* Chicago, Ill., 1972.

LUNDBERG, DONALD E., and KOTSCHEVAR, LENDEL H. *Understanding Cooking.* University of Massachusetts Bookstore, Amherst, Mass., 1965.

NATIONAL CANNERS ASSOCIATION, School Lunch Recipes Using Canned Foods. Washington, D. C., 1949. (Free)

RICHARDS, LENORE, and TREAT, NOLA. *Quantity Cookery.* Boston: Little, Brown & Co., 1939.

SMITH, FRANCES LOWE, and STODDARD, FLORENCE P. *Recipes and Menus for Fifty.* New York: M. Barrows & Co., Inc., 1948.

STOKES, JOHN W. *How to Manage a Restaurant or Institutional Food Service.* Dubuque, Iowa: Wm. C. Brown Company Publishers, 1967.

SULLIVAN, LENORE M. Quantity Recipe File (4th ed.). Ames, Iowa: Collegiate Press, 1945. (455 recipes on 4 x 6 cards with file and guide cards)

U.S. DEPARTMENT OF AGRICULTURE, Production & Marketing Division, School Lunch Recipes for 25 and 50. Washington, D. C.: 1949. (Free)

WENZEL, GEORGE L. Wenzel's Menu Maker. Austin, Texas.

CHAPTER 9

Distribution and Service of Food

Once the food has been prepared and cooked, it must be taken to the location where it is to be served.

In the Industrial Food Service these may include:

1. Employees' Cafeterias and Snack Bars
2. Executive Dining Rooms
3. Mobile units covering various routes in the plant.
4. Canteens located in areas remote from the cafeterias
5. Automatic vending machines

In the Hospital and Institutional Food Service these may include:

1. Service to patients' rooms or dining areas (directly or via Floor Kitchens)
2. Cafeterias for employees and staff
3. Staff dining rooms
4. Coffee shops for visitors and others (if served by the Dietary Department)

In Schools and Colleges these may include:

1. Dining Rooms or Cafeterias for students
2. Snack Bars in student centers
3. Cafeterias for employees
4. Faculty Dining Rooms
5. Banquet Service for special groups

CAFETERIA SERVICE

Cafeterias are operated in factories, stores, and offices, and in institutions of all types. Essentially the cafeteria consists of a service counter and a dining area. The counter is made up of various sections for holding or displaying food and beverages. It includes both heated and refrigerated units. In the line cafeteria, patrons enter at one end, pick up a tray, pass through the entire line, and select the menu items they desire. A tray-rail usually runs the full length of the counter—on it the patron rests his tray while passing through the line. The aisle through which the line moves is usually separated from the dining area by a half-partition or rail. An accounting for the food selected is made at the end of the line where the cashier's booth or stand is located. In some cases the patron receives a check at the end of the cafeteria line and upon leaving pays the amount at the door.

Another type of so-called cafeteria is often found in commercial eating places in which the counter is open and customers give their orders to the counter attendants. These are filled by the counter people or short-order cooks who prepare certain dishes to order behind the counter. This service is similar to that of the snack bar. Obviously it requires more counter employees than the line cafeteria.

Some cafeterias combine self-service with short-orders. For breakfasts, for example, one section may be set aside for griddle cakes, eggs to order, and various breakfast meats.

Where large numbers are to be fed, double cafeteria lines may be installed (see Figure 9.4). These may be in the form of parallel lines and counters with the serving facilities in between. In other instances, a straight cafeteria line may be divided into two or more identical sections with supporting service facilities. Patrons may enter at the center and proceed either to the right or left along the line, with cashier's stations at either end. A reversal of this is seen in some cafeterias where the patrons enter the line at either end and leave at the cashiers' booths in the center. Another arrangement is to have the straight line divided into two or more sections; the traffic flow in each moving in the same or different directions, sometimes to different dining-rooms.

The Free-Flow or Hollow-Square Cafeteria (see Figure 9.2)

An increasing number of cafeterias are being designed on what is variously called the "Free-Flow," "Hollow-Square," "Shopping-Center," or, as on the West Coast, the "Scramble System" type of counter. Of these names, "Free-Flow" would seem most appropriate, although as Shakespeare said, "What's in a name?" In this layout, the counter may form three sides of a square with the fourth side open for traffic. In some instances the counter extends around all four sides of the square with openings left for patrons to enter and leave.

In the hollow-square type of counter, hot and cold food stations may be positioned at right angles to the counter instead of in the usual parallel position. In institutional adaptations of this layout, these stations are often portable hot and cold food tables or bulk food trucks. This position of the food station allows the counter attendant to dish out the food with a minimum of unnecessary body motions. Whether arranged at right angles or in the conventional manner parallel to the counter, the hot food stations are preferably located as near as possible to the kitchen.

Patrons, instead of following in line as with the conventional counter, enter the square and make their selections from the various hot and cold food stations around its sides. A stand for beverages is often placed in the center of the square so as to be readily accessible.

The arrangement of the Free-Flow Cafeteria at Duke University, Durham, North Carolina, is shown in Figure 9.2.

In some institutions, both the straight line and the free-flow types of counters are used. When volume is low, one or more of the hollow-square counters may be shut off by means of sliding panels.

Cafeteria managers who have investigated the free-flow or hollow-square type of counter summarize its advantages as follows:

1. *No waiting in line:* When a large group of patrons arrive at the Cafeteria at a meal hour, from 100 to 150 may be allowed to enter a hollow square at once, whereas under the conventional arrangement they would form a queue and wait until the line moved on. Although it appears confusing at first, patrons seem to disperse more rapidly in the hollow square.

2. *Greater flexibility:* As the plant expands, the hollow-square plan allows greater room for expansion.

3. *Improved labor utilization:* This layout permits greater use of self-service—such as in the dispensing of hot beverages. Thus it tends to reduce labor costs.

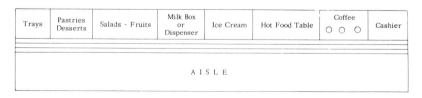

Trays	Pastries Desserts	Salads - Fruits	Milk Box or Dispenser	Ice Cream	Hot Food Table	Coffee ○ ○ ○	Cashier

A I S L E

Fig. 9.1.   Conventional arrangement of counter sections.

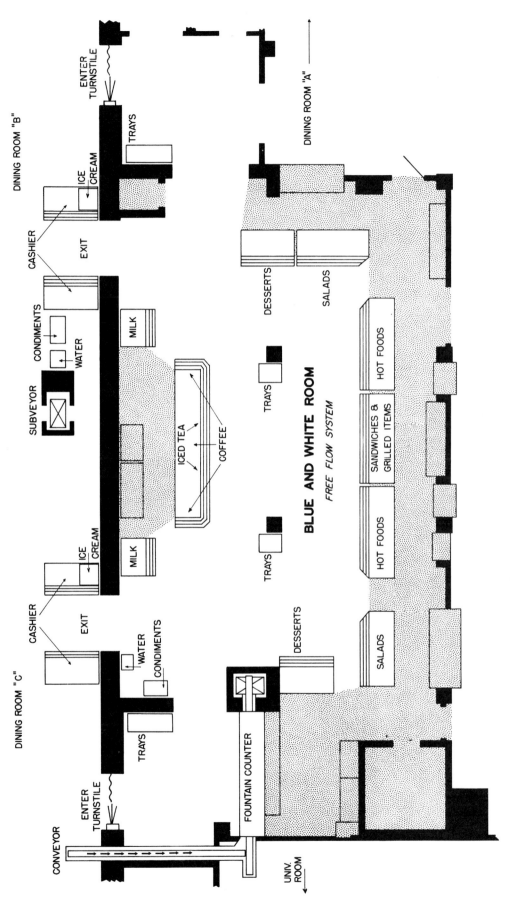

Fig. 9.2. Free-Flow Cafeteria, Duke University, Durham, N. C. (Courtesy Theodore W. Minah, Director, Dining Halls Operations.)

1. ENTER FREE FLOW SERVING AREA THROUGH THE TURNSTILE LOCATED AT EITHER END OF DINING HALL.

2. PICK UP TRAY FROM ONE OF THE TRAY DISPENSERS.

3. DO NOT LINE UP AS IN A CAFETERIA.

4. PROCEED, AS YOU WOULD IN A SUPERMARKET, TO THE COUNTER OFFERING THE FOODS AND BEVERAGES OF YOUR CHOICE.

5. SERVE YOURSELF SALADS, DESSERTS AND BEVERAGES.

6. LEAVE THROUGH THE TWO CASHIERS LINES -- PLEASE HAVE MONEY OR COUPONS READY.

7. WHEN YOU HAVE FINISHED EATING, PLEASE CARRY YOUR TRAY AND SOILED TABLEWARE TO THE TRAY CART OR SUBVEYOR NEAREST YOU.

Essentials of the Cafeteria Line

The essential characteristics of the cafeteria line are:

1. *Food items are prepared in advance* and are ready for service. Short-order items are not offered on the regular cafeteria line.

2. *A maximum of self-service prevails.* With the exception of hot entrées which are served from hot food tables by counter attendants, all food items are picked up or dispensed by the patrons themselves.

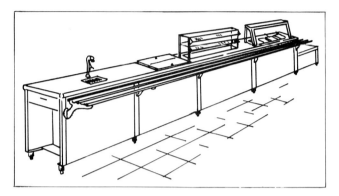

Fig. 9.3. Small cafeteria counter—perspective.

3. *Emphasis is placed upon display.* Foods are displayed so as to appeal to the patron and to emphasize the wide range of choice offered.

4. *Self-bussing of dishes.* Upon completing the meal, the patron carries his tray—upon which are placed soiled dishes, utensils, and waste paper—to a point near the Dishwashing Room where it is deposited. Frequently a conveyor belt is extended into the dining area upon which soiled dishes are deposited and conveyed to the Dishwashing Room.

College Cafeterias

In many college food services students may have as many helpings of food as they wish, although they are usually limited to a single helping of the main entrées. These entrées—meat and vegetable dishes—are usually plated by the cafeteria attendants while all other items are self-served.

An experiment was conducted at a large university in the Spring of 1972 to see if complete self-service would be feasible. During a one month period, the students were allowed to help themselves to all items including the meat and vegetable dishes. It was found that the food-cost percentage for this period increased by six per cent—more than offsetting the labor savings effected. In addition, the quantity of meats and food left over and wasted seemed to be substantially more when using the self-service method.

THE CAFETERIA COUNTER

The counter may vary in length from 20 feet or less to 45 feet or longer, depending upon the number of sections it contains. Its length varies with the quantity and variety of food items offered, rather than upon the number of patrons to be served. For adult service, the counter should be 42 inches above the floor, and the aisle in front of it 4 feet wide to allow for "by-passing" (the passing around one patron by another who was behind him in the line).

The conventional tray-rail is 10 to 12 inches in width, usually constructed of three pieces of one-inch stainless-steel tubing. For easier cleaning and to prevent spillage on the floor, a flat piece of stainless steel, 10 to 12 inches wide, with three ridges tooled in it upon which the tray can slide, may be used. The tray rail should be so designed that the top of the tray, when on the rail, is level with the counter surface.

The counter surface is often constructed of stainless steel or covered with a plastic material such as formica.

Figure 9.3 shows a front view of a small cafeteria counter.

Counter Arrangement

When the patron enters the line he first obtains a tray. Trays may be dispensed from a simple shelf, a truck, or a portable, self-leveling tray dispenser. Next comes the display of salads and desserts. In commercial eating-places these are placed first on the theory that the hungry customer will select a dessert upon first entering the line, whereas he might not do so after he has loaded his tray with the entree and other items. This pattern seems to be followed in institutional cafeterias as well. Hot entrees and hot beverages are generally placed last in line, or near the end of the line, for a more logical but less commercial motive—less time is consumed before they reach the dining table and consequently less loss of heat.

Figure 9.1 shows the conventional arrangement of the various food items with the approximate space given to each. However, there is no hard and fast rule with regard to arrangement. The various sections may be interchanged in accordance with the ideas of the planners and the special conditions prevailing.

Speeding Movement of the Counter Line

Where large numbers are to be accommodated within limited meal periods, it is well to consider where certain facilities are to be located. If the silver dispenser, for example, is located at the beginning of the line, patrons will take a maximum supply of knives, forks, and spoons—more than they really need. This increases the dishwashing load. If the dispenser is positioned at the end of the line, just before the cashier's stand, traffic will be held up while silver is being selected. It is well, therefore, to place the silver dispenser at a point away from the line but accessible to patrons after they leave the cashier's stand. It may well be combined with the water-cooler. In some cafeterias condiments have also been taken off the counter and placed on a stand which includes the water-cooler and silver dispenser.

In one of the cafeterias at the University of Pennsylvania, Philadelphia, some years ago, the line capacity was increased approximately 23% by moving the silver station away from the end of the aisle. A similar result was achieved at a large automobile assembly plant more recently, when increased production required greater capacity. Here, not only were the condiments and silver moved away from the line, but an auxiliary line was pressed into service during peak periods.

In some industrial cafeterias, containers for milk and ice cream are placed along the side of the line opposite the counter. This makes it necessary for patrons to turn around to select these items, and thus tends to slow the movement in the line. If all food items are placed on the counter it will not only speed up the service but also make it more convenient for the patrons to select them.

Signs which are hung so as to be above the line of vision of those passing through the line also tend to impede the rate of flow. Institutional planners might well follow the commercial cafeterias in this respect by placing small, easily-read signs at each section showing the names and prices of the items displayed.

THE CASHIER'S STAND

The cashier's stand should be equipped with a modern cash register having several keys so that a record may be kept of the various types of meal tickets presented—in addition to cash sales. Such special keys are also useful if items other than food are sold. The cashier should be positioned to see each tray as it approaches. Thus an experienced cashier can quickly scan the tray and mentally add up the check by the time the patron reaches her stand.

LEGEND

1. REFRIGERATOR	6. MILK DISPENSER	11. DUMB WAITER	16. PIE CABINET
2. COLD PAN	7. HOT BEVERAGE	12. TRAY STAND	17. TOASTER
3. HOT FOOD TABLE	8. CANDY DISPLAY	13. ROLL FOOD WARMER	18. SANDWICH BAR
4. DESSERT SECTION	9. CASHIER	14. GRILLS (2)	19. ICE CREAM
5. ICED DRINKS	10. CONDIMENT STAND	15. FRYER	20. ICE MAKER

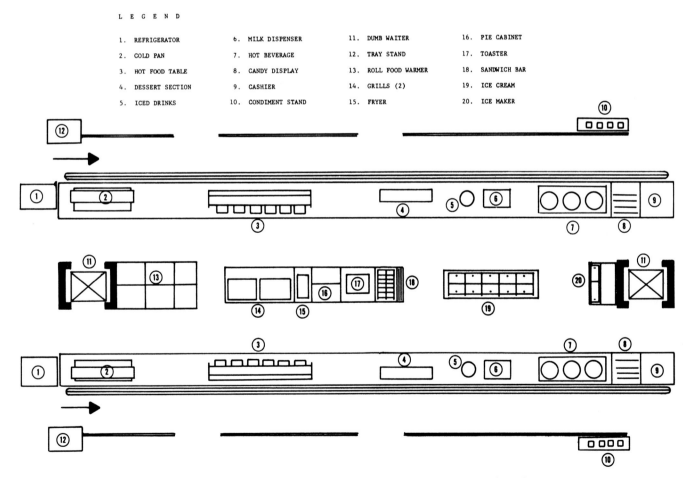

Fig. 9.4.   Double Line industrial cafeteria supplied by dumbwaiter from kitchen on floor above.

COUNTER EQUIPMENT

Marked advances have been made within recent years in the equipment offered for counter use. As previously pointed out, when selecting equipment consideration should be given to lasting qualities, appearance, ease of cleaning, and accessibility for repairs and maintenance. In general, stainless steel remains unchallenged as the most widely used material in food-service equipment.

An integral piece of counter equipment has always been the hot-food container, popularly known as the steam table or "bain-marie" (from the French word for double-boiler). Originally this was a shallow tank of steam-heated hot water in which the pots and pans of water were immersed for warming.

Much good food has been spoiled by being allowed to stand too long in these steam-tables. Not only is food often overcooked and dried out, but it may also lose valuable nutrients which are leached out through prolonged exposure to heat, air, and moisture. Meats shrink considerably under these conditions, and the effect of overheating has been particularly noticeable with respect to vegetables.

Although steam tables are equipped with thermostatic devices which may be set at the required temperatures for various types of foods, employees may be careless or not trained to adjust these temperature settings. Modern types of food warmers utilizing dry heat and fired by gas or electricity are capable of more exact thermostatic control. These have done much to correct the misuse of hot food tables. Nevertheless, a better solution to the problem is the cooking of food in small quantities at more frequent intervals. Modern food warmers have greater flexibility. They are provided with interchangeable top-panels so that the standard 12x20 inch openings may be subdivided for various sized inserts.

Salads, butter-chips, and other cold items are often displayed on a pan of cracked ice known as a "cold bain-marie." Modern counter refrigerators are available which eliminate the use of ice. Nevertheless, many cafeteria managers prefer ice because of the psychological effect of its appearance upon the patrons.

Refrigerated chests for milk in 1/2 pint containers and for individual portions of ice cream have long been used on cafeteria counters. Deep chests require much bending on the part of patrons as well as employees. Through carelessness, individual containers at the bottom of such chests may not be properly rotated on a "first in, first out" basis. Modern shallow-type chests keep the contents more readily accessible, and make for greater convenience of the patron if he is to serve himself. Bulk-milk dispensers have come into vogue in cafeteria service recently, and are generally approved by health authorities. By dispensing the milk directly from bulk containers (10 quarts or larger) a saving is effected over the cost of individual half-pints. These dispensers are refrigerated and in many institutional cafeterias are self-served.

Hot Beverage Service

Because of the volume required, coffee urns are widely used in cafeteria service, although in some cases glass coffee bowls with warmers are also used. The urn has the advantage of also providing boiling water for tea and hot chocolate. Coffee may be self-served or served by a counter attendant who adds cream if desired. Cream may be supplied from a dispenser which can be adjusted to the quantity required. In some cafeterias cream is supplied in small glass "creamers"—however, labor is required to fill and wash these receptacles. Modern coffee urns can be obtained with a "by-pass" valve which when rotated in one direction will dispense black coffee, and in the other will add a predetermined portion of cream.

Instant or soluble coffee for restaurant use has simplified cafeteria coffee service in institutional and industrial food services where it is used.

Dishes and Utensils

Hotel and restaurant china is widely used in institutional and industrial food services. This comes in a variety of patterns and colors. Heavy hotel ware is preferred for cafeteria use, and lighter china for patient service. In selecting dishes for the cafeteria, a plate no larger than 9 inches in diameter should be chosen for service with the standard 14 x 18 inch tray. Cups with a gross capacity of 7 ounces are preferable. These will accommodate 5½ ounces of coffee plus the quantity of cream given (½; ¾; or 1 oz.), and still leave sufficient clearance to prevent spillage. In a food service conducted by the author, coffee cups and soup bowls were marked with colored lines which appeared to be part of the decoration, but were actually indicators of the levels to which these receptacles should be filled.

Breakage costs run high when china is used, frequently amounting to 1% of gross sales. For this reason, many institutional food services have substituted plastic ware for part or all of the service. Hospitals cite breakage rates on plastic dishes ranging from 6% to 8% annually (mostly cups). This is only a fraction of comparable china breakage rates, which may run as high as 50% or more per annum.

The preferred material for institutional plastic ware is the melamine resin heavy-duty type. This is pro-

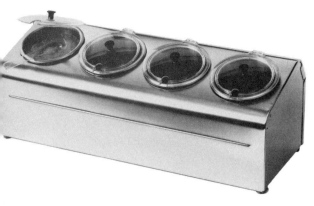

Hole Condiment Dispenser No. 345. (Courtesy Bloomfield Industries, Inc., Chicago, Ill.)

ST5½   ST6½   ST10½
ST8½

Stainless Steel Insets and Covers. (Courtesy Bloomfield Industries, Inc., Chicago, Ill.)

No. 402 Ice Cream Scoop. (Courtesy Bloomfield Industries, Inc., Chicago, Ill.)

No. 403 Ice Cream Spade. (Courtesy Bloomfield Industries, Inc., Chicago, Ill.)

No. 2593WC—3 Compartment Swedish Regent Susan. (Courtesy Bloomfield Industries, Inc., Chicago, Ill.)

No. 355 Lazy Sue Server. (Courtesy Bloomfield Industries, Inc., Chicago, Ill.)

No. 1071 Silverware Bin. (Courtesy Bloomfield Industries, Inc., Chicago, Ill.)

Hospital-Tray Size Salt & Pepper Shakers. (Courtesy Bloomfield Industries, Inc., Chicago, Ill.)

Relish Salver #523. (Courtesy Bloomfield Industries, Inc., Chicago, Ill.)

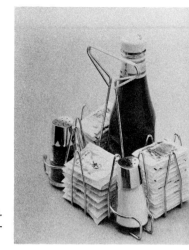

No. 22 Multi-Purpose Rack. (Courtesy Bloomfield Industries, Inc., Chicago, Ill.)

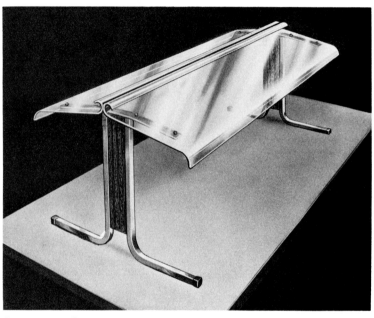

Sneeze Guard for Cafeteria Line. (Courtesy Crescent Metal Products, Inc., Cleveland, Ohio.)

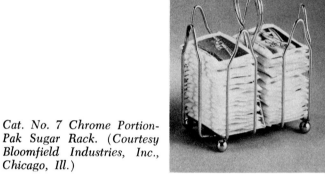

Cat. No. 7 Chrome Portion-Pak Sugar Rack. (Courtesy Bloomfield Industries, Inc., Chicago, Ill.)

No. 14 Sauce Rack. (Courtesy Bloomfield Industries, Inc., Chicago, Ill.)

Cres-Cor Infra Red Warmer with adapters to fit two ½ size Bun Pans. (Courtesy Crescent Metal Products, Inc., Cleveland, Ohio.)

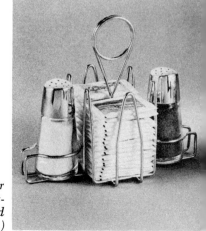

Chrome Portion-Pak Sugar Rack with Shaker Compartments. (Courtesy Bloomfield Industries, Inc., Chicago, Ill.)

No. 615 Five stainless steel shelves. (Courtesy Bloomfield Industries, Inc., Chicago, Ill.)

Vinyl Bussing Cart. (Courtesy Bloomfield Industries, Inc., Chicago, Ill.)

Tote and Stack Cart. (Courtesy Bloomfield Industries, Inc., Chicago, Ill.)

Bus 'N Tote Mobile Cart. (Courtesy Bloomfield Industries, Inc., Chicago, Ill.)

No. 624 China Clipper. (Courtesy Bloomfield Industries, Inc., Chicago, Ill.)

duced under various brand names. In addition to its low breakage rate, other advantages are its light weight and less noise in handling. As plastic is a nonconductor of heat, little preheating is required and foods cool less rapidly. For elementary school cafeterias, the safety factor incident to low breakage is also important. Hospitals using plastic dishes and tumblers claim ready acceptance by patients as well as cafeteria patrons.

Disadvantages of plastic ware are the staining of cups and the loss of gloss from the use of chlorine rinses to remove stains. Plastic plates also become marred by sharp table knives.

Although plastic dishes should not be subjected to temperatures above 200° F., they can be put through the dishwashing machines. Plastics, being nonconductors of heat, require longer time to dry, and, as will be explained in connection with Dishwashing in Chapter 10 "Sanitation," the introduction of wetting agents in the rinse water is often advisable.

Melamine dinnerware has been improved in quality during the past decade with the result that lighter ware, semitranslucent, with decorations, and more resistant to scratches, is now available. It is said to be more resistant to stains as well.

Translucent ribbed tumblers of plastic materials are used in many institutional food services. Although not as attractive as glassware, they are lighter and show a much lower breakage rate. In addition, new types of glassware have been developed within recent years that are more resistant to breakage.

Heavy plated silverware of the type used in hotels has been favored by many institutional food services. More recently, attractively-designed stainless steel knives, forks, and spoons have replaced silver in many institutions. The greatest loss of utensils ordinarily is through pilferage on the part of patrons rather than employees. For this reason, it seems wise to use the least expensive utensils that will suit the purpose of the food service.

Quantities of Dishes and Utensils Required (see Figure 9.5)

A sufficient supply of dishes and utensils to meet peak-load requirements is essential. Shortages will play havoc with the movement of the cafeteria line and require intermittent operation of the dishwashing facilities at loads less than normal capacity. An adequate stock will prevent embarrassing delays in the line and be conducive to an efficient dishwashing operation.

Where china is used, some food services maintain four complete sets in use, two in reserve, and two on

order, or eight in all. Reordering, of course, depends upon the loss and breakage rate as recorded through actual experience. Another consideration is the time required for deliveries. In these food services quantities are checked and orders placed every three month

To assure an adequate supply of dishes and utensils in a new food service, the initial order might well be based upon the estimated total number of patrons who will be served during the peak period of the day—

Item	Initial Supply of Dishes and Utensils (Per peak-period patrons)	
	Number required	Notes
Dinner Plates	1	
Bread & Butter Plates	2	(Used also for desserts)
Fruit Saucers	1	
Cups	1	
Saucers	1	
Soup Bowls	3/4	
Oatmeal Bowls	1/2	
Teaspoons	2	(Used also for desserts)
Dessert Spoons	1/2	
Knives	1	
Forks	1 1/2	(Used also for desserts)
Glasses	1 1/2	(For milk and water)
Trays	1	

Fig. 9.5.   Initial supplies of dishes and utensils.

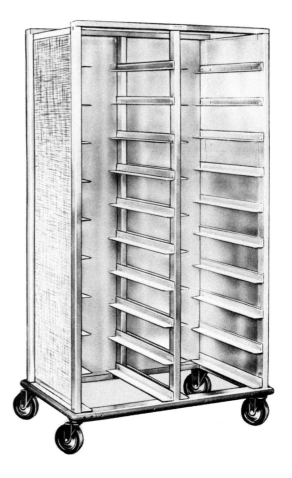

Cres-Cor Double Rack enclosed on three sides with Corax. (Courtesy Crescent Metal Products, Inc., Cleveland, Ohio.)

usually the noon hour. Based upon this maximum, the table in Figure 9.5 may be used as a guide:

Other items, such as casserole dishes, custard cups, iced-tea spoons, bouillon spoons, cocktail forks, etc., will depend upon the needs of the individual food service.

Self-Leveling Devices

Self-leveling devices which raise the trays, dishes, cups, saucers, or glasses one at a time to the counter level for easy handling are widely used in industrial and institutional food services. Portable units of this type may be loaded in the dishwashing room and wheeled directly to the point of service. These devices may also be heated or refrigerated, making possible hot dishes for hot foods, and cold plates for cold entrees, salads, or desserts. The use of these self-leveling devices eliminates double handling, speeds up service, and reduces labor cost. At the same time, sanitation is enhanced as dishes are protected from contamination. Figure 9.6 illustrates the use of self-leveling mobile equipment on the cafeteria counter.

Trays

Trays are available in many sizes and shapes. Most employee cafeterias prefer the 14 x 18 inch rectangular tray. A slightly larger tray, 15 x 20 inches in dimension, is generally used for patient service. Small trays are used for special purposes. For bussing and special service, larger oval and round trays are in use. Recently a plastic tray with corners cut off has been designed to fit a square cafeteria table for four.

Trays are made of various materials: metal (aluminum or stainless steel), hard rubber, plastics, and fiber-glass. Aluminum trays are lighter than those of stainless steel, but become dented and pitted through use. Plastic and fiber-glass trays may be obtained in a variety of colors and designs which add to the appeal of the meal. Fiber-glass trays are usually reinforced by metal rods imbedded in their edges, and are said to withstand warping from the dishwashing process much better than the plastic trays.

Stainless steel trays divided into sections were widely used in military establishments during World War II. They are also used at present in some elementary school cafeterias. Up to six sections are provided in which food is served directly. This principle is also used with plastic trays and both types eliminate the expenditure for dishes and the problem of washing them.

SNACK BARS

Snack bars are set up in large industrial food services to meet the needs of employees who bring their own lunches but may want supplementary desserts and beverages. They may also be used in institutional food services to provide short-order service for egg dishes, sandwiches, etc., off the cafeteria line. Snack bars meet a need in student centers for those desiring soda-fountain service of sundaes, sodas, and other drinks.

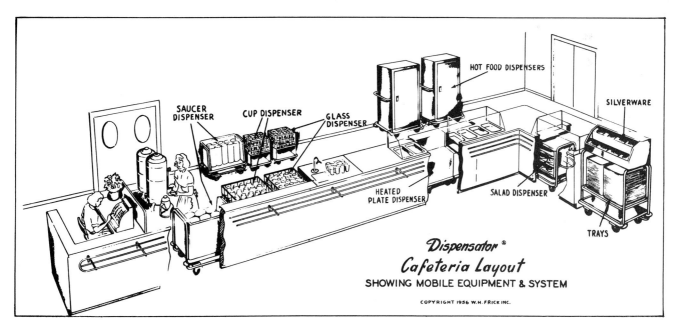

Fig. 9.6. Mobile equipment in the cafeteria. (Courtesy Wear Ever Food Service Equipment, Fort Wayne, Indiana.)

Wear Ever Streamline Cafeteria. (Courtesy Wear Ever Food Service Equipment, Fort Wayne, Ind.)

Wear Ever Buffeteria. (Courtesy Wear Ever Food Service Equipment, Fort Wayne, Ind.)

Essentially the snack bar is a soda-fountain luncheonette service. If located in the same room as the cafeteria, it should be placed at one end, away from the line. Equipment generally included in the snack bar includes:

Soda-fountain or "bob-tailed" units with ice-cream box, syrup containers, mixers, and hot chocolate dispenser.

Sandwich Unit with cutting board and refrigerated receptacles containing various spreads and fillings.

Coffee-Maker (Urn, automatic, or vacuum type) with warming stoves, cream dispenser, sugar envelopes, etc. Hot water should be available for making tea and other hot beverages.

The counter top should be 42 inches above the floor, and should be covered with stainless steel, formica, or a similar plastic material. Its size depends upon the volume of service required.

MOBILE UNITS AND CANTEENS

In some industrial plants, mobile food units cover designated routes, either supplementing the cafeteria service or supplying between-meal snacks. Mobile units are particularly useful in continuous-process industries where employees must remain within reach of their machines, even during meal periods. These units range from simple food trucks carrying sandwiches, pastries, and hot coffee (in thermos containers), to the more elaborate heated and refrigerated mobile food containers.

Canteens, either portable or fixed, are food-service units located in plant areas remote from the cafeterias. Service is usually limited to sandwiches, pastries, coffee, milk, ice cream, and soft drinks. Portable units may be loaded in the main kitchen and wheeled or carried in automobile trucks to location. Fixed canteens are generally supplied with food dispatched from the main kitchen. In many plants both the mobile units and canteens have been replaced by automatic vending machines.

AUTOMATIC VENDING MACHINES

Vending machines have long been used in food services to dispense cigarettes, candies, and soft-drinks. In some cafeteria layouts, a room is set aside, near the dining area, where a battery of vending machines containing cigarettes and candy bars is located. This removes the machines from the cafeteria traffic and from the dining room.

Formerly cigarettes and candy were sold by the cashier. The use of vending machines for these items enables the cashier to concentrate upon the food sales and reduces the possibility of errors. It also minimizes pilferage. To illustrate: the loss of a carton of cigarettes might wipe out the profits from a day's sales of this small-margin item.

Vending machines dispensing sandwiches, wieners, hot coffee, cocoa, and cold milk have also been introduced in many plants. As they are conveniently located near the work areas, their use reduces the time required for employees to travel to and from the cafeteria for the midday coffee breaks.

Commissions (Current Rates—1972)

Cigarette and candy vending machines are supplied by concessionaires who service the machines regularly and keep them in repair. They pay a commission to the food service based upon the volume of sales through the machines. Although this commission is generally less than the gross profit possible through direct sales, it is sure and can be accounted for.

Item	Unit Price	Commission
Candy	15¢	8%
Cigarettes	50¢	3¢
Coffee	15¢	10%-15%
Soft Drinks	15¢	15%

Fig. 9.7. Commissions on Vending Machine Sales.

Economics of Vending Machine Operation

Machines vending foods and beverages are expensive, ranging from about $600 to $2,400 in first cost. They become obsolete rapidly and have a correspondingly high rate of depreciation. With their electronic controls, automatic mechanisms, coin and bill changers, cup dispensers, and electrical heating and refrigerating equipment, they are complicated pieces of apparatus. It is necessary to have expert technicians available for repairs and maintenance, and employees to keep the machines supplied and collect the money.

Although the net return from the automatic cafeteria may be small, the income of the contractor will be augmented if he has numerous vending machines distributed throughout various departments.

THE AUTOMATIC CAFETERIA

Along with the automation of manufacturing processes it is not strange that the automatic cafeteria has appeared on the industrial scene. This has been made possible by the invention of automatic, coin-operated vending machines which dispense sandwiches, hot soups (usually in cans), salads, pastries, puddings, desserts, and fruits.

Automatic cafeterias are generally installed in smaller plants or offices. The vending machine service may be offered by a contractor who maintains a central commissary and services plants within, say, a 50-mile radius. This facility is attractive to small plants or offices where it has not seemed feasible to operate a complete cafeteria service.

In some plants, the workers prefer to bring a sandwich from home and supplement it by purchasing a beverage and dessert from the vending machine.

Future of the Automatic Cafeteria

From a management standpoint, the automatic cafeteria presents the possibility of providing food service for employees without subsidization. In industrial plants where round after round of increases in wages and fringe benefits have been granted, management is not likely to be sympathetic to the idea of subsidizing the meals of highly paid workers.

The situation may be different in offices where the food service is an inducement for attracting desirable workers and may also be a form of additional compensation.

There is no doubt that a well-managed cafeteria, staffed by real live people, is preferred to the anonymity of the vending machine. Many business executives believe that the manually-operated cafeteria makes definite contributions to teamwork and productivity.

While the automatic cafeteria will make its contribution to smaller establishments in which it would not be economically feasible to install a conventional food service, it does not seem likely that well-managed plant cafeterias will be replaced by automatic cafeterias in the near future.

THE COFFEE BREAK

The widespread popularity of the "coffee break" has added to food-service volume in industries and institutions. If the cafeteria is utilized for this purpose, the effect has been to interject busy periods during the hitherto quiet midmorning and midafternoon hours. Where two or three shifts are maintained, "coffee breaks" have become customary in between the night meal periods as well.

While this added volume has tended to level the daily activity curve in the cafeteria, it has presented real problems to management. In many establishments the travel time to and from the cafeteria and the time spent during the coffee break itself has unduly interfered with the progress of the work.

To meet this situation various strategies have been devised. Bells and buzzers have been utilized to mark the beginning and ending of the coffee break—like the recess bells in school. In one large insurance office a corps of girl employees carry baskets of doughnuts and cups of coffee to the various departments and the employees are served at their desks. In industrial plants mobile units are used, as well as automatic vending machines, as previously described.

Manufacturers of water coolers have capitalized on the coffee-break custom by furnishing dispensers supplying both hot and cold water. With the use of individual envelopes of soluble coffee, sweet cocoa mix, tea, and soups, the employees of even the smallest office or shop may have their coffee break.

Although many conflicting claims have been made, there is scientific evidence to indicate the physiological and psychological value the coffee breaks have in terms of increased productivity. This is especially true in the case of calorie-conscious women employees who eat scanty breakfasts and extremely light luncheons. For many workers, the coffee recess breaks the monotony and freshens enthusiasm for the tasks ahead. Persons working under pressure find this relaxation conducive to sustained effort.

TABLE SERVICE (see Figure 9.8)

Table service for students, faculty, and staff is maintained in some colleges and secondary schools. Dining rooms are operated for executives in many industrial and institutional food services, usually in addition to the cafeteria.

Table service presents problems similar to those of the commercial restaurant. Food is prepared in the main kitchen and carried to the table by waiters or waitresses. In educational institutions these are generally students. In other establishments food-service employees are assigned to this task. Service facilities must be properly planned and the waiters or waitresses trained and supervised to perform properly.

Kitchen Layout for Table Service

The kitchen layout for table service differs from that of the cafeteria kitchen. Where all service is to tables, food is dished out in the kitchen by the chef or head cook. The food may be placed directly on the plates, or on platters for "family-style" service. A shelf should be arranged above the cook's work table where dishes may be picked up by the waiters. Infrared lamps are often installed over this serving shelf to keep food warm.

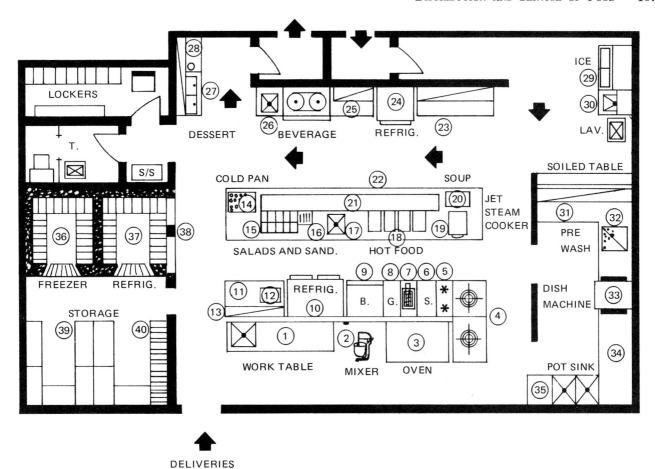

Fig. 9.8. Detail of Kitchen Layout for Table Service.

A key to the list of equipment in Figure 9.8 is as follows:

1. Work table with sink
2. Kitchen mixer
3. Roast and bake oven
4. Two hot-top ranges
5. Open burner range unit
6. Spreader plate
7. Deep fat fryer
8. Grill
9. Broiler
10. Cook's refrigerator
11. Pantry counter
12. Slicer
13. Wall cabinet
14. Cold bain-marie
15. Open top sandwich refrigerator
16. Toaster and bread drawer
17. Sink
18. Hot food wells
19. High compression steam cooker

20. Hot soup well
21. Pass-out shelves (Infrared warmers)
22. Plate storage and tray rest
23. Waiters' utility cabinet and shelf
24. Waiters' refrigerator
25. Utensil storage section
26. Beverage stand, urns, and sink
27. Ice-cream cabinet
28. Dessert cabinet and dipper well
29. Ice machine
30. Water station
31. Soiled dish table—overhead shelf
32. Prewash sink and disposal unit
33. Door-type dishwashing machine
34. Clean dish table
35. Pot sink
36. Walk-in freezer
37. Walk-in refrigerator
38. Reach-in doors
39. Storage shelves
40. Dunnage racking

The kitchen serving area should be laid out so that there is a one-way entrance door on one side and a one-way exit door on the other side. This enables the flow of traffic in one direction only. These doors should have glass panels to prevent collisions. Self-opening doors, equipped with "electric eyes" or electronic treadles are a boon to the oncoming waitress with both hands occupied in carrying a heavy tray.

Generally, as the waitress or waiter enters the kitchen, the first station is a table or window provided for the disposal of soiled dishes. The next stop is at the cook's serving table where the dishes containing the hot entrées (meats and vegetables) are picked up. The route then leads past the salad, dessert, and beverage stations where these items are obtained. This may be done at the same time, or on successive trips.

Figure 9.8 shows a kitchen layout for table service.

Serving Pantries

Where staff dining rooms are maintained auxiliary to cafeteria service, it is advisable to locate a serving pantry adjoining the dining room. This pantry should be equipped with a gas or electric range (domestic type), dishwarming ovens, coffee-maker, refrigerator, sink, work table, and storage shelves for dishes and utensils.

The food may be sent in bulk food trucks to the serving pantry and dished out there by an attendant, who may also be the waitress. Where the dining room is some distance from the main kitchen, the food may be kept at the proper temperature in the serving pantry. If it is dished out in the pantry, attention may also be given to the niceties of plate arrangements.

Dining Room Layout and Equipment

With respect to the seating arrangements, the same considerations in the use of tables and chairs and for the layout of the room, previously discussed with regard to the cafeteria dining room, apply.

In the furnishing of the school or college dining hall, custom and tradition often play an important role. In the staff or executives' dining room, other considerations besides food service must be made. A single large table may be desirable so that the executives may carry on business conferences following the meals.

Service Stations

In large dining halls where the distance from the kitchen is considerable, service stations are most useful. These vary in size and complexity, ranging from a small stand where coffee may be kept on an electric warmer to an elaborate station equipped with a water cooler, coffee warmer, ice container, cooler for butter chips, and shelves for silver, glasses, napkins, and various condiments.

These service stations are stocked before each meal, and make it unnecessary for the waitress to walk to the kitchen for ice water, silver, condiments, etc. This speeds up the service and also saves many steps. In some dining rooms where soluble coffee is used, the waitress makes up the coffee at the service station.

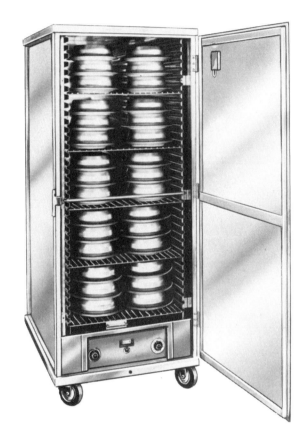

Cres-Cor Banquet Service Cabinet. (Courtesy Crescent Metal Products, Inc., Cleveland, Ohio.)

At the Faculty Club of a large university some years ago, we found that the installation of service stations of this kind would speed up service and at the same time reduce the number of waitresses required, presenting a potential saving of more than $5,000 annually.

Training of Table Service Employees

In addition to the indoctrination and training suggested for food-service employees in Chapter 4 "The Food-Service Organization," table service employees require specific schooling. Cooks and pantry servers should be instructed in portion control in accordance with previously established standards. They should also be trained to arrange food so that it will present an attrative appearance on the plate.

Waitresses and waiters should be taught methods of taking orders, setting the table, and carrying the food from the kitchen and the soiled dishes from the dining area. Many food services make it a point to train serving employees in personal hygiene and appearance, as well as the proper handling of patrons' questions or complaints.

In a well-managed food service it is customary to hold a brief meeting of all serving employees at the beginning of each meal period. At this time the menu is discussed in detail so that each one is familiar with the various dishes and can intelligently answer questions which may arise.

Quality Control

In commercial hotel dining rooms it is the practice to station a "checker" at the kitchen exit. As each waiter or waitress passes by, the food on the tray is inspected and the check totalled. This is done primarily from a food cost control point-of-view. However, the checker also notes the appearance of the food, and may reject any item below standard. Although checkers are not usually employed in institutional food services, it is important that the supervisory staff check constantly on the quality and appearance of the food as it goes to the patron's table. In some institutions one person is assigned the task of checking quality, particularly as the plates leave the kitchen for the dining room.

Quality Control Teams

In our work with institutional food services we have found that tests carried out by teams of two or three supervisors and/or employees bring good results in quality control. Periodically such teams are assigned to various locations, such as the kitchen, employees' cafeteria, or patient tray-assembly areas. Each team member independently records his appraisal of the dishes being tested on forms supplied for this purpose. The findings are recorded and later discussed at a team meeting. Suggestions for improvements are offered, and a tabulation of the findings is posted in the particular production or service location.

This method precludes the limitations of judgment based upon one individual's taste. It also stimulates interest on the part of production personnel and enables them to accept constructive suggestions more readily.

FOOD SERVICE TO HOSPITAL PATIENTS

The serving of meals to patients presents many complications not found in cafeteria or dining room service. In the first place, the patient requires three or more meals daily—unless his physical condition precludes them—not only on weekdays, but also on Saturdays, Sundays, and holidays. Secondly, the patient's room is at some distance both vertically and horizontally from the main kitchen. In the third place, many patients require special or therapeutic diets, prescribed by the physician and prepared under the supervision of the dietitian. Finally, the physical and mental condition of many patients is such that their reactions toward food may be quite different from those of individuals in normal health.

It can be seen, therefore, that the Chief Dietitian or the Food-Service Manager, whether responsible for the feeding of 50, 100, or 1200 patients, faces many problems. Assuming a well-organized kitchen staff, one of the chief problems is to get a patient's food to him three times daily, served in an appealing manner, with the hot entrées *hot* and the cold foods *cold*.

Food Distribution to Patients

As previously stated, there are two general types of food distribution to patients, Decentralized and Centralized. The distinguishing characteristic is the preparation of the patient's tray. When the tray is prepared away from the kitchen service area, the service is considered to be "decentralized." Where trays are prepared at one central point and then dispatched to the patients' rooms, the service is said to be "centralized."

We have previously considered the physical layout and equipment for food service. Here we will consider more particularly the layouts and equipment used for distributing food to patients under the two general methods, and the variations of these that are being used in actual practice. We will also consider the service problems of some of these systems, and list some of their advantages and disadvantages.

Decentralized Service

We list this method first because until recently it has been most widely used. Essentially, The Decentralized Service involves the following steps:

1. Food for up to sixty patients is loaded into electrically heated bulk food trucks in the main kitchen.
2. Each bulk food truck is taken to one of the floor kitchens.
3. In the floor kitchen, trays are prepared for the patients in the area served by it.
4. Trays are served to patients by employees of the dietary, nursing, or housekeeping departments.

Adams-Veyor tray make-up conveyor for hospital kitchens. (Courtesy Adamation, New-ton, Mass.)

Disadvantages of Decentralized Service are:

1. It is difficult to supervise the serving of food in the various floor kitchens.
2. It involves double handling of the food—first in the main kitchen and then in the floor kitchens.
3. Food may remain too long in the bulk food trucks and become overcooked and dried out.
4. More man-hours are required than in centralized service.
5. Space is taken up by the floor kitchens that might be put to more profitable use.

The Mobile Cafeteria

About twenty five years ago, the steward of a Norfolk, Virginia, hospital designed a food truck which he felt would improve the distribution of food to patients. Known as a "mobile cafeteria," the truck was designed to carry all of the foods, juices, beverages, dishes, glasses, utensils, and trays for 30 to 100 patients. It had both heated and refrigerated food compartments, was loaded in the main kitchen, and conveyed by elevator to the various floors. It was stationed at a given location on a floor where it could be connected to an electrical outlet. From this point 16 or 17 patients were served in their rooms nearby. It was then moved to other locations where a like number of patients was served.

Although the mobile cafeteria when fully loaded weighed about 1,800 pounds, it was easily wheeled about by a high school boy in a hospital where its use was observed by the author. In this institution, two trucks were used, each covered two floors and served approximately 100 patients in 40 minutes.

The advantages of the Mobile Cafeteria are:

1. Food is served at proper temperatures soon after being cooked;
2. Patients select their diets just before serving time, thus avoiding waste of food selected, then later rejected;
3. Portions can be large or small according to patient's wishes;
4. Labor cost was said to be about one-half of that under decentralized service; and
5. Space formerly used for floor kitchens was made available for other purposes.

Objections have been raised to the mobile cafeteria on account of its size and weight and the fact that the trays are served in the hospital corridor, subject to possible contamination.

Centralized Service

Within recent years many hospitals have changed from Decentralized to Centralized service. Chief advantages of Centralized Service are:

1. *All patient trays are prepared in one area*—usually the service section of the main kitchen and under the direct supervision of the dietitians. This makes for uniformity and portion control, attractive arrangement on the plate, and complete supervision of tray preparation in one area.
2. *Food is served at proper temperatures.* The use of Centralized Service permits more effective service of hot foods *hot* and cold foods *cold* to patients.
3. *Double-handling of food is eliminated* with the result that food is not overcooked in the bulk food conveyors, and considerable labor saving results.

4. *Floor kitchens are eliminated.* Thus the space formerly used by them can be diverted to more profitable purposes.

Distribution of Food Under Centralized Service

The foregoing advantages apply in general to all types of Centralized Service. However, there are several distinct systems in use. These differ with respect to:

1. Types of equipment in use and methods of tray assembly so that food will remain at proper temperatures until served.
2. Methods of conveying trays to patients.

Tray Trucks

Under this method, trays are prepared centrally and placed in tray trucks carrying up to 30 trays. In one type of truck, electrically heated drawers are pro-

vided to hold plates containing hot food. Partially set up trays are carried in a central rack, and other compartments carry cold foods and special diets. Thermos containers are provided on top of the truck for beverages and juices. Space is also included for cups, glasses, and utensils. Some types of tray trucks also provide refrigeration (dole plates or mechanical refrigeration units).

In other cases, hot soups, hot beverages, and cold desserts such as ice cream are placed in preheated or precooled individual stainless steel thermos containers and carried on the truck.

When loaded, the truck is wheeled to the corridor outside the room and trays are served.

Figure 9.9 visualizes central service with mobile food trucks.

Self-Contained Mobile Food Units

This unit contains thermostatically-controlled, mechanically-refrigerated cold-plate storage sections, an

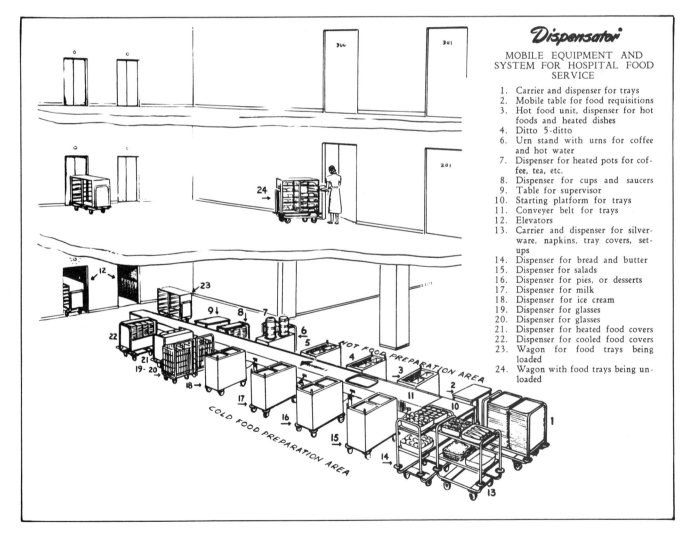

Dispensator

MOBILE EQUIPMENT AND SYSTEM FOR HOSPITAL FOOD SERVICE

1. Carrier and dispenser for trays
2. Mobile table for food requisitions
3. Hot food unit, dispenser for hot foods and heated dishes
4. Ditto 5-ditto
6. Urn stand with urns for coffee and hot water
7. Dispenser for heated pots for coffee, tea, etc.
8. Dispenser for cups and saucers
9. Table for supervisor
10. Starting platform for trays
11. Conveyer belt for trays
12. Elevators
13. Carrier and dispenser for silverware, napkins, tray covers, setups
14. Dispenser for bread and butter
15. Dispenser for salads
16. Dispenser for pies, or desserts
17. Dispenser for milk
18. Dispenser for ice cream
19. Dispenser for glasses
20. Dispenser for glasses
21. Dispenser for heated food covers
22. Dispenser for cooled food covers
23. Wagon for food trays being loaded
24. Wagon with food trays being unloaded

Fig. 9.9. Central service with mobile conveyors. (Courtesy Wear Ever Food Service Equipment, Fort Wayne, Indiana.)

ice-cream freezer, and an ice compartment. The hot plate compartment is automatic, electrically heated, and has *temperature and humidity control*. It also has a self-leveling cup and saucer dispenser, individually heated coffee and hot water urns, and an automatic four-slice toaster. The unit is designed for soiled dish and tray storage, and has interchangeable hot and cold section drawers.

Complete service for 24 patients is provided by each of these trucks. Specially-designed china is used with the unit. Saucers are designed to seal the cups and thus retain heat during service. Cups, saucers, and dishes are designed to resist chipping and breakage, and may be obtained in a variety of colors and patterns. Paper snap-on covers are used on juice glasses, soup cups, and creamers to prevent spillage. Wheels

are arranged so that this truck will turn on its axis and is completely maneuverable.

The design of the unit is such that the various heating and cooling members may be readily replaced. With the truck is supplied a complete array of repair parts likely to require replacement.

Mechanical Conveyor Type

In this type of service, trays are assembled on a moving belt in the main kitchen which leads to a high-speed dumbwaiter or trayveyor (an endless tray conveyor moving up and down a vertical shaft). One trayveyor is used to carry the trays upward and another to return trays containing soiled dishes to the dishroom. Four to eight trays may be placed upon the dumbwaiter at one time. On the trayveyor, the

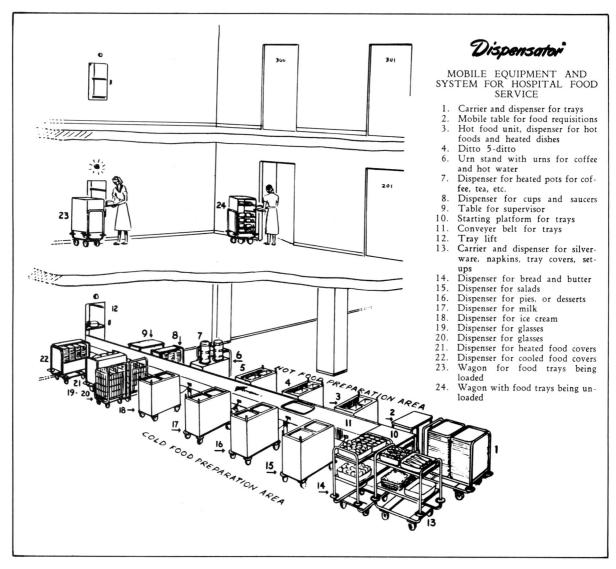

Dispensator

MOBILE EQUIPMENT AND SYSTEM FOR HOSPITAL FOOD SERVICE

1. Carrier and dispenser for trays
2. Mobile table for food requisitions
3. Hot food unit, dispenser for hot foods and heated dishes
4. Ditto 5-ditto
6. Urn stand with urns for coffee and hot water
7. Dispenser for heated pots for coffee, tea, etc.
8. Dispenser for cups and saucers
9. Table for supervisor
10. Starting platform for trays
11. Conveyer belt for trays
12. Tray lift
13. Carrier and dispenser for silverware, napkins, tray covers, setups
14. Dispenser for bread and butter
15. Dispenser for salads
16. Dispenser for pies, or desserts
17. Dispenser for milk
18. Dispenser for ice cream
19. Dispenser for glasses
20. Dispenser for glasses
21. Dispenser for heated food covers
22. Dispenser for cooled food covers
23. Wagon for food trays being loaded
24. Wagon with food trays being unloaded

Fig. 9.10. Central service with vertical conveyor. (Courtesy Wear Ever Food Service Equipment, Fort Wayne, Indiana.)

trays move one at a time in rapid succession. Upon reaching the patient floors they are delivered to the patients' rooms. Banquet covers are used to retain the heat in the food on the plates. Figure 9.10 shows a schematic drawing of central service with vertical conveyors.

Thermally-Sealed, Insulated Containers

Under this system, specially designed pyrex dishes are preheated in an infrared oven. It is said that the penetrating radiation saturates the dishes in the 40 to 80 seconds of travel in the circular oven with the same heating effect as would be obtained in 30 to 40 *minutes* in a 300° to 375° conventional oven.

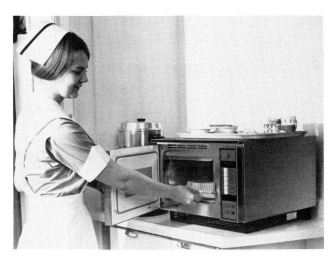

Pre-plated meals are reheated in a ward outside a patient's room at the Hennepin County General Hospital, Minneapolis, Minn. Microwave ovens, either permanently located at nourishment stations in wards or on mobile carts, enable hospitals to make certain meals are heated to proper serving temperatures when delivered to the patients. (Courtesy Atherton Division, Litton Industries, Minneapolis, Minn.)

As the hot dishes come out of the traveling oven, they are placed (by an employee wearing asbestos gloves) in the lower part of an insulated container on a conveyor belt assembly. As the belt travels, hot food is placed in the heated pyrex dish and the cover of the insulated container sealed on it. The sealed dish is placed on the trays, and other items are added during the assembly process, including cold foods. Trays are placed in unheated tray trucks and conveyed to the patients' rooms. Here each tray is taken out of the truck and served to the patient. On each truck thermos containers for beverages and soups are carried. These are dispensed as the trays are served. Each truck carries trays and meals for up to 20 patients.

In one hospital using this method of service we found that difficulty was being experienced with hot beverages. Upon investigation it was agreed that the thermos containers had not been properly preheated. In the same institution it was found necessary to provide special dishwashing facilities for the insulated containers, and in addition the covers and gasket required frequent replacement.

Dry Heat System

A system that has been employed in a number of hospitals is known as the Dry Heat System. An insulated container is used similar to the thermally insulated containers previously mentioned. In the Dry Heat System the food is kept warm by a preheated metal disk or pellet which is inserted in the insulated bottom shell of the container. The pellets are heated to temperatures of 550° F. in special ovens. These ovens have various capacities of 120, 210, or 300, depending upon the number of meals served.

Manufacturers of these systems have now integrated the pellets with the bottom shell of the container. The plate, platewarmer, and plate cover (with built-in pellet) are heated to proper temperature in self-leveling mobile dispensers which heat and dispense 65 plates, 65 plate warmers, and up to 150 plate covers. For large institutions, these dispensers can be provided so that the exact number of components needed is dispensed.

The integrated pellet system is in use at the U.S. Naval Hospital in Bethesda, Maryland; Massachusetts Eye and Ear Infirmary in Boston, Massachusetts; The Osteopathic Hospital, Portland, Maine; Nashoba Community Hospital, Ayer, Massachusetts; and the Barnes Hospitals in St. Louis, Missouri, to name a few.

The Temp-Rite System

A new system which is being used in a number of hospitals is known as the "temp-rite" or "Metro" system. The food for patients is plated in the kitchen in china, plastic, or disposable ware and placed in plastic containers that fit snugly together, one over the other, to keep the food warm. These containers are placed on trucks, and because of their light weight the trucks can be propelled by dietary employees. Each container becomes a serving tray for the patient, much as in airline service. It is claimed that the system is conducive to labor savings, less dishwashing, and more efficient tray preparation.

The company offering this system will install it with little or no initial capital outlay. Supplies, components, and services are purchased as they are used.

Hot-Pak® Integrated Unit. (Courtesy Dietary Products Division, American Hospital Supply Corp., Evanston, Ill.)

Finessa Built-In Pellet and Plate Warmer, Plate and Plate Cover. (Courtesy Ipco Hospital Supply Corp., Valhalla, N. Y.)

Heater for Hot Pak® Units. (Courtesy Dietary Products Division, American Hospital Supply Corp., Evanston, Ill.)

Ambulatory Service

In some hospitals, such as those operated under military auspices, ambulatory patients are served in the cafeteria. This is done in some of the large tuberculosis hospitals as well. It gives the patient an opportunity to eat away from his room and also saves a certain amount of serving labor.

Evaluation

One of the advantages of our form of government, it has often been pointed out, is the opportunity afforded any of the fifty states to experiment with social or economic reforms. This can be done without involving other states or the Federal Government.

In a similar sense, this is true of the various methods of food distribution to patients used in hospitals today throughout the United States and Canada. The many new types of service have come about through experimentation growing out of dissatisfaction with conventional methods, and through a desire to provide better food and service to patients.

Each type of service has its ardent supporters, and each some critics. It is difficult to give a definite evaluation because defects found in existing systems are being corrected and new methods and new types of equipment are being introduced constantly. However, some general conclusions may be fairly stated:

1. Much depends upon the human equation. *Any system whether centralized or decentralized can be made to work*—given sufficient trained personnel and proper supervision and leadership.
2. Each hospital differs with respect to such factors as: physical structure and layout of buildings; needs, desires, and economic status of patients; financial condition and administrative policies. The best method of food distribution is the one that more nearly meets the peculiar needs of a given institution.

Selecting a Food Distribution System

The selection of the food distribution system best suited to conditions existing in a given institution should be made the subject of a careful study. Outside assistance should be sought in order to get a broad, experienced viewpoint.

Methods and equipment under consideration should be studied *in actual operation* in other hospitals.

Even if a given system is found satisfactory in another hospital in which similar conditions exist, a decision should not be made until the equipment in question has been tried out in the institution where it is to be used. This is especially wise where new types of food trucks are being considered. However, it would not be practicable where the installation of an automatic conveyor system is contemplated.

In one hospital where the kitchen was to be relocated in a new wing under construction, favorable consideration had been given to a certain type of food truck. When a careful check was made of the plans, it was found that a ramp would connect the new kitchen with the elevators. This ruled out the use of the food truck selected. It was necessary to use a lighter weight truck with less tray-carrying capacity, thus increasing the labor cost involved.

Careful study should also be made of the construction of the equipment, its requirements for maintenance, and facilities for repairs and service.

SCHOOL LUNCHROOMS

School lunchrooms are rapidly increasing in number in public and private day schools, whether at elementary, junior high, or high school levels. As the great majority of these food services are of the cafeteria type, the principles set forth earlier in this chapter with respect to the cafeteria can be applied in large part.

While formerly only the noon meal was served, the trend is to serve breakfasts as well. The menu is limited, with usually one or two hot entrées. Considerable attention is paid to nutritional values.

CENTRAL KITCHEN

In a growing number of communities, central kitchens have been established where food for the various school lunchrooms is prepared. It may be chilled or frozen and is reheated at the lunchroom sites. Under this centralized system the number of pieces of equipment in the different lunchrooms is greatly reduced with consequent cost savings. No labor is required in the lunchroom for food preparation and cooking, although help is needed in unwrapping the packaged food and reheating it.

Where there is no central kitchen, the equipment for the school lunchroom is similar to that used in industrial cafeterias. Tray rails and counters are, of course, lower, ranging from 28 inches high in elementary schools to approximately 34 inches in height in secondary schools. Tables and chairs are adapted to the ages of the children and preferably should be adjustable. Plastic ware is widely used as are the compartmented metal or plastic trays in which the food is deposited and which save cost of china and some of the dishwashing labor. Paper service is also used in many school lunchrooms to save labor and for safety and sanitary reasons.

SUGGESTED READING

American Hospital Association, *Readings in Hospital Dietary Administration* (an anthology). Chicago, 1952.

Bryan, Mary de Garmo. *The School Cafeteria*. New York: F. S. Crofts Co., 1946.

Chartrand, Maurice, Cafeteria Manager, Norton Co., Worcester, Mass. *The Design of Cafeteria Counters*, privately printed, 1958.

May, Ernest N. *The Economics of Hospital Food Service*. Wilmington, Delaware: Charitable Research Foundation, 1955.

National Industrial Conference Board Inc., *Company Food Services* (Study in Personal Policy No. 104), New York.

North Carolina, State of, *Food Service in North Carolina Public Schools* (Publication No. 274). Raleigh: State Department of Public Instruction, 1950.

Stokes, John W. *How to Manage a Restaurant or Institutional Food Service*. Dubuque, Iowa: Wm. C. Brown Company Publishers, 1967.

CHAPTER 10

Sanitation, Safety, and Fire Protection

Every well-managed business establishment insists on cleanliness and good-housekeeping in work areas, storerooms, offices, and restrooms. Hospitals go to great lengths to insure aseptic conditions in operating rooms and patients' areas. Yet in industrial and institutional food services one often finds inadequate attention paid to sanitary practices.

Food-service management must exert eternal vigilance against the contamination of food with toxic substances and against the transmission of food-borne disease. Constant safeguards must also be maintained to prevent the spread of infectious diseases through ineffective sanitizing of glasses, cups, and utensils.

While regulations of local and state health authorities with respect to food-service sanitation must be complied with, industrial and institutional services should go beyond the letter of the law. Because of the human equation involved, it is necessary to keep everlastingly at it in order to maintain sanitary practices. To protect the health of those who work in the food service and those who are its patrons, nothing short of the highest possible standards of cleanliness and sanitation should be maintained.

The accident rate in industry and institutions has been greatly reduced in recent years by insistence on safety standards and through safety education programs. As the use of machinery has become widespread in food services, these same standards and programs need to be applied in this area.

Every step should be taken to prevent fires and to train employees in fire prevention. Because of the cooking process and the accumulation of grease in flues and chimneys, fire is a constant hazard in food services. This has been somewhat alleviated through modern systems of ventilation which collect the grease in filters and these filters can be regularly removed and cleaned.

MAIN POINTS IN SANITATION

To ensure high standards of sanitation, the following essentials should be complied with:

1. Physical equipment and layout should be conducive to good sanitary practices.
2. Food should be handled, stored, and refrigerated so as to prevent spoilage and contamination.
3. Food should be safeguarded in distribution and service.
4. Washing of dishes, glasses, utensils, and equipment should result not only in a thorough cleansing, but also in the practical sanitation of these items.
5. Floors, walls, ceilings, counters, tables, and chairs should be cleaned regularly.
6. Vermin and rodents should be eliminated from food areas.
7. Adequate employee supervision, as well as a constant program of education in sanitation should be maintained.

Planning for Sanitary Operation

In planning a new food-service layout, much can be done with the materials and types of equipment now available to ensure safe and sanitary operation. Ceilings and walls should be made of washable materials. The floors of the kitchen and serving areas preferably should be constructed of quarry tile or similar slip-resistant material that is easy to mop, and should be made to slope toward central drains for flushing. A modern alternative, however, is to make the floors level to facilitate movement of mobile equipment, and to install trap drains around cooking areas where moisture collects. These drains may be cleaned with a brush, using a good detergent.

Formerly the various pieces of cooking equipment were mounted on or close to the floor, making cleaning difficult. Modern practice is to mount equipment on legs well above the floor so as to permit mopping underneath, or to cement it in place directly on the tile so that dirt cannot get underneath. Counters are now built without shelves under them, and ranges without ovens or cabinets underneath. Hollow legs of equipment can be used for electrical conduits.

Many pieces of equipment are now made so that they may be moved out of line for cleaning. This also facilitates repairs and replacements. Drawers of cabinets and food trucks should be removable for cleaning.

Air-conditioning has not only alleviated the intense heat in kitchens and serving areas, but has also brought cleaner air into these areas.

In older installations, equipment must be constantly watched to make sure it is contributing to sanitary food production. Crevices or cracks in wooden cutting tables may harbor harmful bacteria. Butcher's chopping blocks are a constant source of danger, and should be resurfaced when worn, or discarded if beyond repair. Cracks in floors and counter surfaces should be repaired. Apertures under counters and pavement allow moisture to enter. They should be sealed. Pots and pans that have become dented and pitted should be discarded. Here, as everywhere, the ounce of prevention is worth far more than the proverbial pound of cure.

An example of lack of care in sanitation was seen in a large cafeteria surveyed recently. A swab test of the meat block revealed, according to the bacteriologist, "definite fecal contamination, as well as probable contamination from nose and throat secretions."

Handling and Storage of Food

We have already emphasized the importance of selecting good food products, checking food items for quality when delivered, and placing them under proper conditions of storage as soon as possible after delivery.

Food in storage must be constantly watched. Modern methods of canning, freezing, and pasteurization have removed many of the difficulties experienced in the past. Nevertheless, excessive temperature and humidity may cause meats and seafood to spoil or cans to swell. Recent tests by food technologists indicate that canned foods lose vitamin content if kept at room temperatures (60° to 72° F.) for a considerable number of days. Butter may take on the flavor of other foods with which it is stored. Milk, even though pasteurized, should not be allowed to become warm.

When pans of sliced meats, poultry, or other leftovers are placed in the refrigerator to be used later, they should be tagged with the storage date so that first-in items will be first to be used.

Bacteria require warmth, moisture, and food upon which to thrive. For this reason, extra precautions must be taken with food in warm, humid seasons of the year. This is especially true of such desserts as eclairs, and of pastries with cream or custard fillings. In humid weather these provide perfect media for the development of harmful bacteria. Such items should be kept under refrigeration even when on display. To be on the safe side, it is advisable to keep such cream-filled items off the menu during the warm months of the year.

Poultry and certain other meats also provide excellent hosts for bacteria if left unprotected for some time after cooking. They should be immediately refrigerated even though still warm.

Pork should always be thoroughly cooked to avoid the dangers of trichinosis. In tropical and subtropical areas, lettuce and similar leafy vegetables should be carefully washed with chlorinated water to prevent disorders such as dysentery caused by amoeba.

The use of packaged, prefabricated cuts of meats and other packaged foods also makes for better sanitation in that it affords protection in the handling of these items.

Sanitary Service and Distribution of Food

The story of the waitress with her thumb in the soup is an example of how not to serve food in a sanitary manner. Yet how often we see a counter attendant hand rolls, doughnuts, or cakes to the patron with the bare hands. In a beautifully equipped employees' cafeteria, we observed a counter girl serve a piece of pie to a patron with her hands. To make matters worse, this girl earlier had put her hand to her mouth, sans handkerchief, to stifle a cough!

The widespread vogue of packaging crackers, cookies, and prepared sandwiches makes these articles sanitation-sound. With items that are not so protected, the rule should be that a serving utensil (serving knife or fork or tongs) should be used in serving food on the counter. Glasses or paper cups should be grasped with fingers well away from the rim, and china cups grasped by the handle.

"Banquet rings" or covers on plates being carried away from the serving area are helpful not only in keeping the food warm but also in preventing contamination. This applies to the distribution of food to patients in hospitals, particularly when trays are carried from the floor kitchen down a long and busy corridor where there is the possibility of exposure to contamination.

PROCEDURES FOR WASHING DISHES, UTENSILS, AND EQUIPMENT

The best practice in washing dishes includes the following steps:

1. *Scraping* and removal of leftover food and waste from soiled dishes. Waste should be put through an opening in the soiled dish table leading to a garbage receptacle underneath or into a garbage disposer.

2. *Pre-rinsing* in luke warm or cold water to remove food particles or soil which otherwise may "bake" on during the washing process.

3. *Washing* in clean water at 140° F. (except in handwashers) containing a good soap or detergent for at least three minutes.

4. *Rinsing* in clean rinse water at 170° F. or higher for at least two minutes. This treatment will sanitize the dishes which may then be removed and allowed to dry in the air.

Note: Temperatures and times given above are those in general use. These may vary with the method of washing (i.e., automatic dishwashers use water at 190° F. and higher and require a shorter rinsing cycle). In any event, the local health authorities should be consulted to make sure that the method of washing complies with the sanitary regulations prevailing. These regulations differ somewhat in different localities.

5. Another step—soaking—may also be employed in washing pots and pans, silver, or dishes with heavy coatings of food or grease.

Dishwashing By Hand

The foregoing steps in good dishwashing practice can be taken by the smallest food service as well as the largest. Washing dishes by hand in a three-compartment sink will do the job just as well as an expensive dishwashing machine if baskets are available for immersing the dishes in hot rinse water. A hose with spray nozzle should also be provided for pre-rinsing.

Pre-Rinsing

When large numbers of dishes are to be washed, the use of machinery is necessary. One effective pre-rinsing device is equipped with a water pump and with a strainer to catch silverware, creamers, and other utensils which otherwise might find their way into the garbage.

Dishwashing Machines

There are six general types of dishwashing machines on the market. Their use depends upon existing conditions, including the number of dishes to be washed daily. These are:

1. Immersion washer with an agitator or oscillating basket
2. Single tank-single basket-door spray type
3. Rack push through curtain type
4. Rack conveyor with single tank
5. Rack conveyor with two or three tanks
6. Dish conveyor type

In dishwashers of types 1 and 2 the dishes are placed in baskets, and in types 3, 4, and 5 in racks which are either pushed through (type 3) or carried through the machine on a conveyor. In type 6 the dishes are placed on a conveyor which forms a continuous rack through the dishwasher.

Adamation Model CA-2 at Abington Hospital, Abington, Pa. (Courtesy Adamation, Newton, Mass.)

Adamation Dishwasher at TWA Flight Kitchen J.F.K. Airport, New York, (Left: Loading; Right: Clean Dish Removal). (Courtesy Adamation, Newton, Mass.)

Hobart Condenser (removes moisture from air in Dishroom). (Courtesy Hobart Mfg. Co., Troy, Ohio.)

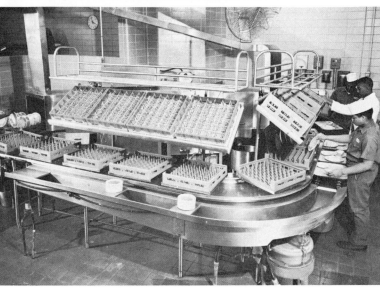

Adamation Model C, Triangle at I.S. Radvin Institute, University of Pennsylvania Hospital, Philadelphia, Pa. (Courtesy Adamation, Newton, Mass.)

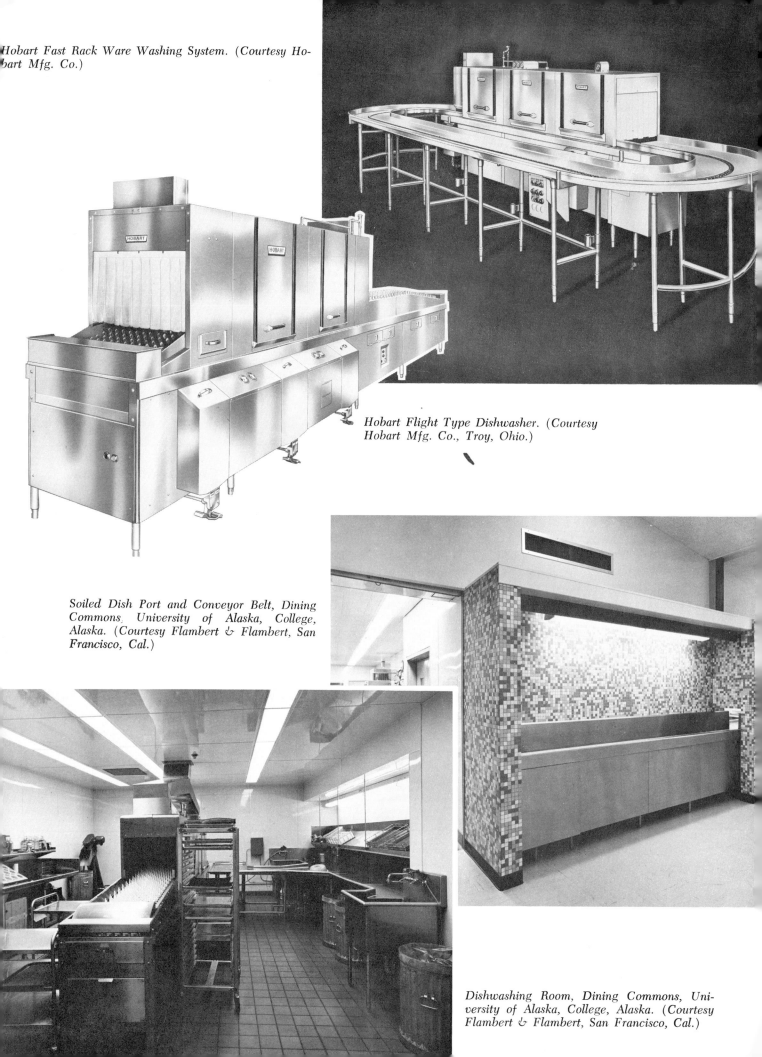

Hobart Fast Rack Ware Washing System. (Courtesy Hobart Mfg. Co.)

Hobart Flight Type Dishwasher. (Courtesy Hobart Mfg. Co., Troy, Ohio.)

Soiled Dish Port and Conveyor Belt, Dining Commons, University of Alaska, College, Alaska. (Courtesy Flambert & Flambert, San Francisco, Cal.)

Dishwashing Room, Dining Commons, University of Alaska, College, Alaska. (Courtesy Flambert & Flambert, San Francisco, Cal.)

Gravity Rollers at cafeteria in Place de Justice (Court House) Montreal and at Residence des Filles (Girls' Dormitory) Laval University, Cité Universitaire, Quebec. Patrons place trays of soiled dishes on rollers leading to dishroom where they stack up awaiting washing. Said to be only a fraction of the cost of conveyors. (Courtesy Bernard et Associés, Montreal P. Q. Canada.)

Gravity Rollers from dishroom side. (Courtesy Bernard et Associés, Montreal P. Q. Canada.)

With the single tank type of machine the sequence depends upon the manual operation of a valve which shuts off the dishwater and turns on the rinse water. Because of the human equation involved, more uniform and positive results can be relied upon with the automatic types of machine having two tanks, one for washing and the other for rinsing. Nevertheless, the single-tank machines are doing an excellent job in many food-service operations.

Some operators find the smooth-bar type of conveyor belt advantageous over the pin-type belt. The smooth-bar belt is useful in washing silver in baskets, cups, and glasses in racks and bus pans.

No machine is foolproof, and the results achieved depend upon the operator, his capacity and interest in the work and the type of training and supervision he receives.

Washing Glasses

Because glasses touch human lips it is necessary that they be sanitized in the cleansing process to prevent the spread of infectious diseases. This can be accomplished through ordinary washing methods by hand or machine, if the rinsing water is hot enough. Milady's lipstick marks, however, present another problem. To remove this deposit brushing is required.

Special glass washers have been devised in which the glasses are placed upside down in a holder which subjects both the inside and outside of each glass to brushes revolving in hot water to which a detergent has been added. The glasses are then immersed in a rinse tank containing a bactericide solution.

Caterers have found that the use of ordinary galvanized wire baskets tend to chip the lips of china cups and glasses. By having these baskets chromium-plated they present smooth surfaces which will not chip the cups or glasses. This can be accomplished at nominal cost.

Silverware

Knives, forks, and spoons can be washed in the baskets of the dishwashing machine. However, when these utensils are piled in layers in the basket, it is not possible for the detergent solution or the rinse water to act on all surfaces of each utensil.

Perforated metal or nylon cylinders are on the market in which knives, forks, and spoons are placed vertically in respective cylinders with the "business end" of the utensils protruding from the cylinder and the handles at the bottom. These cylinders allow the utensils to air dry after rinsing. After drying, their contents are "poured" into other cylinders so that the handles protrude. The cylinders are then placed on the cafeteria counter. The use of these cylinders prevents contact with any part of the utensil except the handle until it is picked up by the user. Baskets can be used for putting these cylinders through rack-type dishwashing machines. (See Figure 10.1)

Special washing machines for silver are in use in larger operations. Burnishing machines, in which silverware is polished by being rolled in tanks containing tiny metal balls, are also in common use.

Use of Towels

Drying with towels is generally unnecessary and is not recommended as good sanitary practice. If towels must be used to polish glasses and silver, clean, dry, lintless towels should be provided.

Hot Water Supply

Plenty of hot water is a "must" if dishes are to be properly sanitized. This entails a supply of water at from 170° to 190° F. for rinsing. It is dangerous and wasteful to maintain such temperatures in the regular hot water lines supplying washrooms. Recourse must be had to special hot water units supplying the kitchen, heaters under the rinse water tank, or "boosters" on the hot water lines on the dishwashing machines. Special attention should be given to the hot water supply in providing for dishwashing facilities.

Bactericides

There are a number of bactericides on the market for use in rinsing to provide for positive sterilization. Some of these are said to be highly effective. In situations where it is difficult to maintain proper rinse water temperatures, their use should be considered—providing the local health authorities approve.

Detergents

Detergents are specially prepared cleaning agents which are designed to wash dishes thoroughly, without forming suds, thus facilitating the rinsing process. Many brands of effective detergents are on the market. Special dispensers, mounted on the dishwashing ma-

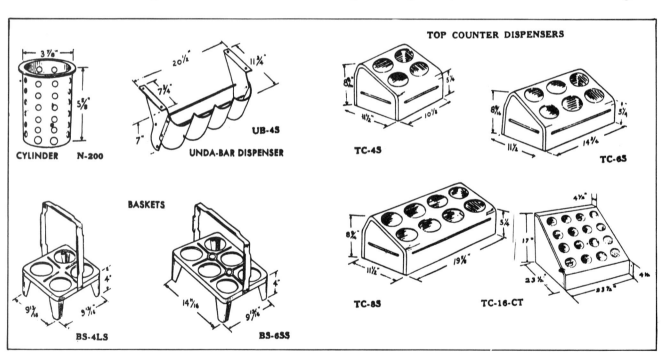

Fig. 10.1. Steril-sil equipment. The Steril-sil cylinders are perforated and made of stainless steel or nylon. Soiled knives, forks, and spoons are put in separate cylinders, each with the handles down and the "business ends" (blades, tines, and bowls) exposed as they go through the washing process. When it comes out of the Washing Machine, the cylinder is turned upside down and its contents transferred to an empty cylinder, but with the handles protruding. This protects the "business end" of the utensil from contamination. (Courtesy Steril-Sil Company, Boston, Mass.)

chine (the most modern, electronically operated), are adjusted to provide the correct amount of detergent in the wash tank when the machine is operating.

Some detergents contain a "wetting agent"—a chemical which prevents the formation of droplets. This is particularly desirable in areas where water contains more than 7 grains per gallon of calcium or magnesium, causing it to be termed "hard." The use of wetting agents is desirable in washing plastic ware and nonmetal trays. These materials are low in conductivity and consequently do not retain heat as does china or metals. Wetting agents also permit air drying of china and utensils free from "spotting."

Detergents are also available containing oxygen-liberating elements which are said to remove stains from plastic ware without impairing the finish. When chlorine rinses are used to remove stains in plastics, the gloss finish is eventually removed.

Conveyor Type Dish Machines—Drying Space

With the automatic conveyor type of dish-washing machines, sufficient drying space must be allowed at the end of the conveyor line. Because these machines require considerable floor area, the lack of adequate space sometimes causes the conveyor line to be curtailed at the drying end. Up to eight feet of drying space should be allowed on this type of machine.

The Unlimited Horizontal Conveyor

This device was invented by two Massachusetts men, C. R. Weihe and Edward Gratto.

Instead of revolving like a belt wholly within the machine, the new conveyor carries up to twenty or more dish racks on a shallow, stainless-steel table which runs in an elliptical shape outside the machine. The tracking mechanism, actuated by the machine itself, moves continuously at the rate of approximately eight feet per minute. The table may be varied in shape and even be carried outside the dishroom, hence the term "unlimited."

Because of the ample external radius and slow continuous motion, soiled dishes may be loaded directly by bus boys or waitresses. As clean dishes emerge from the machine they can be visually inspected and if any have not been thoroughly cleansed they are allowed to remain on the racks for a second washing cycle.

The use of this new device eliminates the need of a dishwashing machine operator for many food services. In one hospital, where this new conveyor is in use, two women employees strip trays from 145 patients and place dishes, glasses, and trays upon the racks. The same women store all of these when washed, ready for the next use. The horizontal conveyer is said to save 18½ man hours daily in this institution and requires 40% less floor area.

One of the features of the unit is a powerful automatic pre-wash device which reuses clear rinse water. A rubber squeegee is attached under every third dish rack to carry food particles along the table to a garbage disposal unit placed just ahead of the pre-rinse cabinet.

Chief advantages cited in addition to the labor savings economy of floor space are thorough cleansing of glasses; effective pre-wash mechanism; reduction of breakage; low water consumption; and visual inspection of dishes. The garbage disposal unit is optional.

Storage of Clean Dishes and Utensils

It is not enough merely to be assured that dishes and utensils have been properly washed and sanitized. They should be stored on clean shelves, and protected against dust, vermin, or other contamination. The use of portable, self-leveling devices, in which the dishes are placed immediately after washing and drying, is preferable. By this means, the dishes are fully protected against contamination, and can be wheeled to the serving area, thus eliminating further handling. If desired, these devices can also be equipped with heating or refrigerating elements.

Washing of Cooking Utensils and Equipment

The conventional method of washing pots, pans, and food containers has been by hand in a sink in the kitchen in what is known as the pot-washing area. A three compartment sink is preferable, with one compartment for soaking, a second for washing, and a third for rinsing.

An electrically-operated revolving brush can speed up the cleansing process.

A number of mechanical pot washers have appeared on the market recently and are in use in many food services. In these devices, the utensils are subjected to heavy sprays of water, to which detergents are added. Where these are operated according to directions, they have been found satisfactory. The opinion is, like any other mechanical contrivance, the operator must be trained in its use.

Not only should pots and pans be subjected to the pot-washing process, but also inserts from cafeteria counters and from mobile food conveyors. Where possible, some of these items can be sent through the dish machine. Many pieces of food equipment, such as tray trucks, are now equipped with removable drawers and tray slides which should also be washed along with the other containers in which food has been stored.

Cres-Cor Dish Dolly. (Courtesy Crescent Metal Products, Inc., Cleveland, Ohio.)

Cleansing of Equipment

The same precautions taken in washing dishes should be applied to all the pieces of equipment in which food is stored or processed. Unfortunately, this is not always the case. A city health inspector recently stated that he frequently finds kitchen employees who do not know how to take apart for cleaning such machines as slicers, grinders, choppers, and mixers.

Recently in one of the leading general hospitals noted for its high standards, we found that the meat-grinding machine had not been taken apart daily as prescribed by the Dietary rules. Extremely high bacteria counts were registered when the hospital pathologist made an examination. Again, this illustrates the importance of proper supervision.

Bacteriological Tests

Health inspectors in most localities take frequent bacteriological counts of restaurant dishes and utensils. Many food services have found it advisable to have such tests made on their own account. In some

concerns, this is done by the company's own technicians. In other instances, competent consulting bacteriologists are engaged to make periodic inspections, not only of the dishes and utensils, but of all phases of the food-service sanitation.

In hospitals, this work is often done by laboratory technicians working under the direction of the pathologist.

In any food service, such bacteriological examinations should be made regularly without advance notice to the food-service management. Swab tests should be made not only of clean dishes and utensils, as a check on the functioning of the dishwashing operation, but also of the various food processing machines such as meat grinders and slicing machines, and of chopping blocks, tables, and counters on which food is prepared.

A written report of the findings should be made directly to the management of the institution or business establishment, and a copy given also to the food-service manager or chief dietitian. Thus a constant check is maintained on the effectiveness of the sanitary measures being taken. Figure 10.2 shows an inspection form used in checking food-service establishments. These checklists insure that nothing important in the way of sanitation is overlooked by the inspector, and speed up the inspection process.

Cleaning of Rooms and Furniture

Tables, chairs, and counters should be cleaned daily. Floors should be swept and mopped. Walls and ceilings also should be washed frequently and refinished periodically.

A bright, clean dining room and kitchen not only reduces dangers of infection, but adds to employee morale and patron satisfaction.

Elimination of Vermin

The term "vermin" applies to insect pests such as flies, mosquitos, roaches, and includes rats and mice. Vermin not only destroy food, but carry infection. Flies are known to spread disease by traveling from filth to food.

Food should be stored in rodent-proof and insect-proof containers. Foundations of buildings should be made tight. Holes in walls and partitions should be closed with rat-proof materials. Garbage should be stored in covered metal containers which do not leak. Windows and doors should be provided with screens. Sprays, flypaper, and other precautions can be used against flies, but the best safeguard is absolute cleanliness, inside and outside the food-service area. Many food services regularly employ the services of qualified professional exterminators to eliminate vermin.

Where insecticides and other poisons are used, care must be taken that they do not come in contact with food. Such materials should be stored separately and kept under lock and key.

Disposal of Garbage and Rubbish

As previously pointed out, garbage from the dishwashing operation is usually dropped into a receptacle placed under an opening in the soiled dish table. Where local regulations allow its use, a mechanical waste disposer is preferable. This device grinds and carries waste into the pipes connecting with the sewage system. There are a number of disposers on the market. It is important that the disposer selected be large enough and powerful enough to care for the garbage volume to be handled. In selecting a garbage disposer, it is wise to insist upon a guarantee of performance. It is also well to look into the provisions for service and repairs, in case a breakdown should occur.

In addition to the garbage from the Dishroom, there will be considerable garbage from the food preparation area in the main kitchen. If a disposer is not installed in this area, it will be necessary to carry the garbage to another room to await collection. Such a room should be vermin and rodent-proof. It should be screened, with walls and floor free from cracks or openings.

Preferably, the garbage room should be refrigerated to prevent odors.

In many areas garbage is collected by the proprietors of piggeries who feed the garbage to the pigs. In some cases the food service receives compensation for the garbage. In others, the collection is made without charge. In some areas garbage from hospitals cannot be used for animal food. An increasing number of health boards are ruling that garbage must be boiled before being used for this purpose. The boiling is usually done by the piggery proprietor.

The disposal of rubbish, boxes, cartons, wastepaper, and cans also involves good sanitary precautions. A separate room—with precautions against vermin and rodents—is recommended. Rubbish should be removed regularly (daily where large quantities accumulate). Collections can be made by local governmental authorities or by private contractors.

Garbage and rubbish rooms should be constructed so that they can be flushed out with a hose after collections are made. It is good practice to follow this flushing process with a disinfectant spray.

Compactors

Bottle crushers and rubbish compactors are available and used by food services. Some companies offer a service whereby a compactor is furnished the food-service operator and the compacted rubbish collected weekly by the contractor. Because of the principle of the compactor's operation, more frequent collections are unnecessary.

Incinerators

Food services use incinerators to dispose of garbage and rubbish. Where the material is dry, no external fuel is required. If wet garbage is to be incinerated, an oil, natural gas, or bottled gas burner will be necessary. Of these, oil is the least expensive. It is claimed that an incinerator so equipped will reduce 500 pounds of mixed waste or garbage, wet or dry, to one pound of dry ash within a few minutes. The use of an incinerator also makes it possible to inspect

Hobart Food Waste Disposer. (Courtesy Hobart Mfg. Co., Troy, Ohio.)

FOOD SERVICE ESTABLISHMENT
INSPECTION REPORT

ESTABLISHMENT _____ DATE _____ NSD _____

ADDRESS _____ TYPE _____ PERMIT POSTED _____

Regulations: Article X, Sanitary Code "Minimum Sanitary Standards for Food Service Establishments." 1. Definitions:

_____ 2. FOOD SOURCES: Clean, wholesome, safe. No spoilage, adulteration or misbranding. Milk products: legal, pasteurized, in original container. Shellfish: approved, identified, Meat inspected. Other food approved.

_____ 3. FOOD PROTECTION: Not contaminated while stored, prepared, displayed, served or transported. Perishable foods under 45 F, hazardous under 45 F or over 150 F, frozen under O F. Minimum handling of food, fruits and vegetables washed, pork and stuffings thoroughly cooked, straws wrapped, poisons properly handled.

_____ 4. DISEASE CONTROL: No employee with communicable disease or infection. Manager to report to Health Department.

_____ 5. CLEANLINESS OF PERSONNEL: Employees wear clean garments, wash hands, wear hair restraints, not use tobacco.

_____ 6. EQUIPMENT AND UTENSILS (CONSTRUCTION): Smooth, cleanable, and in good repair. Food contact surfaces accessible, clean, nontoxic corrosive or absorbent. Installed to facilitate cleaning adjacent areas.

_____ 7. EQUIPMENT AND UTENSILS (CLEANLINESS): Tableware cleaned and sanitized after use. Air dried. Kitchenware cleaned and sanitized prior to use. Other equipment as tables, counters, mixers, slicers, hoods, fans, stoves, etc., kept clean. Tableware, kitchenware, and equipment stored and handled to prevent contamination.
MANUAL DISHWASHING: 3 section sink, detergent, sanitize by immersion 30 sec 170 F, or 1 min chlorine 50 ppm.
MACHINE DISHWASHING: Proper operation, cleanable design, thermometers, wash water 140 F, rinse 180 F.

_____ 8. WATER: Hot and cold water under pressure, adequate and approved. Ice approved, handled in sanitary manner.

_____ 9. SEWAGE: Public system or other in compliance with Article XI of the State Sanitary Code.

_____ 10. PLUMBING: According to code. No nuisance, contamination, insanitary condition, or cross connection.

_____ 11. TOILETS: Adequate, convenient, clean and in good repair. No odors. Self closing doors, hand washing sign.

_____ 12. HANDWASHING: Adequate, convenient, hot and cold water, soap in dispenser and sanitary towels. Kept clean.

_____ 13. GARBAGE AND RUBBISH: Garbage in nonabsorbent covered containers. Other waste handled in sanitary manner.

_____ 14. VERMIN: Effective measures to prevent the entrance and breeding of rodents, flies, roaches, and other vermin.

_____ 15. FLOORS, WALLS, CEILINGS: Floors smooth, clean, nonabsorbent. No sawdust. Walls washable and light color.

_____ 16. LIGHTING: Food preparation rooms and all working surfaces well lighted. Toilets well lighted.

_____ 17. VENTILATION: Food preparation areas well ventilated. Areas free from excessive heat, steam, vapors, smoke and fumes. No grease or condensate. Filters removable for cleaning. Exhaust fans, -no nuisance outside.

_____ 18. DRESSING ROOMS: Facilities provided for storage of employees' clothing and personal belongings. Kept clean.

_____ 19. HOUSEKEEPING: Premises neat and clean. Not used for living. Soiled linens in container. No animals.

REMARKS: _____

_____

_____

_____

_____

_____

_____

_____

_____

_____

_____
PERSON INTERVIEWED   SANITARIAN

Fig. 10.2.   Food Service Inspection Report. (Courtesy Harlan W. Kingsbury, Chief Sanitary Officer, Newton Health Department, Newton, Mass.)

waste as it is loaded into the incinerator and to salvage pieces of silverware, china, or glassware which may have been thrown out with the garbage.

Incinerators are still used by many institutions; however, the growing tendency to restrict such burnings in order to reduce air pollution has tended to curtail their use.

FOOD-SERVICE EMPLOYEES

High standards of food-service sanitation can only be attained through the cooperation of the food-service staff.

There are three principal groups of communicable diseases that must be guarded against in public feeding operations. These are:

1. Respiratory
2. Intestinal
3. Skin diseases

All three can be transmitted by food handlers who are infected. Some of these, it is true, can also be transmitted by patrons; but it is the employee who handles the food, utensils, and equipment.

Fortunately, most food is sterilized in the cooking process. Public health records indicate that the incidence of food poisoning is low in established food-service operations where proper equipment is provided and sanitary standards maintained. Nevertheless, precautions must be taken to avoid possibility of infection.

Medical Examinations

The first step is to make sure that food-service employees are in good health, and are not carriers of communicable diseases. Medical examinations for employees, including chest X-rays and blood tests are required in many food services upon induction and periodically thereafter. Although these are highly desirable, there is no guarantee that an individual who passes an examination one day may not become infected at a later date.

Supervisors must constantly check the health of their staff members. Workers who are obviously ill or have infected sores, particularly on the hands or exposed parts of the body, should be excused from work until fully recovered.

First Aid

First aid facilities should be provided so that cuts and burns may be cared for immediately to prevent infections and serious complications.

Employee Cooperation

Employee attitudes play a large part in food-service sanitation—more than is generally realized. If workers *want* dishes to be sterile, if they *want* floors to be clean, if they *want* food to be free from the hazards of infection, it is likely that their wishes will come true.

To develop such attitudes, food-service workers must first be brought to understand the necessity for sanitary precautions. This is a matter of education, and should begin with the initial interview when the new employee is hired. It should also play a part in the orientation of the new employee. A continuing program of education in food sanitation should be carried on for all employees. (See "Group Meetings," Chapter 4.)

Rules for Employees

Every food-service employee should be required to follow sanitation rules, such as the following:

Clean uniforms should be worn at all times. Some kitchens are now built with glass partitions so that the work of food preparation and cooking is in full view of patrons. This has had a salutary effect upon the morale and sanitary habits of employees in such kitchens.

Employees should cover coughs and sneezes with handkerchiefs. Hands should be washed frequently, particularly after using handkerchiefs and after visits to the toilet. To make sure that this is done, a wash basin should be installed in the kitchen, in plain sight, with soap and paper towels. Every employee entering the kitchen or food-service area should first wash his hands regardless of his reason for leaving the room.

Hair nets should be worn by women and/or caps by male employees, especially those wearing long hair. Workers should be trained not to touch the nose or other parts of the face or head with fingers when serving food or when on duty behind the cafeteria counter.

No smoking in kitchens or behind counters. Not only is it unpleasant to find a trace of tobacco in one's food, but food may acquire an off-taste from tobacco fumes.

Employee Education

The fundamentals of food-service sanitation can be covered in a series of weekly or fortnightly employee meetings. Local and state boards of health will gladly furnish speakers, and also slides, strip films, or moving pictures. In some cases, the health authorities will present certificates to those attending who evidence satisfactory grasp of the subject.

Posters may be used to inculate proper habits of food handling. The Boston Health Department in cooperation with the Massachusetts Restaurant Association developed a series of posters which illustrate such points, as shown in Figure 10.3.

Moving pictures and filmstrips on sanitary food handling are also available through state and local health departments, restaurant associations, manufacturers of dishwashing machines and detergents, and some of the large restaurant chains. Among several audiovisual filmstrips put out by the National Restaurant Association is an excellent one on food-service sanitation. The United States Public Health Service also provides booklets and many visual training aids.

A FEW REMINDERS

Handle Glasses Without Touching The Rim

Use An Ice Scoop

Use A Fork To Pick Up Butter

Pick Up Knives, Forks, And Spoons Only By The Handles

Keep Fingers Out Of Food

Cover Coughs And Sneezes

Fig. 10.3. (Courtesy Boston Health Department.)

In food protection meetings conducted by the author, it has been interesting to note the reactions of employees. When, for example, they look through a microscope for the first time and see bacteria on a slide, it makes a deep impression. They come to understand some of the rudiments of bacteriology and its place in food sanitation. The understanding enhances their feelings of responsibility to the public. It increases their pride in their daily work. They cannot help but be better workers.

Sound worker attitudes toward sanitation can be nurtured. They develop best where the environment reflects a sincere desire on the part of management for sanitary practices.

A fundamental point to emphasize is the responsibility of the employee for the health of the patrons in so far as the food service is concerned. If the dishwasher or other worker can be brought to think of

himself not as a menial but rather as the guardian of the health of his customers and fellow employees, it increases his feelings of importance. He gains what the sociologists call "status." He will be a happier and better worker because he realizes that his work is important. And important it is!

In a food service where the manager had been unable to keep dishwashers, he advertised for a "Dish Machine Operator." Among the applicants was an older man of excellent character and background who had found it difficult to get a job because he was over sixty. The manager stressed the importance of the job as that of seeing that dishes were sanitized so that the health of patrons would be safeguarded. The man accepted the job and did outstanding work. The manager made it a point to visit with him each day to talk with him. He was made to feel that he was one of the supervisory staff, and that his job was just as important as any in the organization. As a result, dishwashing was no longer a problem in that food service.

Positive employee attitudes toward sanitation can be built by the supervisor and his assistants in daily contacts with employees. They can be developed in discussion meetings where workers are not scolded or lectured, but rather their suggestions sought. (See Two Types of Meetings, Chapter 4, "The Food-Service Organization.")

With sanitation, as with other food-service problems, teamwork will bring to light latent capabilities hitherto not recognized. Given proper understanding and cooperation between management and workers, all problems of food service can be solved.

SAFETY

Accident prevention and safety education are standard procedures in institutions and industrial plants today. These programs should be applied in food services so that the occupational hazards in them may be guarded against and minimized.

The new Federal Occupational Health and Safety Law, which is now in effect, provides drastic penalties for institutions in which conditions are found to be unsafe or dangerous to the health of employees.

Making the Food Service Safe

The first step in a safety program is to make sure that, as far as possible, the physical structure and the equipment located in it are safe. Stairways should be well lighted and protected by handrails. Elevator shafts should be equipped with safety gates. Doors should have a panel of glass to permit vision both ways. This applies particularly to doors leading to and from kitchens.

Food processing machines such as bread and meat slicers and chopping, mixing, or grinding machines should be equipped with safety guards and emergency stops. In some cases such machines can be made virtually accident-proof by making it necessary that one hand press upon a spring switch to keep the device running while the other hand is engaged in feeding it.

The use of color can be extremely helpful in bringing out the contrasts between moving and nonmoving parts of machines and equipment—as warning signals. Brilliant yellow, for example, against a contrasting background will arouse even the day-dreaming employee because of its effect on the senses. Contrast-

ing colors on the steps and risers of a stairway will tend to prevent stumbling and falls. Proper illumination does much to enhance the safety of the food service, and at the same time increase the productivity of the workers. (See Chapter 5)

Training for Safe Work Practices

Not only should the premises be made physically safe, but, in addition, food-service employees must be trained in safe practices. Storeroom workers are especially susceptible to strains, bruises, and cuts. They can be taught how to lift using the legs rather than putting the strain on back or abdominal muscles. The use of gloves in handling cartons and cases will often save the hands.

Fig. 10.4. What can you do about falls. (Courtesy Liberty Mutual Insurance Company, Boston, Mass.)

Kitchen employees are subject to burns and cuts. The latter can be minimized by instruction in the proper use of knives in food preparation, meat slicing, etc. Burns from grasping hot metal objects can be prevented by the use of potholders and gloves. Burns from flying grease may be extremely painful, and can be guarded against only by extreme care on the part of the worker.

In operating kitchen machinery such as meat choppers, grinders, and slicing machines, a wooden guide should be used to feed the machine rather than using the fingers. It is not only a matter of education but also of supervision to see that this and similar regulations are enforced.

Some food services will instantly dismiss an employee who flagrantly violates a safety rule.

Slippery floors are one of the greatest hazards for waiters, waitresses, and serving employees. Here they are often due to careless spillage of liquids from receptacles or containers or the dropping of slippery bits of food or refuse on the floor. The rule should be that any foreign substance should be removed from the floor *immediately* by sweeping or mopping. This should apply in every part of the food service.

Dishwashing employees are often injured by cuts from broken glass or china or from burns from the dishwashing machine. The use of gloves will lessen these hazards. Cartoons and posters are always useful in safety education. (See Figures 10.4, 10.5, and 10.6.)

Foreign Substances

When the food-service patron finds a piece of metal, glass, or wood in his food it distresses him and reflects

DON'T OVERLOAD TRAYS!

WE GET BREAKAGE

YOU GET A SORE BACK

THE *WRONG* WAY TO LIFT
DON'T LIFT WITH YOUR BACK

THE *SAFE* WAY TO LIFT
BEND YOUR KNEES AND USE YOUR LEGS

Fig. 10.5. Two important causes of strains. (Courtesy Liberty Mutual Insurance Company, Boston, Mass.)

Fig. 10.6. First aid is important. (Courtesy Liberty Mutual Insurance Company, Boston, Mass.)

upon the institution. If this happens in a commercial restaurant, he may bring suit for damages. The elimination of foreign substances begins with the purchasing and receiving of food items. Metal and cardboard containers are preferable to wooden ones because they practically eliminate splinters, tacks, and nails. The opening of containers should be carried on in a segregated area. Loose pieces of material and nails should be picked up immediately lest they find their way into food. One source of foreign substances is the breaking of dishes or tumblers at the counter. Pieces of flying glass may get into open ice-cream containers or other food in open pans. Electric light bulbs should not be hung over exposed ingredients or food products. Cracked or chipped pieces of china or glassware should be discarded.

The only solution of this problem is constant vigilance! Food should always be inspected before it goes to the patron. Dishes and utensils should be checked as they come from the dishroom and before being put into service. Sieves, brushes and whiskbrooms used in handling food should be inspected often for loose wires, bristles, and other foreign substances which might get into the food. Overhead pipes and ceilings should be protected so that chips of rust or paint do not fall upon food.

How Employees Are Injured

According to insurance companies, food-service employees are injured in the following ways: bumps and cuts; slips and falls; strains; burns; objects in eyes; cuts from glass and china; injuries from hand tools and implements; elevators; razor blades; machinery. By isolating the causes of accidents, it is possible to correct the hazards and prevent serious consequences.

Safety Training Pays Dividends

Safety training should be given on the job as part of the induction of new employees, and should be followed up at the regular employees' meetings. Visual material for such meetings can be secured from insurance companies and from such agencies as the National Safety Council.

Safe and sanitary practices pay for themselves many times over in increased productivity, reduced absenteeism, and greater confidence on the part of patrons. Where employer's coverages for workmen's compensation, public liability, and product liability are based upon actual performance, as is usually the case, lower accident rates mean lower insurance premiums, affording direct savings. Under retrospective rating policies, the causes of accidents are usually listed—and from these indicators steps can be taken to prevent similar accidents in the future.

Fire Protection

Fires most frequently occur in food-service kitchens in the exhaust flues connected with the conventional hoods over the principal cooking appliances. Grease and dirt which accumulate in these flues should be removed and the flues cleaned periodically. This can be done by the institution's maintenance department or by contractors who make it their business to do this work.

In modern kitchen installations filters are provided in the ventilating system which collect grease and dirt. These filters can be removed and cleaned at regular intervals.

Nevertheless, fire extinguishers should be provided in convenient locations in storerooms, kitchens, dining-room and other areas where fires may occur. Some of these extinguishers are equipped to emit a chemical foam which will smother grease fires. Steam is also effective as an extinguishing agent.

In any event, employees should be trained in the use of fire-fighting equipment through periodic fire drills. Care should be taken to prevent accumulations of waste materials—boxes, cartons, waste paper, etc. —which might become ignited through spontaneous combustion. Draperies and decorations in dining areas should be made of materials that are resistant to fire. Arrangements will, of course, be made for prompt notification of the local fire department, in case of fire, either by telephone or through fire alarm boxes located in the institution.

SUGGESTED READING

ASSOCIATION OF FOOD INDUSTRY SANITARIANS. *Sanitation for the Food Preservation Industries.* New York: McGraw-Hill Book Company, 1952.

KLEINER AND COLEMAN. *Sanitation Manual.* New York: Ahrens Book Co., Inc.

LIBERTY MUTUAL INSURANCE COMPANY, Boston, Mass. Publications of Loss Prevention Department.

LIBERTY MUTUAL INSURANCE COMPANY, Boston, Mass., booklet "Hazard Hunt at the Hotel."

MICHIGAN, UNIVERSITY OF. Publications of the National Sanitation Foundation. Ann Arbor, Michigan.

NATIONAL SAFETY COUNCIL, Publications. Chicago, Illinois.

NATIONAL FIRE PROTECTION ASSOCIATION, Publications. Boston, Mass.

RICHARDSON, TREVA M. *Sanitation for Food Service Workers.* Chicago: Cahners Publishing Co.

STOKES, JOHN W. *How to Manage a Restaurant or Institutional Food Service.* Dubuque, Iowa: Wm. C. Brown Company Publishers, 1967.

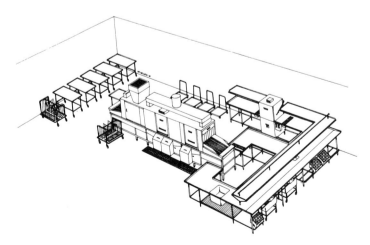

Illustration of Cost Saving Dishwashing System. (Courtesy Hobart Mfg. Co., Troy, Ohio.)

CHAPTER **11**

Control of Food Cost

Costs of operating industrial and institutional food services are generally considered under three headings:

1. Raw food cost
2. Salaries and Wages
3. Other Expenses

As food costs are subject to day-to-day fluctuations more than any other class of expense, it has long been considered a basic criterion of economic success in food-service operation. Menu prices in commercial restaurants as well as in industrial and institutional cafeterias are customarily based on the cost of "raw food" in a given dish.

RAW FOOD COST

There was a time when all food purchased by a public feeding establishment was "raw food." Today ice cream, bread, pastries, and many other processed or partially processed foods are purchased. Potatoes and apples, for example, may be delivered already peeled or potatoes purchased in powder form for instant use. Nevertheless, the term "raw food cost" embraces the cost of all food items brought into the food service. It includes transportation and delivery charges, but it should not include any item of labor, fuel, or other expense entailed in the handling or processing of the food once it has been delivered.

Food-Cost Percentage

Where meals are accounted for when served,[1] such as in cafeterias, the raw food cost is expressed as a percentage of the sales price. Thus if a given portion

---

[1]The term "accounted for" is used because in institutional cafeterias some meals (such as those served to student nurses) may be served free of charge, but are accounted for and may be charged to the Nursing Service.

of food costs 25¢ and is sold for 50¢ the "food-cost percentage" is said to be 50%. If food sales for a given period total $1,000 and the total cost of raw food for the same period is $600, the food-cost percentage for the period is 60%. The amount left over, in the latter case 40%, is known as Gross Profit.

In the industrial or institutional cafeteria it is essential that a definite objective be set in terms of food-cost percentage. In the commercial restaurant this percentage must be set so that the Gross Profit is sufficient to cover Salaries and Wages and Other Expenses (including rent) and still leave a margin of profit (termed Net Profit).

However, industrial and institutional food services are usually operated on a nonprofit basis. This allows a higher percentage of food cost than can be afforded in the commercial establishment. In other words, the patron of the institutional cafeteria should receive greater food value for the money he pays than the patron of the commercial restaurant. Whether or not he actually gets more for his money will depend upon the efficiency of the operation, and also upon management policy.

By "management policy" we mean the amount of subsidy management is willing to provide. In some food services management is satisfied if the income received from the operation covers only the actual food cost. Generally management supplies space, equipment, and utilities; and the food service is expected to provide for salaries and wages and other expenses. However, as wages and fringe benefits have increased in recent years, the percentage available for food cost has had to be reduced.

The raw food cost percentage of any given item depends chiefly upon three factors: (a) Purchase Cost, (b) Portion Size, and (c) Menu Price. It can be seen, therefore, that by adjusting these factors, the food-cost percentage may be set at any desired figure. However, if the percentage is too low, the patron will get too little in food value for his money and will become dissatisfied. If the percentage is too high, there will be an insufficient amount of the sales dollar left over (i.e. Gross Profit) to cover costs of labor and other expenses of the operation.

As in the old Greek fable of Scylla and Charybdis, it is necessary to steer a middle course between the two hazardous alternatives. This can be done by settling upon a food-cost percentage that will give adequate food value and at the same time provide sufficient gross profit to cover other necessary costs of the operation. When the food-cost percentage is decided upon, it should be maintained uniformly within

a reasonable degree of accuracy. This can be accomplished through an effective food-cost control system.

Raw Food Cost Per Meal

With respect to meals served away from the cafeterias to patients in hospitals, students in schools or colleges, or inmates in institutions, it is not feasible to operate upon a food-cost percentage basis, as no sales figure is available. Common practice is to compute the food cost per meal. This is done by dividing the total cost of food for a given day, week, month, or year by the total number of meals served during the period.

In governmental institutions it is the general practice to compute food costs upon a per diem or a daily ration basis (i.e. three daily meals combined) rather than upon the number of meals served. This, of course, presents no problems in control.

Food costs can be controlled effectively whether food is served in cafeterias, dining rooms, or to patients in their rooms.

STEPS IN FOOD-COST CONTROL

Assuming that proper methods of purchasing, receiving, storing, preparing, and cooking are being followed, the essential steps in controlling food costs are:

1. Establishing standard portions and making sure that these standards are adhered to.
2. Determining the exact unit cost of each standard portion.
3. Fixing of uniform cafeteria menu prices based on these unit portion costs and the overall food-cost percentage that has been decided upon.
4. Setting standard per diem costs or meal costs on meals served away from the cafeteria.
5. Instituting a system of control to make sure that the various food-cost objectives are attained.

Standard Portions

The standard portions to be served will depend principally upon the current market price of the raw food item, the price at which the cooked item is to be sold, and the markup desired. Thus all of these factors—costs, portions, prices, and food-cost percentages—are interrelated.

Other important, though less tangible, factors have to do with the type of workers to be fed, and the portions which have been customarily served. In this connection, the appearance of the cooked portion on the plate is one criterion.

After the standard portion has been determined, it is necessary that steps be taken to see that it is served uniformly to patrons. With poultry and meat items it is often possible to weigh out the portions in advance and separate them with waxed papers ready to be placed on plates. Reliable scales giving exact weights in ounces should be provided for this purpose. Casserole dishes are also helpful in making up uniform portions in advance. With soups, stews, and soft dishes, instruction must be given as to the size and type of ladle, spoon, scoop, or dipper to be used. Figure 11.1 shows how this information may be noted on a Cost and Portion Card.

Determining Unit Costs

To determine unit costs it is necessary to carry on a series of tests in the kitchen and bakery. Records must be kept of weights and quantities as purchased, with costs computed at market prices. Cooked weights and numbers of usable portions are determined and recorded. Due allowance must be made for inevitable shrinkage and waste (for food which adheres to pots and pans, losses in serving, etc.). An allowance of 10% is recommended for this purpose.

On dishes in which various ingredients are used, the necessary data as to items and quantities will be obtained from the formula cards or records. The preparation must be carefully observed to make sure that the formula in question is being followed as recorded. The costing process is time-consuming, but once an item is costed the cost record should remain valid indefinitely, or until the formula is substantially changed.

Cost and Portion Card

Figure 11.1 shows a form of Master Cost and Portion Card. This is the Master Card which is kept in the Food Service Department office. On this card the quantities and costs of the ingredients are listed for the batch as cooked. The unit portion cost is found by dividing the total cost by the number of cooked portions yielded. To this unit cost is added the allowance for waste.

It will be noted that the standard portion and service is outlined on the card. The standard portioning instructions on this card may be duplicated separately for the kitchen and counter people concerned with serving, so that uniformity in portioning may be maintained.

On the Cost and Portion Card provision has been made for price fluctuations of the principal ingredient. In this example the card deals with Beef Stew with Dumpling, and unit portion cost is shown with beef chuck, the principal ingredient at varying prices.

The prices shown in this instance and in other figures in this book are those which prevailed at the time the form was in use and are given here merely for illustrative purposes.

Portion costs may be recorded on any sort of card, although the visible index form is recommended for its convenience and use in the typical employees' food service. Combining several types of information on one form, as in this illustration, makes for savings in time and expense.

Pricing

The normal method of pricing is to first obtain the unit portion cost, then divide by the desired overall food-cost percentage. In the Portion Cost Card shown in Figure 11.1, 60% was the objective. It will be noted that the unit cost of Beef Stew with Dumpling was $.1458. This divided by .60 gave $.243.

In commercial restaurants the food-cost percentage is often set at 33 1/3%, 40% or 50%. In such cases instead of dividing the unit portion cost by the appropriate decimal, it is easier to multiply by 3, 2½, or 2, respectively.

			Cost and Portion Card BEEF STEW DUMPLING			
Lbs.	Ingredient	Per lb.	Total	Unit Cost	Portion and Service	
18	Beef Chuck	$.58	$10.44		Place dumpling in Soup Bowl with fork. Add one 4-oz. ladle of meat and vegetables (4 or 5 pieces of meat) and one 4-oz. ladle of liquid.	
14	Turnips	.045	.65			
8	Carrots	.0875	.70			
30	Potatoes	.04	1.20			
3	Onions	.07	.21			
	Total (108 orders)		$13.20			
					Cost Range	
Cost per order of stew Dumplings				$.1222	Beef at Cost	%
3 Biscuit Mix .1925 Makes 56 Dumplings		.5775			.48 .1274 50.96%	
					.53 .1366 54.64%	
Cost per Dumpling				.0103	.58 .1458 58.32%	
Total per order Allowance for Waste 10%				.1325 .0133	.61 .1513 60.52%	
Cost per order Divided by .60 Sales Price			.243	.1458 .25		

Fig. 11.1. Master cost and portion card.

In Figure 11.1 the selling or menu price set was 25¢, because at the time this was figured it appeared that the cost of beef chuck (the principal ingredient) was likely to become lower. If beef prices were moving upward, it would be more prudent to set the price say at 26¢ or 28¢, so as to minimize further menu price changes in the future.

On this card, costs and percentages have been figured with beef ranging from 48¢ to 61¢ per pound;

the latter figure being the top limit. Cost, portion, and price figures here, of course, are for illustrative purposes only.

Adjusting for Fluctuations in Food Cost

If all cafeteria items are costed correctly based on standard portions, and all prices could be set based on these costs as described, it would be comparatively easy to attain the desired food-cost objective.

When the physical inventory is taken, however, and the actual food cost is computed, it may be found to be out of line. One reason for this is that it is almost impossible to mark up all items on the desired percentage basis. Milk, for example, may be sold for say 15¢ per 8 ounce container. The cost of the milk may at times be 8¢, thus giving rise to a 53.3% food cost. For policy reasons it may be undesirable to increase the menu price of the milk. This may be true of other staple items.

It is therefore necessary to set the food cost for some items lower than the stated objective, in order that the overall percentage will average out to the desired figure. High food cost items are often offset by low cost items such as macaroni, hash, cheese dishes, chop-suey, soups, and gelatin desserts.

Odd-Cent Pricing (See Chapter 7—Menu-Planning)

As previously pointed out, it has been customary in many institutional food services to price menu items in odd cents rather than to the "nearest nickel" as is usually done in commercial restaurants. In the industrial cafeteria from which the cost card on Beef Stew with Dumpling was taken, odd-cent pricing was in use.

"Prime Cost" Method of Pricing

The increasing use of foods that are fully or partially prepared outside of the kitchen, coupled with rising labor costs, is causing food service operators to revise their thinking regarding methods of costing and pricing.

Food prepared outside of the kitchen carries with it two cost factors: (1) the cost of raw materials, formerly expressed in the food service by the term "raw food cost"; and (2) the cost of the preparation labor involved. This "built-in" labor, supplied by the manufacturer of the product, should relieve the food service of some portion of the preparation labor in the kitchen.

When a prepared item is *costed* under conventional methods, no account is taken of this labor performed outside. But when the item is *priced* on the menu, the cost of the "built-in" labor should be considered. This can be seen by contrasting the pricing of an item prepared outside with that of an item prepared in the kitchen.

As a simple illustration let us consider the conventional pricing of a 4 ounce hamburger, premixed, preshaped and delivered to the food service ready for the griddle at a cost of, say, 16 cents including the roll. We will compare this with a salad having a food cost of 9 cents.

Conventional Pricing Method	4 oz. Hamburger & Roll	Salad
Food cost	16¢	9¢
Menu price at 40% (x 2 1/2)	40¢	22 1/2¢

Under the conventional method, the hamburger is priced at a figure nearly twice the salad price.

Let us assume that making the salad required 3 minutes of the salad maker's time. At $2.00 per hour this amounts to a labor cost of 10 cents. The hamburger, on the other hand, required no kitchen labor and only a minimum of service labor at the griddle.

Under the Prime Cost Method advocated by Harry H. Pope of Pope's Catering Co. of St. Louis, the food cost and direct labor (production labor) cost are combined and are known as the "Prime Cost" of the item.

Since the prime cost includes part of the total food service labor cost, it is obvious that in computing the menu price by this method it will not be necessary to have as large a percentage devoted to gross profit.

In fact, in the average food service the kitchen or production labor represents about one-third of the total labor cost. If the total labor cost is 30 per cent, the production labor would represent 10 per cent, so 10 per cent could be deducted from the gross profit required. If a 60 per cent gross profit would be necessary under a 40 per cent cost percentage objective by the conventional method, only 50 per cent would be required under the Prime Cost Method. This means that instead of multiplying by 2 1/2 it would only be necessary to multiply by 2 under the Prime Cost Method.

The menu prices for the hamburger and salad would then be set as follows:

Prime Cost Method of Pricing

	Hamburger & Roll	Salad
Food Cost	$.16	$.09
Direct Labor	.00	.10
Prime Cost	$.16	$.19
Menu Price (x 2)	$.32	$.38

In actual practice, these prices would probably be rounded off to 35 cents and 40 cents, respectively. Under the conventional method the hamburger would be priced at almost twice the salad price.

The Prime Cost Method gives the hamburger a better break from a price standpoint. The salad price is equitable as it includes the direct labor cost.

There is another consideration: the increasing cost of labor is forcing food-service operators to devote more attention to labor costs and their effect upon prices. The Prime Cost Method takes labor costs into account. This is discussed in Chapter 12 "Controlling Labor Cost."

The multiplier used in the foregoing example was 2. This would vary with different food services, depending upon total labor cost percentages and the amount of gross profit required to cover operating expenses after prime cost. Some operations could use a multiplier of 1 1/2 while others might require multipliers of 1 3/4 or 2. In any event the multiplier used with the Prime Cost Method of pricing would be lower than that used under the conventional system.

Applied to costly meat, fish and seafood items the Prime Cost Method enables each operator to base the price of each item upon the actual food and labor cost incurred. Steaks and chops, for example, can be priced more equitably from the customer's standpoint. They can also be priced more attractively from a merchandising point of view.

Figure 11.2 shows prime costs of various dishes used in food services. Production costs in this table are calculated at three cents per minute. This may seem high but is conservative if fringe benefits, time lost through coffee breaks, rests and waiting periods are taken into account. Careful study of this table will show that labor costs involved in preparing relatively small items, such as pies, often exceed those for entrées. It also reveals that labor costs are lower when canned or frozen items are used in place of fresh ones.

EVALUATION OF FOOD COST

It is necessary to provide for periodic evaluations of the food cost to determine whether or not the desired percentage is being attained.

The Physical Inventory

There are several methods of evaluation. One is the periodic physical inventory, taken at the end of each week, month, or accounting period. This consists of the listing and counting of all foods on hand in the kitchen, storerooms, and refrigerators. Quantities on hand are extended (multiplied by the unit costs) and the total inventory values computed.

Prime Costs For Typical Dishes (With production time estimated at three cents per minute)					
Item	Portion	Food Cost (Dollars)	Prod. Time (Minutes)	Prod. Cost (Dollars)	Prime Cost (Dollars)
Bean Soup	3/4 cup	.022	.3	.009	.031
Beef Noodle Soup	3/4 cup	.039	.3	.009	.048
Chicken Rice Soup	3/4 cup	.045	.3	.009	.053
Chopped Beef Steak	3 1/2 oz.	.215	1.1	.033	.248
Fried Chicken	6 oz.	.198	1.2	.036	.234
Baked Meat Loaf	4 oz.	.167	.6	.018	.185
Yankee Pot Roast	4 oz.	.315	.3	.009	.324
Swiss Steak	4 oz.	.238	.6	.018	.256
Roast Turkey	3 oz.	.224	2.3	.069	.293
Breaded Veal Cutlet	3 1/4 oz.	.186	1.4	.042	.228
Fresh Frozen Lima Beans	1/2 cup	.059	.2	.006	.064
Boston Baked Beans	2/3 cup	.047	.8	.024	.071
Fresh Carrots	1/2 cup	.039	.6	.018	.057
Fresh Frozen Corn	1/2 cup	.041	.2	.006	.077
Baked Macaroni and Cheese	2/3 cup	.034	.5	.015	.049
Canned Onions	3 oz.	.068	.1	.003	.071
American Fried Potatoes	3/4 cup	.034	.3	.009	.043
Mashed Potatoes	1/2 cup	.028	.4	.012	.04
Buttermilk Biscuits	1 biscuit	.01	.4	.012	.022
Cornsticks	1 stick	.01	.4	.012	.022
Dinner Rolls	1 roll	.014	.6	.018	.032
Muffins (Blueberry)	1 muffin	.025	.3	.009	.034
Cole Slaw	3/4 cup	.035	.7	.021	.056
Combination Salad	2/3 cup	.034	.7	.021	.055
Fruit Salad		.122	2.0	.06	.182
Tuna Fish Salad	1/2 cup	.125	.8	.024	.149
Apple Pie (Canned Apples)	1 pie	.449	3.0	.09	.539
Blackberry Pie (Frozen Berries)	1 pie	.436	3.0	.09	.539
Coconut Cream Pie	1 pie	.457	5.0	.15	.607
Lemon Meringue Pie	1 pie	.454	7.0	.21	.664
Devils Food Layer Cake	1 slice	.045	.5	.015	.06

Fig. 11.2. Prime costs for typical dishes. (Based on studies made by Pope's Cafeterias, Inc., St. Louis, Mo.)

In taking the inventory, cooked foods are included if the quantity is appreciable. For example, a pound of butter would be included whereas a fraction of a pound would not be considered. This is done on the theory that there is always a certain quantity of foodstuffs on hand, the value of which is nominal but fairly constant month in and month out.

When the total value of the inventory is computed, the food cost is determined in the following manner:

Computation of Food Cost

Food Inventory at beginning of period	$ 3,500
Add: Food Purchases during period:	10,500
	$14,000
Less: Inventory at end of period	$5,000
Cost of food sold	$9,000

If the food sales for the period were say, $25,000, the food cost percentage would be 36 per cent (9,000 ÷ 25,000 = .36). One might desire to determine the food cost per meal. Assuming that 30,000 meals had been served during the period, the food cost per meal would be 30 cents (9,000 ÷ 30,000 = .30). This would be a mean or average figure. Probably the luncheons and dinners may have cost more than the breakfasts, but this is an average of all three meals.

How to Take a Physical Inventory

Steps to be followed in taking a physical inventory are:

1. Prepared typed or mimeographed sheets listing the items by location (storeroom, kitchen, cafeteria, etc.), the description of the items, the unit quantity (gallons, pounds, cases, etc.), and include spaces opposite each item for the quantity on hand. See Figure 11.3.

2. These items may be listed alphabetically under each location or by commodity groups (such as canned fruits, canned vegetables, meats, etc.).

3. The inventory should be taken by two people, one calling out the items and quantities, the other verifying each count and marking it on the sheet. In some establishments, the inventory is taken by the manager together with a representative from the accounting department. This enables the management to spot items that should be moved out of the inventory.

4. Items should be taken by location as they are stored, not as they may be listed on the sheet. If a storeroom inventory is being taken, for example, each shelf should be covered from one end to the other, regardless of the listing on the sheet. This method minimizes the possibility of overlooking

items. In the inventory book to which the data are transferred, the items may be arranged alphabetically or by commodity groups.

When the sheets are completed, they are entered in a permanent inventory record and extended. Inventory cards are often used. However, many prefer a book with half pages on which the extensions are made, the descriptions being on the full page. Such a book eliminates recopying descriptions, and may last a year or more.

Checking the Inventory

The inventory should be carefully checked to make sure that it is accurate. Adding machine tapes should be verified. Extensions should be compared with those of previous periods and unusual variations investigated. When the food-cost percentage or cost per meal is computed and substantial variances are found, they may be due to an error in taking or extending the inventory. In other words, in checking for variances the first thing to investigate is the inventory itself.

Valuing the Inventory

Standard accounting procedure usually requires that industrial inventories be valued either at cost or market prices, whichever are lower.

In food services, however, as inventories are usually relatively small and turn over rapidly (or should do so), it is the general practice to value the inventory at cost.

Inventories of Supplies

The same procedures should be followed with respect to supplies used in food services—such as soap, cleaning powder, brooms and brushes, and paper. If these represent any substantial investment they should be inventoried each month and a figure brought out known as "Cost of Supplies Used."

Daily or Weekly Food Cost Evaluations

If physical inventories are taken monthly, or at the end of the organization's accounting periods, several days may pass before the food-cost percentage or cost per meal is compiled. When the cost figure is obtained, it may be five or six weeks after the beginning of the period to which the figure applies. If an adverse trend is disclosed it may have affected the gross profit for an even longer time before corrective measures can be instituted.

For this reason it is wise to establish some form of daily or weekly evaluation which will give management prompt information on the current food cost

Inventory Date __March 31-__   Sheet __1__

Location __Store Room__   Value of Sheet __$2485.90__

Size	Description	Inventory Phy.	Book	Unit Value		Amount		Remarks
6/10	Apples - Pie	25				152	40	
30#	Apples - Dried	3		18	20	54	60	
6/10	Apples - Sauce	20				94	—	
24-2	Asparagus	8				85	55	
6/10	Apricots	6				58	25	
6/10	Beans - Green	127				583	80	
6/10	Beans - Lima	12		3	85	46	20	
6/10	Beans - Red Kidney	33				121	80	
6/10	Beans - and Pork	20				66	50	
6/10	Beans - Sprouts	—				—	—	
24-2 1/2	Barbecued Pork	4				90	15	
24-2#	Beef - Prepared	1		35	75	35	75	
6/10	Beets	14				49	98	
6/10	Blackberries	—				—	—	
6/10	Catsup	37				224	65	
6/10	Cherries - Red Sour	—				—	—	
6/10	Chili	6		8	80	52	80	
24-10 oz.	Codfish Cakes	3		3	75	11	25	
6/10	Corn Beef Hash	10		6	50	65	—	
6/10	Corn - Cream Style	14				67	80	
6/10	Corn - Whole Kernel	23				111	40	
24-2	Corn - W.K. Fancy	—				—	—	
6/10	Cranberry Sauce	2		6	95	13	90	
6/10	Carrots - Diced	27				126	45	
6/10	Dehydrated Onions	6		9	20	55	20	
Lb.	Dehydrated Vegetables	—				—	—	
6/10	Fruit Cocktail	12		6	45	90	90	
12-46 oz.	Grapefruit Juice	—				—	—	
6/10	Hominy	14		2	95	41	30	
24-1#	Hominy Grits	—				—	—	
6/10	Jelly	-1		3	45	8	45	
6/10	Kraut	15				54	50	
48-1#	Milk - Evaporated	6		6	—	36	—	
6/10	Mixed Vegetables	6				26	50	
Case	Mushroom Buttons	3				29	90	
Case	Noodles - Prepared	—				—	—	
6/10	Okra	—				—	—	
4-1	Olives	1				16	00	
12-46 oz.	Orange Juice	6				19	92	

Fig. 11.3. Sample inventory sheet.

trend. Several methods may be employed to obtain such frequent evaluation. These include:

1. Weekly Physical Inventories
2. Daily Purchase Records
3. Daily Food Cost Estimates

Weekly Inventories

Many chain organizations such as fountain luncheonettes, snack bars, and various franchise operations take a physical inventory each week end, bringing out weekly food costs. While this method is not feasible in all institutional food services it provides an excellent and accurate evaluation as a means of control.

Daily Purchase Records

Another method of evaluation is through the use of a columnar sheet on which the cost of food items delivered daily are listed under the various commodity group headings. The daily total is computed and compared with the daily sales figures. A weekly computation is also made and a comparison made with sales volume. As purchases may fluctuate from day to day, the weekly totals are more reliable as a guide to cost trends. A Daily Purchase Record form of this type is shown in Figure 11.4.

This record is simple to maintain but it is of course an approximation of the food cost, as issues from storerooms are not included. In reading the Purchase Report, the operator will have to make allowance for large or unusual purchases which can be carried over beyond the week in question. If meats, for example, show an unusual percentage increase during the week, however, an investigation may be necessary. This is also true of poultry, fish and shellfish, which normally make up a substantial percentage of purchases. The investigation may show that the prices of the commodities in question may have increased, or that more higher-priced items have been placed upon the menu than is ordinarily the case. Errors may have occurred in receiving, excessive spoilage may have occurred in storage, or shrinkage in preparation and cooking may be greater than planned.

Comparison of purchase percentages is valuable under any circumstances even though it may not be

Daily Purchases, Sales and Food Cost—October, 19																
												Total Purchases		Total Sales		%Cumulative Pur. to Sales
Oct. 1949	Purveyor	Meats	Poultry	Sea Food	Vege- tables	Fruits	Dairy Products	Ice Cream	Gro- ceries	Baked Goods	Total	Daily	Cumula- tive	Daily	Cumula- tive	
3	City Baking Co.									1.08	1.08					
	Jones Ice Cream Co.							59.50			59.50					
	Towne Fish Co.			5.00							5.00					
	Wholesale Grocers Inc.								26.58		26.58					
	United Packers	84.40					36.45				120.80					
	Farmer's Dairy						4.54				4.54					
	J. Brown		16.30								16.30					
	Cavallo's Market					9.50					9.50	$243.35		$185.49		126%
4	City Baking Co.									16.38	16.38					
	Farmer's Dairy						20.30				20.30					
	F. Smith				7.00						7.00	43.68	$287.03	198.15	$ 383.64	74.7%
5	Cavallo's Market				16.15	4.00					20.15					
	Doe Grocery Co.								65.53		65.53	85.68	372.71	201.45	585.09	63.7%
6	Farmer's Dairy						35.73				35.73					
	Blank Meat Co	48.40					20.16				68.56					
	Green's Bakery									2.08	2.08					
	Towne Fish Co.			17.00							17.00					
	Cavallo's Market					13.00					13.00					
	United Packers	4.90					24.70				29.60	165.97	538.68	220.30	805.39	66.9%
7	Farmer's Dairy						13.74				13.74					
	City Baking Co									.88	.88					
	Cavallo's Market				5.00						5.00					
	F. Smith		16.50								16.50					
	Wholesale Grocers Inc.								42.55		42.55	$ 78.67	$617.35	$242.50	$1,047.89	58.9%
	Total for week	$137.70	$32.80	$22.00	$37.65	$17.00	$155.62	$59.50	$134.66	$20.42	$617.35					
	%to Total Purchases	22.3%	5.6%	3.5%	6.1%	2.6%	25.3%	9.6%	21.8%	3.2%	100%					

NOTES: "Vegetables" and "Fruits" include fresh and frozen varieties. Canned varieties are listed under "Groceries." "Dairy Products" includes Milk, Cream, Butter, Cheese and Eggs. A better analysis would be afforded if "Milk and Cream" and "Butter, Cheese and Eggs" were separate headings. Some cafeterias list "Butter" as a separate commodity heading.

For the following week the cumulative totals for Purchases and Sales are carried forward. Weekly totals are taken at the end of each week in order to compare weekly percentages. These weekly totals are not accumulated.

Fig. 11.4. Daily Purchase Record Form.

as accurate as other methods in determining the food cost trends.

Daily Food Cost

The most effective and immediate method of control is through a Daily Food Cost system of evaluation. This is done by keeping track of all food deliveries and issues made each day directly to the kitchen. A total of the cost values of all of these items can then be compared with total sales and a daily food-cost percentage or cost per meal figured. While this will not be as accurate as an evaluation based upon a physical inventory, it is sufficiently accurate to indicate the daily trend.

Departmental Food Costs

Where food is prepared in a main kitchen and delivered to several different food services within the establishment, as in a hospital, a daily food-cost evaluation showing differential costs is useful as indicating the costs of different menus which may be served in the different services. Figure 11.5 shows this type of daily summary of purchases and issues.

While Figure 11.5 shows the differential costs of the services of a hospital, the same type of form can be used where different dining rooms of an industrial food service provide meals perhaps with different menus and prices. Where only one dining room is involved, it will be necessary to use only columns "A," "B," and "C," thus providing a daily food-cost estimate.

Food Cost Summary Date:_____19__	(A) Store room	(B) Main Kitchen	(C) Cafe- teria	(D) Ward	(E) Semi- Private	(F) Private	(G) Nourish- ments	(H) Total
Jones Meat Co.	$ 47.20	$150.20	$	$	$	$	$	$197.40
Brown Groceries	110.00							110.00
Wholesale Produce Co.		79.00						79.00
City Dairy		20.00	32.40					52.40
National Baking Co.		10.00	9.60					19.60
U.S. Ice-Cream Corp.		17.50	27.50					45.00
Issued from Storeroom	(265.30)	143.00	122.30					-
Issued from Main Kitchen		(415.20)	105.23	118.30	113.40	66.20	12.07	-
Issued from Cafeteria			(3.00)				3.00	-
Totals	($108.10)	$ 4.50	$294.03	$118.30	$113.40	$66.20	$15.07	$503.40
Meals Served				409	303	108		820
*Avg. Food Cost Per Meal				$ .289	$ .377	$ .612		$ .363
Cafeteria Sales			490.18					
*Est. Cafeteria Food Cost			60%					

*These figures, of course, are subject to adjustment when the physical inventory is taken.

Fig. 11.5. Summary of Purchases and Issues—daily or monthly.

In a hospital or similar institution, food may be served in two or more cafeterias, in staff dining rooms, and also to several groups of patients (i.e. ward, semi-private, and private patients). In addition, nourishments may be sent from the main kitchen several times daily to patients. There may also be a special diet kitchen to which food is sent for the preparation of therapeutic diets. In many industrial food services food is prepared in the main kitchen not only for the cafeteria but also for executives' dining rooms, special luncheons, and in some cases for mobile food trucks or canteens.

Obviously in such cases an overall raw food cost per meal or food-cost percentage is of only limited value. For food-cost control purposes it is necessary to bring out separate food costs for each of the areas served. In this way the costs of each of these services can be analyzed and the necessary control measures taken.

Bringing Out Departmental Food Costs

In bringing out these departmental food costs, the following records are kept:

1. Food issued to the main kitchen and to the different dining areas from the storeroom.
2. Food delivered directly to the main kitchen.
3. Food delivered directly to the dining room (daily deliveries of bread, milk, ice-cream, etc.). This is often true of cafeterias.
4. Food issued from the main kitchen to the various dining rooms, guest or patients' services.
5. Food issued from the cafeteria in certain cases.

Items (B) and (C) are recorded directly from the vendors' invoices. Items (A), (D), and (E), involve the use of food issue forms.

Food Issue Forms

These vary with the different systems in use. In Figure 11.6 is shown a requisition form also used as an issue form in many institutions, and in Figure 11.7 is shown an issue card used with the McBee Key Sort system.

Key sort cards are marginally punched for quick selection or for placing into numerical or alphabetical sequence. The classification of a given card is indi-

STORES REQUISITION   REQUISITION NO _____

DEPARTMENT_____DATE_____19_____

FLOOR OR DIVISION _____DATE REQUIRED_____19_____

QUANTITY		DESCRIPTION OF SUPPLIES NEEDED	TO BE USED IF PERPETUAL INVENTORIES ARE KEPT			
WANTED	DELIVERED		PRICE	PER	AMOUNT	ACCT. NO.

REQUESTED BY	APPROVED BY

SEND ORIGINAL TO STORE ROOM CLERK. DUPLICATE IS RETAINED BY DEPARTMENT HEAD.

Fig. 11.6.   Issue and Requisition Form. (Courtesy Physicians Record Co., Chicago, Illinois.)

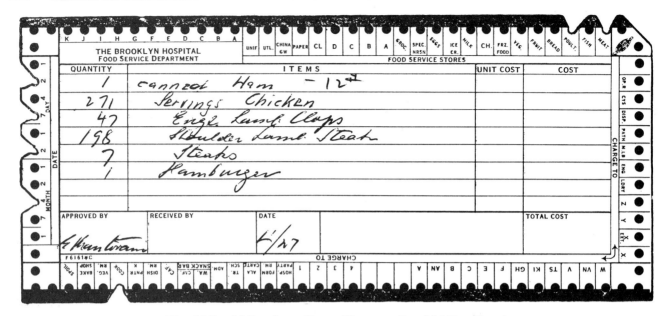

Fig. 11.7. McBee Issue Form. (Courtesy Royal-McBee Corp.)

cated by one or more notches in the margin. When the Key Sorter (a long steel needle) is inserted through the cards in a file, the notched cards fall out. These cards can be sorted or classified, it is stated, at the rate of 1,000 per minute per hole.

This form is used in connection with the McBee Key-Sort system in the issuing of food and supplies from a central storeroom. It will be noted that the left margin of the card indicates the date, the upper margin the type of commodity, and the right-hand and lower margins the various areas to which the items are issued. This makes for easy sorting and collating. Spaces for Quantity, Items, Unit Cost and Total Cost, Date, Signatures, etc., are provided on the face of the card. Different colored margins on the cards distinguish those used for different classes of food and supply items.

Essentially each issue card should include the following information, usually in pencil:

1. Date of issue.
2. Issuing department: storeroom, main kitchen, cafeteria, etc.
3. Department to which issued: main kitchen, cafeteria, dining room, etc.
4. Quantity and description of food issued.
5. Space for inserting cost value of the food issued. This is usually computed in the office when the issue forms are tabulated.

Establishing Cost Values

The use of issue forms entails computation of costs of cooked food in volume (i.e., quarts of mashed po-

tatoes or chicken à la king, pints of gravy, tins of chocolate cake, etc.). Such computation is made through tests, and involves considerable detail. Absoluate accuracy cannot always be achieved, and certain costs must be established arbitrarily.

The same problems are encountered in industrial cost accounting. Contrary to popular belief, cost accounting is not an absolutely exact science. The essential goal is to make sure that all costs are spread with a reasonable degree of accuracy so that management is provided with information on costs upon which it can safely rely.

For this reason it is well to include the allowance for waste, for which ten per cent is recommended as shown on the Cost and Portion forms. This covers the cost of food which inevitably adheres to receptacles, spillage, mistakes in portioning, spoilage and other forms of food waste.

Using the Daily Summary of Purchases and Issues to Control Food Cost

Each day the issues and direct deliveries of the preceding day are summarized and allocated to the different departments as shown in Figure 11.5.

This summary is in effect a record of purchases taken from vendors' invoices—as well as a record of issues. While this duplicates the record of purchases kept in the general accounting office in the voucher register or other records, it is desirable for enabling the food-service department to keep its own record for purposes of control. This record can be adjusted at the end of the month to the purchase figure issued by the general accounting office.

It will be noted from Figure 11.5 that the main kitchen issued $4.50 less than the value of the daily deliveries. In other words, there should be $4.50 worth of food in the kitchen refrigerators at the end of the day. This should not represent losses in waste or shrinkage. If such losses have been costed correctly, the values shown should cover these losses. It is thus possible to check the accuracy of costing and control losses.

The storeroom column shows that $108.10 more in food value was issued than received. A tabulation of these daily purchases and issue figures in connection with the beginning inventory will serve as a check on the closing storeroom inventory figure.

In case it is felt that the compilation of the complete summary as shown in Figure 11.5 requires more clerical labor than is available, columns showing purchases can be eliminated and only the columns from C to G, showing issues, retained in the form.

OTHER FACTORS AFFECTING COST

Although the purchase cost, the portion size, and the menu price are the primary elements, there are other factors affecting food cost. In particular there are ten items that must be watched constantly to insure effective food-cost control:

1. Errors in delivery
2. Spoilage in storage
3. Waste in preparation
4. Shrinkage in cooking
5. Carelessness in portioning
6. Losses in serving and distribution of food
7. Discrepancies in cash
8. Excessive leftovers
9. Pilferage
10. Meals to employees

In previous chapters we have discussed procedures to be taken in connection with purchasing, receiving, storage, preparation, cooking, portioning, and serving in order to avoid losses. Here are methods to be used in avoiding some of these other losses.

Handling of Cash

If mistakes are made in ringing up cash on the cafeteria register—or in making change if a cash register is not used—these errors will be reflected in the food cost.

Such errors are either intentional or unintentional. In the first category come the failure to ring up checks; ringing up less than the proper amount as a favor to friends; and the changing of meal checks where wait-ress service is used. The answer to this problem is to have the cashier checked by observers from time to time. This can be done internally—or there are outside shopping and checking agencies which render this service.

From our observation, most errors in the handling of cash are unintentional. This is often a matter of employee selection. Frequently people hired as cashiers do not have the ability to perform the mental arithmetic the job requires.

When applicants are hired as cashiers or for counter work where food checks are issued, it is advisable to give them simple tests to make sure that they have the mental ability to add quickly and correctly.

Waste Through Leftovers

The ability of a chef used to be gauged in proportion to his facility in making use of leftover food items. Today an excessive number of leftovers is considered an indication of improper ordering of food to be cooked.

Care in advance ordering can reduce leftovers to a minimum. The astute manager keeps posted on factors that may reduce a given day's patronage below the normal volume. The quantity of food ordered and prepared in the kitchen should be just sufficient to meet the demand. Cooking in small quantities and kitchen scheduling play a part in reducing leftover food items.

When there are leftovers, ingenuity is required in disposing of them. For example, when chicken or turkey is served, it is customary to serve wings, croquettes, and soup respectively on the following days in order to use the leftover portions. This pattern can be reversed, by placing turkey wings on the menu a day or so before the main dish is featured, as an example.

Most chefs and kitchen supervisors can make good use of leftover food provided they realize the importance of keeping waste at a minimum.

Pilferage

Management must be constantly on the alert to prevent pilferage of food. Some employees have a "split morality" in this respect. While they would not steal money, they apparently see no wrong in taking food. We have encountered numerous instances of this kind in mass-feeding operations. The loss of a pound of butter, a steak, or a can of tomatoes may be small in itself, but in the aggregate such leaks seriously affect the food cost. To meet this problem, the following rules should be obseved:

1. Storerooms and refrigerators should be kept locked at all times when unattended. Keys should be entrusted only to responsible individuals.
2. Employees should be required to enter and leave through an employees' entrance. All bundles should be checked when the employee enters. Bundles should not be allowed to be taken from the premises without being inspected.
3. Eating by employees should not be allowed except at regular employees' meal hours and in areas designated for employees' meals.

Employees Meals

It is still the general practice to serve employees in institutional food services at least one free meal each day they are at work. While this was the custom in restaurants also, owing to the increased costs of wages and fringe benefits in recent years, the tendency is to take advantage of the charge allowed for meals by the various state wage laws. Where meals are served without charge, it is expected that such employees will be readily available during their meal period to give assistance to the employer. It is also considered desirable that food-service employees be familiar with the food which they have a part in producing. A generous policy with respect to employees' meals is believed to promote goodwill and to reduce pilferage.

Limits are generally placed upon the free items employees may have. Steaks or other expensive entrées generally are not available to employees unless paid for.

It is well to insist that employees do not eat while on duty—except during periods set aside for employees' meals. It is also desirable to have a room set aside for employees' meals.

Employees' meals may constitute as much as 5 per cent of total food cost. At present they are considered an additional income in figuring total wages for minimum wage, social security, and workmen's compensation insurance purposes.

DISPOSITION OF ENTRÉES PRODUCED

Under any system of food-cost control it is desirable to have a record of the number of principal entrées produced compared with those sold to determine the disposition of the unsold items. This can be accomplished through the following records:

1. *Daily Production Report.* This is simply a list of items produced in the kitchen during the day, prepared by the chef or kitchen manager.
2. *Record of Entrée Sales.* This is a record of the number of principal entrées sold.

3. *Disposition Report.* From the information given in the daily production report and the record of entrée sales, a disposition report is prepared as shown in Figure 11.8. If, for example, 25 steaks were prepared and the sales record shows that only 24 were sold, the question arises, "What happened to the one not accounted for?" Investigation may bring several possible answers to this question.

Where the cafeteria checking systems are installed, the tabulation of the numbers of different entrées sold is done automatically. One system has 99 keys for as many different food items, another system has a somewhat smaller number of keys. Under such systems an exact tabulation of sales by items is available and can be recorded for different meal periods or for the daily total. (See Figures 11.9, 11.10, 11.11.)

MANAGEMENT FUNCTIONS IN FOOD-COST CONTROL

To recapitulate, effective food-cost control depends upon the management functions of planning, organizing, supervising, controlling, coordinating, and evaluating.

1. *Planning.* Food-cost control involves planning in advance. An objective is set and plans made to attain it. The objective may be in terms of a percentage of sales, as in cafeterias; cents per meal, as in schools and hospitals; or in dollars per daily ration, as in military establishments and some institutions.

The planning is predicated upon proper menu planning, purchasing, receiving and storage procedures. Menu items are precosted and priced, based upon the standard objective set and also upon:

a. Standard recipes
b. Standard portions
c. Standard menu-pricing methods

2. *Organizing.* The staff must be organized so that each individual responsible for food-cost control will be informed, trained, and motivated to do his part in achieving the desired standard objective.

3. *Supervising.* Each department head and supervisor must see that standard procedures are being followed in his area of responsibility.

4. *Controlling.* Guided by the daily, weekly or monthly food-cost evaluations, management will exercise control through supervision, devoting attention, under the exception principle, to any areas that may not be functioning properly.

5. *Coordinating.* To effectuate food-cost control will require coordinated effort on the part of all departments and individuals concerned. For example, the

Disposition Report _____ 196 __

Item	Prepared	Sold	Over	Remarks
Roast Beef	40	12/28	0	
So. Fried Chicken	30	11/17	2	Employees Meals
Baked Ham	14	5/8	1	Left Over
Baked Beans and Frank	18	3/15	0	
Fried Clams	10	1/9	0	
Br. Veal Cutlet	10	2/7	1	
Fr. Br. Shrimp	15	1/13	1	Employees Meals
Br. Swordfish	8	2/5	1	Left Over
Rump Steak	23	5/18	0	
Hamburger	22	7/15	0	

Note: Under "Sold" figures above the diagonal lines show luncheon sales and below the line, dinner sales.

Fig. 11.8. Disposition Report

Fig. 11.10. Cafeteria Checking Machine. (Courtesy National Cash Register Co., Dayton, Ohio.)

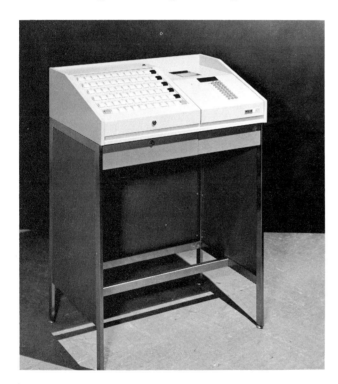

Fig. 11.9. Cafeteria Checking Machine. (Courtesy National Cash Register Co., Dayton, Ohio.)

Fig. 11.11. Monroe Sweda Data Register. (Courtesy Monroe International Inc., Orange, N. J.)

purchasing department will inform the menu-planners if price fluctuations occur which may necessitate changes in the menu. The menu department will check with the chef or kitchen manager regarding special menu items which may place an unusual load on cooking equipment. The service supervisor will work with the kitchen to see that standard portions are maintained. Such coordination may be through channels or may be informal. It will be constantly taking place, however, in a well-organized food service, where management sees to it that all concerned have their attention focused upon the main objectives to be accomplished.

6. *Evaluating.* Responsibility will be placed upon an individual or department to conduct periodic evaluations of food-cost results. This may be in the form of daily reports or weekly or monthly statements based upon physical inventories. Whatever the method used,

the information should be placed promptly before management so that executive action, if called for, can be immediately initiated.

CONSTANT SUPERVISION AND COOPERATION

To keep food costs under control requires not only an effective control system but also constant supervision. Food-service managers must be "everlastingly at it" in their efforts to minimize food waste and losses.

Cooperation of employees plays a vital role. If workers understand the importance of food cost, they may be more careful of the food they handle. Such understanding may be inculcated through meetings of food-service workers and through leadership by supervisors and key employees.

In some food services the kitchen supervisor, the chef, and other key personnel are paid a weekly or monthly bonus, depending upon the attainment of the food-cost percentage goal. This is dangerous unless carefully thought out. It is usual to set upper and lower limits so that the food cost will not be reduced at the expense of the customers.

In more than 100 food services in which we have made surveys within recent years, we have yet to find one where food costs could not be reduced by at least 10 per cent. In every case in which a sound food-cost control system has been installed, it has en-

hanced, rather than reduced, food quality and standards of service.

Although this may seem paradoxical, it is sound logic. The introduction of a food-cost control system brings about better management methods. It also serves to focus attention upon food quality and service, to the improvement of both.

SUGGESTED READING

AMERICAN HOSPITAL ASSOCIATION, Food Cost Accounting, Chicago, 1948.

BRODNER, JOSEPH; CARLSON, H. M.; AND MASCHAL, H. J. Profitable Food and Beverage Operation. New York: Ahrens Book Co., Inc., 1962.

BRYAN, MARY DE GARMO. The School Cafeteria. New York: F. S. Crofts Co., 1946.

DUKAS, PETER, AND LUNDBERG, DONALD E. How to Operate a Restaurant. New York: Ahrens Book Co., Inc., 1960.

FAIRBROOK, PAUL. "Starting and Managing a Small Restaurant," Small Business Administration, Washington, D. C., 1964.

LUNDBERG, DONALD E., AND KANE, C. V. Business Management in Hotels, Motels and Restaurants. Florida State University Bookstore, Tallahassee, 1959.

NATIONAL RESTAURANT ASSOCIATION, "A Uniform System of Accounting for Restaurants," Chicago, Illinois, 1958.

STOKES, JOHN W. How to Manage a Restaurant or Institutional Food Service. Dubuque, Iowa: Wm. C. Brown Company Publishers, 1967.

CHAPTER 12

Controlling Labor Cost

At one time food cost was the largest single cost item in a food-service operation. However, with increased minimum wages required by state and federal laws, and with wage rates in industry and institutions mounting year by year, labor cost in some food services is higher than food cost. In figuring labor costs, we must take into consideration all of the charges relating to labor cost, such as:

Salaries and wages (including overtime pay)

Social Security taxes

Vacation and holiday pay

Employees' meals

Workmen's compensation insurance

Life, health, and accident insurance

Pensions or retirement plans

Social Security taxes are slated to increase, and other "fringe" benefits for employees might be added to this list. It is not unusual for all labor charges to total 125% of the payroll itself.

RELATION OF LABOR COST TO SALES

Percentage-wise, labor cost varies with the total sales, while food cost tends to remain constant. As sales increase, labor cost drops and as volume shrinks, labor cost goes up percentage-wise. For example, if a cafeteria is staffed to feed 1,000 meals daily, and only 800 customers arrive on a given day, the staff cannot readily be decreased. Conversely, an increase up to 1,200 could probably be taken care of by the same staff. Assuming a normal labor cost say of 40% with a volume of 1,000, a decrease in volume to 800 would increase the labor cost to 50%, while an increase in volume to 1,200 would cut labor cost to 33 1/3%. (See Figure 12.1.)

Meals Per Day	1,000	%	800	%	1,200	%
Sales @ $1.00 Avg. Check	$ 1,000	100%	$ 800	100%	$ 1,200	100%
Food Cost @ 40%	400	40	320	40	480	40
Gross Profit	$ 600	60%	$ 480	60%	$ 720	60%
Labor Cost	350	35%	350	43.75%	350	29.16%

Fig. 12.1.   Effect of Volume Upon Food and Labor Cost Percentages.

Effect of Increased Volume

It is well to keep in mind the fact that one way of reducing labor cost percentage-wise is to increase volume. Methods of increasing volume are discussed later in this text.

PAYROLL RECORDS

Normally, two records are used to keep track of regular payrolls:

1. Daily Time Card or Record
2. Weekly Time Sheet

Daily Time Record

Where time clocks are used, a card is assigned to each employee who, by "punching the clock," records on the card the time he begins and ends his work each day.

Where time clocks are not in use, a simple Daily Time form may be ruled on an 8½" x 11" sheet of paper. This is posted on the bulletin board, and on it each employee or a supervisor records in pencil the time of starting and finishing work daily. Spaces may be provided for a week.

Weekly Time Sheet

At the end of each week, the information on the daily time cards or time sheet is transferred to the organization's weekly time sheet—usually made up in duplicate. The original may be sent to the employment office for approval, and then to the Payroll Department for making up the weekly payroll.

The duplicate time sheet is filed in the Food-Service Office for reference.

The time sheet lists only the hours worked by each employee for the week. Rates of pay are usually supplied and computations made by the Payroll Department.

Payroll Receipt

When the payroll envelopes are brought to the food service by one of the payroll department staff, the supervisor checks the envelopes against the list made out on a payroll receipt form. If they are correct, he signs the receipt for the number of envelopes received.

ANALYSIS OF LABOR UTILIZATION

In order to control labor cost it is first necessary to analyze the work being done in terms of individual tasks to determine whether or not labor is being utilized effectively. The terms used in such analysis are: *Job Analysis:* The actual procedure of observing a given job, interviewing the worker and recording the results; *Job Description:* The organized written description resulting from job analysis, usually done away from the job, based upon notes taken during the observation and interview; and *Job Specification:* A list of the skills and personality traits required to perform a given job. In its more concise form it is termed a *Job Definition.*

Steps to be Taken in Job Analysis

1. Sell your department heads on the need for job analysis and point out the advantages that will result from analyzing jobs.
2. Inform your employees as to the purpose of job analysis and present its benefits to those who are doing their work well.
3. In a small food service, the proprietor can make the analysis himself. In a larger organization the work will be done by the personnel manager or some other interested individual.
4. Expert assistance can be obtained and forms procured from your state employment service. These forms include: (a) Job Analysis schedule; (b) Physical Demands form (for listing the physical demands of the job); and (c) Job Specification form.
5. Use both the questionnaire and personal interviews in obtaining job information, as one will supplement the other.
6. Keep department heads informed of progress being made. Get their advice and suggestions in rearranging job tasks and time schedules.

Methods of Conducting Job Analysis

1. One method is to develop a suitable questionnaire and have it filled out by several workers doing the same job. The job analyst then assembles and compares the questionnaires, selecting representative items for the various replies, to make up a complete job description. Because most workers are not sufficiently trained to make analyses or observations on their own, it will be necessary for the job analyst to supplement the questionnaires by observation and interviews.

2. Another method is to train each department head so that he can perform the analysis within his department. This is advantageous in that the department head will be interested in his own department and more willing to make any changes which result from his own recommendations.

3. A third method combines the two foregoing procedures. The job analyst is responsible for the overall program but delegates as much responsibility to others as possible.

Figure 12.2 shows a Job Description Questionnaire. In Figure 12.3 the analysis of the work of a Salad Girl is depicted.

Figure 12.4 shows the job description of a kitchen supervisor in a large hospital, with his duties scheduled throughout the hours of his workday.

PRODUCTION SCHEDULES

Once the requirements of the various jobs and the tasks comprising these jobs are known, the personnel should be scheduled to fit the work load. Knowledgeable food-service executives estimate that up to one-third of the labor in restaurants and institutions is wasted through lack of proper scheduling. The employee cannot be held responsible if he is not told exactly what he is expected to do during his work period. Figure 12.5 shows a Cook's Production Schedule with tasks clearly outlined.

Individuals vary greatly in their work habits. Some are "self-starters." When they complete one job they look around for another to tackle. Many employees, although willing, seem unable to direct themselves. They are happier when someone else plans their schedule and tells them what to do next. Most people like to be busy and find that time passes more quickly when they are occupied with consecutive tasks. Scheduling thus generally increases worker satisfactions as well as productivity.

Among the practices by which scheduling is used to promote efficiency in food services are the following:

1. *Split-Shift Scheduling.* Waiters and waitresses and counter people can usually be scheduled for a noon meal period and then released until an evening meal period. This is especially feasible when the employees concerned live within easy reach of the food service. Care should be taken in scheduling split shifts to observe Work Span Laws in those states which require the hours worked to fall within a given span of hours.

2. *Irregular Scheduling.* Some employees may be scheduled to start at noon one day, in the morning another day, and in the late afternoon on still another day. Through careful scheduling no one is overworked or too greatly inconvenienced and efficiency is increased.

3. *Use of Part-time Workers.* Part-time workers are used extensively in many food services. If volume is centered around the noon and dinner hours, only a core of full-time employees are needed. Married women are often free to devote a few hours daily and welcome the extra earnings as well as the opportunity for a respite from household chores. With training, such part-time employees can become effective workers.

4. *Use of Staffing Tables.* The staffing table is an effective labor control device. It is based upon the number of patrons expected for a given meal on a given day. Thus it takes into account the day-to-day and meal-to-meal fluctuations in patronage. Figures 12.6 and 12.7 depict two hypothetical staffing tables for a restaurant kitchen and dining room, respectively.

5. *Labor Cost Budgets.* Whether full or part-time personnel is involved, modern management principles call for budgeting manpower as well as money, materials, or machines. Chain restaurants budget the labor cost to be allowed for a given dollar volume of sales. Based upon past experience, tables are worked out indicating the labor dollars that can be expended given a specific daily sales figure.

LABOR COST COMPARISONS

As a means of checking upon actual labor costs, comparisons are useful. There are various methods used of which the following are examples.

Comparative Profit and Loss Data

Where the profit and loss statement is prepared on a comparative basis, labor cost figures are available periodically as in Figure 12.8.

These figures, which are illustrative, indicate that despite greater sales during the current period, labor costs have increased by ½ of 1 per cent. Normally, in-

JOB DESCRIPTION QUESTIONNAIRE

Name of your position_____ Date_____

Other Title(s)_____

How long have you held this position?_____yrs._____mons._____

How long have you worked at this hotel?_____yrs._____mons._____

Who is your supervisor?_____

What is your Age_____Height_____Weight_____Sex_____

Education: – Circle the last grade you attended.

Grade School	1	2	3	4	5	6	7	8
High School		1		2		3		4
College		1		2		3		4
Trade School		1		2		3		4

1. What time do you come to work? (If you work different shifts, state the different times you come to work.)

2. What time do you actually begin to work?

3. What do you do between the time you come to work and the time you begin to work?

4. What time are you through work for the day?

5. Is your work evenly divided during the day or are any hours particularly busy or slack? Please be definite!

6. What do you consider the most important part of your job?

7. Are there any special tasks connected with your job for which you believe a new person should be trained before he could do the work satisfactorily?

8. List any jobs that you may perform at times, which are not daily parts of your job.

9. Do you believe being able to read is important in your job? (Yes or No)

10. Do you believe being able to write is important in your job? (Yes or No)

11. Describe in detail on reverse side what you do in an average day at work. Try to remember everything. Try to account for every minute of your working day. Describe not only what you do, but how you do it, and when you do it, and why you do it. Use extra paper if you need it.

Signature_____

Fig. 12.2.   Job Description Questionnaire. (From the Management of People in Hotels, Restaurants and Clubs.)

```
                - JOB ANALYSIS -
Name of Employee - Mary Jones        Position - Salad girl
Date - November 10, 19          Checked by - H.L.
─────────────────────────────────────────────────────────────
 From  |  To   |Total|  DUTIES
       |       |Hrs. |
─────────────────────────────────────────────────────────────
7.30A.M|9.30A.M|  2  | On counter - serving bar., prepares coffee,
       |       |     | waffles and toast, eggs and cooks short order
       |       |     | items to customers' orders and places on the
       |       |     | serving shelf for counter people
─────────────────────────────────────────────────────────────
9.30A.M|11.00AM| 1½  | Sets up serving bar by filling containers
       |       |     | with vegetables, fruits, fish and meat (which
       |       |     | have been prepared in the kitchen)
─────────────────────────────────────────────────────────────
11.00AM|11.45AM|     | Eats luncheon in employees' dining room
─────────────────────────────────────────────────────────────
11.45AM|4.00PM | 4¼  | Fills orders from waitresses involving
       |       |     | preparation of salads, short orders & meat
       |       |     | plates. Assists in serving from steam table.
       |       |     | Orders additional food from kitchen. Relieves
       |       |     | regular steam table operator. Keeps
       |       |     | serving counter and work area clean.
─────────────────────────────────────────────────────────────
TOTAL HOURS   | 7¾  |
─────────────────────────────────────────────────────────────
```

Fig. 12.3.   Job Analysis Sheet

creased volume should bring labor cost percentage down. Investigation may disclose that wage rates have increased or it may indicate less efficient scheduling. Whatever the cause, the comparison will alert management to the need for remedial measures.

Comparison of Unit Costs

Where more than one eating place operated under the same management, comparison between the different units is enlightening. This is shown in Figure 12.9.

This indicates that Unit C, although lowest in sales volume, is also lowest in percentage of labor cost and in labor cost per meal. Unit B, with greatest volume, shows higher labor costs in dollars and percentagewise than the other two food services. Labor cost per meal is shown in this illustration, as in feeding patients or inmates in institutions, the cost per meal is the criterion generally used.

Man-Hour Comparisons

Because of changing wage rates, the most accurate method of comparing labor costs is the man-hour comparison. The man-hours, that is, the total hours worked by all employees in the department being studied, for one period are compared with those of

another period. The comparison is valid only if the work load in both periods is the same or approximately so. In Figure 12.10 is an illustration based upon an actual study of a dishwashing department in a food service of a hospital.

This comparison was undertaken for a two-week period after improvements had been made in the utilization of personnel and arrangement of equipment. The comparison was made with a two-week period sixty days earlier. Savings as shown amounted to 164 man hours and $179 in payrolls for the two-week period. Actual savings in this food service totaled approximately 4,300 man-hours and more than $5,200 in payrolls annually, not including fringe benefits, in the dishwashing department alone.

Man-Hours Per 100 Meals Served

Another method of comparing man-hours is to relate them to the number of meals served. This is often done on the basis of *man-hours per 100 meals served* and provides a valid yardstick for institutional food-service operation. As advocated by C. Graham Hurlburt, Food Service Director of Harvard University, man hours of all kitchen and service employees are included but those of managers and chefs are excluded in making these comparisons.

ANALYSIS OF HOURLY SALES AND LABOR COST

A Labor Analysis chart of a company cafeteria is shown in Figure 12.11. The cafeteria had been open from 7 A.M. to 1 A.M. the following morning. The hours of operation are indicated by the horizontal lines. The heavy vertical lines indicate the hours of the employees on duty, with the total daily hours and rates of pay of each shown underneath. In addition to the light horizontal lines, the heavier horizontal lines indicate the nine periods into which the day was divided and for which cash register readings were taken. The five horizontal columns at the right of the chart show for each period; (1) customer count; (2) sales; (3) gross profit (in this case figured on a 40 per cent food cost); (4) labor cost; and (5) the percentage of labor cost to sales for the period.

After studying the chart, it was decided to close the cafeteria at 9 P.M. This and other economies resulted in savings of approximately $1,000 per month.

WAYS OF REDUCING LABOR COST

In addition to increasing the sales volume, which has the effect of lowering labor cost percentage-wise, there are a number of other ways of reducing dollar labor costs.

NAME OF JOB   Main Kitchen Supervisor   EMPLOYEE'S NAME   Mr. Davis

HOURS: 9 A. M. - 5:30 P. M.

JOB DESCRIPTION

DUTIES AND RESPONSIBILITIES

1. Responsible for the supervision of all the work in the cooking, bakery, and refrigerator units, and, on the assistant's days off, also for the work in the nourishment, ice cream, and salad units.
2. Checking in all receipts of meat regarding specifications, quality, and prices.
3. Daily work sheets
4. Weekly day-off schedule.
5. Daily storeroom requisition.
6. Training of employees in meat and vegetable cookery, and baking.

9:00   Check menus for the day to see if all supplies are in.
Check schedule to see if all employees are in.
Go over the baker's work for the day.
Check #2 refrigerator to see what leftovers can be used, and decide the cafeteria menu specials.

Monday and Tuesday: menu conference and meat quotations on Monday. Call in meat orders for the following week. Purchase orders to be typed by typist, and originals mailed same day to vendors. Carbon copies given to Sister.

Check porters to see that their work is being done properly.

Check heated trucks to see if all dials are set at #9, and that the trucks are heating properly.

10:30   Check out food to the cafeterias with the assistant when she is on, and by checking the work sheet.

11:15   Check all food for patients with the assistant, using the work sheet.

11:20   Check heated trucks out to the floors, using the work sheet, with the assistant.

11:45   Check out the Sister's truck.

12:00   Check the cafeterias for adequate food, serving, etc.

12:15   Return to Main Kitchen. Check cleaning, putting away of food into refrigerator, etc.

12:45   Lunch.

1:15   Check all units. Check Dinner menu. Check cleaning.
Desk work.
General supervision.
Check with refrigerator man to see if there is enough milk, if more is needed or if it should be cut down or cancelled for the following day.
Check out the cafeteria food.

3:30   Check to see that all trucks are set at #9, and that they are heating.

4:00   Check part-time employees to see that they are on duty, and they understand their duties for the afternoon.

4:15   Stop all work, and check the food, according to the work sheet, with the assistant.

4:30   Check the heated trucks out as at noon-time, using the work sheet, and working with the assistant.

Fig. 12.4. Job Description of Kitchen Supervisor in Hospital.

NAME OF JOB ___Main Kitchen Supervisor___   EMPLOYEE'S NAME ___Mr. Davis___

HOURS: ___9 A.M. - 5:30 P.M.___

JOB DESCRIPTION

DUTIES AND RESPONSIBILITIES

4:45   Check out the Sisters' truck.

5:00   Check cafeterias to see that there is enough food, serving, etc.

As soon as all food trucks are returned to Main Kitchen, combine foods, return the food to refrigerators. Make certain all stoves and equipment are off. Lock refrigerators, bakery, closets.

5:30   Off duty.

Note: When there are priests in the dining room, check out the priests' food at 11:50 for lunch; 4:50 for dinner.

ADDITIONAL NOTES:

Write recipes stating quality and quantity of ingredients, total yields, portion size, and cost.

Instructor in employee training program.

Checks cooked and baked foods for appearance, texture, color and flavor.

Fig. 12.4 (Contined)

DATE Tuesday - May 18, 1965

COOKS' MORNING PRODUCTION SCHEDULE

Employee	1. Mary	2. Jane	3. Lillian	4. Ruth
6:45 to 8:00	Check refrigerator for leftovers. Put on (1st) beef roast. Prepare braised beef	Make sauce. Cook noodles and	Prepare soup. Bread and pan veal steaks.	Clean and cut chickens. Prepare chicken batter.
8:00 to 9:00	Cook potatoes and carrots for stew. Prepare all gravies and sauces.	Prepare lasagna for baking. Wash pots.	Slice, dip, and bread onions for frying.	Butter sole for broiling. Clean fresh ear corn.
9:00 to 10:00	Put on (2nd) beef. Bake (1) ham. Bake lasagna. (48 orders)	Prepare vegetables for counter. Steam potatoes.	Prepare sweet potatoes Wash pots.	Cut lemons. Clean parsley. Peel potatoes. 200 lbs.
10:00 to 11:00	Bake veal steaks (30 orders) Set up counter. Put on (3rd) beef.	Broil sole (9 pc's). Fry chicken (8 pc's). Fry onions. Whip potatoes.	Cut ham cheese. for sandwiches. Help set up counter and clean dept.	Help set up counter. Wash pots.

ADVANCE PREPARATION

1. Cut chuck for beef steak pie—22 lbs. (3/4 inch cubes).
2. Cube (1/2 inch) 20 lbs. potatoes.
3. Cook corned beef.
4. Prepare chicken and dressing for p.m. menu. Check time with manager.
5. Tenderize steaks.
6. Clean cabbage—33 lbs.
7. Peel onions, check peeled potatoes and tartar sauce.

Fig. 12.5. Cook's Production Schedule. (Courtesy Pope's Cafeterias, Inc., St. Louis, Mo.)

STAFFING TABLE FOR KITCHEN

Jobs to be Filled	For 0-49 Patrons	For 50-99 Patrons	For 100-175 Patrons	For 175-plus Patrons
Chef	1	1	1	1
Cook	1	2	3	4
Salads -- Pantry	1	2	2	3
Dishwasher	1	2	3	3
Potwasher	1	1	1	1
Cleaner	0	1	1	1
Storeroom Man	0	1	1	1
Baker	0	1	1	1

Fig. 12.6.   Kitchen Staffing Table.

1. Use of machinery to replace or assist manual work.
2. Rearrangement of kitchen and service areas and equipment to save steps.
3. Application of work simplification methods to all tasks and procedures.
4. Rescheduling of employees to fit fluctuations in work.
5. Development of participation of employees and improved team work.

Replacing Manual Labor By Machines

Machinery is now available to supplement or replace manual labor in many tasks such as food preparation, dishwashing, and other areas of the food service. The use of conveyors, trayveyors, lowerators, and various types of material handling equipment saves many footsteps in the course of a day. "Put it on wheels!" is the motto adopted by progressive food-service managers in their efforts to expedite the handling of foodstuffs and supplies. In selecting machines for institutional use, the following questions should be asked (assuming that the design and construction of the piece of equipment are satisfactory):

1. *What are the alternatives to the use of this machine?* For example, the alternatives to the purchase of a potato peeler might be that preparation people may have free time to peel by hand or ready peeled or dehydrated potatoes might be purchased. Relative costs would need to be figured on which a decision could be based.
2. *Will this machine be economical for our operation?* A belt conveyor might save the wages of one or

Labor Costs as per Profit & Loss Statement		
	Current Period	Previous Period
Sales	$ 30,000	$ 28,000
Labor Cost	10,200	9,380
Percentages	34.0%	33.5%

Fig. 12.8.   Labor Costs from Profit and Loss Statement.

Comparison of Labor Costs			
	Unit A	Unit B	Unit C
Sales for Period	$ 36,000	$ 45,500	$ 22,000
Customer Count	60,000	70,000	40,000
Average Check	$ .60	$ .65	$ .55
Labor Cost	$ 12,240	$ 15,925	$ 7,370
Labor Cost %	34.0%	35.0%	33.5%
Labor Cost Per Meal	$ .2040	$ .2275	$ .1835

Fig. 12.9.   Comparison of Labor Costs.

Comparison of Man-Hours—Dishwashing Department				
	Current Period		Previous Period	
Employees	Hours	Wages	Hours	Wages
Breakfast	148	$ 185	208	$ 260
Luncheon	204	$ 255	220	$ 275
Dinner	188	$ 235	222	$ 278
Supervisors	40	$ 80	94	$ 141
Totals	580	$ 755	744	$ 934

Fig. 12.10.   Man-Hours Comparison.

more bus boys but the actual savings should be figured before purchasing the equipment.
3. *Is this machine the proper size for our food service?* A mixing machine, for example, should ordinarily be large enough to handle the largest batch for which it might be used. On the other hand it is impractical to purchase a large machine if it is to be used at capacity only a small part of the time. Consideration should be given to whether or not to buy a smaller machine in which several smaller batches might be mixed.

STAFFING TABLE FOR DINING ROOM
(Based on number of patrons)

Jobs to be Filled	For 0-37	For 38-58	For 59-75	For 76-95	For 96-112	For 113-129	For 130-145	For 146-166	For 167-Plus
Hostess	1	1	1	1	1	1	1	1	1
Waiter -- Waitress	2	3	4	5	6	7	8	9	10
Bus Boy	1	2	2	3	3	3	4	5	
Bar Waitress	1	1 1/2	1 1/2	2	2	2 1/2	2 1/2	2 1/2	2 1/2

Fig. 12.7.   Dining Room Staffing Table. (From the Management of People in Hotels, Restaurants, and Clubs.)

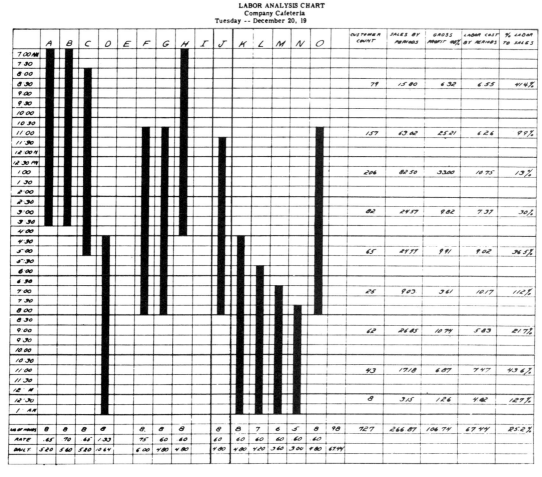

Fig. 12.11.   Labor Analysis Chart.

4. *Where should it be located so as to be most useful?* Some machines such as dishwashers and baking equipment will be located in the departments in which they are used. A coffee maker might be set up in the dining area where it is most used, even though coffee made in it might be served in other areas. With respect to the mixer previously discussed, it might be found that a portable mixing machine could be used in several areas and thus be more useful than one in a fixed location. As far as possible, kitchen machinery should be located so that it will be convenient to the worker or workers who will use it most frequently. If there is a question as to which of these employees is to be inconvenienced, it would seem advisable to locate the machine near the highest paid worker in order to save his time as much as possible.

Other questions about machinery pertain to the training of the operator and maintenance of the equipment. These have been covered in previous chapters.

How Much To Invest?

A machine may be installed for various reasons. Perhaps better, more uniform, or more sanitary results can be secured through its use. It may speed up a given process, and thus aid the entire operation.

Where the question involves investment in a machine in order to save labor costs, careful study should be made. Perhaps the machine will save labor but not enough to fully replace a single employee. In this case can the time saved be used profitably elsewhere, or can a part-time worker be engaged?

Factors to be considered are cost of the machine; its estimated life; cost of maintenance and repairs; interest on capital invested; and the estimated value of labor to be saved.

For example, assume that a new dishwashing machine is to be installed at a cost of $10,000. It will save the full time of one worker now being paid, including fringe benefits, $3,500 annually. On a ten-year basis, conservative tabulation of the savings would be set up as follows: (See Figure 12.12).

Gross savings ($3,500 per year for 10 yrs.)		$35,000
Cost of machine	$10,000	
Interest on invested capital, 5% for 10 yrs.)	5,000	
Estimated repairs and maintenance (10 yrs.)	3,000	
Total estimated cost 10 yrs.		18,000
Estimated savings for 10 yr. period		$17,000
Average annual savings		$ 1,700

Fig. 12.12. Estimated savings through installation of dishwashing machine.

To this, of course, would be added the intangible considerations such as improved sanitation, greater speed of service, and convenience.

Let Machines Prove Need

If in the layout of a new food service there is doubt as to whether or not a given machine or piece of equipment should be installed, it may be well to leave it out temporarily and let its use be proven through subsequent operating needs.

Rearrangement of Kitchen and Service Areas

A study of the kitchen and service areas will often reveal that labor could be more efficiently utilized if changes were made in the layout. In such an analysis, material flow plans are of great value.

Material Flow Plans

In studying a kitchen layout, charts can be made of the flow of the principal raw materials such as meats, vegetables, fruits, dairy products, and groceries. This can be done very simply by making up a large scale floor plan of the kitchen and using a colored crayon or colored thread (thread requires no erasing) to mark the progress of the various food items. As they make their way from the delivery entrance to the storeroom or refrigerator and thence through the various processing operations in the kitchen, suitable locations for various pieces of equipment will be made clear. Another method is to plot the actual routes of the material on a floor plan. See Figure 12.17.

Work Simplification

The term "work simplification" may sound formidable, but it is merely the application of common sense principles to all sorts of work situations. The objectives are to make work easier and generally more efficient. Present methods are *analyzed* and new methods are built up or *synthesized*.

Unnecessary forms, useless motions, and red tape are discarded. Steps are saved and workers are enabled to do quicker and better work by the rearrangement of tools, work places, and processes. Needless fatigue and unnecessary back-breaking labor are eliminated.

Work simplification can be applied to the work done by an individual food handler. It can also be applied to the routes followed by a food product through the kitchen; by a dish on its way to the customer; or by a paper form going through the office. In any event, the essence of the study is to get the essential facts down in black and white. It is surprising how much can be learned about an everyday routine operation once it is properly recorded.

Five Steps

There are five steps ordinarily followed in work simplification:

1. A definite job is selected for improvement.
2. The job is broken down into its elements or detailed steps. (Analysis)
3. Each detail is subjected to questioning.
4. An improved method is devised (Synthesis)
5. The improved method is placed in operation.

Here is how these five steps are carried out:

1. *Select the Job to be Improved.* Usually the job selected is the one causing the most trouble, or perhaps the one involving the greatest increased expense. It may be that the dishwashing operation or the distribution of certain foods or utensils during the rush hour is the "bottleneck" in the operation.

2. *Break Down the Detail of the Job.* Every job can be broken down into three parts:

   a. *Make-ready*—setting up equipment, preparing food for cooking, getting utensils with which to work.

   b. *Performance*—doing the job.

   c. *Put-away*—Clearing up and putting away tools and utensils, bussing dishes, etc.

It is often found that "make-ready" and "put-away" require more time than the actual work. One therefore will often find substantial room for improvement in these two steps.

For example, in one food service a study revealed a disproportionate amount of time taken by counter girls in getting replacements of clean silver from the three boxes on the back bar.

When supplies of clean silver were provided in advance at each of the thirteen counter stations, a substantial saving in time resulted. This made for speedier service, increased customer turnover, and reduced labor cost percentage.

Duplication is often found in these "make-ready" and "put-away" activities in the operation. This may be covered up due to fear of criticism, ignorance, mistrust of others, or other human weaknesses.

It is therefore important that the confidence and cooperation of the employees and supervisors be secured at the very start. This can be done by explaining to them in advance about work simplification.

Process Charts

To analyze a job or detail, a form known as the "process chart" or "flow chart" is used. This can be as simple or as elaborate as desired. The essential thing is to get the details down in the order in which they occur.

To make a process chart there are four things to keep in mind:

a. Be sure of and state the activity you are studying.
b. Follow the individual, material, or form you are studying through the entire process.
c. Have definite starting and stopping points.
d. Write down all steps briefly, but be sure to get all important details listed.

Symbols

To portray the activity graphically so that it can be quickly grasped and understood, work simplifiers generally use a "sign language" consisting of four symbols. (Different symbols are used in various systems of Work Simplification. Those cited here are given for illustrative purposes.)

a. *Operation*: When an action takes place which changes something (cutting off a chop, cooking a roast, washing dishes) a large circle is used. ◯
b. *Transportation:* When something is being moved (a bag of potatoes to a storeroom, a roast to an oven, etc.) use a small circle. ○
c. *Storage:* When something remains in one place awaiting action (food in a refrigerator or storeroom), use a triangle. △
d. *Inspection:* When something is inspected or verified (goods weighed at the delivery entrance, food inspected at checker's desk, etc.) use a square. ☐

When transportation occurs, it generally is advisable to note the distance involved. Usually the time in minutes for various activities is recorded.

In Figure 12-13, a flow process chart depicts the original analysis of motions performed in a typical kitchen operation: the delivery of potatoes at the receiving entrance and the subsequent movements. The activity taking place at all stages of the process is observed and graphically recorded.

3. *Question Each Detail.* When the entries made on the Process Chart are completed, each detail is then subject to such questions as:

WHAT is its purpose?
WHY is it necessary?
WHERE should it be done?
WHY should it be done here?
WHEN should it be done?
WHY should it be done at that time?
WHO should do it?
WHY should *he* do it?
HOW should it be done?
WHY should it be done this way?

The answers to these questions, if any, are placed in the NOTES column on the Process Chart.

4. *Devise an Improved Method.* After you have studied the way in which the job is now being done and have questioned the details on the Process Chart, you are ready to work out a better way of doing the job.

This is done by writing up a Proposed Process Chart showing the new method. It may be found that certain details can be eliminated, or that one or more steps can be combined. It may be advisable to change the order to simplify certain details.

Figure 12.14 shows a proposed chart based on the study of potatoes shown in Figure 12.13. This flow process chart is in distinct contrast to the original. Following an analysis of the actual operations, the work simplifier has set up this chart in which two operations have been eliminated, together with one transportation and storage. In addition 70 minutes and 235 feet of walking distance were saved. Similar savings can be accomplished in many of the daily routine tasks in any food-service establishment. Add all these time savings together and several days' work for an employee can be eliminated.

5. *Place the Improved Method in Operation.* As soon as the proposed improvements have been decided upon and approved, they should be put into effect.

Work simplification also involves motion-economy, the areas in which workers can operate normally without undue fatigue, the use of labor-saving machinery and other factors.

If the proposed new method is sound, it will be found to have saved some operations, some time in minutes and distance in transportation, and perhaps several storages and inspections. All of these make for payroll savings.

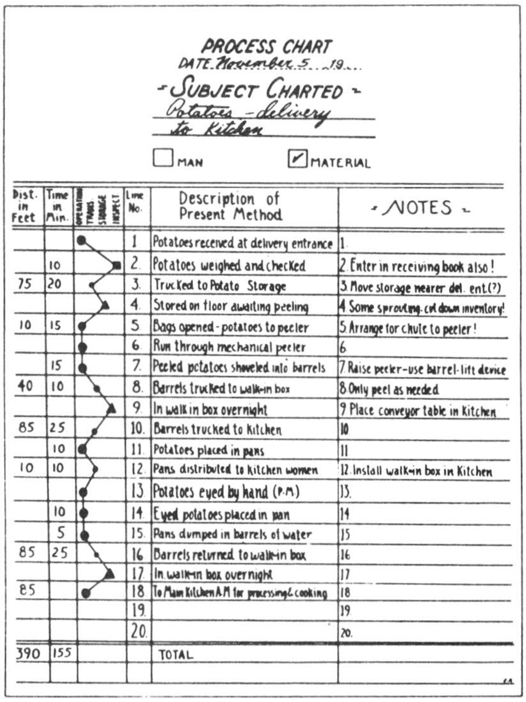

PROCESS CHART
DATE November 5, 19......

— SUBJECT CHARTED —
Potatoes - delivery
to Kitchen

☐ MAN   ☑ MATERIAL

Dist. in Feet	Time in Min.	Line No.	Description of Present Method	— NOTES —
		1	Potatoes received at delivery entrance	1.
	10	2	Potatoes weighed and checked	2 Enter in receiving book also!
75	20	3	Trucked to Potato Storage	3. Move storage nearer del. ent.(?)
		4	Stored on floor awaiting peeling	4 Some sprouting-cut down inventory!
10	15	5	Bags opened - potatoes to peeler	5 Arrange for chute to peeler!
		6	Run through mechanical peeler	6
	15	7	Peeled potatoes shoveled into barrels	7 Raise peeler-use barrel-lift device
40	10	8	Barrels trucked to walk-in box	8 Only peel as needed
		9	In walk-in box overnight	9 Place conveyor table in kitchen
85	25	10	Barrels trucked to kitchen	10
	10	11	Potatoes placed in pans	11
10	10	12	Pans distributed to kitchen women	12 Install walk-in box in kitchen
		13	Potatoes eyed by hand (P.M.)	13.
	10	14	Eyed potatoes placed in pan	14
	5	15	Pans dumped in barrels of water	15
85	25	16	Barrels returned to walk-in box	16
		17	In walk-in box overnight	17
85		18	To Main Kitchen A.M. for processing & cooking	18
		19.		19.
		20.		20.
390	155		TOTAL	

This flow process chart depicts the original analysis of motions performed in a typical kitchen operation—delivery of potatoes at the receiving entrance and subsequent movement. The activity taking place at all stages of the process is observed and graphically recorded by means of symbols—big circle for OPERATION; little circle for TRANSPORTATION; triangle for STORAGE; and square for INSPECTION—along with distance traversed and time elapsed.

Fig. 12.13. Original Process Chart (material) analyzing delivery of potatoes.

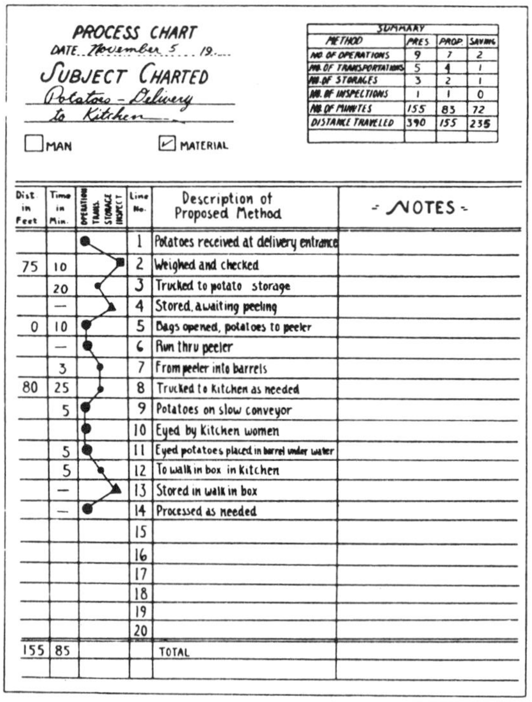

PROCESS CHART
DATE November 5, 19......

SUBJECT CHARTED
Potatoes - delivery
to Kitchen

☐ MAN   ☑ MATERIAL

	SUMMARY		
METHOD	PRES	PROP	SAVING
NO. OF OPERATIONS	9	7	2
NO. OF TRANSPORTATIONS	5	4	1
NO. OF STORAGES	3	2	1
NO. OF INSPECTIONS	1	1	0
NO. OF MINUTES	155	83	72
DISTANCE TRAVELED	390	155	235

Dist. in Feet	Time in Min.	Line No.	Description of Proposed Method	— NOTES —
		1	Potatoes received at delivery entrance	
75	10	2	Weighed and checked	
	20	3	Trucked to potato storage	
	—	4	Stored, awaiting peeling	
0	10	5	Bags opened, potatoes to peeler	
	—	6	Run thru peeler	
	3	7	From peeler into barrels	
80	25	8	Trucked to kitchen as needed	
	5	9	Potatoes on slow conveyor	
		10	Eyed by kitchen women	
	5	11	Eyed potatoes placed in barrel under water	
	5	12	To walk-in box in kitchen	
	—	13	Stored in walk-in box	
	—	14	Processed as needed	
		15		
		16		
		17		
		18		
		19		
		20		
155	85		TOTAL	

This flow process chart is in distinct contrast to the original. Following an analysis of the actual operations, the work simplifier has set up this proposed chart, in which two operations have been eliminated, along with one transportation and storage. In addition 72 minutes and 235 feet are saved. Similar savings can be accomplished in many of the daily routine tasks in any food service establishment. Add all these time savings together and several days work for an employee can be eliminated.

Fig. 12.14. Proposed Process Chart (material) showing results of analysis in Figure 12.13.

The improvements here illustrated made possible savings of $1,500 per annum in labor costs in this one operation. The principal expense entailed was the building of a walk-in box in the kitchen in which the potatoes could be stored. This cost approximately $1,800 at the time, and the cost was offset within about 15 months.

Figures 12.15 and 12.16 show the application of Process Charts to an individual worker (man charts). These figures illustrate an analysis of the movements of a working-chef in an industrial cafeteria during part of a typical busy period in the kitchen (from 8:30 A.M. to 12:05 P.M.). In Figure 12.16 (the proposed method), after giving effect to the changes in the location of walk-in boxes, meat cutting equipment, the telephone, and the pot racks, savings of 728 feet in distance travelled and 15 minutes in time are shown.

Work Flow Layouts

The Work Flow Layout is similar to the Material Flow Layout, only in this case the movement of the individual worker, rather than that of the material, is charted.

Figure 12.17 shows the paths of travel of the same employee (working-chef) studied in the Process Chart shown in Figures 12.15 and 12.16. Circled figures denote the number of trips made to and from the same destination by the chef.

In Figure 12.18 the proposed rearrangement of the kitchen is shown. As the walk-in refrigerators were old and in poor repair, two new portable walk-in boxes—a meat box, and a dairy and bakery box— were installed. The old refrigerators were given over to storage purposes. Changes were made in location of the scales, meat block, grinders, etc. A new telephone for the chef was proposed, and changes made in location of work tables and equipment for the bakers.

Most of the changes shown here were actually placed in effect. The result was twofold: actual savings in labor and increased efficiency which enabled the staff to handle a larger sales volume without added labor cost.

A collateral saving was effected through the use of old walk-in boxes for storage purposes. It was found that at least one hour less of the janitor's daily time was required than when canned goods, groceries, and

DIST. IN FEET	TIME IN MIN.	LINE NO.	DESCRIPTION OF PRESENT METHOD	NOTES
	9	1	MIXING HAMBURGER	
150	21	2	TO TELEPHONE (ORDERING)	BRING PHONE CLOSER
	6	3	STUDIED MENU	
	7	4	BASTED ROASTING CHICKENS	
80	3	5	TO MEAT BOX FOR BACON	RELOCATE MEAT BOX
	9	6	SLICED BACON - PUT IN OVEN	NEW BLADE ON SLICER -TEARS
	2	7	PREPARED GRAVY	
	3	8	REMOVED BACON FROM OVEN	
180	4	9	TO OFFICE (TELEPHONE)	
	7	10	PREPARED SPAGHETTI	
	3	11	BASTED CHICKENS	
	3	12	TO COUNTER AND RETURN	
	2	13	PUT SPAGHETTI ON RANGE	
	11	14	WORKED ON RANGE STIRRED -TASTED	
70	4	15	TO COUNTER AND RETURN	
80	3	16	TO POT RACK FOR LADLE	RELOCATE POT RACK
60	8	17	TO SCALES TO CHECK MEATS	RELOCATE SCALES
	10	18	PREPARING MEATS	
80	5	19	RETURNED MEATS TO BOX	
180	3	20	TO OFFICE (TELEPHONE)	
40	2	21	TO BAKERY SECTION	
80	2	22	TO WALK IN BOX	
	17	23	PREPARING SPAGHETTI SAUCE	
70	3	24	PLACED SPAGHETTI ON STEAM TABLE	
	12	25	CARVING CHICKEN	
	6	26	TESTED COFFEE	RELOCATE COFFEE MAKER
60	2	27	SOILED POTS TO POT SINK	
150	5	28	TO OFFICE(TELEPHONE)	
70	12	29	CHECKING COUNTER	
	38	30	SUPPLYING COUNTER	
1330	215			

Fig. 12.15. Original and Proposed Man Process Charts showing Movements of Working Chef in Industrial Cafeteria (8:30 A.M. to 12:05 P.M.) (PRESENT METHOD)

DIST. IN FEET	TIME IN MIN.	LINE NO.	DESCRIPTION OF PROPOSED METHOD	NOTES
	9	1	MIXING HAMBURGER	SUMMARY
12	18	2	TO TELEPHONE (ORDERING)	
	5	3	STUDIED MENU	
	7	4	BASTED ROASTING CHICKENS	
52	2	5	TO MEAT BOX FOR BACON	
	9	6	SLICED BACON-PUT IN OVEN	
	2	7	PREPARED GRAVY	
	3	8	REMOVED BACON FROM OVEN	
12	6	9	TELEPHONE	
	7	10	PREPARED SPAGHETTI	
	3	11	BASTED CHICKENS	
70	3	12	TO COUNTER & RETURN	
	2	13	PUT SPAGHETTI ON RANGE	
	13	14	WORKED ON RANGE STIRRED-TASTED	
70	4	15	TO COUNTER & RETURN	
0	0	16	POT RACK FOR LADLE	POT RACK OVER COOK'S TABLE
28	4	17	TO SCALES TO CHECK MEATS	
	10	18	PREPARING MEATS	
52	3	19	RETURNED MEATS TO BOX	
12	1	20	TELEPHONE	
40	2	21	TO BAKERY SECTION	
52	1	22	TO WALK IN BOX	
	11	23	PREPARING SPAGHETTI SAUCE	
70	3	24	PLACED SPAGHETTI ON STEAM TABLE	
	12	25	CARVING CHICKEN	
	6	26	TESTED COFFEE	
40	2	27	SOILED POTS TO POT SINK	
12	2	28	TELEPHONE	
70	12	29	CHECKING COUNTER	
	38	30	SUPPLYING COUNTER	
592	200			

Summary (NOTES box):

METHOD	PRES.	PROP.	SAV.
NO. OF OPERATIONS	11	11	
NO. OF TRANS.	14	14	
NO. OF STORAGES	1	1	
NO. OF INSPECTIONS	4	4	
NO. OF MINUTES	215	200	15
DISTANCE TRAVELED	1330	592	738

Fig. 12.16. (See Figure 12.15) (PROPOSED METHOD)

supplies had to be transported to and from the former storerooms in the basement.

In the industrial cafeteria to which these figures apply, rearrangement of the kitchen, improved labor utilization, and savings in food costs made possible total savings of approximately $28,000 per annum.

Man-Machine Charts

Another device used in industry is known as the man-machine chart. In factories, the purpose of this chart is to point up idle time on the part of the machine and the operator. By changing the sequence of the operation, it is often possible to have the operator perform set-up or preparatory tasks while the machine is operating.

In kitchens where costly material, machinery, and equipment are provided, an analysis of the use of the machinery and equipment may be profitable.

By making a simple chart of the times each machine is used, by whom, and for what purposes, much useful information may be found. Such a chart may show, for example, that:

1. A much-used piece of equipment or machine may be located so as to require considerable walking time on the part of the kitchen employees.
2. Conversely, a machine which is seldom used may be taking up valuable space which might well be allocated to a more important piece of equipment.
3. Work may be being done on machines which could better be done by hand.
4. Small batches (as in the bakery) may be demanding the time of a large machine when they could be processed more economically on a smaller machine or by special attachments on larger machine.

Rescheduling of Employees. Charts such as the foregoing point up the importance of scheduling employees in relation to the work volume at hand at different periods of the day.

In Figure 12.19 are shown the results of a study of cooks in a large kitchen. In order to cover the work load over the seven day period, it had been customary to have each cook work five days weekly with two successive days off each week.

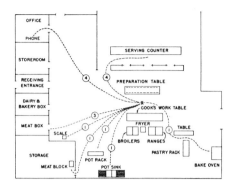

Fig. 12.17. Work flow layout showing movements of Working Chef as originally studied in Figure 12.15.

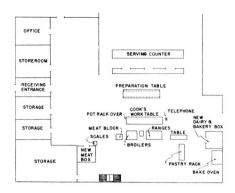

Fig. 12.18. Proposed layout of kitchen after study of Figure 12.17.

By carefully studying the work requirements, it was found possible to reschedule the assignments so that the work could be done with five instead of six cooks. Each man received his two consecutive free days as before.

Development of Teamwork

The possibilities of increasing productivity through improved teamwork are infinite, not only in employee food services, but also in industry as a whole.

If productivity is defined as production per man-hour, it readily can be seen that increased productivity will result in lower unit labor costs.

By "development of teamwork" we mean the providing of such a work atmosphere that each employee will be constantly motivated to do his or her best for the success of the enterprise.

This has been discussed in detail in Chapter 4 "The Food-Service Organization."

Incentives

Incentive systems are not as common in industrial and institutional feeding as they are in commercial food-service operations. In the hotel and restaurant field, such systems range from bonuses based on monthly operating ratios to outright profit-sharing plans. Excellent teamwork results in many instances.

For example, in one institution each employee is given 1/6 of a day's extra vacation for each week without absences or tardiness. Six weeks of a perfect record would entitle him to one extra day's vacation. A 48 weeks' perfect record would entitle him to eight extra vacation days.

NAME			SUN	MON	TUE	WED	THU	FRI	SAT	SUN	MON	TUE	WED	THU	FRI	SAT
6-3	Black	2nd			off	off									off	off
6-3	Brown	(Cook & Baker)						off	off	off	off						
6-3	Doe	(Relief Baker)	off	off								off	off			
8:30-5:30	Roe	1st						off	off	off	off						
9-6	Smith		off	off								off	off			
9-6	White				off	off									off	off
					PROPOSED WORK SCHEDULE											
6-3	Doe		off	off								off	off			
7-4	Roe				off	off									off	off
8-5	Black		off	off								off	off			
9-6	Smith				off	off									off	off
	White		6-3	6-3	9-6	9-6	9-6	off	off	off	off	6-3	6-3	9-6	9-6	9-6

Fig. 12.19. Present and proposed cooks' work schedule.

Bonuses are often allowed for achieving a given food or labor cost objective. To illustrate: One cafeteria manager gives a bonus of $25.00 to his chef each month, provided the desired food-cost percentage is achieved. In this case the objective is 40 per cent. If the food cost runs no higher than 40 per cent of cafeteria sales, *but no lower than 38 per cent*, the bonus is paid.

The setting of a lower limit, in this case 38 per cent, is extremely important. It prevents those responsible from cutting portions or in other ways lowering the food value received by the patron below a reasonable minimum.

ACCURATE COSTING OF PRODUCTION LABOR

The food-service kitchen is, in many respects, similar to the manufacturing plant. Raw materials are processed and partially-processed materials are finished ready for service to the customer.

An important key to success in manufacturing is accurate cost knowledge. The institutional food-service operator needs to have accurate cost knowledge today for two compeling reasons: first, in order that he can set menu prices to greatest advantage under current conditions; and second, that he can decide whether "to make or to buy" certain products which may be either produced in the kitchen or purchased in fully or partially prepared form.

The Prime Cost Method of menu-pricing, advocated by Harry H. Pope of St. Louis, stresses the importance of determining the cost of production labor involved in the preparation of various menu items. There are two kinds of labor to be considered, namely direct and indirect.

Direct labor is the labor involved in the direct processing of the product such as the work of the preparation people, cooks, bakers, and salad makers.

Indirect labor is the work done by those employees who, while not directly engaged in processing, assist in making possible the work of those so directly engaged. Under this heading comes the work of receiving and storeroom people; dishwashers and pot washers; cleaners, janitors, porters, handy men; checkers, if any, and the kitchen manager or superviser if other than the chef.

The first step in determining production labor cost is to divide the kitchen into a number of departments in accordance with the groups of menu items produced. These departments might be salads, pastries; meats; vegetables, sandwiches; bread and rolls, and desserts and beverages, depending upon the type of the food service.

One method of applying production labor cost to specific menu items is to compute the total sales of each of the foregoing items for a given period and also the direct and indirect labor attributable to each of the corresponding departments. The ratio between departmental labor and departmental sales is then expressed as a percentage and this percentage of the sales price of each menu item is taken as the production labor cost.

The chief problem is the exact determination of direct labor cost. This is done most accurately by the use of time study, which is described in detail in a following section and involves the use of a stop watch. It can be done, however, by the use of a wristwatch or the clock on the wall. The object is to measure the amount of time devoted in the actual processing of a given entrée or food item. Work is observed as it is being done and the time intervals are noted on a time study sheet, clipped for convenience on an observation board.

By-products of Time Study

In addition to determining the time devoted to the processing of various food items, a time study program will bring many valuable by-products to the restaurant or institution.

As previously mentioned, it will assist management in determining whether to "make or to buy" a given product which is available in prepared or semiprepared form. Most important of all, the time study will often disclose ways of improving the effectiveness of various processes and procedures in the food service.

For example, in all processing, whether in industry or in the food service, waste motion is often discovered in the beginning and at the ending of the process. In a factory, the worker often lost considerable time in getting together the tools and materials required to perform a given task. This has been remedied in most plants by having tools and materials delivered to the work place by less highly paid employees.

Similarly, savings in labor costs have been attained in food-service kitchens by having the recipes for the day analyzed and the ingredients assembled and delivered to the cooks at the beginning of the work period. Many food services have special departments set up for the assembly of ingredients and their delivery to the kitchen. This solves the problems of "make-ready" and "put-away" in the kitchen.

Waiting Time. Time spent waiting for foods to cook, waiting for another employee to pass on a material, and the like, is a considerable factor in kitchen operation. This waiting time is not chargeable to direct labor as no labor is performed. In costing, however, it must be accounted for by spreading it over the total direct labor cost. Much can be done to reduce waiting time by arranging for the cook, for example, to perform some useful task rather than waste his time gazing at the oven. Thus time study discloses many ways of improving the effectiveness of the entire operation.

Time Study and Motion Economy

For many years industry has made use of time study, primarily in setting work standards upon which various types of incentive wages have been based.

In recent years, greater attention has been paid to the principles of motion economy in devising easier, quicker, and less costly methods of performing tasks.

Time Study

Any operation, whatever its nature, can be simplified to some extent by rule-of-thumb methods, provided the observer is competent and knows what to look for. The techniques of motion and time study, however, enable the observer to do a more thorough and accurate job.

The equipment required to make a time study consists of a timing device and certain auxiliary equipment. Usually a stop watch and observation board are all that are necessary for time study in its simplest form.

A decimal minute stop watch is used in which the dial is divided into 100 equal spaces. Instead of running from one to 12 as in an ordinary watch, the "hours" run from one to 10 (10 being designated by zero). The large hand of the watch makes one complete revolution per minute, so each dial division represents 0.01 minutes. The small dial is divided into 30 spaces, each of which represents one minute, the small hand making one complete revolution in 30 minutes. A decimal stop watch is pictured in Figure 12.20.

The watch is started or stopped by pressing the slide on the side. By pressing the winding stem, the hand will return to zero, but it will start immediately when the stem is released. Thus it is possible to time each operation separately by using the stem, but it is safer and better practice to allow the watch to run continuously during an operation and note the readings on the observation sheet, subtracting from the previous reading to secure elapsed time.

For purposes of illustration, a sample observation sheet is shown in Figure 12.21. This was used in observing a cafeteria employee wrapping knives, forks, and teaspoons in paper napkin rolls.

On the left of the sheet there are spaces for the various elements into which the operation was broken

Fig. 12.20.   Decimal Stop Watch. (Courtesy Meylan Stop Watch Corp., New York City.)

down, in this case four in number. The actual time is recorded in the lower spaces opposite the name of each element, and the elapsed time computed by subtraction and entered on the upper line. In this case, only ten observations were taken—although there is space on the sheet for fifteen. At the right are columns for the minimum time, the average time, the time selected, and the number of times the element occurs per cycle.

Given a few minutes' practice, almost anyone can learn how to use a stop watch. In a short time it is possible to note the elapsed times for different elements and to record them while keeping the entire operation under observation.

Chief Difficulties

The chief technical difficulties which require some training and experience to master are:

1. *Breaking down the elements.* The operation must be broken down into elements, or groups of related motions. Each element should be as short as can be accurately timed (less than .03 minutes is difficult to measure with a stop watch). Manual time should be separated from machine time. Elements that are "constant" (regardless of the size and shape of the articles handled) should be distinguished from "variable" elements (those that vary with the size and shape).

2. *Selecting a representative time.* The selected time is generally the arithmetical mean or average of the various elapsed times.

   There are other ways of arriving at the selected times—such as the "modal" method. Under this pro-

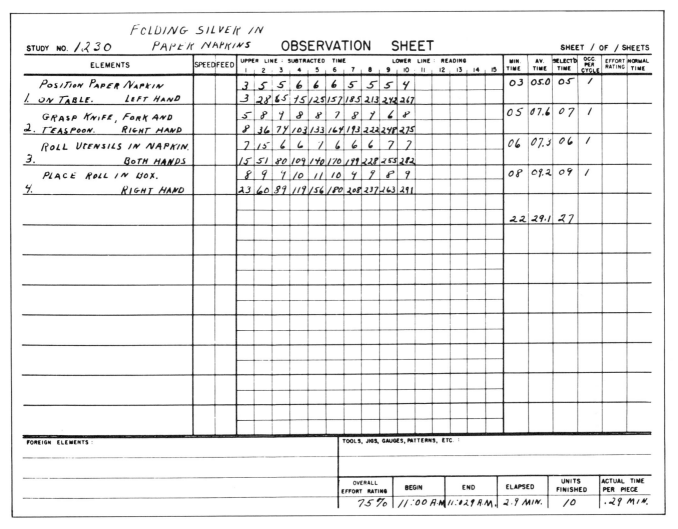

STUDY NO. 1.230   FOLDING SILVER IN PAPER NAPKINS   OBSERVATION SHEET   SHEET / OF / SHEETS

ELEMENTS	SPEED	FEED	UPPER LINE : SUBTRACTED TIME / LOWER LINE : READING (1–15)	MIN. TIME	AV. TIME	SELECTD TIME	OCC. PER CYCLE	EFFORT RATING	NORMAL TIME
1. POSITION PAPER NAPKIN ON TABLE. LEFT HAND			3 5 5 6 6 6 5 5 5 4 / 3 28 65 95 125 157 185 213 242 267	03	05.0	05	1		
2. GRASP KNIFE, FORK AND TEASPOON. RIGHT HAND			5 8 9 8 8 7 8 9 6 8 / 8 36 74 103 133 164 193 222 248 275	05	07.6	07	1		
3. ROLL UTENSILS IN NAPKIN. BOTH HANDS			7 15 6 6 7 6 6 6 7 7 / 15 51 80 109 140 170 199 228 255 282	06	07.3	06	1		
4. PLACE ROLL IN BOX. RIGHT HAND			8 9 9 10 11 10 9 9 8 9 / 23 60 89 119 156 180 208 237 263 291	08	09.2	09	1		
				22	29.1	27			

FOREIGN ELEMENTS :

TOOLS, JIGS, GAUGES, PATTERNS, ETC. :

OVERALL EFFORT RATING	BEGIN	END	ELAPSED	UNITS FINISHED	ACTUAL TIME PER PIECE
75%	11:00 A.M	11:02.9 A.M.	2.9 MIN.	10	.29 MIN.

Fig. 12.21. Time Study Sheet.

cedure, the number appearing most frequently is taken as the selected time. In the sample time study, (Figure 12.21) .05 occurs five times in the elapsed times of the first element (top row of figures); .06 occurs three times; .03 one time, and .04 once. In this case .05 was taken as the selected time.

3. *Rating the operator.* Rating is the process of comparing the performance of the operator under observation with the observer's own concept of normal performance. This is where the judgment of the observer enters in, and there is no way of establishing a time study without that element of judgment. In the Observation Sheet shown, the operator was rated at 75 per cent.

As an example: Some people walk at a slow pace while others walk rapidly. If walking at a rate of three miles per hour is considered normal, walking at two miles per hour would be 66 2/3 per cent of normal, and walking at four miles per hour would be 133 1/3 per cent of normal.

Motion Economy

Motion study was originated by the late Frank Gilbreth aided by his wife, Dr. Lillian Gilbreth, well-known today through the book and movie *Cheaper by the Dozen.* The original motion studies of brick laying were made by Mr. Gilbreth in Boston about the turn of the century. At first, motion study was carried on separately from time study, but in recent years it has been seen that motion and time study supplement each other. Today they are widely used in combination.

THE GILBRETH PRINCIPLES

The Gilbreths developed 17 fundamental principles of motion economy which permit the maximum amount

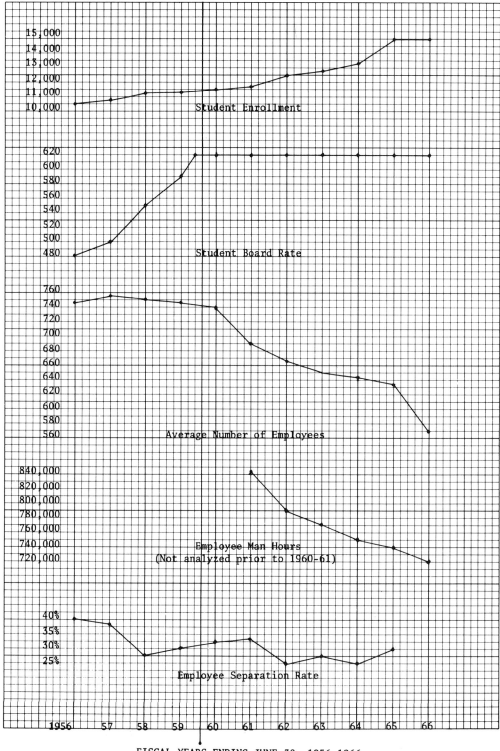

FISCAL YEARS ENDING JUNE 30, 1956-1966

Chart showing improvement of labor utilization in large university food service resulting from better methods of selection and training; application of production schedules and use of labor-aiding machinery. Note that while student enrollment has increased since latter part of 1959 the average number of employees and the man-hours worked per 100 meals has been reduced while the student board rate remains the same and the turnover, or employee separation rate has been fairly constant. (Vertical line from end of 1959 denotes opening of new dining hall feeding 400 students.) (Courtesy C. Graham Hurlburt, Director Food Service, Harvard University, Cambridge, Mass.)

Fig. 12.22. Labor Utilization Chart.

of production effort with a minimum of fatigue. To attain the greatest economy of motion, the principles should be followed as far as practicable.

These principles can be applied to improve an existing job and also in setting up new work. Eight of the most important principles having application to food services are listed here. Each principle warrants a separate discussion.

1. Arrange work within the proper working area.
2. Pre-position tools and materials.
3. Make use of bins or fixtures.
4. Use motions of least body movement wherever possible.
5. Perform the work with both hands wherever possible.
6. Use drop delivery.
7. Provide good conditions for posture and sight.
8. Reduce to a minimum the holding of work by either hand.

1. *Proper Working Area:* There is a limited area which the employee can use with a normal expenditure of effort. There is a normal working area for the right hand, for the left hand (working separately), and for both hands working together. These areas are shown in Figure 12.23.

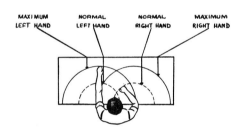

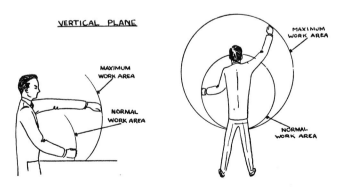

Fig. 12.23. Normal and Maximum Working Areas. One principle of motion economy is to arrange work within the proper working area. How to figure this area for both the horizontal and vertical planes is illustrated.

The normal working area for the right hand is determined by drawing an arc with a sweep of the right arm across the working area. Only the forearm is extended, with the upper arm at the side of the body in a normal position. The normal working area for the left hand is determined in the same manner. The area enclosed in the arcs represents the zone in which two-handed work can be done most conveniently.

The maximum working area for both hands is determined by drawing an arc with a sweep of the right arm across the working area with the arm pivoted at the right shoulder. The maximum working area for the left hand is found in the same way. The area between the two arcs, normal and maximum, represents the zone in which two-handed work cannot be performed without causing disturbance of posture and consequent fatigue.

The hands have a normal work space in the vertical plane as well as in the horizontal plane. In placing materials or equipment, the location should be within the normal working area. This applies to tasks which require a standing position at the work place.

2. Materials and tools used on the job should be located between the normal and the maximum working areas. They should be pre-positioned and placed in holders or containers so that they can be grasped in a position ready for use.

3. The use of bins or fixtures plays an important part in the proper arrangement of the work place. The effort of the worker can be reduced to a minimum by placing supplies in such fashion that they are easily accessible.

4. In laying out a table or working area, it is desirable that motions be confined to the lowest classification with which it is possible to perform the work properly.

Manipulation motion can be divided into the following general classifications:

Finger motions.
Motions involving fingers and wrist.
Motions involving fingers, wrist and forearm.
Motions involving fingers, wrist, forearm, and upper arm.
Motions involving fingers, wrist, forearm, upper arm and shoulder.

In other words, arm movements should not be used if wrist or finger movements will serve as well. It is also essential that materials and tools should be as near as possible to the point of use, and that motions of the hand should be as short as the work permits.

5. *Work with Both Hands.* In line with this principle, work should be arranged, and the actions of the two hands balanced so that both hands start and end each motion at the same time. This tends to build up a smooth operating rhythm. It is much easier to do something when the hands move at the same time, especially when both hands do the same thing. Idleness of hands singly cannot be eliminated in many cases, but idleness of both hands at the same time, except when rest is required, is undesirable. One hand should not have more work than the other; preferably the hands should do the same or similar things at the same time if the job permits.

The arms should move in opposite directions at the same time.

6. *Use Drop Delivery.* Wherever possible the work should be so arranged that the finished work can be disposed of by releasing it in the position in which it is completed and delivering it to its destination by gravity. Work can be dropped into a chute or conveyor without moving to dispose of it or it can be dropped as the hands are on their way to handle the next unit of work. In one institution, for example, carrots are sliced by inmates who are handicapped to some extent. The workers sit in a row on a platform and the sliced carrots are dropped into chutes leading to a large pan.

This saves the time necessary to carry the finished work to its destination, and the disposal of it frees the hands so that they may begin the next cycle without disturbing the rhythm.

7. *Posture and Sight.* Wherever possible, the worker should be permitted to vary his or her position by either sitting or standing as preferred. This enables the employee to rest certain muscles, and a change of position improves circulation. Sitting or standing for long periods of time produces more fatigue than alternately sitting or standing at will. The height of the work place should be so arranged as to be suitable for the average employee.

Proper illumination should be provided as indicated in Chapter 5.

8. *Minimize Holding by Hand.* Frequently we find that either hand may do nothing except hold the work so that the other hand can work on it. Wherever possible this holding should be eliminated, perhaps by the introduction of a holding fixture which would release both hands for more useful work.

WHAT TO OBSERVE

Eight questions can be asked with respect to any job to determine whether the principles of motion economy are observed in the work:

1. Is the work arranged to best advantage?
2. Are tools and materials pre-positioned?
3. Can bins or fixtures be used?
4. Is the work being performed with the fewest body movements possible?
5. Are both hands working together rhythmically?
6. Can drop delivery be employed?
7. Are conditions for posture and sight as good as can be provided?
8. Is work being held by either hand?

For the food-service manager, the objective is to learn to think in terms of motion economy. Apply the principles and learn to recognize what is good and what is bad from a motion economy standpoint.

How will the application of work simplification and its basic techniques—time and motion study—aid the food-service manager? Here are three ways:

1. It will minimize fatigue and make work easier for employees—thus reducing labor turnover.
2. It will reduce costs and improve quality.
3. It will further the growth and personal satisfactions of the manager by enabling him to do a constantly better job.

In the case of the time study shown in Figure 12.21, the wrapping of silverware in paper napkins, much could have been done to improve the operation. For one thing, a pile of napkins could have been positioned in the center of the table and the silver placed upon it. The uppermost napkin could then be wrapped around the utensils. This would save the time and effort required to grasp for each napkin separately. In addition both hands could have been used in grasping the silver, one hand picking up the knives, for example, and the other hand the fork and spoon. As observed, the right hand was used to gather the silver and the left hand to grasp a napkin each time.

A further improvement might have been to have a slot in the table with a box under it so that the rolled utensils could be dropped through the slot when completed.

Actually, in this case when the time consumed in the entire operation was computed, it was decided to abandon this procedure and use Steril-sil cylinders. This afforded better protection from a sanitary point of view, and at the same time an opportunity for substantial labor saving.

Industrial engineers now realize that the principles of both motion economy and time study should be employed in bringing about greater productivity and eliminating unnecessary fatigue. The use of micromotion picture film, in addition to conventional stopwatch techniques, has made possible more accurate visualization of finger, hand, arm, and body movements, as well as elapsed time.

The Work Simplification procedures outlined in this chapter are based essentially upon this new concept of motion economy and time study as an integrated whole. While relatively little work has as yet been done in the mass-feeding field, new applications are now being made daily. With the growing interest, it is likely that much progress will be made in the future. Increasing labor costs in other industries have brought about the necessity for a means of increasing productivity. In a like manner, rising costs in the food-service field undoubtedly will focus more attention upon the application of motion and time study techniques and other modern scientific management procedures.

SUGGESTED READING

BARNES, RALPH W. Motion and Time Study. New York: John Wiley & Sons, 1949.

BARNES, RALPH W. Work Methods Training Manual. Dubuque, Iowa: Wm. C. Brown Company Publishers, 1950.

CHARTRAND, MAURICE, Cafeteria Manager, Norton Co., Worcester, Mass. The Design of Cafeteria Counters, privately printed, 1958.

LUNDBERG, DONALD E., AND ARMATAS, JAMES P. The Management of People in Hotels, Restaurants and Clubs. Dubuque, Iowa: Wm. C. Brown Company Publishers, 1965.

MAY, ERNEST N. "The Economics of Hospital Food Service." Wilmington, Delaware: Charitable Research Foundation, 1955.

STOKES, JOHN W. How to Manage a Restaurant or Institutional Food Service. Dubuque, Iowa: Wm. C. Brown Company, Publishers, 1967.

THOMAS, ORPHA MAE. A Scientific Basis for Design of Institutional Kitchens. New York: Columbia University Teachers College, 1947.

CHAPTER 13

Control of Other Expenses and Overhead

In addition to the cost of food and labor, there are certain other expenses involved in operating an industrial or institutional food service. These may be grouped as follows:

Supplies
Office supplies
Paper supplies (cups, plates, napkins, etc.)
Cleaning supplies
Dishes, utensils, and small equipment

Utilities
Fuel
Heat
Light
Power
Telephone
Water
Ice

Services
Laundry (towels and uniforms)
Exterminating
Trucking and expressage
Repairs and maintenance
Garbage and rubbish disposal
Window cleaning
Cleaning of exhaust flues

Occupancy Charges
Rent or Space Charges
Taxes
Insurance
Depreciation
Administrative Overhead

Not included in this list are capital charges such as the cost of equipment involving substantial expense and designed to last one year or more. The original cost of dishes, glassware, and silver is usually considered a capital item, but replacements are treated as expense. Capital units are charged off by depreciation over their period of useful life.

FIXED AND VARIABLE EXPENSE

Expenses may be classified under two headings: fixed and variable. *Fixed* expenses are those which do not vary with the volume of sales—for example, rent, taxes, and depreciation. All of these charges go on at a given rate regardless of sales.

Variable expenses are those which vary with the volume. To illustrate—as sales increase, there will be increased usage of supplies, certain utilities and services—all of these are *variable expenses.*

Utilities vary to some extent with volume and the season of the year, although there are certain minimum rates and demand charges which tend to limit the variations. Some service charges, such as maintenance, are variable, but not with respect to volume. Most of the items in the service group are fixed expenses. Under occupancy, all of the items are fixed. That is, they accrue regardless of sales volume. Some forms of insurance, such as those based upon payrolls or inventory values, vary with the activity of the operation.

Regardless of these classifications, there is much that can be done to keep other expenses under control.

Supplies

This item often amounts to as much as 2½% of cafeteria sales. It may also represent a substantial charge to patient's service. A careful check of purchases and usage may reveal opportunities for savings.

Paper goods are an important item of supplies. Prices from different suppliers should be compared. Studies may be made to find less expensive substitutes for certain items and to prevent waste of paper goods. The use of a type of dispenser which makes it difficult to pull out more than one napkin at a time is an example.

Where paper cups or containers are used for items taken from the food services, a charge should be made to cover this extra cost. If such charges are substantial, they should be separated from the food sales figure so that the food-cost percentage will not be distorted.

As in the purchase of food, savings may be effected through careful checking of prices. On frequently-used supply items it is often possible to save through buying larger quantities at one time. Delivery charges can also be reduced by placing orders for a number of small items at one time, so that they can be delivered in one truckload.

Analysis of the ways in which supplies are being used may also reveal possible economies. The use of acceptable types of dispensers for soaps, detergents, paper towels, and similar items may help to cut costs and at the same time make for more effective use of such supplies.

The possibility of effecting savings through the use of the plastic ware now on the market may well be studied. Breakage rates as compared with china, porosity, and other factors should be analyzed—as well as the customer appeal of the new materials.

In the same manner, economies may be found through the use of new and improved types of glassware and utensils. For example, the new heat-treated glasses are a better buy, even though more costly than untreated glasses.

Utilities

Light, heat, fuel, and power are often supplied from the institution's own plant. Nevertheless, savings can be effected, as in any eating place, by care in turning off incandescent lamps when not needed, and in using proper-sized bulbs and fluorescent lighting where possible.

Considerable progress has been made in industry generally in the use of proper illumination and color in increasing productivity and in reducing accidents. The same principles may be profitably applied in industrial food service. (See Chapter 5 "Design and Equipment" and Chapter 10 "Sanitation, Safety and Fire Prevention"). *Electrical heating elements* in ranges and food warming equipment should be turned off when not in use to save electrical energy, as well as to reduce kitchen heat.

Where electrical energy is purchased from a power company, it is well to investigate the rate in effect. Often by placing all motors and heating elements on a separate power meter it is possible to get a lower rate on electrical energy used for power and heating purposes.

Steam is used in many institutions for steam kettles, steam cookers, etc. This is often supplied by the establishment's power plant. Care in the use of steam may result in economies.

In one of the industrial food services we studied, a substantial annual expenditure was incurred to provide fuel for an oil burning heater to warm the building housing the cafeteria. As the result of a concerted effort to reduce other expenses, it was found that this building could be heated by exhaust steam, a by-product of the Company's power plant. It was estimated that the cost of the steam line could be amortized within three years through the savings in cost of fuel oil.

Water shortages in many sections of the country during recent years point up the importance of preventing waste of water. The use of spring faucets that shut off automatically is one way of doing this. Leaky faucets and other water leaks should be reported immediately to the maintenance department.

Telephone bills are a substantial cost in any establishment. Many institutions have found it profitable to have studies of the rate schedule in effect made by telephone experts. It may be found that changes in equipment will make possible savings in telephone costs—under a more favorable schedule. It is also wise to consider ways of preventing unauthorized use of telephones. Locks may be provided for dial phones when not in use. Regulations as to the use of telephones should be made clear and enforced.

Ice is a necessity in food services, both in industries and cafeterias. Many of the older institutional plants are equipped with ice-making machinery operating on an ammonia and brine system. This involves considerable labor in making and crushing the ice and delivering it to the various points where it is to be used.

In a New York City hospital when this problem was studied by one of our engineers, it was found that the operation of the ice plant entailed the employment of a licensed operator at a substantial wage rate. This also added to the cost of the operation; although the workload, due to use of many self-contained units throughout the institution, had been cut down. Thus an additional reason was presented for de-centralizing ice production throughout the entire hospital. Modern self-contained units located in the cafeteria and on various patients' floors eliminate considerable labor, and make ice continuously available either in the form of cubes or flakes. This method represents considerable improvement in sanitation.

Services

Hospitals and other like institutions generally maintain well-equipped and efficiently operated *laundries.* Cost of this service is usually charged to the food service on the basis of usage. Industrial cafeterias usually depend upon commercial laundries or linen services for uniforms, hand-towels, etc. Many food services, however, find it economical to have household type automatic washers, dryers, and small mangles to handle dish towels, aprons, and other flat work.

About two years ago, in the food-service center of a university graduate school, a washing machine and a dryer were installed in a room set aside for the purpose and a competent woman engaged to operate

them. Perma-press materials requiring no ironing are used for tablecloths, napkins, uniforms, etc. As a result, laundry charges which formerly ran as high as $17,000 per annum have been reduced to approximately $12,000.

Exterminating service may be provided by the Maintenance Department, by an outside exterminating agency, or by a combination of both. A monthly checkup by a qualified exterminator agency with its expert know-how is sound insurance for any food service in making sure of vermin control.

Trucking and express charges can be substantial where the food service is at some distance from its suppliers. Some institutions find it economical to operate their own equipment, usually a one-ton pick-up truck. Vendors will usually deliver free when the load is sufficiently large or in the course of a regular route (such as for bread, milk, ice cream, coffee, etc.) It must not be forgotten, however, that delivery costs have to be absorbed, and the supplier must include these costs in the prices he quotes. Where deliveries are made by trucking companies, minimum charges prevail. A load weighing less than 100 lbs., for example, will be charged the 100 lb. rate, and so on. Care in ordering to make sure that delivery costs are kept at a minimum will be found profitable to the food service.

Repairs and Maintenance is usually the responsibility of the Maintenance Department of the industry or institution in which the food service is located. As indicated in Chapter 5, a Preventive Maintenance program is the most efficient way of handling this problem.

When the service of the Maintenance Department is required to make emergency repairs or to change existing facilities, a special Maintenance Order form is usually filled out. This sets forth the nature of the work to be done, and usualy requires the approval of an administrative officer. The Work or Job Order (See Figure 13.1) form made out by the Maintenance Department should set forth the time the job started and was finished, and a list of parts or supplies used. This should require the signature of the Food-Service Manager or one of his assistants. Needless to say, the one signing this order should see that it is factually correct.

From our observation, the cafeteria is often an attractive resting place for some maintenance workers. A simple chore like the replacement of an electric bulb may involve many extra minutes over a cup of coffee. Unless the Food-Service Manager is on the alert considerable extra labor time may be charged unnecessarily to the food service.

Newton-Wellesley Hospital
MAINTENANCE WORK ORDER

N.° 1950

Date:_____

Requested by:_____

Location of Job: Bldg._____Floor_____Rm._____

Approved By: Dept. Head_____Administrator_____

Charge to:_____ Account No.:_____

Nature of work:

_____

_____

_____

_____

_____

_____

_____

_____

Plant Supt. Approval:_____

To be completed by:_____

COST	SUMMARY
Labor	
Materials	
Direct Purchases	
Total	

Order of Assignment	
Carp.	
Painter	
Plumb.	
Elect.	
Mason	
Repairman	
Machinist	
Trucks	
Grounds	
Refrig.	

Work Completed:
Date_____19
Per:

Checked by:	Posted:	Remarks:

For Maint. Use:

Fig. 13.1. Maintenance work order form. (Courtesy Newton-Wellesley Hospital, Newton Lower Falls, Mass.)

In requesting the services of the Maintenance Department, much time can be saved if the Food-Service Manager gives full details, as far as possible, of the work to be done, including the exact location. If this is done the Maintenance Department can send the qualified mechanic to cope with the problem together with the necessary tools and repair parts. Thoughtfulness on the part of the food-service people in this respect will prevent time-absorbing trips "back to the shop," and keep the expense at a minimum.

Garbage may be collected by the local municipality, or by the proprietor of a nearby piggery. In some cases the food service is paid for this garbage—in which case it is accounted for under Other Income on the Operating Statement. However, local sanitary regulations will have to be observed (see Chapter 10, "Sanitation"). Where garbage grinders or disposers are used, the garbage problem is minimized.

Rubbish (cans, bottles, cartons, boxes, paper, and other refuse) presents a problem. Rubbish may be disposed of by the Maintenance Department (a service for which the Food Service is usually charged), by the local municipality, or by a contractor.

In the last named case, it will be advisable to periodically scrutinize the contract to see if improvements and savings can be effected. The use of compactors to reduce the volume of rubbish has been mentioned previously. With respect to waste paper, some institutions have found it economical to install a compressing machine, and to sell the baled wastepaper. Usable wooden boxes can generally be resold. Here again, the money received is credited to Other Income.

When the food service occupies its own quarters, it is often advisable to have the windows cleaned by outside contractors rather than by its own staff. Window cleaning, particularly of the outsides of windows, often presents problems and hazards with which the food-service staff is not equipped to cope.

Other services include such matters as: the care of plants and shrubbery within or around the premises; the painting of signs, which may be done by the staff or by an outside artist; and decorations, for which an interior decorator is usually relied upon. Painting of the walls and ceilings may be done by painters on the Maintenance Staff. In most institutions this work is done upon a regular schedule throughout the establishment. The Food-Service Manager must be alert to see that the cafeteria and kitchen are not overlooked in this overall schedule. Dingy walls and ceilings in work areas absorb light, and lower the efficiency of the workers. Light and attractive dining rooms draw patrons, and thus help to maintain volume.

Occupancy Charges

Many food-service managers feel that they can do nothing about overhead charges such as taxes, depreciation, and insurance—as these are generally allocated by top management.

Nevertheless, the manager should make it a point to check into all of these so that he understands the basis of each charge. Frequently, in so doing, possibilities for savings are disclosed.

Rental charges on rented land and buildings or local real estate taxes are often charged throughout the entire establishment, including the food service, on a square foot basis.

The federal and state employment-security taxes are based upon the employment experience of the establishment. By reducing labor turnover, the food service aids in keeping this at the minimum rate.

In some localities, special licenses and taxes are required for all food services (victuallers licenses, milk licenses, etc.). These are a direct charge to the food service.

Insurance

Insurance in many forms affects the food service. Fire insurance on buildings and contents usually involves the largest premiums. The installation of sprinklers, maintenance of fire extinguishers, and regular fire drills of employees may result in lowering premiums paid for this coverage, both in the food service and elsewhere. However, this is usually handled by management on an overall basis. Premiums charged depend upon the construction of the building, the nature of the industry, and local fire protection facilities.

Fire insurance on contents cover furniture, equipment, and merchandise in inventory. An analysis of the coverage in relation to the present value of these items may establish that the food service, taken by itself, is over- or under-insured. If merchandise inventories are substantial and fluctuate from month to month, it is possible that savings may be effected

under a monthly inventory-reporting plan of coverage which is available in most areas.

Prior to the passage of Workmen's Compensation Acts, about fifty years ago, employers were liable under the common law for accidents suffered by their employees in the course of their employment. Employers' Liability Insurance was carried to indemnify employees against this liability. With the passage of Workmens' Compensation Acts by the various states and Canadian provinces, specific rates of compensation were provided to reimburse employees for costs incurred as a result of accidents in the course of their employment. Employers are generally required to carry insurance to cover such compensation.

As there is still the possibility of liability under the common law as well as under the compensation acts, the coverage for these hazards is known as Workmen's Compensation and Employers' Liability Insurance.

Rates are set for different occupations according to the hazards involved. This coverage for food-service employees generally costs at least 1% of the annual payroll. Under some policies, such as the "retrospective-rating" plan, the cost varies in proportion to the amount previously paid out for accident claims. By preventing accidents, this cost may be substantially reduced.

Other insurance coverages carried by food services are:

Public liability: Protection against claims for damage by persons other than employees who may sustain injuries on the premises. While institutional cafeterias are usually provided for the use of employees, other persons may frequently be among the patrons. Hospitals and similar institutions regularly carry special forms of insurance to cover injuries to patients, suits for malpractice, etc. Although eleemosynary institutions have not been liable to suits for damages in many jurisdictions, because of the charitable nature of their organizations, the trend in this respect is said to be changing. According to lawyers familiar with this field, the courts of several states have held hospitals and similar institutions liable for legal action. For this and other reasons, it is important that care be taken to avoid accidents of all kinds.

Product liability necessitates protection against claims for damages by persons for injuries caused by food poisoning, foreign substances in food, etc. These types of claims may be obviated by attention to sanitary precautions (see Chapter 10, "Sanitation"), and care in food preparation. Fraudulent claims sometimes arise on the part of unscrupulous individuals. In every case, a careful investigation should be made and all facts verified and recorded. Witnesses to the alleged happening should be required to prepare statements at the time in written form so that all facts may be available in case the need arises.

Fidelity Bonds

These provide protection against defalcations by employees handling cash or other valuables. As the bonding companies usually make a thorough investigation of each applicant, it is common practice to bond not only supervisory employees and cashiers, but also all employees responsible for handling cash or merchandise. This often prevents the employment of individuals who may be dishonest.

Burglary and Armed Robbery Insurance

Where substantial sums or valuable merchandise are subject to theft, these policies are advisable. The number of hold-ups of payrolls—and even of sums less than $100 which currently occur—make this protection worth considering.

Other Forms of Coverage

There are many other forms of insurance coverage—forms such as health and accident, hospitalization, death benefits, etc.—which apply to food-service employees. In this same category are retirement and pension plans, and in some industries stock-purchase, profit sharing, and savings plans. In industrial and institutional food services these are generally handled by the management for the establishment as a whole.

Depreciation

This is a charge based upon the fact that all physical assets except land—buildings, machinery, equipment, furniture and fixtures—eventually wear out or become obsolete or inefficient to operate and must be replaced. The life of some of these assets is longer than others. Buildings may last for several hundred years, but from an accounting standpoint usually are considered to have a life of approximately 40 years; and consequently would be depreciated, if a straight-line basis is used, at the rate of 2½% per annum.

Some machinery and equipment may be depreciated at the rate of 10% (10 years' life). Automobiles are depreciated at the rate of 20% or 25% per annum. (5 yrs. or 4 yrs.)

Although many pieces of equipment may not actually wear out, there comes a time when they become inefficient to operate. This may be the result of wear, or because they can be replaced by another piece of equipment which costs less to operate and will do a much better job. This is known as

obsolescence, which in this day of rapid change is a factor that must be taken into account.

It might be supposed that the amount charged off to Depreciation would always be deposited in a bank account each year and be available for the purchase of new equipment. In the rare instances where this is done, it is known as *Funded Depreciation.* Under modern accounting practice, however, this is not usually done. The amount charged to depreciation goes to increase the funds of the establishment for general purposes including equipment purchases. In this case, Depreciation is not an actual expense, but rather an accounting charge that essentially accomplishes the purpose for which it is intended, even though not specifically funded.

For establishments coming under the provisions of the federal income taxes, depreciation is recognized as a deductible expense. The Federal Income Tax authorities have set up certain regulations governing methods of depreciation and allowable rates on different types of assets. These regulations provide that the computation of annual depreciation may be made in any manner consistent with regular trade practices; however, the regulations set forth three methods of depreciation known as:

1. "Straight-line"
2. "Declining Balances"
3. "Sum-of-Digits"

Under straight-line depreciation the life of a given asset is taken as being a certain number of years. Each year an amount of depreciation, expressed as a percentage, is allowed on that asset. For example: a piece of food-service equipment valued at $1,000 and having an estimated life of ten years would be depreciated at the rate of 10% per annum.

Both the "Declining Balance" and "Sum-of-Digits" methods are "accelerated" forms of depreciation. In other words, a greater portion is allowed in the earlier years than in the later years of the asset's life.

"Declining Balance" method is in reality "Double Depreciation on the Declining Balance." Assuming the piece of equipment previously mentioned, valued at $1,000 with 10 years' life, the first year 2 x 10% of $1,000 or $200 is taken. This is subtracted from the total, leaving $800 undepreciated. The second year 20% of the $800 or $160 is taken, leaving $640 as an undepreciated balance, and so on until the tenth year when the amount remaining is written off.

The "Sum-of-Digits" method is another form of accelerated depreciation. Let us again use as an illustration the $1,000 piece of equipment having a ten year life. We then take the digits representing the ten years, 1, 2, 3, 4, 5, 6, 7, 8, 9, 10. Adding these together we find the sum of the digits to be 55.

Applying the "Sum-of-Digits" method we work backwards taking the first year 10/55 of $1,000 or $181.81; the second year 9/55 or $163.63; the third year 8/55 or $145.45 and so on until at the end of ten years the full amount is depreciated.

The general rule is that once having adopted a method of depreciation, the taxpayer must continue that method unless he secures the government's permission to change it. However, if the "Declining Balance" method is being used, it is possible at any time to change to the Straight-Line method without requesting permission.

Although many institutions are nonprofit corporations and hence exempt from income taxes, the practice of allowing depreciation has been generally following as it is based upon sound accounting principles.

Administrative Overhead

Administrative Overhead of any institution or industry includes the cost of the administration as separate from departmental expense. This is often spread over the various departments including the food service. It is often done on the basis of the ratio of the Food-Service Department Budget to the total budget in forms of a percentage of Administrative Overhead.

The cost of certain staff departments such as Accounting, Purchasing, and Maintenance (including the Power Plant) may be allocated to the Food-Service Department on the basis of the service rendered.

Policy With Regard to Occupancy and Overhead Charges

This raises the question as to whether or not Occupancy Charges and Administrative Overhead should be allocated to the food-service operation, and if so, to what extent?

This is a matter of management policy. From one point of view, as the company or institution pays for all of these charges, it only duplicates paper work to make these allocations to the food service.

On the other hand, such allocation is good accounting practice in that it helps all concerned to understand just where these costs are incurred. From a psychological standpoint, it is also well for those responsible for food service to know what the total costs are. It provides an incentive toward economical operation. Also, it is felt that the employees should know the total costs of the operation and the amount subsidized by the company or institution.

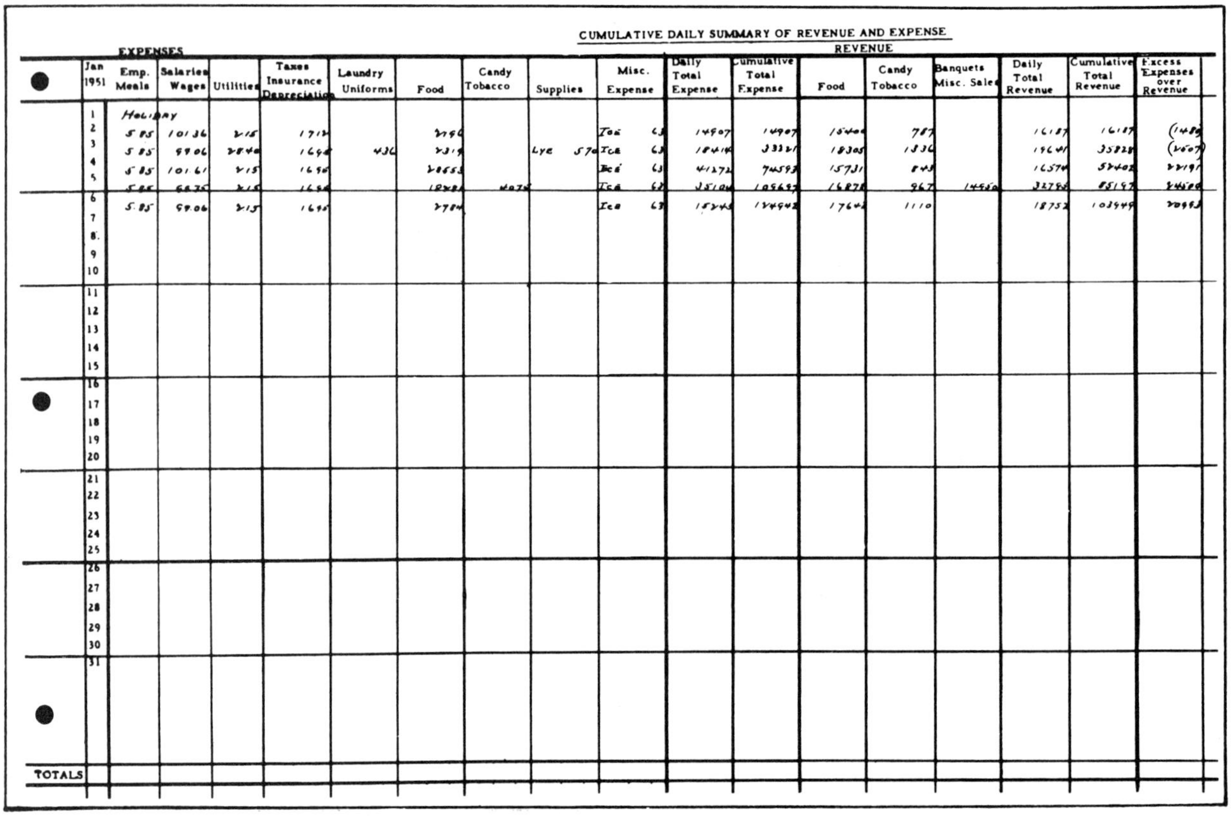

Fig. 13.2. Cumulative daily summary of revenue and expense.

Daily Summary of Revenue and Expense

A practice followed by many food services is to keep a daily record of all revenues and expenses. These are accumulated each day and the difference between total income and total charges gives an approximation of the excess of charges over income, if such is the case.

Figure 13.2 shows such a Daily Summary Sheet. It will be noted that this sheet combines some of the suggestions previously made in connection with food cost and labor cost control.

This Summary is based on the assumption that inventories of food and supplies remain fairly constant. As it does not allow for inventory fluctuations, there will usually be some variances between the amount shown on this sheet and the final results shown by the Operating Statement. Nevertheless, this Daily Summary is an excellent guide to overall operating trends.

Like the other controls suggested in this text, it has the advantage of focusing the attention of the supervisor on the salient points of the operation from a cost standpoint.

CHAPTER 14

Operating Statements, Reports, and Budgets

Business establishments and institutions generally require a statement or report covering the operations of the Food-Service or Dietary Department for each calender month or accounting period. This report is usually compiled as soon after the end of the period as the necessary figures are available.

Whether required or not, such a monthly statement or report is essential to the sound operation of the food service for the following reasons:

1. It serves as a check on the financial control of the entire food-service operation.
2. It affords a basis of comparison for preceding and future periods.
3. It provides a statistical source for compilation of annual reports.
4. It gives information for the preparation of budgets where such forecasts are required.

ACCOUNTING PERIODS

As previously stated, many business establishments and institutions operate on the basis of "accounting periods" rather than upon calendar months. One method is to divide the year into thirteen four-week periods. Another plan is to divide each quarter into one five-week and two four-week periods. In either case, each period ends on a Saturday, making it convenient to take physical inventories on that day if desired. Furthermore, each period is comparable to the same period in other years as it contains the same number of days.

STATEMENTS OR REPORTS

There are two types of statements or reports which are used in connection with food services:

Dietary or Food-Service Reports
Operating Statements

These may cover the operations of the food service for a day, a week, or month, or a year. Regardless of the period covered, the content of the report is basically similar.

Dietary or Food-Service Reports

In hospitals and other institutions a monthly report is generally prepared by the Dietary or Food-Service Department, giving the following information:

A. *Number of Meals Served.*

This may include the Cafeteria and the total number of patients served. In larger institutions it may show the number of meals served to each of the following:

1. Ward patients
2. Semi-private patients
3. Private patients
4. Special diets
5. Nourishments
6. Cafeteria meals
7. Meals to special groups (such as Student Nurses, internes, staff, etc.)

(See Departmental Costs, Chapter 11, "Control of Food Cost")

B. *Cost of Food Consumed*
C. *Salaries and wages*
D. *Other Expenses*
E. *Raw Food Cost Per Meal*

This in turn may be broken down into the Raw Food Cost per meal for each of the various categories of patients, other groups, and cafeteria.

F. *Labor Cost Per Meal*

As with Raw Food Cost this may again be broken down into the separate categories served. However, as labor cost does not usually vary with the different types of patients (except those on Special Diets), it is general practice to show an overall Labor Cost Per Meal (By dividing total Labor Costs by the total meals served during the period).

G. *Overall Cost Per Meal*

This is computed by dividing Total Dietary Costs by the total number of meals served during the period under review.

Meal Count

Obviously the various costs per meal (Raw Food, Labor and Overall) will depend upon two factors: (1) the Total Meals Served; and (2) the various total costs (Raw Food, Labor, and Other Expenses).

In any hospital or similar institution there are generally some patients who for one reason or another (operative and postoperative cases, for example) do not eat certain meals.

If the meal count is based merely upon the daily census multiplied by three, including such cases and also newborn infants (who are fed by special formulas usually handled by the Nursing Department), it will be inflated. This will show costs per meal that are lower than is actually the case.

In one 300-bed city hospital where this method had been in use, The Raw Food Cost per Meal was reported as $.367. When an accurate count of meals served was made, we found that the Raw Food Cost per Meal was actually $.416, a difference of almost 5¢ per meal. On the 407,000 meals served annually, this meant a difference of more than $20,000.

Furthermore, an inflated meal count will add to food cost in at least two ways: (1) more food will be prepared than is needed, thus increasing waste; and (2) extra trays sent to the floors may be surreptitiously consumed by employees instead of patients.

There are various methods by which accurate counts may be obtained, depending upon the practice of the institution. Where centralized service is in use and each tray is prepared for a specific patient in a central distributing point of the Main Kitchen under the supervision of the Dietitian, more accurate counts generally result. The use of selective menus, whereby each patient's selection is recorded on a menu slip, also makes for greater accuracy. Unfortunately, in many hospitals where selective diets are in effect, the patient's selections are made the day before the meals are served. Frequently it occurs that the patient's condition changes so that by the time the meal is served he cannot eat it.

This condition may be overcome by allowing patients to make their selections on the same day (see Chapter 9, "Distribution and Service of Food").

Frequently a patient is discharged before a meal period and the discharge notice does not arrive in the Dietary Department until the meal has been prepared and sent to the patient's floor. This may be prevented by closer cooperation between the Nursing and Dietary Departments.

In any event it is well to have an actual count made by the Dietitian or Supervisor in charge of each floor or nursing unit of the number of meals actually served. The counts from the various floors are then assembled in the Dietary Department and checked with the number of meals prepared. If there are substantial variances in thes figures, the reason for the discrepancies should be investigated.

Care in the compilation of meal counts can bring rewards in the form of substantial savings. The waste of only one meal, three times daily, will amount to several hundred dollars in the course of a year.

Sources of Cost Figures

Total costs of Raw Food for the period should be based upon the physical inventories and the total Food Purchases (see Chapter 11, "Control of Food Cost"). These figures should coincide with the records of the Accounting Department.

Labor Cost will be obtained from the Accounting Department. Accounting records are usually kept on an accrual basis, so that actual salaries and wages for the period can be obtained. Otherwise, for example, a period containing five pay days would show a distorted labor cost.

Under standard accounting procedure, payrolls and certain other expenses are "accrued" for a given period. This means that the payroll expenses for the actual number of days in the period are charged to the period whether actually paid or not. For example, hourly employees may be paid on Tuesdays for wages due for the preceding week's work. A Tuesday pay day might fall on the 1st of the following month, but under the accrual method the wages due for that week and also for Monday would be charged to the preceding month.

Other Expenses would be obtained from the Accounting records as well. However, supply items, if of substantial value, should be based on physical inventories. To illustrate:

Usage of Paper Goods November 19

Beginning Inventory Nov. 1	$550
Purchases during month	275
	$825
Closing Inventory, Nov. 30	700
Cost of Paper Goods Consumed	$125

In this case in which a large purchase had been made during the month, the Accounting Records would probably show the Cost of Paper Goods as $275 (based upon Purchases), whereas the actual figure would be $125. On the monthly Food Service report the actual figure ($125) would be used (with the approval of the Accounting Department), and the accounting figure used in the annual report. By the end of the year, usage should more nearly equal purchases.

Accuracy and Conciseness

It is essential that Dietary Reports be accurate. It is also advisable that they be concise, as the Administrator or Board to whom they are made will also have to go over reports from other departments as well. Usually all of the information required can be set forth on one 8½" x 11" type-written sheet. Figures 14.1 and 14.2 show Dietary reports; from a small hospital of less than 100 beds, and from a 1000-bed institution, respectively.

Operating Statements

Businesses and institutions generally issue two kinds of statements: (1) The Balance Sheet, which lists the Assets, Liabilities, and Capital and strikes a "balance" between them, hence its name. Essentially it is a cross-section view of the financial position of the establishment at a given time, usually the end of a fiscal period; (2) The Operating Statement, or Profit and Loss Statement, showing Income and Expenses during given periods. The difference between the two latter items is either a Profit or a Loss, hence its name.

Operating statements are used to show the results of cafeteria operation. In form they are similar to the "Profit and Loss Statements" used by commercial business operations of all kinds. As institutional and industrial cafeterias are not operated for profit, the term "Operating Statement," "Statement of Revenue and Expenses," or similar title is preferable.

The Operating Statement includes the following data: (see Figure 14.3).

A. *Income for the period,* including
   1. Cafeteria Sales
   2. Income from Other Sales (candy, tobacco, etc.)
   3. Other income (special parties, banquets)

B. *Cost of Food Consumed*
   This is determined by adding opening Physical Inventory value to value of Purchases, and subtracting the value of the Closing Inventory. It is good accounting practice to deduct the value of Employees' Meals from the Food Cost.

C. *Gross Income*
   Obtained by subtracting values of Food Cost from Total Income. (it is the amount left over after food cost has been covered).

D. *Labor Cost*
   This may include:
   1. Salaries and wages
   2. Employees Meals
   3. Holiday pay
   4. Vacation pay
   5. Social Security Taxes
   6. Workmen's Compensation Insurance
   7. Other "fringe benefits"

Where employees' meals are provided free of charge, it is good accounting practice to consider them as a

_____ HOSPITAL
MONTHLY DIETARY REPORT

Date   December 11, 19

I.   MEALS SERVED FOR THE MONTH OF NOVEMBER

	Breakfast	Lunch	Supper	2:00 A. M.	TOTAL
1. Patients	1151	1149	1152		3452
2. Sp. Diets	538	548	567		1653
3. Employees	592	1581	721	328	3222
4. Guests	--	1	12		13
5. TOTALS	2281	3279	2452	328	8340

II.   MEALS SERVED TO THIS DATE THIS YEAR
(For 12 months of the Fiscal Year)

	Breakfast	Lunch	Supper	2:00 A. M.	TOTAL
1. Patients	12,837	12,752	13,044		38,633
2. Sp. Diets	5,636	5,717	5,734		17,087
3. Employees	7,633	22,181	9,136	4193	43,143
4. Guests	27	107	97		231
5. TOTALS	26,133	40,757	28,011	4193	99,094

III.   MONTHLY DIETARY INVENTORY:

1. Beginning Inventory	11-1-	$ 5393.40
2. All Food Purchased		$ 3974.40
3. Total Food		$ 9367.80
4. End'g Inventory	11-30-	$ 5802.13
5. Difference-Monthly Food Cost		$ 3565.67

IV.   Food Costs:

	This Month	To Date This Year
1. Raw Food Cost:-	$ 3565.67	$ 42,905.42
2. RAW FOOD COST PER MEAL:-	.4275	.4329
3. Prepared Food Costs:-	$ 6280.60	$ 74,058.44
4. PREPARED FOOD COST PER MEAL:-	.753	.7473

Fig. 14.1.   Monthly Dietary Report.

labor cost—which they actually are. In this case, the value of Employees' Meals is estimated, and this amount (deducted from the Cost of Food Consumed) is included under Labor Cost.

Yearly Comparison

	1970-71 Meals Served	1970-71 Raw Food	1970-71 Raw Food	1969-70
Total Patients	1,059,096	$713,378.79	$.674	$.666
Non-Patients Cafeteria	1,396,272	479,897.25	.344	.313
Grand Total	2,455,368	$1,193,276.04	$.486	$.475

Fig. 14.2.   Annual Dietary Comparison Report.

Where it is necessary to hire replacements for employees granted vacations, the cost of this is spread over the year. This is done so that Labor Cost during the period when the vacation occurs will not bear an undue proportion of expense. For two-week vacations, four per cent is charged off each month, as two weeks is approximately four per cent of a year. A similar plan is followed in some food services with respect to holiday pay.

Social Security Taxes are of two kinds:

1. *Unemployment Insurance,* under the Federal Employment Security Act.

2. *Old Age and Survivors Insurance,* under the Federal Insurance Contributions Act. (F.I.C.A.)

Employees' Cafeteria _____ Company

Statement of Revenues and Expenses
Month Ending September 30, 19   (20 Working Days)

Sales - Regular Food Sales		$ 7062.	
Banquets and Misc.		832.	$ 7894.	100%
Cost of Raw Food			
Inventory 8/31/	$ 2363.		
Food Purchases - Sept.	4894.		
	$ 7257.		
Less: Inventory 9/30/	2710.		
Cost of Raw Food	$ 4547.		
Less: Cost Empl. Meals	234.		
Net Cost of Raw Food		4313.	54.6%
Gross Profit - Food		$ 3581.	45.4%
Tobacco Sales		$ 97.	
Cost of Tobacco Sold		68.	
Gross Profit - Tobacco		29.	29.9%
Total Gross Profit		$ 3610.	
Operating Expenses			
Labor Charges			
Salaries and Wages	$ 3510.		
Vacation Pay (4%)	140.		
Soc. Security Taxes (6.00)	211.		
Compensation Ins. (1%)	35.		
Employees' Meals	234.	$ 4130.	(51.6% to Total Sales)
Supplies - Services			
Supplies Consumed	$ 135.		
Laundry	22.		
Ice	16.		
Fuel Oil	64.		
Exterminating	20.	$ 257.	
Meal Taxes			
Pro Rated Items			
Insurance - General	$ 69.		
Depreciation	187.		
Taxes (Real Estate)	160.		
Maintenance & Repairs	70.		
Total Operating Expenses		$ 486.	
		$ 4873.	
Excess of Expenditures			
Over Income		$ 1263.	

Fig. 14.3. Cafeteria Operating Statement.

Unemployment Insurance

The Federal Employment Security Act was designed to encourage the various states to provide their own insurance against unemployment. This has been done, although the provisions of the plans vary from state to state.

At present (1972) the tax (which is paid by the employer) is 3.2% on the first 4,200 of annual earnings of each covered employee. However, some states have increased this percentage during recent periods of high unemployment.

Under the merit-rating plans set forth by various states, the actual rate paid by the employer might be reduced if he maintained stable employment. How-

ever, due to rising unemployment and increasing benefit payments, merit rating has been suspended in most states, a condition which is to be deplored.

Employees of hospitals and other nonprofit institutions have now been brought under the provisions of the Act.

Federal Old Age and Survivors Insurance (FICA)

This is provided for by a tax on a portion of the wages of the employees covered, paid equally by employer and employee. The employee's share is deducted from his wages, along with withholding taxes, and paid to the Federal Government at the end of each quarter. (See Chapter 16, Figure 16.2.)

The FICA base is scheduled to go to $9,000 or more in the near future, depending upon the action of Congress.

Workmen's Compensation Insurance

As previously stated, this coverage provides compensation for the employee when he is injured in the course of his employment. Laws in most states require that this coverage be carried either by the employer in an insurance company of his own choice, or that he maintain a self-insurance plan to provide for such protection.

Cost of Workmen's Compensation coverage is based on what is known as the "manual" rate. This is set at various amounts, per $100 of payroll, depending upon the occupation and its hazards from the underwriters' viewpoint.

Hospitals and other institutions vary in their policies with regard to Workmen's Compensation Insurance. Some cover all employees and others only non-professional workers.

Proprietary institutions and all business concerns are required to carry such protection for all employees. Adjudication of cases arising out of industrial accidents are usually handled by a state regulatory body known as the Industrial Accident Board.

E. *Supplies and Services*

These have been fully discussed in Chapter 15, "Control of Other Expenses and Overhead."

F. *Prorated Items*

Some items such as insurance are usually paid for in advance.

The practice in connection with the purchase of general insurance is that a rebate is allowed if the premium for several years is paid in advance. For example, on a premium paid for three years, the rate was formerly 2.5 times the annual rate. In most states this ratio has been changed to 2.7.

Real estate taxes are usually paid annually. The general practice is to prorate or spread tax and insurance payments over the year, so that the statement for the month in which the payment is made is not distorted. For example, if a certain insurance premium covering the ensuing three-year period amounted to $3600, it would be prorated at the rate of $100 per month.

In a like manner, the year's Depreciation Expense may also be prorated. Maintenance and Repair Charges may also be estimated, based on the preceding year's experience, and prorated on a monthly basis.

G. *Excess of Expenses Over Income (or vice-versa)*

Often in an employees' cafeteria operated by an industry or institution, the total of expenses, including Food, Labor Costs, and Other Expenses, will be in excess of the Total Income. There may be times when Income will cover all expenses shown in the Operating Statement. In this case the caption would be "Excess of Income over Expenses."

This item (G) might also be captioned Operating Deficit (or Revenue). The use of the word "Operating" indicates that the deficit or revenue is based on charges directly attributable to the Cafeteria Operations. If Administrative Overhead is added, this would increase the deficit or decrease the revenue accordingly. The resulting figure would be called Total Deficit (or Revenue) or Net Deficit (or Revenue), to distinguish it from the operating results.

Percentages

In preparing an Operating Statement, it is well to show percentages; particularly for Food Cost, Labor Cost, Supplies, and Prorated items. These percentages show the ratio of these various costs to the total Income figure which is taken as 100%.

The key figure is the Food-Cost Percentage, as volume has little effect on this ratio. By comparing the Food-Cost Percentage from month to month, an index to the effectiveness of the operation can be obtained.

Figure 14.3 shows an operating statement from the actual operation of an industrial cafeteria in a plant employing approximately 1000 workers.

In this case, tobacco and cigars are sold at the Cashier's stand (cigarettes, candy, etc. are handled through automatic vending machines). It will be noted that the food cost is shown as a percentage to Food Sales only, while Labor and other Expenses are shown as a percentage of Total Sales (including tobacco).

Holiday pay is not shown as the plant is normally closed on holidays, and it is not necessary to employ replacement for cafeteria workers.

Round Dollars

It is noted that the figures shown are not carried out to the exact cents, but were expressed in "round dollars." Where the amount is 50¢ or more it is carried as a dollar. Amounts below 50¢ are not considered.

This method saves considerable time, and makes the statements easier to study and understand. In order to make the totals add correctly, one or more figures may have to be increased or decreased by One Dollar. Business firms are increasingly using "round dollars" in their statements in order to simplify and make comparison easier.

Analysis of Sales and Customers

In many employee food operations, it is customary to compile an additional statement to accompany the operating statement. This gives an analysis of sales by dollars and customers for the various food services. Such a form is shown in Figure 14.4. This also shows Average Checks (sales values divided by number of customers).

Cumulative and Comparative Statements

In some operations, statements are prepared showing cumulative figures for the year to date; and also in some instances, comparative period and cumulative figures for the corresponding period of the preceding year.

Two Kinds of Statements

In hospitals and other institutions operating both cafeterias and food service to patients, it is customary to prepare the Monthly Dietary Report and the Cafeteria Operating Statement.

BUDGETS

A budget is an estimate of income and expenditures for a given future period. When adopted, it becomes a means of control. In many establishments, particularly governmental institutions, the total expenditures allowed in the budget may not be exceeded, except under unusual circumstances. It is, therefore, important to make sure that the budget is prepared with the greatest of care.

Estimating Income

In preparing estimates of income, as much information as possible should be obtained as to the prospective volume. In industrial plants this will depend upon the expected levels of employment. Employment, in turn, depends upon expected sales—which may reflect general business conditions. Ordinarily, in preparing budgets, top management will set production goals upon which the food service volume may be estimated.

In hospitals or other institutions, much depends upon the number to be fed during the period being budgeted—usually the ensuing year. The administrator will know whether or not new beds or departments are to be added, additional services offered, or changes in policies made which will increase or decrease the patient load.

Enrollments in schools and colleges have been increasing for many years, and this trend is likely to continue. The food-service manager must be informed of the administration policy with respect to enrollment, and can then base his income estimates accordingly.

Estimates of Expenses

In estimating expenses for a forthcoming budget period, many factors should be considered such as: (1) trends in prices of commodities and services; (2) wage rates; and (3) need for additional personnel if volume increases. In all of these problems it is advisable to obtain information from suppliers and counsel from top management.

Past Results

Formerly, much reliance was placed upon past results in making budgets. Sometimes results, as shown by monthly and annual reports for as far back as five

---

_____Company Cafeteria

Month Ended - September 30, 19___

Location	Customers	Sales	Average Checks
Cafeteria "A"	5246	$ 2548.	$ .485
Cafeteria "B"	7322	1907.	.260
Total Cafeteria Sales	12,568	$ 4455.	$ .354
Food Trucks			
Route # 1	8988	$ 1174.	$ .131
Route # 2	8946	1474.	$ .163
Total Food Truck Sales	17,934	$ 2648.	$ .147
Total Regular Sales	30,502	$ 7103.	$ .233
Charge Sales	89	56.	
Banquets and Miscellaneous	420	832.	
Total Sales	31,011	$ 7991.	
Recapitulation			
Total Food Sales		$ 7894.	
Total Tobacco Sales		97.	
Total Sales		$ 7991.	

Fig. 14.4. Analysis of Sales and Customers.

or ten years, were felt to be of value. At present, events move with such rapidity that figures of even the past year can hardly be relied upon for guidance.

Budgeting Costs

Food cost, either as a percentage (in case of the cafeteria) or as a cost per meal, can normally be kept within bounds (see Chapter 11 "Control of Food Costs").

Labor costs will fluctuate depending upon volume. If a larger volume can be handled with the same number of employees, labor cost, either per meal or percentage-wise, will be reduced. This is only true, of course, if wages remain at the same rates.

Usage of supplies, of course, closely follows volume as, to a certain extent, does the cost of fuel for cooking. However, light, heat, and power would not vary directly with volume.

Other charges such as taxes, insurance, and depreciation are more or less fixed without regard to volume.

Preparing the Budget

In preparing the budget the following steps should be taken:

1. Determine food-service volume in terms of cafeteria sales and number of meals served. By use of either the Food-Cost Percentage or the estimated raw food cost per meal, an estimated total Food Cost is obtained.
2. Labor Cost may be obtained by:
   a. Taking total of fixed salaries for supervisory and salaried workers.
   b. Estimating hours of labor required for estimated volume.
3. *Supplies and Services*
   These will be estimated on basis of current usage and costs.
4. *Fixed Expenses*
   Listing fixed expenses required, and making allowances for such items which may be varied through changes in volume or rates.

CHAPTER 15

Merchandising the Food Service

If an employees' cafeteria is efficiently operated, its benefits should be extended as widely as possible. In a school or college cafeteria, where students eat three meals daily, much can be done to add variety and appeal to the meals and to the environment. This comes under the heading of "Merchandising."

EMPLOYEE CAFETERIAS

A successful food service plays an important part in developing morale and good relations between management and workers. It also makes for good public relations. Furthermore, if prices and costs are in proper relationship, increased volume will normally reduce operating costs. There is every reason, therefore, to build patronage and to do everything within reason to maintain and increase sales volume.

Sales opportunities in the typical employees' food service are limited as compared with commercial eating places. Clientele is usually confined to the employees on the premises, and often only one meal is served daily. Nevertheless, there are many things that can be done to broaden the scope of the food service and to make it of greater usefulness to the employees and the institution as a whole.

Let the Employees Know!

The first step is to make sure that all present employees know about the food service. A sound method is to inculcate in new employees the habit of eating in the cafeteria from the very start of their employment. Some organizations give each new employee a ticket entitling him to a complete meal in the cafeteria, free of charge, on the first day of employment.

News of the food service is generally featured in employee news organs. Posters, bulletins, and announcements are also used to advertise seasonable dishes, holiday specials, and the like. In some establishments such posters are displayed on the traveling food trucks.

Special "inducements" may be arranged, and prizes may be given to stimulate interest in the cafeteria. For example, a free meal may be given to a lucky patron each day, the 10th or 100th person in line, for instance. Cash register checks may be signed and dropped in a box from which "lucky tickets" are drawn each day. Contests to select names for new and unusual dishes are another means of arousing interest on the part of patrons.

Combination meals at a special price are always attractive. Some cafeterias feature at least one complete, one-price special combination each day, and make sure that it is advertised throughout the establishment. Employees look forward to Thursday's New England dinner combination or Friday's Seafood Newburg Special.

Banquets and Special Parties

One way of increasing sales is to encourage luncheons, banquets, and special parties which can be held —so as to more fully utilize the existing facilities— without interfering with the regular food service. Such parties can be put on for employees' organizations and various other groups connected with the business or institution.

Sample menus should be prepared from which selections can be made. By concentrating upon one entrée, it is possible to do a better and more profitable job. It is well to insist upon a guarantee of a definite number with the proviso that 10 per cent more can be taken care of if necessary. Usually 10 per cent is allowed if less than the guaranteed number are served. In many cases the sponsors of such banquets are overoptimistic in their estimates of the number of people who will attend.

It is well to keep a day-book or diary or other handy record in which the details of each special function can be entered: the menu; prices charged; actual costs incurred; number guaranteed; and number actually served. When the same group is served each year, this data will be useful in making preparations for future functions.

Experienced catering organizations set an example in this respect. One outstanding Boston caterer, for example, serves from 4,000 to 5,500 persons at special functions given several times each year by a large fraternal organization. Because of the detailed records of these functions which have been kept year after year, the caterers are able to forecast the attendance and probable food preferences of those attending more accurately than the officers of the fraternal organiza-

tion themselves. Some time before each affair is scheduled to begin, employees equipped with counting devices are stationed at the entrance doors. Every ten minutes the count of arrivals is reported to the caterer's manager, who checks it with the data from previous functions. From these records, the manager can estimate the total number that will have to be served. If it appears that more food will be required, he telephones the company's commissary a few blocks away, and the chefs immediately go into action.

There has always been plenty of food at these gatherings, although attendance may vary by as much as 1000 from one function to another. On the other hand, the leftover food has always been kept to a minimum. This attention to detail, both in quantity and quality, is one of the reasons for the success of this eighty-year-old catering organization, now being operated by the grandsons of the original founder.

Costs of banquets and special functions should be carefully figured in advance, including extra help, overtime for regular help, additional Social Security taxes, and meal taxes involved, if any. In addition, costs of decorations, rental of additional dishes, utensils, chairs, tables, and other equipment if necessary, and extra supplies and laundry should be taken into consideration.

It is customary to figure upon a higher margin of profit (lower food-cost percentage) for such parties than that which prevails regularly in the food service. A lesson may be learned from the hotels in this respect. Many of them figure on a 25 percent or lower food cost for banquet service. Prices are generally set at a definite figure per plate based on the food-cost percentage determined.

Each party should be carefully planned with adequate supervision to make sure that preparation, cooking, and serving are properly carried on. Provision should be made for checking of hats and coats, designations of tables, and collection of tickets.

Where feasible, family-style service may be used to advantage in handling such affairs. Under this method fewer serving employees are required, and patrons enjoy serving themselves and each other. Generous portions can be provided so that "seconds" are available for those who desire them. It costs relatively little to serve extra cups of coffee at affairs of this kind, and doing so adds greatly to the enjoyment of the meal.

In a company-operated cafeteria in Virginia recently we saw an unusually successful banquet served to 250 in one of the dining rooms by the food-service staff. Colorful and appealing Cold Plates, which had been prepared in advance and chilled in the refrigerators, constituted the main entree. Since the weather was warm, this was an appropriate choice.

While the guests were assembling in another room and a few minutes before they were admitted to the dining room, the cold plates were placed on the tables, along with receptacles of hot and cold beverages and platters of rolls and salads. Practically the entire meal was served in advance, and the program went forward without a "hitch."

Sales of Food to Take Out

Another opportunity for increasing volume lies in the sale of food to be taken out. If the food service operates its own bakery, business in pies, cakes, doughnuts, cookies, and the like can be developed—particularly on Fridays for home consumption over the weekend. Fruit cakes can be sold at Christmas time. Birthday and wedding cakes may become another source of income if the baker is skilled in pastry decoration.

Precooked frozen foods are also another possibility, provided proper freezing facilities are available.

Candy, Tobacco, and Gifts

Most employee cafeterias offer bar candy, nuts, cigars, cigarettes and other tobacco products, and accessories for sale. As previously pointed out, candy and cigarettes are preferably handled through vending machines.

At holiday seasons, gift-wrapped boxes of candy and of cigars are sold by some food services.

Souvenirs and gifts are frequently displayed near the cashier's stand and sold from time to time.

While daily sales of candy, tobacco, and gifts may not be large, in the aggregate they mount up and play their part in reducing the annual deficit.

Care should be taken that such sales are not thrown in with the regular food sales. If this happens, the food-cost percentage, which is the basic economic indicator of the operation, will be distorted. Furthermore, it is important to know whether or not candy, tobacco, or other items are each standing on their own feet, profit-wise. Daily Inventories are helpful, but are often too time-consuming for practical use.

If vending machines are not used, there are several ways of keeping track of such sales. Many cash registers, of course, are equipped with special keys so that candy, tobacco, or other sales may be segregated. Where such keys are not available, a pencil mark may be made on the register tape. Separate cash boxes may be kept for these other sales or a notation made on a slip of paper for each sale of a nonfood item.

Coffee Breaks

As previously indicated, "coffee breaks" serve to augment sales in cafeterias and to level the curves of daily volume. Variety can be injected by alternating the types of doughnuts and other pastries offered with the beverage.

Care should be taken by the cafeteria management that employees do not abuse the privilege, and make the coffee break an excuse for loafing on the employer's time.

Quality and Service Best Volume Builders

Although every effort should be made to increase sales, the best way of maintaining and building sales is through quality and service. The history of the restaurant industry shows that, other things being equal, those eating places that serve good food and give courteous service invariably attract patronage. "Word-of-mouth advertising" is the most effective volume-builder for the well-managed cafeteria.

Check the Operation Periodically

Because any deficit accruing from the employee food service will be met by the establishment, there is always the danger that an attitude of complacency may characterize its policies and management. It is well, therefore, to check its operation from time to time, to see whether it is doing the job that it should be doing. The best way of doing this is to have an experienced, impartial, outside consultant make a comprehensive survey of the operation. Invariably such studies reveal ways of improving food quality and service, and often lead to substantial savings that will offset the nominal cost involved.

Successful business executives make it a practice to call in outside consultants to assist them in doing a better management job. Food service involves so many fields of knowledge that no one individual can hope to be an expert in all. Experienced food-service managers realize that the more one learns about food and food service, the more there is to know. For that reason, they welcome the assistance that the experienced food consultant can give.

Employee Questionnaires (See Chapter 2, "Patron's Questionnaire")

To supplement this, or as a part of the survey, a questionnaire may be sent to all employees, preferably at their home addresses, to learn their attitudes and preferences with respect to the food service.

Questionnaires, if properly handled, will supply answers to such questions as "Why is it that some employees do not patronize the cafeteria?"—"Is the food good?"—"Are prices reasonable?"—"Is service prompt and courteous?" It is surprising how revealing such answers can be if the questionnaires are properly handled.

Such questionnaires are also useful in planning for new food services. They will give an indication as to how many will use the new service, what their food needs and desires are, and how these can be met.

Decor

Decor has much to do with the appeal of a dining room. One of the dining rooms in the graduate school of a university has recently been redecorated with colorful walls and ceiling, attractive drapes and wall-to-wall carpeting. Matching colors are used for table-cloths and napkins and backs of chairs. To eat in this room, which was formerly drab and uninviting, is now a joy.

In the dining room of another food service, a corner is set aside for a display, appropriate to the season, that can be seen from all parts of the room. This display is changed every six or eight weeks and presents Winter, Spring, and Summer scenes as well as traditional harvest and Christmas themes in the Fall and at the end of the year. These displays are arranged by the food-service manager, who has a flair for such things and who also from time to time changes the greenery in the attractive planter which is used as a room divider.

Thus much can be done through decor to make the atmosphere of the dining room attractive and appealing.

COLLEGE CAFETERIAS

In the school or college cafeteria serving three meals daily to students, the food service is apt to become monotonous and the constant waiting in the cafeteria line a source of frustration. Steps can be taken to alleviate some of this. The meals can be made varied and appealing, as indicated in Chapter 7, Menu-Planning; the use of the "Free-Flow" type of cafeteria, as shown in Chapter 9, Distribution and Service of Food, will lessen some of the inconvenience of the conventional cafeteria lines. In addition, there are many ways in which the school or college cafeteria may be made more attractive to its patrons.

At Laval University in Quebec, there is a large room adjoining the 700-seat cafeteria dining room. This is known as the *Casse Croute* (Snack Bar). It contains 300 seats and is in addition to the cafeteria. It is used for student entertainments and meetings and is often decorated for special parties and dances. The *Casse Croute* thus provides an alternative to eating in the cafeteria.

For added interest many colleges hold special nights when the cafeteria is decorated in Spanish, Japanese, French, German, or some other national style with cafeteria employees dressed in native costumes and the appropriate types of food served. It may be a "Wild West Night," a "Chinese Night" or a "Western European Night." At Duke University the "Soul Food Night" is popular. Duke also holds a "Just Because" night, and when students ask what it signifies, they are told "just because we love you."

SOLICITING PATRONS' COMMENTS

Another way of maintaining volume is to ask for the comments and suggestions of patrons. In a fine commercial cafeteria we visited in Atlanta recently, there were attractive business reply post-cards on each table with a space on the reverse side which stated "We treasure your opinion of our service and food. Mail in this card and register with us your suggestions as to how we may better serve you."

VISITS TO OTHER OPERATIONS

One of the best ways to keep abreast of the times is to visit other similar food-service operations. Food-service managers who follow this practice find it profitable. Visits of this kind by other supervisory and key employees can also be conducive to leadership development. Arrange for such visits in advance, and make sure that the time chosen is mutually convenient. Most food-service managers will welcome you if they know about your visit in advance.

COURSES, BOOKS, PERIODICALS

Evening and summer courses in Food-Service Management are offered in various colleges and universities, and by such schools as the Culinary Institute of America. Many experienced food-service managers and their associates find it profitable to supplement their knowledge and practical experience through participation in refresher courses.

There are many books available on various aspects of food-service management. In the references given at the end of several of the chapters in this book, we have listed some of the most useful of these. Through these and the current information contained in the monthly trade magazines, any progressive food-service executive may keep abreast of the latest developments in the field so that the operation under his charge will provide the kind of food and service that will attract and hold patronage.

TRADE ASSOCIATIONS

The National Restaurant Association with headquarters in Chicago and the various state and local restaurant associations hold many meetings and welcome the attendance and membership of food-service executives. The American Hospital Association and the National Education Association also provide sections on food service at their national and regional meetings.

At these meetings and conventions, opportunities are afforded to meet and compare notes with other mass-feeding operators, and to hear talks by leaders in the industry. In connection with the national conventions and at many of the regional and state conferences, exhibits are conducted in which the latest types of equipment are displayed and demonstrated.

In addition, the trade associations provide regular information to members regarding food research, accounting practices, sanitation, pertinent legislation, market trends on foods and supplies, new operating techniques, and other valuable services. Food-service managers can profitably avail themselves and their organizations of the advantages of membership in such associations.

In addition to the associations mentioned, there are numerous professional societies such as the American Dietitic Association, the International Stewards and Caterers Association, the National Educational Buyers Association, the Industrial Food Service Managers, the Hospital Food Service Managers Association, National Association of College and University Food Services, The Club Managers Association, Food Service Executives Association, and The International Military Club Executives Association. There are also specialized groups such as the Society for the Advancement of Food Service Research and the Council on Hotel, Restaurant & Institutional Education. Organizations for the chefs include Les Amis d'Escoffier and the International Geneva Association. These organizations, which have branches in the principal cities, conduct meetings and conferences and carry on educational and social programs.

Other technical organizations such as the Society for the Advancement of Management with headquarters in New York City and branches throughout the United States and Canada welcome the membership of food-service executives interested in advancing the principles of scientific management.

Thus are provided many opportunities whereby food-service managers, dietitians, chefs, and others interested in industrial or institutional food services may gain from contacts with others in their respective professional and vocational fields.

CHAPTER 16

Laws and Regulations Affecting Industrial and Institutional Food Services

Industrial and institutional food services are affected by many federal and state laws and by the regulations of federal and state agencies as well as by local ordinances. These statutes and regulations are frequently changed by legislative action and by the interpretations of the courts, and new laws are constantly being enacted. In the minds of some legislators, the easy solution to any problem is to "pass a law." While the fallacy of such action has been demonstrated time and time again, bad as well as good laws continue to be enacted.

The food-service executive should be fully informed about laws and regulations affecting his operations, particularly in view of the current trend toward regulating public food services. Such organizations as the National Restaurant Association and the American Hospital Association employ counsel and maintain an office in Washington to inform their members regarding federal legislation affecting food services. The various state restaurant associations perform similar services for their members with respect to laws introduced in the state legislatures.

Because laws and regulations are constantly changing, we can only list the principal statutes affecting food services and about which the food-service executive should keep informed. Full details of these laws can be obtained through the various associations previously mentioned.

MINIMUM WAGE LAWS

Figure 16.1 shows the states having minimum wage laws and those not having such statutes, as of November, 1970.

STATE WAGE BOARDS

The inflexibility of statutory wage rates as applied to the food-service industry and other types of em-

STATE MINIMUM WAGE LAWS

November 1970

Forty-one jurisdictions (38 states, the District of Columbia, Guam, and Puerto Rico) currently have minimum wage laws and minimum wage rates in effect:

Alaska	Hawaii	Nevada	Pennsylvania
Arizona	Idaho	New Hampshire	Puerto Rico
Arkansas	Indiana	New Jersey	Rhode Island
California	Kentucky	New Mexico	South Dakota
Colorado	Maine	New York	Texas
Connecticut	Maryland	North Carolina	Utah
Delaware	Massachusetts	North Dakota	Vermont
District of Columbia	Michigan	Ohio	Washington
Georgia	Minnesota	Oklahoma	West Virginia
Guam	Nebraska	Oregon	Wisconsin
			Wyoming

Three additional States—Illinois, Kansas, and Louisiana—have wage board laws on their statute books, but no minimum wage rates are in effect.

The remaining nine States do not have minimum wage laws:

Alabama	Mississippi	South Carolina
Florida	Missouri	Tennessee
Iowa	Montana	Virginia

Fig. 16.1.   State Minimum Wage Laws. (U.S. Department of Labor, Washington D.C.)

ployment has brought about the establishment of Wage Boards in a number of jurisdictions. Wage Boards are set up for various industries, usually composed of representatives of employers, employees, and the public. Statutory rates apply except to employees covered by the orders of these Wage Boards. These orders are usually subject to the approval of official bodies such as the State Minimum Wage Commissions.

Wage boards generaly differentiate between the minimum wages applying to "service employees" (i.e., those receiving tips or gratuities) and others, known as "non-service employees."

Other regulations concern principally minimum daily hours for which employees must be paid; travel time and expenses; deductions for meals and lodging; and uniforms and deposits. They also set forth the minimum nutritional requirements for employees' meals.

A number of states have "Restaurant Orders." In other states institutional and industrial food services are included in what are known as "Public Housekeeping Orders." These orders apply to all establishments offering food, beverages, rooms, or lodging (for remuneration) to employees, guests, students, or other members of the public. They cover all types of food services operating for profit, as well as hospitals, hotels, motels, tourist homes, camps, convalescent homes, private schools, colleges, and other similar establishments.

Some of these Housekeeping Orders exempt women working in executive or professional capacities such as managers and supervisors, and a few specifically exempt students and student and graduate nurses.

THE FEDERAL MINIMUM WAGE LAW

Food-service employees were brought for the first time under the minimum wage provisions of the Federal Fair Labor Standards Act of 1938 by amendments passed by Congress in September, 1966.

Restaurants and food-service establishments having gross sales volume of $500,000 or more per annum were covered as of February 1, 1967 and those with annual sales of $250,000 or more came under the provisions of the amended act of February 1, 1969. Minimum wage rates for newly covered employees, such as food services, were set to reach the amount of $1.60 per hour on February 1, 1971.

Wages paid to a "tipped employee" (one receiving $20 or more per month in tips) were deemed to be increased by an amount determined by the employer up to 50% of the applicable minimum wage rate.

Restaurants, hotels, and motels (but not hospitals and related institutions) were exempted from the provisions requiring payment of time and one-half for overtime.

Currently (1972), several legislative proposals are pending in Congress which would increase the minimum wage rate to $1.90 or more per hour.

EMPLOYMENT OF WOMEN AND MINORS

Laws regulating the employment of women and children in industry had their beginnings in the child-labor laws enacted in England in the early nineteenth century. In the United States and Canada over the years, these statutes have been broadened to cover "mercantile employment," a term which includes food-service workers.

In general, they restrict the number of hours per day and the total weekly hours that women and minors may work. They also include health and safety provisions such as those requiring toilets, lockers, and dressing rooms; safe working conditions; and prohibiting or limiting employment of women during pregnancy.

Penalties are provided for violations of these regulations. In most jurisdictions, enforcement is in the hands of inspectors who make regular visits to places of employment. Certain notices are required to be posted in conspicuous places on the premises.

One of these is the "Time Sheet" listing the employees working on various shifts. Records of hours worked by employees are also required to be kept subject to inspection by enforcement authorities.

"Working-span" laws are in effect in some states. These apply especially to restaurants, and stipulate that women and minors must complete their daily working period within a certain span of hours. For example, where the span is 10 hours and the daily maximum work period 8 hours, a waitress starting work say at 7 A.M. would be required to complete her eight hours by 5 P.M. However, she might work in two or more shifts, say from 7 A.M. to 9 A.M. and from 11 A.M. to 5 P.M.

This law has caused dissatisfaction in waitresses eager to earn tips who may have formerly worked, for example, from 7 A.M. to 9 A.M., 11 A.M. to 2 P.M., and from 6 P.M. to 10 P.M. As a result in some jurisdictions the law has been amended so that the length of the "span" may be increased upon petition to the state labor department by the employees concerned.

In some states, minimum ages are prescribed for the employment of minors in various occupations. Minors are also barred from engaging in certain hazardous occupations. Maximum daily and weekly hours of employment are set forth, and work during specified night hours prohibited for minors. Employment certificates are required in many jurisdictions for minors under 18 in any gainful occupation. These certificates are usually obtained from the local school departments.

ANTI-DISCRIMINATION LAWS

Many states have enacted laws forbidding discrimination in employment with regard to race, color, religious creed, nationality, or ancestry. Under these statutes the employer is prohibited from refusing to employ an applicant on any of these grounds. He also may not discharge an employee solely on such grounds, nor may he discriminate on these grounds with respect to the advancement or promotion of a worker.

Under these laws, employment application forms may not include questions concerning the race, color, or creed of the applicant. In cases where applications are sent through the mails, the employer may not ask for a photograph of the applicant. Furthermore, advertisements offering employment may not be worded so as to include or exclude individuals of any race, color, or creed.

Anti-discrimination boards have been set up in the various states for the enforcement of these statutes. Individuals who claim to have been discriminated against may file complaints with these boards which have the power to summon employers and conduct hearings on the complaints.

In some states laws prohibit discrimination in employment because of age. These provisions are designed to protect workers in the 45 to 65 year age brackets.

Legislative proposals have in addition been introduced to extend the coverage of these laws to prevent discrimination in wages paid because of sex. These would require equal pay to men and women where the job content is equal.

CIVIL RIGHTS ACT OF 1964

The Civil Rights Act of 1964, which has been held constitutional by the U.S. Supreme Court, prohibits primarily (a) discrimination or segregation on the ground of color, religion or national origin by any "place of public accommodation" and (b) like discrimination by an employer, a union, or an employment agency.

Under Title II of this Act, an establishment which serves the public is defined as a "place of public accommodation" if "its operations affect commerce or if discrimination or segregation by it is supported by state action."

Places of public accommodation include motels, hotels, restaurants, cafeterias, lunchrooms, lunch counters, soda fountains, and other facilities engaged in selling food for consumption on the premises including those located on the premises of retail establishments or gasoline stations. Theatres and places of entertainment or exhibition are included. Bona fide private clubs are exempted and hotel and motel restaurants are covered by the Act.

Food services are covered if they serve, or offer to serve, interstate travelers, or if a substantial part of the food or beverages they serve has moved in interstate commerce. In a case involving a family-owned restaurant, where it was shown that 46 per cent of the purchases consisted of meat bought from a local vendor who in turn procured it from outside the state, the restaurant was held to be subject to the Act.

Under the Act, eating places do not have to serve undersirable customers. Individuals who are drunk, disorderly, unclean, rude, improperly dressed, or otherwise undesirable on legitimate grounds other than color, race, or religion, need not be served. There are no criminal penalties for the violation of Title II of the Act. Enforcement is by suit, brought by the person affected. If such person is not able to bring suit, under certain circumstances the Attorney General of the United States may intervene.

The Civil Rights Act of 1964 is such a far-reaching piece of legislation that all food-service operators should be conversant with its provisions.

LABOR LAWS

Federal and state laws concerning the recognition of labor unions and collective bargaining are subject to the interpretation of the National and State Labor Boards. As these interpretations vary from time to time it is essential that the food-service management have available the advice and counsel of a competent attorney who is conversant with current rulings and experienced in labor negotiations.

If unions attempt to organize his employees, the food-service operator should know his rights under the law and not hesitate to take advantage of them. He can be sure that the union representatives will be fully informed. Theirs is a full-time job and the prospect of augmenting the monthly income of their organizations by adding a substantial number of dues-paying members provides a strong motivation. The union leader has nothing to lose. If he fails this time, he can try again. The food-service operator, on the other hand, has to run his business and at the same time face the possibility of the added burdens and costs that unionization will bring. Clearly he needs counsel and assistance.

SANITATION

For a complete exposition of the regulations relating to sanitation in food services, it is recommended that the reader procure a copy of the Recommendations of the United States Public Health Service, set forth in their Food Service Manual which includes a Model Food Service Sanitation Ordinance and Code.

(Public Health Service Publication No. 934, Superintendent of Documents, U.S. Government Printing Office, Washington D. C. 20402)

THE OCCUPATIONAL SAFETY AND HEALTH ACT OF 1970

The Occupational Safety and Health Act of 1970 requires all employers to provide safe employment and safe work places for their employees, and makes all employers virtually insurers of their safety. The Act provides severe penalties for violations and places the responsibility for enforcing the Act in the hands of the Occupational Safety and Health Administration. The Administration has already cited a number of food-service operators for violations of the Act. Every food-service manager should make sure that moving parts of machinery are protected and that all parts of the food service are in accordance with high standards of safety. (See Chapter 10, Sanitation, Safety, and Fire Protection.)

BUILDING CODES AND REGULATIONS

Holocausts and panics in "places of public assembly" (defined in many jurisdictions as places where 50 or more people may assemble) have brought about drastic revisions of state and local building codes. These concern food services mainly with respect to means of egress (doors, windows, stairways, and fire escapes) and minimum areas required for tables, chairs, and aisles. Use of flammable materials for equipment and decorations is generally prohibited. Fire extinguishers and emergency lighting facilities are usually required, as is the presence of members of fire and police departments under certain conditions.

Readers are advised to consult their local and state building departments for particulars.

LICENSES AND TAXES

Many states and municipalities require licenses for the operation of public eating establishments. In Massachusetts these are known as "Common Victuallers Licenses." In addition, there are special licenses required in some jurisdictions for the sale of certain commodities such as milk and ice cream. The service and sale of malt and spiritous liquors, of course, is hedged about with many restrictions and licenses in most jurisdictions, and entirely prohibited in some areas.

In dairy states such as Wisconsin and Minnesota, the use of oleomargarine in public eating places is restricted. The importation from other areas of citrus fruits is restricted in California.

Retail sales taxes in many states and municipalities generally exempt food products. In one state (Massachusetts), however, a meals' tax is imposed upon all meals sold for $1.00 or more. This tax was amended to allow food-service operators to deduct a portion (1 per cent) of the tax collected to cover costs of collection.

Income Taxes

Provisions of federal and state income taxes on corporations, partnerships, and individual proprietorships are so complicated and subject to change as to require the services of a tax expert. With respect to income taxes on individuals, many food services provide expert assistance to employees in making out their returns. Nonprofit institutions, as such, generally are exempt from such taxes. Food services in industry and proprietary institutions are usually operated on a nonprofit basis, and in any event tax problems are usually handled by the accounting department for the establishment as a whole.

Employers are required to report to the tax authorities all wages paid to employees.

Withholding of Income and Social Security Taxes

Regulations require the withholding of federal, income, and Social Security taxes from wages paid each pay day. Amounts withheld are forwarded to the local federal income tax office on or before the last day of the month following the end of each quarter. Where the total amount withheld is $100 or more per month, including Social Security taxes, the regulations require that it must be deposited in a special bank account. In some states, statutes require the withholding of state incomes taxes as well.

When an employee is hired, he is required to fill out a form (W-4) giving his name, home address, Social Security number, and the number of dependency exemptions to which he is entitled. The amount of the tax to be withheld is computed from tables given in the instructions issued by the federal income tax division. If a new employee does not have a Social Security number, he should obtain it at the nearest field office of the Social Security Board.

At the end of each calendar year a form (W-2) must be filled out in triplicate showing:

1. Name and identification number of the employer. (This identification number is issued by the income tax division to new employers when they start in business.)

2. Name and Social Security number of the employee.
3. Total wages paid to the employee during the year.
4. Total taxable wages of the employee under the Federal Insurance Contribution Act (Old Age and Survivors Insurance).
5. Total federal income tax withheld from the employee's wages during the year.
6. Total FICA tax deducted from the employee's wages during the year.

One copy of this form is retained by the employee for his records, and another is sent in with his income tax return. A third copy is sent in by the employer along with a reconciliation sheet covering all taxes withheld, to the local office of the director of internal revenue. Employers find it advisable to make a fourth copy for their records. Where state income taxes are levied, an additional copy is supplied to the employee to be filed with his state income tax return.

FICA WITHHOLDING

Deduction Based on Tips Received by Employees

As of January 1, 1966, tips amounting to $20.00 per month or more received by employees must be included in determining the taxable wage base for FICA deductions. Employees are required to give their employers a monthly accounting of all tips received within ten days after the end of the month. The employee's deduction is based upon the total of wages paid and tips reported. Employers are not required to match the portion of the FICA tax based upon tips nor are they held accountable for the accuracy of the reports made to them by employees.

SOCIAL SECURITY AND MEDICARE

Under the 1965 Medicare Act, all individuals, 65 years of age or over, whether or not covered by Social Security, are entitled to receive certain number of days of hospital care for any period of illness. The provisions of the Act also provides out-patient hospital diagnostic services, post-hospital nursing-home care, and home visits by nurses or technicians.

A voluntary medical insurance program is also provided for which those 65 and over pay a monthly premium ($6.30 as of July, 1973). This amount is deducted from the Social Security check each month. This program covers doctors' and surgeons' bills in hospital, office or home, and certain other medical expenses. Over and above a nominal deduction, the insured is reimbursed for 80 percent of these charges.

Figure 16.2 shows the contribution rate schedule pertaining to employers and employees for Social Security and Hospital insurance. Under the law the base will be $10,800 in 1973 and will increase to $12,000 in 1974, with automatic adjustments thereafter as earnings' levels rise.

As the provisions of Social Security and Medicare may change from time to time, it is suggested that the reader can obtain up-to-date information by contacting the local office of the Department of Health, Education, and Welfare, or write to the Superintendent of Documents, U.S. Government Printing Office, Washington, D. C. 20402.

Year	Retirement, Survivors, and Disability Insurance	Hospital Insurance	Total
Employer-Employee, each			
1973-77	4.85	1.00	5.85
1978-80	4.80	1.25	6.05
1981-85	4.80	1.35	6.15
1986-92	4.80	1.45	6.25
1993-97	4.80	1.45	6.25
1998-2010	4.80	1.45	6.25
2011+	5.85	1.45	7.30
Self-employed			
1973-77	7.00	1.00	8.00
1978-80	7.00	1.25	8.25
1981-85	7.00	1.35	8.35
1986-92	7.00	1.45	8.45
1993-97	7.00	1.45	8.45
1998-2010	7.00	1.45	8.45
2011+	7.00	1.45	8.45

Figure 16.2.   Social Security Contribution Rate Schedule. (Percentage of Base Amount.)

EMPLOYMENT SECURITY TAXES

All states and territories now have funds from which benefits are paid to eligible unemployed workers for prescribed periods. These periods and the amounts of benefits paid vary from state to state. (See Chapter 14.)

UNION CONTRACTS

Some industrial and institutional food services operate under contracts with labor unions. Usually, the negotiations with the unions are conducted by the Personnel or Industrial Relations Department of the institution. However, there are factors affecting food-service employees which are different from the working conditions of other employees. These should be brought to the attention of the negotiators.

In instances where food-service employees receive free meals, this should be considered in the setting of wage rates. Even more important is the fact that food-service employees should be free to do any job that is required during the rush periods preceding and during the serving of meals. Adherence to rigid union jurisdictional requirements makes for difficulties.

The problems of the food service should be considered when union contracts are being negotiated. Once the contract is in effect, it is difficult to make changes.

KEEP POSTED ON CHANGES IN LAWS AND REGULATIONS

In this chapter we have summarized principal types of laws and regulations affecting institutional food services. These rules and statutes vary from community to community and in the different states. They are changed from time to time by amendments, the enactment of superseding statutes by Congress and the state legislatures, by the ordinances of local governing bodies, and also by the interpretations of the courts and administrative agencies.

The food-service executive should be informed about the laws in effect in the area in which his establishment is located. This information can be secured from the local or state restaurant associations and the National Restaurant Association. These organizations keep their members posted upon pending legislative proposals.

Particular attention should be given the following points:

Records
What records are required to be kept under the various regulations?

Reports
What reports must be made? When? To Whom?

Posting
What notices are required to be posted on the premises?

Inspection
What inspectors have the right to enter and inspect the premises or to examine records? How can they be identified?

Above all, food-service operators should avail themselves of competent counsel. There is a saying, current in the legal profession, that "the man who acts as his own lawyer has a fool for a client."

Index